THE
PĀLI LITERA
OF CEYLON

ABOUT THE AUTHOR

G.P. Malalasekera (1899-1973) was one of the leading lights of the Buddhist Renaissance in Sri Lanka and a chief architect of international Buddhist unity in the twentieth century. Having obtained a Ph.D. degree in England in 1925 at the School of Oriental Studies, London University, he served as the Head of the Department of Oriental Languages at the University College (Colombo) and as Professor of Pāli and Dean of the Faculty of Oriental Studies at the University of Ceylon (Peradeniya). In 1950 Dr. Malalasekera helped to found the World Fellowship of Buddhists, which he served as its first President for eight years. He was also a long-time President of the All-Ceylon Buddhist Congress.

In the field of Buddhist scholarship Dr. Malalasekera is best known for his magnum opus, *A Dictionary of Pāli Proper Names*, a work of over 2,500 pages in two volumes, first published in 1937 and still maintained in print by the Pali Text Society. In 1956 he initiated the international *Encyclopaedia of Buddhism*, a project to which he devoted his talents as its Editor-in-Chief until his death in 1973.

THE PĀLI LITERATURE OF CEYLON

G.P. MALALASEKERA

BUDDHIST PUBLICATION SOCIETY
KANDY SRI LANKA

Published in 1994

Buddhist Publication Society
P.O. Box 61
54, Sangharaja Mawatha
Kandy, Sri Lanka

Originally published in 1928 by the Royal Asiatic Society of Great Britain and Ireland.

ISBN 955-24-0118-6

Printed in Sri Lanka by
Karunaratne & Sons Ltd.
Colombo 10.

To

M A L L I K Ā

(M.H.R.)

“ Whatever she touches she transforms into Music, into Beauty, into Joy.”

PUBLISHER'S NOTE

The Buddhist Publication Society is delighted and honoured to bring back into print the late Dr. G.P. Malalasekera's excellent and important study, *The Pāli Literature of Ceylon*, which first appeared in 1928 as a Prize Publication of the Royal Asiatic Society of Great Britain and Ireland. I.B. Horner, late President of the Pāli Text Society, described this work as "masterly" and "invaluable," adding that it is "not very likely ever to be superseded." In retrospect such praise does not seem to be excessive. In a little over 300 pages Dr. Malalasekera admirably surveys Sri Lanka's rich heritage of Pāli Buddhist literature, a legacy which has justly merited its international reputation as the stronghold of the Theravada Buddhist literary tradition. Beginning with the story of the Sinhala people's conversion to the Sublime Doctrine of the Buddha, the author traces, in impeccable prose, the development of Sri Lanka's Pāli literature from its origins, through the glorious Anuradhapura and Polonnaruva periods, down to the early twentieth century. Since the history of the island, its Buddhist faith, and its Pāli literature are inseparably intertwined, his book is at the same time a gracefully written history of Sri Lanka as reflected in its literary heritage.

This BPS edition of *The Pāli Literature of Ceylon* includes a Supplement by Dr. Somapala Jayawardhana, formerly Senior Lecturer in Pāli at the University of Ruhuna. The Supplement contains corrections to a sprinkling of minor errors in the original edition and helps to clarify some points requiring elucidation. The publisher's thanks are due to Dr. Jayawardhana for compiling this Supplement, and also to Professor N.A. Jayawickrama for allowing us to incorporate into it several corrections from the marginal notes to his personal copy of the 1928 edition of the book.

The publisher would also like to thank Mr. Vijaya Malalasekera, the author's son, and other members of the Malalasekera family, for granting the BPS permission to publish this work by their esteemed father.

BHIKKHU BODHI

PREFATORY NOTE

I am deeply beholden to the Council of the Royal Asiatic Society of Great Britain and Ireland for having accepted this little volume to be issued under the ægis of their Prize Publication Fund. My obligations are due to the numerous scholars who have gone before me and explored the fields of Pāli Literature in Ceylon. Their pioneer work has made my efforts pleasanter and more fruitful than they would otherwise have been. I wish also to express my thanks for guidance and inspiration to my teachers at the School of Oriental Studies, Professor R. L. Turner, Dr. L. D. Barnett, Dr. W. Stede, and Mr. M. de Z. Wickremasinghe, and to Mrs. A. de Z. Elliot for various assistance received. I have no words sufficient to convey my heartfelt gratitude to my *Ācariya*, Mrs. Rhys Davids, but for whom this work would never have seen the light of day. The two years I spent in London as her *antevāsika* have been one of the happiest periods of my life, and I am indebted to her, more than I can express, for the very great honour she has conferred on me by revising this, the result of my first researches. *Ciraṃ jīvatu!*

G. P. M.

COLOMBO,

January, 1928.

CONTENTS

The Pāli Literature of Ceylon

Introduction

THE Pāli Literature of Ceylon is of great extent and importance and also of multifarious interest; it is of value alike to the historian and the student of folklore, to the philologist and the student of comparative religion. Broadly speaking, it may be classified under three main heads: first, the Buddhist Scriptures, or *Tipiṭaka*, which form the Pāli Canon; second, the Commentaries (of Buddhaghosa, his contemporaries and successors), exegetical expositions of the text of the *Tipiṭaka*, compiled, as we have them now, only after the fifth century of the Christian era, but alleged to be based upon records of distinctly greater antiquity; and third, historical, grammatical and other works on secular subjects, which have been produced by scholars at various times from about the fifth century to the present day.

Pāli had probably ceased to be a spoken language by the time it was introduced into Ceylon; but that does not seem in any way to have lessened the interest which it evoked in the minds of the scholars of the island. To them it was of no pagan stock; they had no difficulty in assimilating the philosophic culture of a religion, which had come into birth and attained to power in a country which they themselves claimed as the motherland; they were *orasa-jātā* (bosom-born) spiritual children of India, their lives and minds nourished on her age-long, yet living and growing, traditions. When Buddhism was introduced into the island, under the ægis of the Emperor Asoka, they found in its teachings the development of essentially their own genius. Pāli was the language consecrated as the instrument of, as it is called, "the Buddha's word," and in order, therefore, to realize to the fullest extent the value of the heritage which the Master had bequeathed to them, they devoted their attention to the study of that language. To a nation little accustomed to traffic, and therefore free from the endless difficulties and anxieties which trade produces on society in general, the cultivation of letters was not only an indispensable pursuit, but a delight. In the Scriptures of the religion which thenceforward became the national faith Ceylon found material for endless contemplation; each succeeding sovereign, interested in the people's welfare and in the development of his own spiritual nature, rendered them essential service in this respect, extending his munificent patronage to all whose lives were engaged in the pursuit of literary study.

Within a moderate period men of the Sinhalese race had acquired proficiency in the use of the Pāli tongue; its phraseology, at once soft and sonorous, smooth-flowing and capable of employment as a language of culture and science, appealed to their imagination and kindled their power of expression. Pāli became their literary dialect, raised to a position of dignity which, in spite of many vicissitudes, it still retains. Quite soon afterwards scholars began to compose works in Pāli, so that the knowledge which they had garnered in the course of their studies might be recorded for the benefit of generations yet unborn.

The earliest attempt at such writings that has come down to us is the *Dīpa-vaṃsa*, a work generally assigned to the fourth or fifth century.[1] From that time onwards there was a succession of authors of literary compilations, who wrote unremittingly, though there were periods of special activity. The Pāli language continued to be assiduously cultivated; kings and princes, nobles and statesmen vied with one another in Pāli composition, and laymen and monks contributed Pāli works, some of which can rank among the notable productions of the literature of the world. Books were written on all conceivable subjects: exegesis and law, medicine and poetry, religion and folklore, history and philosophy, prosody and rhetoric—an array of extensive volumes on all that in

[1] See discussion on the *Dīpa-vaṃsa* in Chap. VII.

their day chiefly engaged the attention of mankind. The high degree of the intellectual attainments and the culture and refinement to which the Sinhalese had reached in the hey-day of their prosperity is fairly indicated by what now remains of the art displayed in the design and decoration of their religious edifices, the science exhibited in the conception and execution of their stupendous irrigation works, and in the beautiful ideals of love and service and devotion which appear to have been the staple of their best poetry.

Unfortunately for us, however, a large part of this ancient literature has been irretrievably lost.

The Sinhalese have ever been a domestic, not a political people. Lulled by a sense of security in their island-home, set in the silver sea, the people did not provide sufficient safeguards for the protection of their possessions and industries. Having but few needs of their own, they lavished their wealth upon their religious edifices, which they decorated with a profusion of precious metals and valuable gems, such as were highly prized and could easily be carried away. They thus attracted the attention of their rapacious neighbours, who from time to time swooped down upon their defenceless coasts, ravaging and plundering the wealth of the land. On several occasions these marauders succeeded in establishing themselves on the throne of the island, and in exercising supreme power. Their rule was marked by much cruelty and oppression, and not the least of the damage they perpetrated was the systematic destruction of whatever literary records fell into their hands.

But the country's foes were not all from without. More than once in the course of its history the Saṅgha in Ceylon was rent asunder by violent schisms, resulting from the propagation of heresy within its ranks. Like a hydra-headed monster, the *Vaitulya-vāda* every now and then showed signs of vitality, until its final destruction by Parākrama-Bāhu the Great, in A.D. 1165. And sometimes it came to pass that the heretics gained the confidence of the ruling monarchs, who, to show their hatred of the recusant *Theriya Nikāya*, because of their obstinate adherence to the orthodox religion, commanded that their temples should be confiscated and demolished, and their books be collected and a bonfire made of them. Of the literature of the *Vaitulya-vādins* themselves not a trace is left; for the kings of Ceylon, in the excess of their zeal for the preservation of the purity of the faith, born of their passionate attachment to the Thera-vāda fraternity, saw to it that not a vestige of their heretical teachings should survive. And finally, towards the close of the sixteenth century, Rāja Siṅha I of Sītāvaka, embittered against Buddhism, because of the treachery of certain members of the Saṅgha, openly embraced a foreign faith, became virulently hostile to the Buddhist priesthood, drove them from their temples and destroyed their libraries.

Amidst all these ravages, however, a good deal of the Pāli literature of Ceylon has survived, due mainly to the pious care of its loyal custodians. Regardless of personal danger and steadfast in their devotion to all learning, humble and ascetic in garb, the monks have preserved for us through the ages something of that heritage of wisdom which drew to Ceylon's shores in ancient times men from Burma and Siam and distant China in search of her intellectual treasures far more valuable than her pearls and rubies, her elephants and peacocks. And it happened that these seekers of knowledge carried back with them into their native lands copies of the books which they had come across in their travels; and, when Ceylon had lost many of her books of priceless value, the Sinhalese were able to restore them from copies collected elsewhere.[1]

Ever since the advent of the Portuguese into the island in the sixteenth century European scholars had evinced a certain amount of interest in the literature of the Sinhalese,

[1] Thus Oldenberg says that all the copies of the *Dīpa-vaṃsa* which he saw bore marks of being copies from one Burmese original. (*Dīp.*, Introd., p. 11.) And Turnour (*Journ. As. Soc. Bengal*, vi, p. 790) says that his copy was obtained from MSS. brought to Ceylon from Siam.

particularly in the books dealing with the history of Ceylon. But for quite a long time it was believed that the Sinhalese annals were devoid of materials of historical value; that their religious literature contained nothing but the ravings of fanaticism; that their other works were all myth and romance, wearisome in their monotonous inanity.[1] It was not till about 1826 that the discovery was made that Ceylon was in possession of continuous written chronicles in Pāli, not only rich in authentic facts about the history of the island, but also yielding valuable materials for unravelling the meshes of Indian chronology. A young civil servant, George Turnour, in charge of the administration of the district at the foot of Ceylon's holy mountain, Samanta-kūṭa (Adam's Peak), had been studying Pāli under the guidance of a Buddhist monk; and the investigations which he made into certain rare and valuable manuscripts, led him to publish a series of articles in the *Journal of the Bengal Asiatic Society*, under the heading of "The Pāli-Buddhistical Annals". Therein he demonstrated that Ceylon possessed a connected history of over 2,300 years, authenticated by the concurrence of every evidence which could contribute to verify the annals of any country.[2] At the moment Prinsep was endeavouring to decipher the mysterious Buddhist inscriptions of "Piyadassi", scattered over Hindustān, and the identification of "Piyadassi" with Asoka, made possible by the discovery of the Ceylon chronicles, proved to be to him of the utmost importance.

The value of the Buddhist records in the scholarship of the East was thus brought home to research students more than ever before; and a new zest was added to their greater and closer scrutiny. In 1833 Edward Upham made at the request of Sir Alexander Johnston, Chief Justice of Ceylon, translations of the *Mahā-vaṃsa,* together with two chronicles in Sinhalese (the *Rāja-ratnākara* and the *Rājāvalī*) and published

[1] See e.g. Valentyn, *Oud en Nieuw Oost-Indien,* 1725, iv, p. 60.

[2] V, p. 521; vi, pp. 299, 799, 1049.

them in three volumes under the title *The Sacred and Historical Books of Ceylon.*[1] Upham's translations included eighty-eight of the hundred chapters of the *Mahā-vamsa.* It was found, however, that his pioneer work was full of inaccuracies; and in 1837 Turnour made a fresh translation of the *Mahā-vaṃsa.* Only thirty-eight chapters of this work were published, accompanied by the Pāli text, Turnour dying before his task was completed.[2] In the Introduction to this translation Turnour gave a résumé of the contents of his articles written for the Bengal Asiatic Society's *Journal,* and added a short dissertation on the Pāli language and a few of its more important grammatical works. In addition to this he gave, in an Appendix, a detailed account of the *Tipiṭaka,* as to its arrangement and divisions. He also drew the attention of scholars to the fact that in no part of the world were there greater facilities for the study of Pāli than in Ceylon, and that in addition to the historical material in that language, the importance of which had been hitherto but little understood and imperfectly illustrated, there existed many doctrinal and metaphysical works on Buddhism still extensively and critically studied by the monks of Ceylon.[3]

The missionaries who had come to the island had already addressed themselves to the task of learning both Pāli and Sinhalese, so that they might ascertain the nature of the religion which they were attempting to displace; and, in order to facilitate the work of their fellow-labourers in the field, they published translations in English of several of the books which had come under their notice. But for many years to come no attempt was made by scholars at a systematic study of the literature of Ceylon, whereby their books and their authors might be placed in some sort of chronological sequence. The meagreness of the published materials made the task doubly difficult.

[1] London, Parbury, Allen & Co. (1833).
[2] Ceylon, Cotta Church Mission Press (1837).
[3] Introd., p. xxv.

The first attempt to prepare a Catalogue of the literary works of Ceylon was made by the Rev. Spence Hardy, who, in the course of a residence of twenty years (1825–45) in the island, had made a collection of whatever manuscripts he happened to come across. At a meeting of the Ceylon Branch of the Royal Asiatic Society, held in Colombo on the 26th February, 1848, he read out a list, compiled by him, of "Books in the Pāli and Sinhalese Languages"; this list was published in the Society's *Journal* in the same year.[1] It was a bare enumeration of names of books, often wrongly spelt; no mention was made of their authors, or of the dates of their compilation, and the list was necessarily incomplete. In 1852 James D'Alwis, one of the most erudite scholars of Ceylon during the last century, published his monumental work, an English translation of Vedeha's Sinhalese grammar, the *Sidat-saṅgarā*. In a masterly Introduction, extending to over two hundred pages, he traced the development of Sinhalese and gave a continuous history of the books written in that language from the earliest times to his own day. Unfortunately for us, however, D'Alwis confined himself therein exclusively to compilations made in Sinhalese, and, beside a bare mention of a few Pāli works, no particulars were given of scholars who wrote in Pāli.

In 1869, during the régime of Sir Hercules Robinson, Governor of Ceylon, was established the Government Oriental Library of Ceylon, containing a collection of books in Pāli, Sinhalese, and Sanskrit. D'Alwis was invited by the Governor to undertake to compile a catalogue of the books contained in the Library, and such other valuable and unknown manuscripts as were not available therein, but were to be found in the Temple Libraries of the island. He very public-spiritedly accepted the invitation. But before the work could be even fairly completed D'Alwis departed this life. He had written descriptive accounts of twenty-three books, eleven of which were compilations in Pāli, and these were published in 1870,

[1] *JRAS.* (*Ceylon Branch*), vol. i, No. 3, pp. 189 foll.

as vol. i of *A Descriptive Catalogue of Sanskrit, Pāli, and Sinhalese Literary Works of Ceylon.*[1] D'Alwis did not satisfy himself with merely giving a list of books with their titles and author's names, and specifying the subject of which they treated; he gave detailed descriptions of the books themselves, illustrating his statements with copious quotations.

The work so well begun remained in abeyance until the appointment of Louis de Zoysa, Chief Interpreter *Mudaliar*, to pay official visits to the temple libraries of the island and to find particulars of the literary treasures they contained. In a report submitted to the Government in 1876 he mentions that, in spite of the fact that he was a Christian, on the whole he had met with a very favourable reception from the heads of the various Buddhist monasteries. Only in three or four instances does he seem to have been received with a good deal of distrust, the monks evidently suspecting Government of some design upon their collections! The results of his mission were not inconsiderable; he carried out his task with great tact and energy, and his report is interesting reading. Perhaps the greatest find was a copy of the Sinhalese gloss on the *Dhamma-pada*, which, excepting the Mihintale Inscription, is the oldest known specimen of Sinhalese prose. A strange fate seems to have been ordained for all those who undertook to make catalogues of the temple libraries, and De Zoysa too fell a victim to this unrelenting decree, for he died before his work could be finished. However, the Government issued as much of the catalogue as had been completed.[2] The works were included under several heads: the Pāli MSS. being divided into Canonical works, Commentaries, *Ṭīkā* or Scholia, General Religious Works, Historical Works and Grammatical and Philological Works. In regard to most of the MSS. mentioned no further details were given, except the title of the book, size, place of deposit, author, date (hypothetical in many cases) and subject.

[1] Government Printing Press, 1885.
[2] Colombo, Government Printing Press, 1876.

Mr. M. de Z. Wickremasinghe, then Assistant Librarian of the Colombo Museum Library, was appointed to complete the work that had been assigned to De Zoysa. He paid visits to many of the temples which had hitherto been neglected, and the results of his researches were embodied in the Administration Reports of the Colombo Museum 1890–5. These were later put together under the title of the Catalogue of the Colombo Museum Government Oriental Library.[1]

Meanwhile the British Museum had been acquiring by purchase and presentation a collection of Sinhalese MSS., and in 1899 the Trustees invited Mr. Wickremasinghe to compile a Catalogue of Sinhalese MSS. in the British Museum, as part of the series of the catalogues of the MSS. in the languages of India, which were then in course of publication. This catalogue was finally published by the British Museum in 1900. The historical Introduction to this Catalogue, though it contains only twenty-five pages, forms by far the most authentic account of the literature of Ceylon hitherto published. By the very nature of his work Mr. Wickremasinghe was precluded from giving more than the names of the Ceylon scholars who wrote in Pāli, and the titles of their compositions; but he has done valuable service in fixing the periods of several scholars whose works had till then been floating dateless on the sea of chronology.

Sometime later the library of Hugh Nevill was acquired after his death by the British Museum and joined to their Oriental Collection. Nevill was for many years in the Ceylon Civil Service, and during his stay in the island had travelled extensively in search of rare and unknown MSS. He was immensely interested in the literature of Ceylon, and at the time of his death was engaged in the preparation of a catalogue of his collection, prefaced by a historical survey. His catalogue now forms part of the Nevill Collection of the Oriental Section of the British Museum Library; and it is hoped that steps

[1] Government Record Office, 1896.

may be taken soon to publish some of the works included in it which are at present not known to exist elsewhere.

No account of the attempts to give a continuous history of the Pāli Literature of Ceylon would be complete without a reference to that monumental work, Childers's *Pāli Dictionary*, first published in 1875. There, in his Introduction, besides giving an account of the books of the *Tipiṭaka* and of Buddhaghosa's Commentaries, Childers made brief mention of one or two other works in Pāli, such as the *Sāra-saṅgaha* and the *Abhidhammattha-saṅgaha*. Reference has also to be made to the article published in the *Indian Antiquary* by the Rev. Thomas Foulkes on the *Vicissitudes of Ceylon Literature*.[1]

Among the Pāli compilations themselves but two works devote any attention to chronicling the history of literature. The first is the *Saddhamma-saṅgaha*, by an author named Dhammakitti, who lived probably at the end of the fourteenth century. It is a history of Buddhism in Ceylon, and one of its chapters (ix) is devoted to making a record of the books that had been written from the earliest times down to the end of the reign of Parākrama-Bāhu the Great (A.D. 1164–97). This account contains several inaccuracies, and the author follows no chronological sequence ; but it is of value in showing what works were recognized as authoritative at the period in which it was written. The other is a much later composition, by Ācariya Vimalasāra *Thera*, who completed and published his poem in A.D. 1880. It is called the *Sāsana-vaṃsa-dīpa*, and is a history of the Buddhist church in the island. The eleventh chapter gives a list of the authors who flourished in Ceylon from the time of Buddhaghosa to the reign of Paṇḍita Parākrama-Bāhu (A.D. 1240–75), together with the names of their compilations. This list also contains several works of Burmese authors which were introduced to Ceylon from time to time.

Apart from these Subhūti *Thera*, in the Introduction to his

[1] *Ind. Antiq.*, xvii, pp. 100, 122.

Nāma-mālā, published in 1876, gave a very valuable historical survey of the Pāli grammatical literature of Ceylon. A similar account is contained in Dhammārāma's Introduction to his edition of Rāhula's *Pañcikā-pradīpa*, published in 1896.[1] With these two works and the *Sāsana-vaṃsa-dīpa*, and the *Nikāya-saṅgraha* [2] as his basis, Medhānanda Thera wrote a historical Introduction to his Pāli poem, the *Jina-vaṃsa-dīpanī*, published in 1917,[3] giving an account of the Buddhist Saṅgha in Ceylon and of the works of Buddhist monks.

Short biographical memoirs of individual authors, together with descriptions of their compositions, are also to be found in the various editions of them published by scholars both in the East and the West, and in essays dealing with particular books that have appeared in various journals and periodicals. In this connexion mention must be made of the *Life and Work of Buddhaghosa*, by Bimala Charan Law.[4] There, with commendable energy, the author has gathered together a large mass of valuable material concerning the great Commentator, which will be of the utmost help in any study of Pāli literature.

After these preliminary observations a word may also be said about the method of treatment adopted in this present dissertation. The earliest Pāli work that has come down to our times dates only from the fourth century A.D. Perhaps at first sight, it might appear as if too much space has been allotted in the earlier chapters to a consideration of the history of Ceylon—apart from any literary productions—during the period prior to that date. It should be borne in mind, however, that the literature of a country cannot be separated from the life of its people ; books are but an index to the intellectual development to which men have attained in their reaction to the environment in which they live and move and have their being. To the literature of no country in the world does this observation apply more forcibly than to that of Ceylon,

[1] Colombo, 1876 ; Colombo, 1896.
[2] q.v.
[3] Colombo, 1917.
[4] Calcutta, 1923.

where literary productivity has been mainly a result of the sedulous attention and the munificent patronage of kings and rulers and the support extended to the monks by an ever generous and grateful lay community. Pāli literature grew only with the advancement of Buddhist culture, and some idea of the development of that culture and civilization is essential to enable us to see its literature in a true perspective. The same holds true of the period of the decay of literary activity, which the last three centuries have witnessed and which is a result of the neglect of Ceylon's spiritual heritage, and an undue attention to a civilization extraneous to the genius of the people.

This attempt to give a continuous and connected history of an intellectual movement which, in spite of the many vicissitudes it has undergone during the course of twenty-four centuries, will yet come to be included in the annals of the scholarship of the world, is inevitably full of deficiencies and imperfections. The searchlight of modern critical research has only of late been directed to the study of Pāli literature. Instances are numerous where scholars are not agreed as to the date and origin of particular books, and in the absence of direct evidence conclusions must necessarily be uncertain. But, as time goes on and our knowledge of the subject grows, there is reason to believe that there will come a gradual narrowing of issues and an approximation to concurrence of opinion. Such is the cherished hope in which this effort has been made—the hope that it may serve as an unpretentious stepping-stone to a fuller and a closer study of the history of the Pāli literature of Ceylon.

CHAPTER I

The Conversion of Ceylon

FOR all practical purposes the history of Buddhism in Ceylon, and, therefore, the history of the Pāli literature which records the results of that great spiritual movement, begins from the earlier part of the third century B.C. It starts with the arrival of the missionaries sent from India by the Buddhist Emperor Asoka. It would, nevertheless, be incorrect to suppose that prior to that event the Buddha and his teachings were altogether unknown to the island. Indeed, there is evidence to the contrary.

The primitive history of Ceylon, like the ancient histories of all nations, is enveloped in fable ; and, although latter-day chroniclers have recorded for our benefit events extending far down the vista of time, their accounts afford us very little of historical importance concerning the earliest times. It would almost seem from their manner of describing these remote happenings that they were not prepared to vouch for their strict accuracy, and that they did not regard it as their purpose to record anything anterior to the advent of the last Buddha, Gotama.

For to these chroniclers the history of Ceylon was the history of the Sinhalese people, and the Sinhalese people were, above all else, the custodians, appointed, it was believed, by the Master himself, of that sublime body of teaching which he gave to mankind. To give to the Sinhalese their authority for carrying out the mission that had been entrusted to them the Buddha is said to have visited the island thrice, so that he might honour and purify with his holy presence the land which was to be the future home of the Sinhalese race. The old chronicles, such as the *Mahā-vaṃsa* and *Dīpa-vaṃsa*, give vivid descriptions of these visits—made in the fifth month, the fifth year, and the eighth year after the Enlightenment. How much of truth there is in these descriptions we have no way of ascertaining at this distant date; but that the tradition was a very old one, there is no doubt at all. The oldest of the Ceylon chronicles, the *Dīpa-vaṃsa*,[1] written in the fourth century A.D., mentions it. The *Samanta-pāsādikā*, Buddhaghosa's commentary on the *Vinaya-Piṭaka*, records it in the historical section,[2] and the *Mahā-vaṃsa*, Ceylon's best known chronicle, gives a graphic account of the visits, with a wealth of detail.[3] (The *Samanta-pāsādikā* belongs to the latter half of the fifth century, and the *Mahā-vaṃsa* to the earlier part of the sixth century A.D.) There exist to the present day the remains of a monument, erected in 164 B.C. by King Duṭṭhagāmaṇi, on the spot where the Buddha was supposed to have touched the earth on his first visit.[4] It is quite probable that the *Dīpa-vaṃsa* account, the earliest record which we have at present, was borrowed from an even earlier source. For the author tells us that his work was based on earlier redactions, the *Sīhala-Atthakathā* (the Sinhalese commentaries), which contained besides exegetical matter on the *Piṭaka*, also material of a historical character "twisted into a garland of history from generation to generation like flowers of many kinds".[5] It is significant that the Pāli canon itself, which gives a fairly complete account of the Teacher's doings during the first few years of his ministry, does not make any mention of a visit to Ceylon.[6] We may, therefore, be justified in concluding that the story first gained currency soon after the official introduction of Buddhism into Ceylon owing to the religious enthusiasm of the early converts and their national sentiment, which co-operated in producing a belief associating the founder of their new

[1] Chaps. I and II.

[2] P.T.S. Ed., pp. 1 foll.

[3] *M.V.*, chap. i, vv. 19 ff.

[4] Ibid., i, vv. 40–3.

[5] *Dīp.*, i, v. 4.

[6] It is interesting to note that the Burmese claim a visit of the Buddha to Burma. He is supposed to have stayed at a place now known as the Lohitacandana Vihāra (*Sāsana-vaṃsa*, Introd., p. 13).

faith with the dawn of history in their island home, which was thus made for ever sacred to them by the touch of the Master's feet.

Whatever be the truth underlying the accounts of these visits, there exists other evidence which makes it possible to believe that prior to the arrival of Asoka's missionaries Buddhism was not unknown to Ceylon.

The known history of the Sinhalese begins with the landing in Ceylon of Vijaya with his 700 followers in 543 B.C.,[1] according to the strict orthodox tradition on the very day of the Buddha's death.[2]

There is room for suspecting, as Turnour remarks in his Introduction to the *Mahā-vaṃsa*,[3] that sectarian zeal had led to the assignment of the same date for the landing of Vijaya as to the cardinal Buddhistical event—the death of the Buddha. But we may confidently hold that Vijaya landed in Ceylon about the middle of the sixth century B.C. He was a headstrong and impetuous youth, scion of a royal race, which held sway over the country of Lāḷa (or Lāṭa), whose capital was Siṅhapura[4], Being banished from home because of their misdeeds, he and his followers, after many adventures on the way, landed in Ceylon, and energetically set about colonizing the country.

Ceylon was inhabited by a race of men whom Vijaya and

[1] According to Ceylon chronology (*Ep. Zey.*, i, pp. 155 foll.) Western scholars have long held this date wrong by some sixty years, but recent research, especially a new and more critical study of the Khāravela Inscription in the Hāthigumpha Cave, Orissa, has furnished very strong evidence that the Buddha was contemporary with both Bimbisāra and Ajātasattu. The inscription fixes the latter at about 554 B.C., and Bimbisāra, his father, at *c.* 582 B.C., thus supporting the Ceylon dates. Vide *Bihar and Orissa Research Society Journ.*, vol. iii, pp. 425–507; *JRAS.* 1918, pp. 543–7; *Ceylon Antiq. and Lit. Reg.*, July, 1922, pp. 66–7.

[2] Thus the *M.V.*, vi, v. 47. The *D.V.*, ix, v. 21, refers the event to the time of the *Parinibbāna*. The *Samanta-p.* assigns it to the same year as the death of the Buddha (loc. cit.).

[3] *M.V.*, Transl., Introd., p. li.

[4] Neither the country nor the city has yet been successfully identified. Philological evidence tends to the view that the original home of Vijaya was in E. Bengal; it is not my purpose to discuss the question here.

his companions called Yakkhas, and who evidently belonged to an earlier colony of settlers that had migrated from South India.[1] For there is no reason to doubt that Vijaya's band was only one, perhaps the best known and the most powerful, of colonists who had gone over from India in their southward course.[2] Only a few miles of water separate Ceylon from the mainland. Even to-day people cross over in *kattamarans*, the most primitive of all modes of boat save that of the hollowed log.

The country already possessed a certain degree of civilization. The Yakkhas had their own cities, social institutions, a fairly well-developed language, and indubitable signs of accumulated wealth. Spence Hardy tells us that Lankāpura, the Yakkha capital, which Vijaya visited soon after he had landed, is no mere city of imagination, as its site can still be pointed out in the district of Mātale, in the Central Province.[3] One of Vijaya's first acts was to marry, under romantic circumstances, a Yakkha princess, by name Kuvēṇī. Divested of obvious exaggerations, she appears before us as a very real and fascinating lady, whose ideas, tastes, and language harmonized with the princely character of Vijaya. And she had charms sufficiently real and refinements sufficiently captivating to win him and to obtain the honour of being his wife. It is true that she was later discarded in favour of another ; but that was under the stress of political expediencies. After the marriage Vijaya founded the city of Tambapaṇṇi and settled down there, while his ministers set about to form separate establishments, each for himself, "that the country might be rendered habitable for men," [4]

[1] Tennent, *Ceylon*, i, pp. 327 foll.

[2] Sir W. Jones said that Rāma "conquered Sīlān in 1810 B.C.," basing his authority on the *Rāmāyaṇa*. However that may be, there is no doubt that, invited by its elephants and pearls, the fertility of the soil, and the salubrity and the richness of its products, the Indians settled there quite early, even if their occupation was not coeval with that of India. D'Alwis, *Sidat-saṅgarā*, Introd., p. xi.

[3] *JRAS.* (*C.B.*), i, No. 2, p. 101.

[4] *Rāja-rat.*, chap. i, *M.V.*, vii, v. 39.

in parts widely distant from each other.[1] It may be inferred that the places were well-populated and that the people were of a peaceable character, else the small party would not have dared to separate. Besides, the marvellous nature of the works executed by the Sinhalese and the rapidity with which they were finished in the first century and a half after the conquest (such as, for example, the irrigation tank of Anurādha constructed less than forty years after Vijaya's landing),[2] seem to show that the Yakkhas had a high degree of civilization.

It is most improbable that into a community so cultured and well-established some traces, at least, should not have found their way, of that great Buddhist spiritual movement, which was making rapid strides in the mainland, and whose missionaries, with that enthusiasm which invariably marks allegiance to a new cause, were carrying the glad tidings even into regions hitherto unexplored. It is true that Vijaya's own attention was fully engrossed with the consolidation of his newly-acquired power. But the others who came soon after him, in ever-increasing numbers, were from countries where Buddhism was the dominant faith.[3] This becomes all the more probable when we are told that Vijaya obtained his consort for his coronation from among the daughters of the Pāṇḍiyan king, who reigned at Madhurā in South India, and that she was accompanied by hosts of others, among them being a thousand families of the eighteen guilds.[4] Now these Pāṇḍiyans were originally a Kṣatriya race of Āryans from the Madhya-deśa, the scene of the Buddha's lifelong ministry.[5]

After they had left their original home in their wanderings southwards they kept in touch with those whom they had left behind. It is, therefore, reasonable to suppose that the Pāṇḍiyan families carried over with them to Ceylon some knowledge of the Buddha and his teachings.

[1] *M.V.*, vii, vv. 43–5.
[2] Ibid., ix, v. 11.
[3] Tennent, i, p. 339, and Hiuan-Tsang, *Travels*, chap. iv.
[4] *M.V.*, vii, vv. 57 foll.
[5] D. R. Bhandarkar, *Carmichael Lectures*, 1918, pp. 9 foll.

Hugh Nevill, in the Introduction to the Catalogue, which he prepared for publication, of his collection of Pāli books now in the British Museum, says that when he was in Ceylon he was informed of a tradition among the Tamils there, that Vijaya had actually, after settling down in Ceylon, introduced a colony of persecuted Buddhists from Magadha.[1]

In his Introduction to the *Jinālaṅkāra* James Gray ascribes that work to a monk named Buddharakkhita, born of a distinguished family in Ceylon in 426 B.C. " With the inducements to missionary work in Vijaya's domain our author must have joined the Church and, as an outcome of his devotion to Pāli studies, composed the *Jinālaṅkāra*." " And he was at the head of a congregation of monks in Coḷika-tamba-raṭṭha, the maritime western division of Ceylon, where the Coḷas of the Coromandel coast originally settled." [2] Though there is no historical evidence to support the very great antiquity attributed to this work,[3] yet the Burmese tradition, which Gray has followed in making these statements, serves to show that long before Mahinda's arrival, Buddhism was known in Ceylon.

In this connexion, there is one more fact worthy of notice. Vijaya died, leaving no heir to the throne. Before his death he sent an embassy to his younger brother Sumitta, inviting him to take charge of his domain in Ceylon. Sumitta, having been already crowned king as his father's successor, accepted the invitation on behalf of his youngest son Paṇḍuvāsudeva, who came over and succeeded Vijaya. His queen was a Sākya princess, Bhaddakaccānā, of great beauty. Suitors from many lands sought her hand, and her father, to escape unpleasant complications, put her in a boat with a few friends, and launched it upon the Ganges. The boat, with its precious cargo, reached Ceylon, and Bhaddakaccānā became Paṇḍuvāsudeva's queen.[4] She and her companions, all scions

[1] British Museum, Oriental Catalogue.

[2] *Jinālaṅkāra*, Introd., pp. 7–8.

[3] See my remarks on the *Jinālaṅkāra* further on.

[4] *M.V.*, viii, vv. 18 foll.

of the Sākya clan, were undoubtedly Buddhists, because the *Piṭakas* bear ample testimony to the whole-hearted adherence and the loyal devotion of the Sākyans to the new faith taught by their great kinsman. It would be strange if, with such intercourse with the motherland, the Sinhalese people of that day were not brought into touch with the religious movement which was then growing and spreading in power in the valley of the Ganges.

Both Vijaya and his successors treated all religions with a perfect equality of royal favour, a policy evidently dictated by their eagerness to encourage immigration. Yakkha temples were respected, and even annual offerings were provided for them; halls were built for the Brahmins; residences were erected for them at public expense, one of them being the Titthārāma (the monastery for foreign religions), built by Paṇḍukābhaya, on the spot where Abhayagiri now stands at Anurādhapura.[1] No mention, however, is made of a single edifice having been built for the use of the Buddhists—a silence probably due to a natural tendency on the part of Buddhist chroniclers to concentrate all attention on Mahinda and thus connect the introduction of Buddhism into Ceylon with the most distinguished person conceivable, the great Asoka.[2]

Paṇḍukābhaya was followed by his son Muṭasiva, and he in turn by Devānaṃpiya-Tissa (Tissa Beloved of the Gods). He was Muṭasiva's second son, but was chosen because he was "foremost among all his brothers in virtue and intelligence."[3] At the time of his coronation many miracles came to pass. "In the whole Isle of Laṅkā treasures and jewels that had been buried deep rose to the surface of the earth . . . pearls of the eight kinds . . . came forth out of the ocean and lay upon the shore in heaps."[4]

Soon after his accession Tissa sent envoys to his friend Dhammāsoka with costly presents—an act of friendly homage,

[1] *M.V.*, x, vv. 98–102.
[2] Oldenberg, *Vinaya*, Introd., p. lii.
[3] *M.V.*, xi, v. 6.
[4] Ibid., xi, vv. 8–15.

further evidence of the free intercourse which existed between the two kingdoms. The great emperor returned the courtesy. He sent an embassy of his chosen ministers, bearing gifts marvellous in splendour, that Tissa might go through a second coronation ceremony, and the messengers were directed to give this special message to the king: "I have taken refuge in the Buddha, his Doctrine and his Order. I have declared myself a lay disciple of the religion of the Sākya son; seek then, even thou, O best of men, converting thy mind with believing heart, refuge in these best of gems."[1] Thus was the ground prepared for Mahinda's mission.[2]

In the meanwhile, between the landing of Vijaya in 543 B.C. and the arrival of Mahinda about 243 B.C., many changes had come over India, north of the Vindhya Mountains. In the middle of the seventh century B.C. the paramount power was the great kingdom of Kosala, then at the height of its prosperity, under the great Kosalan (Mahākosala). His dominions extended from the mountains to the Ganges, and from the Kosala and Rāmagaṅgā rivers on the west to the Gaṇḍak on the east. But already in the time of the Buddha's boyhood a new star was rising on the political horizon. This was Magadha, a petty kingdom on the South of Kosala. The exact course of events which made Magadha triumph over all her rivals it is impossible to follow. But one fact stands out clearly: before more than a century and a half had elapsed from the date of the Buddha's death, Candragupta, a scion of the Nanda race, and a youthful adventurer, effected a revolution at Pāṭaliputra (Patna), the capital of the Magadhan monarchy, exterminated the Nanda family, which was then holding sway, destroyed the Macedonian garrison in the Indus basin, and, having thus secured his position against all enemies, worked his way

[1] *M.V.* xi, vv. 34–6.

[2] For this, and the rest of the historical portion about Asoka in this chapter, see Rhys Davids, *Buddhist India*, pp. 272 foll.; Vincent Smith's *Aśoka* (Oxford Univ. Press), Rulers of India Series, *passim*; and *The Oxford History of India* (1923), pp. 72 foll.

to a dominion equalling the mightiest then existing. He made of Magadha a gigantic empire and became the first genuinely historical emperor of India. He was succeeded by his son, Bindusāra, whose title Amitraghāta (slayer of foes) suggests a martial career. Though nothing definite is recorded of his military achievements, it seems almost certain that the conquest of the Dekkhan was effected during his reign.[1] When the reign of Bindusāra terminated after a duration of twenty-eight years, he was succeeded by one of his sons, commonly called Asoka, then the Magadha Viceroy at Ujjenī. His succession was contested; but, in the end, he asserted his rights and was crowned emperor. He inherited a kingdom which was strong and rich and extensive, protected by a large army, administered by a government with elaborately organized departments, and carefully graded officials with well-defined duties. Asoka was a man of peaceable disposition, and did everything in his power to make his subjects happy and contented. His imperishable records, in the shape of those wonderful inscriptions—the most remarkable of their kind in the world, and apparently written for the most part to his own dictation—enable us to form a fairly connected and vivid picture of his life. He waged but one war, and that a war of annexation, upon the kingdom of Kaliṅga, eight years after his consecration. This war is made to appear the turning-point in his career; for to this war was due not only the gradual development of the emperor's character and policy which converted him to the Buddhist faith, but also that movement which he later initiated, whereby Buddhism, from being a local sect, grew to be one of the world religions. The Kaliṅga war thus became one of the decisive events in the history of the world.

Asoka himself tells in the Thirteenth Rock Edict [2] how repentance came upon him when he contemplated the miseries and the sufferings which the indulgence of his

[1] Smith, *Oxford History*, p. 76.
[2] Senart, *Inscrip. de Piyadassi.*

ambition had involved, and how he was driven to seek in the Good Law, which he elsewhere identifies with the teaching of the Buddha, refuge from the hauntings of a remorse-stricken conscience.

There were three stages in this conversion. The Rūpnāth Edict,[1] written about the thirteenth year after his formal coronation, mentions that he had been, for two and a half years, a lay disciple (*upāsaka*), but had not developed much zeal, but that one year before the date of the Edict he had entered the Order.[2] In the Eighth Edict he tells us that in the thirteenth year after his anointing he had set forth on the path to *Sambodhi* (towards the attainment of Arahantship). Thenceforward he devoted his whole energy and all the extensive resources of his vast empire to the realization of the noble ideals which the new faith had given him. With unbounded zeal and a high and lofty devotion, such as was worthy of so great a cause, Asoka devised ways and means of bringing about a change of heart in all men—whom he considered as his children—so that they, "hearing his Ordinance, based on the Law of Piety, and his instruction in that Law, may practise the Law." [3] He taught not merely by precept, but also by personal example. In the thirteenth edict he describes how he had already won success in his ambition in this direction among the people of Egypt, Syria, Macedonia, Epirus, Kyrene, among the Coḷas and Pāṇḍiyas in South India, and in Ceylon.

This last, the only one that may be called historically successful, is the achievement with which we are at present concerned. That Asoka had a special warmth of regard for Ceylon is clear from the message, referred to earlier, which he sent to Devānampiya-Tissa. According to the statements

[1] Senart, op. cit.

[2] What exactly this "Entering the Order" means is not clear. Perhaps it refers to the incident where Asoka consents to his children Mahinda and Sanghamittā entering the Saṅgha, which act made him a *Sāsana-dāyāda* "the inheritor, heir, or kinsman of the Buddha's religion", to the spreading of which teachings he thenceforward dedicated his life.

[3] Edict xiii.

made by the Ceylon Chronicles, which there is no valid reason for disbelieving—especially, in view of the evidence, brought to light by Cunningham in and near the Sānchī Topes, which corroborate, in a very remarkable manner, many of the facts therein mentioned—Asoka dispatched his son [1] Mahinda, with six others, to carry the glad tidings of the Good Law over to Ceylon.

The *Mahā-vaṃsa* describes with ecstatic rapture the advent of Mahinda to the island, his aerial flight, his descent to Ambatthala, the loftiest peak of Mihintale, where, rising suddenly from the plain, the mountain overlooks the city of Anurādhapura. The story proceeds to relate how the king, who was hunting the elk, was miraculously allured to the spot where Mahinda was standing, and how the latter propounded the Doctrine to the ruler of the land, who, together with his forty thousand followers, embraced the new faith.[2] Thus, on the full moon day of Poson (June–July), 236 years after the passing away of the Buddha, the new religion gained official recognition in the island. Mahinda's arrival, and the consequent conversion of the king and his royal retinue, was the culminating event in a process which had been going on gradually and without doubt tolerably rapidly for well nigh two centuries.

No time could have been more opportune for the promulgation of the new and living religion. The two hundred years which had elapsed after Vijaya's arrival had been spent in initiatory measures for the organization of the country. Encouraged by the facilities held out to settlers, fresh colonists had been pouring into the land in ever-increasing numbers. Towns had been built and arrangements made to keep them clean and healthy; suburbs had been laid out and measures

[1] " Aśoka's younger brother " says Smith (*Oxford Hist.*, p. 99) following the Indian tradition and also the evidence furnished by the Chinese. Hiuan-Tsang mentions the name of Mahinda, but calls him Aśoka's younger brother (Beal, *Buddhist Records of the Western World*, vol. ii, pp. 246–7). But I do not see any reason for accepting the Chinese version in preference to the Sinhalese.

[2] *M.V.*, xiv, vv. 1 foll.

adopted to provide the inhabitants with the necessary comforts of life; gardens planned, parks constructed, and fruit-bearing trees introduced. The production of food had been secured by the construction of canals and public works for irrigation. Every one, from the king downwards, took a personal interest in adding to the fruitfulness of the land. Carriage roads facilitated communication between the various settlements; village boundaries had been fixed, and the cultivation of art and science encouraged.[1] The people were contented and happy, and they were at the dawn of a new era of peace and prosperity. By the earlier infiltration of Indian culture the ground had already been prepared to receive a doctrine of life which gave a new purpose to existence and furnished an opportunity for noble endeavour. The seed had only to be sown for it to take root and blossom with amazing vigour.

As a fitting climax to the conversion of Ceylon, which was the most successful and most productive of the missionary efforts of Asoka, he sent his daughter Saṅghamittā, carrying with her, as a token of the king's cordiality and goodwill, a branch of the Pīpul tree at Buddha-gayā, where the Teacher had attained enlightenment. And the honour thus paid to Ceylon was well deserved. "It is doubtful if any other single incident in the long story of their race has seized upon the imagination of the Sinhalese with such tenacity as this of the planting of the aged tree. Like its pliant roots, which find sustenance on the face of the bare rock and cleave their way through the stoutest fabric, the influence of what it represents has penetrated into the innermost being of the people till the tree itself has become almost human. The loving care of some pious observer has left on record in sonorous Pāli and with minute detail the incidents of the day when the soil of Ceylon first received it,[2] and to-day the descendants of the princely escort who accompanied it from India continue to be its

[1] *M.V.*, x, vv. 88 foll.
[2] *Mahā-Bodhi-vaṃsa*, q.v.

guardians. The axe of the ruthless invaders who for so many centuries to come were destined to spread ruin throughout the country was reverently withheld from its base. And even now, on the stillest night, its heart-shaped leaves on their slender stalks ceaselessly quiver and sigh, as they have quivered and sighed for twenty-three centuries." [1]

The spiritual movement introduced under such well-auguring auspices found a permanent abode in the little island home. If the criterion of the greatness of such a movement be the beneficial influence it has exerted on the character of those towards whom it was directed, then, certainly, the mission of King Asoka to Ceylon was amongst the greatest civilizing influences of the world, for it bequeathed to the Sinhalese people a gentleness of disposition and a nobility and refinement of character of which neither the ravages of time, nor centuries of ruthless warfare, nor the insidious attacks of modern commercialism have succeeded in depriving them.

But by no means the least of its results was the impetus it gave to a fresh study of the problems of mankind in the light of its new philosophy—a study which resulted in the production of a voluminous literature, which for centuries commanded the veneration of the whole Eastern world, and the remnants of which even to-day excite our wonder and admiration. "For there, in that beautiful land," as Rhys Davids reminds us, "the province most fruitful of any in India or its confines, in continuous and successful literary work and effort, there have never been wanting, from that day to this, the requisite number of earnest scholars and students to keep alive, and hand down to their successors and to us that invaluable literature which has taught us so much of the history of religion, not only in Ceylon, but also in India itself." [2]

It is the story of that literature, unique in many respects, that we propose to unfold in the following chapters.

[1] P. E. Pieris, *Ceylon and the Portuguese*, pp. 3–4.
[2] *Buddhist India*, pp. 303–4.

CHAPTER II

THE WRITING DOWN OF THE BOOKS

WITH the arrival of Saṅghamittā, and the planting of the sacred Bo-tree in Sinhalese soil, the establishment of Buddhism in the island was complete. Great rejoicings marked the event. A festival of fourteen days, the like of which Ceylon had never before witnessed, was held in honour of the occasion. From the sea to the city gates the road along which the holy sprig was conducted to Anurādhapura was decorated, "sprinkled with white sand, bestrewn with various flowers, and adorned with planted pennons and festoons of blossoms."[1] Saṅghamittā was accorded all the honour due to so distinguished a visitor. When the ceremony of the planting of the tree was over, a state function was held, where the royal princes and other leading men who had escorted the Bodhi-tree were duly presented to the king by Ariṭṭha, the Sinhalese envoy, who had been specially dispatched to Asoka's court, to bring over Saṅghamittā and the sacred Pīpul branch. Titles and honours were conferred on the distinguished ambassadors, and arrangements were made for the custody of the holy tree and for the due performance of religious ceremonies in its honour.

Meanwhile day after day the great *Thera* Mahinda, on the invitation of the king, visited the palace in the forenoon and after being entertained with his companions to the midday meal preached the Good Dhamma to the multitudes who continually flocked to the palace gates to see the *Thera* and listen to his message. Day after day the concourse grew larger and larger, and thousands, hearing the teaching of the Great Elder, became converted and were admitted into the new faith.

A large number of the converts, both high and low, finding the householder's life uncongenial to the practice of the

[1] *M.V.*, xix, vv. 37 foll.

Buddha's message, renounced the world and entered the Order of the Saṅgha. The Prime Minister, Ariṭṭha, who was the king's nephew, and the king's younger brother, Mattābhaya, were among the very first of the Sinhalese Bhikkhus to be ordained.[1] For the residence of the Bhikkhus the king made an offering of the royal park, Mahā-megha-vana (the pleasance of the Great Shower), extending southwards from the city to the banks of the Kadamba river.[2] According to the Chronicles, many were the miracles that accompanied its consecration. The very elements manifested their joy at the glorious event; for on the extensive grounds thus dedicated to the use of the new religion was destined to rise a little while later the Mahā-Vihāra, the Great Minster, which for many centuries held, as a Temple of Learning, a prominent place in the Eastern world. Monasteries were built with all possible speed for the accommodation of the monks, and *Sīmā* (boundaries) were marked out for the holding of the *Uposatha* and other Vinaya acts of the Saṅgha. The women were by no means second to the men in their zeal for the new religion. Indeed, the very first of the converts to attain to the Fruits of the Path were Anulā, the wife of the sub-king Mahānāga, and the ladies of the court who formed her retinue.[3] A few days later, on attaining to the second stage of salvation (*sakad-āgāmi*), they expressed a desire to receive the *pabbajjā*-ordination and enter the Sisterhood of Nuns. They were informed that the Vinaya rules did not allow Mahinda to admit women to the Order, and it was to make their ordination possible that Ariṭṭha was sent to Pāṭaliputra, to Asoka's court, that he might bring Saṅghamittā. Soon after her arrival the Therī admitted Anulā and five hundred other women into the Order, thus founding the Bhikkhunī-Sāsana (the Sisterhood of Nuns) in Ceylon. They had already retired from the world and gone into residence in a nunnery which came to

[1] *M.V.*, xix, v. 66.
[2] The present Malvatu Oya to the south of Anurādhapura.
[3] *M.V.*, xiv, v. 58.

be known as the Upāsikā-Vihāra (the Vihāra of the lay sisters).[1] Saṅghamittā herself, wishing for greater seclusion and pleasanter remoteness, took up her abode in the Hatthāḷhaka (the Vihāra near the Elephant Post),[2] which the king built for her special use. There she remained till the end of her days, " working for the progress of the Doctrine and mindful of the good of the Bhikkhunīs." [3]

The monks and nuns who had thus retired from household life were not actuated, in taking this step, by a desire to live in indolent devotion, supported by the generosity of the rest of the community. Buddhism demands from its votaries ceaseless activity in the service of their fellow men and women, and *pamāda* (indolence) is the greatest of all sins. The members of the Saṅgha could, if they felt so inclined, go for a while into some woodland retreat, or mountain cave, and there meditate on the transitoriness of life, and the sorrows of this never-ending cycle of birth and death. But their rightful place was in the midst of men and women, preaching and discoursing, exhorting them to lead the good life, which alone could bring them to salvation. From its very inception Buddhism was a missionary religion. Quite early in his career as Teacher and Sage the Buddha took a momentous step in bidding his disciples go forth and preach the Dhamma to the whole world. " Go ye, monks," he said, " and wander for the good of the many, the happiness of the many, out of compassion for the world, for the good, for the happiness, and for the welfare of devas and men. Go not alone, but by twos. Preach, monks the Doctrine which is lovely in the beginning, lovely in the middle, lovely in the end, in the spirit, and in the letter ; proclaim the consummate life of holiness, perfect and pure." [4] Thus was the trumpet-call sounded, for the first time in the world's history, for the establishment of a religion, which knew no distinctions of colour or race, but

[1] *M.V.*, xviii, vv. 11–12.
[2] Ibid., xix, vv. 77–85.
[3] Ibid., xix, v. 78.
[4] *Mahāvagga*, i, 10 (*Vinaya Texts*, S.B.E., i, 112).

which was meant for the salvation of all mankind. It was this command of the Master that had sent Mahinda and Sanghamittā over to Ceylon, and they and those whom they admitted into the fraternity of the Buddha's disciples in the island considered it their self-appointed task to make the message of the Dhamma known in every hearth and home throughout the land. Until missionaries trained from amongst the sons of the soil could themselves carry aloft the light of the Dhamma amidst all the people, Mahinda did not consider the Sāsana firmly and securely established.[1] The Buddhist missionaries sought no advantage for themselves or for their own nationalities. It was their endeavour to establish in every land whither they carried the Teacher's message a Saṅgha having its own national character, free to develop along its own lines, untrammelled by external control, temporal or spiritual. Indeed, when on one occasion King Devānampiya-Tissa, after having done all that he thought was necessary for the permanent establishment of the Sāsana in Ceylon, asked the great Thera Mahinda whether the religion of the Buddha was well established in the island, the reply he received was: "The Sāsana has been established, but it has not yet taken deep root." "When will it be deeply rooted, Sir?" asked the king. "On the day when a son born in Tambapaṇṇi (Ceylon) of parents resident in that island has entered the Order in this island, and, having studied the Vinaya in this island itself, expounds it in this island, then, O King, will the Sāsana have taken deep root,"[2] was the memorable reply.

For this purpose and for the purpose of disseminating a knowledge of the Dhamma amongst the people a careful study of the religion was necessary. And Mahinda had provided for this by bringing with him over to Ceylon the traditions of the orthodox Thera-vādin school, contained in the canon which had been handed down by the Thera-vāda-paramparā (the succession of Elders), and which had been completed

[1] *Samanta-pāsādikā* (P.T.S. Ed.), p. 102. [2] Ibid.

and sanctioned by the Three Councils or Recitals held after the Buddha's death.

Devānampiya-Tissa's reign lasted for forty years. It was a period of unbroken peace, devoted entirely to the social and moral welfare of the country. The king had lived sufficiently long to see the accomplishment of the task upon which he had his whole heart—the permanent establishment of Buddhism as the national faith. This work well done, he passed away in the fullness of time, leaving behind him a name whose lustre the lapse of centuries has failed to dim in the memory of a grateful people. The whole island had become the scene of ever-increasing religious activity from Rohaṇa in the south to Pihiṭi in the north. By the time of Tissa's death the new religion had spread into every town, village, and hamlet, and Vihāras and other religious edifices dotted the land from end to end. Some of them soon acquired fame as centres of learning, and chief among them was the Dīghasaṇḍa-senāpati-pariveṇa, built by the king's commander-in-chief, Dīghasaṇḍa, who gave it to Mahinda.[1] In later times it became famous as the residence of the author of the *Mahā-vaṃsa*.[2] The desire for the acquisition of knowledge was also greatly encouraged by the presence of material prosperity. The disposition of the Gangetic population which had taken possession of Ceylon with Vijaya's arrival was essentially adapted to agricultural pursuits, and, helped by the zeal and vigour of the rulers, the people easily secured all the material comforts necessary for a happy life.

Tissa was succeeded by his brother Uttiya, and during his reign the great Apostle Mahinda passed away on the 8th day of the bright half of Assayuja (October), "the light of Laṅkā, the teacher of many disciples, he who, like unto the Master, had wrought great blessing for the people".[3] In the following year the saintly Saṅghamittā herself passed to her

[1] *M.V.*, xv, vv. 212–14.
[2] q.v.
[3] *M.V.*, xx, vv. 30–3.

rest. She had worked strenuously for the religion during twenty-nine long years, and her remains were cremated in sight of the Bodhi-tree which she had brought over from Jaṃbu-dīpa.[1] Uttiya was followed by Mahā-Siva and the latter by Sūra-Tissa, who was an ardent devotee of the religion, and is said before and after his accession to have built five hundred monasteries in all parts of the country. His pious career, however, came to a tragic end. From among the large concourse of foreigners who had come to Ceylon from Jambu-dīpa, two Tamils, sons of a horse-dealer, seized the kingdom and slew the king.[2] Thus began those periodical invasions of the Tamil hordes from the continent which later rendered desolate the greater part of the island and all but completely destroyed its culture and civilization. It is true that the Tamils (or the Malabars, as they are frequently called) brought with them a certain amount of civilizing influence in the form of Hindu culture; but the destruction they wrought was immense. They pulled down all public buildings, put to death the monks, and burnt whatever literary records fell into their hands. The ultimate disappearance of the greater part of the literature and learning of Ceylon was, as we shall see later, directly or indirectly due to the results of these invasions.

The usurpers were driven out after nearly twenty-five years; but very soon others appeared on the scene, with greater strength of arms, under the leadership of Eḷāra from the Coḷa country. They killed the reigning king, and Eḷāra ruled the kingdom for forty-four years, administering "even justice towards friend and foe".[3] Eḷāra himself was a good friend of Buddhism and the Buddhists, and he was one of the most popular rulers of the country; but his followers were not so scrupulous in their behaviour. In the meantime many of the Sinhalese, unwilling to bow the knee to the invader, had gone

[1] *M.V.*, xx, vv. 51–4.
[2] Ibid., xxi, vv. 10–12.
[3] Ibid., xxi, v. 14.

south to Rohaṇa, on the other side of the Mahaväli-gaṅga, and the Sinhalese capital was established at Mahāgāma,[1] where the ruling prince was Kākavaṇṇa-Tissa. He was a devout Buddhist and proved to be a great patron of that faith. In this he was assisted by his consort Vihāra-Mahādevī, whose enthusiasm excelled even that of her husband. Under their auspices the religion was firmly established in Rohaṇa, which later was destined to become the birthplace of many of Ceylon's most distinguished sons and daughters in all spheres of life. More than a half of the best known names in Ceylon literature come from this province, and even to-day the inhabitants of Rohaṇa are reputed for their learning and their ability. The patriotism of the Sinhalese could not tolerate a foreign invader in their midst. No government, however just, if based upon alien domination, could placate national feeling or satisfy national aspirations. Tales of oppression, rumours of the supercilious contempt with which the conquerers treated the country's holiest possessions, reached the Sinhalese band in their exile. Youths of strength and valour and ardent patriotism flocked to Māgama, their hearts burning to avenge their country's insults. But the time was not yet ripe. The old king realized that the expulsion of the Tamils was a task of no small difficulty, and his army and his resources were yet too weak and limited to undertake the reponsibility. But he could help towards that end, so that, when the propitious day dawned, the hated oppressor would no longer be supreme in the land. with this in view he gathered round him at his court all the bravest and the strongest of his subjects. Martial ardour, however, was not his predominant characteristic. It was otherwise with his queen, the noble lady, Vihāra-Mahādevī. She was cast in a much more heroic mould than her husband. The presence of a Tamil usurper on the throne at the sacred city of Anurādhapura was a humiliation which she resented deeply. Her ardent faith, too, strengthened her resolve to

[1] *M.V.*, chap. xxii, vv. 11 ff.

see the emancipation of her motherland, and, when the time came, this noble and sagacious woman played no small part in the national movement to sweep the infidel foe into the sea.

And the hour produced the man.[1] To the king and queen was born Gāmaṇi-Abhaya, who was to rid Laṅkā of the Tamil oppression and help her to regain her lost honour. The omens that attended his conception and his birth indicated that he was no ordinary man.[2]

When he was twelve, his father, lest his son should ruin his chance by any attempts of rash impetuosity, had asked him to take an oath that he would never fight with the Tamils. The brave lad promptly and indignantly refused.[3] We may be sure that the old king secretly rejoiced at having so courageous a son, and the queen-mother openly encouraged the lad's ambitions. He was trained in all the arts and sciences that he might be fit to be a ruler of men. At the age of sixteen he was given a separate establishment, and he gathered round him a famous band of giant warriors whose names have become household words to this day. The prince excelled all others in manly accomplishments—versed in archery, dexterous in swordsmanship, and skilled in guiding elephant as well as horse, he soon showed himself a born leader of men. Soon he sent forth his gallant bodyguard to sound the call to arms, and the nation manfully responded. In a few months the Sinhalese army, compact, thoroughly equipped and eager for the fray, assembled in Māgama, and Gāmaṇi demanded permission to cross the river and attack the foe. He met with a blunt refusal. "Be not rash," wrote the aged king, "and desist from any precipitate action. The Tamils are over a million men. The region on this side of the river sufficeth at least for the present."[4] But Gāmaṇi chafed at the restraint. He sent to his father a pair of bangles and other female ornaments,

[1] I have dealt with the career of Gāmaṇi at some length because it forms the central theme of the greatest of Pāli epics, the *Mahā-vaṃsa* (q.v.).

[2] *M.V.*, xxii, vv. 42 foll.

[3] Ibid., xxii, vv. 82–5.

[4] Ibid., xxiv, v. 4.

declaring "My Royal Sire is a woman, not a man", and hid himself to escape the royal anger. Soon afterwards Kākavaṇṇa-Tissa died, and within a few months of his coronation Gāmaṇi got ready in earnest for the campaign which had been his dream and ambition. With the blessings of the Saṅgha and the good wishes of the people he set out northwards with his army. Vihāra-Mahādevī accompanied her brave son and by her sagacity, enthusiasm, and encouragement kindled him to greater and greater achievements. Fort after fort fell under the charge of the brave Sinhalese band, and after a long siege at Vijitapura the Tamils were completely routed. A little while later Gāmaṇi engaged Eḷāra in a hand-to-hand fight near the south gate of Anurādhapura. Eḷāra was no match for his adversary, and soon fell. Gāmaṇi's victory was complete, and in the hour of his triumph he made a gesture which brought honour not only to himself but also to the nation which produced him. For he decreed that his royal adversary should be accorded all the honours due to a king, and further declared that no man, prince or peasant, should pass the spot where the remains of the Tamil hero lay buried riding in palanquin or litter or with beating of drums.[1] It is to the credit of the people of Ceylon that during two thousand years and more they obeyed this decree and continued to pay their homage to one who was a brave man and a just and humane ruler.

In a few days the king was crowned as supreme ruler of a united Laṅkā (the three Siṁhala provinces), and great were the rejoicings thereat. But the king's outlook on life had changed, the great and glorious success for which he had lived and dreamed gave him no real joy. He thought of the thousands of human lives on whom suffering had been wrought to encompass this end, and he was filled with poignant grief. For he had always been deeply religious in mind and compassionate at heart, and the memory of these miseries caused him great pain. He determined to start a new chapter

[1] *M.V.*, xxv, vv. 71–5.

in his life. Hitherto material conquest had been his one and dominant ambition ; henceforth he would be a man of peace, governing his people like unto a father, and devoting himself to the sacred cause of the Buddha's compassionate teaching. Thus was initiated an era of peace and joy and contentment, an age pre-eminently of faith, beautiful in its simplicity, yet illumined by knowledge and imbued with an extraordinary moral earnestness. It was an age when *devas* walked on earth and in their heavenly abodes declared their wish to be born in Laṅkā as men and women. There was happiness in the land and prosperity. Many are the tales, enshrined in tradition, of the saintly personages that flourished during this period, and some at least of them undoubtedly deal with historical characters. But the accounts of their doings are enveloped in myth and fable, and it is impossible to separate truth from fiction.

Gāmaṇi's munificence was especially directed to the erection of religious edifices, chief among them being the Lovā-Mahā-Pāya (the Brazen Palace, so called because of its being roofed with metal plates), a nine-storied monastery elevated on sixteen hundred columns of monolithic granite, resplendent with gold and silver and precious stones, furnished with costly beds and chairs, a gem-palace designed and constructed after the reputed model of a *devatā's* abode in heaven.[1] This was dedicated to the use of monks of all ranks and positions, and there they studied and preached the Sacred Scriptures. This was a great service rendered by the king to the growth of literature, the providing of a place where scholars could meet and discuss various problems. The *Pūjāvaliya* [2] tells us that books were supplied and all manner of comforts provided for the preachers.

But the greatest of his works was the Mahā-Thūpa, the Ruvanväli Dāgoba (the Relic Chamber of the Golden Sands, so called from its magnificence), the most stupendous and the

[1] *M.V.*, xxvii, vv. 10–20.
[2] Colombo Ed., p. 176.

most venerated of those at Anurādhapura. It was a labour of love, and the king took special precautions that no hardships fell upon the people in consequence of his great enterprise. "No work is to be done here without reward," he caused to be proclaimed, and no labourer was allowed to go away unrequited.[1] We are not here concerned with the building of the glorious edifice, except for one circumstance connected with it. We are told that on the day when the foundation-stone was laid for the Mahā-Thūpa, on the full-moon day of Vesākha (April–May), 144 B.C., the assemblage of monks for the auspicious occasion included not only the *bhikkhus* of Laṅkā, but also large numbers from the principal Vihāras and monasteries of India. The *Mahā-vaṃsa* [2] gives, with a wealth of detail, the names of many of the eminent visitors from India; Candagutta from the Vanavāsa country, Cittagutta from Buddha-gayā, Dhammasena from Isipaṭṭana, Indagutta from Rājagaha, Mānadeva from Pallavabhogga, Mittiṇṇa from Pāṭaliputta, Piyadassin from Sāvatthī, Suriyagutta from Kelāsa, Urubuddharakkhita from Vesālī, Urudhammarakkhita from Kosambī, Uru-saṅgha-rakkhita from Ujjenī, Uttara Mahā-Thera from the Vindhyas, Uttiṇṇa from Kāśmīr, and Mahā-Dhammarakkhita from Alasanda of the Yoṇa country (probably near Kabul). The *Mahā-vaṃsa* was here only following an older tradition, and, whatever we may feel about the chroniclers' statements as to the mode of travel adopted by these distinguished visitors and the numbers of the disciples that formed their respective retinues (sixty thousand, etc.), there is no gainsaying that this points to a historical event, that these eminent *theras* did come to Ceylon at the time and that they were men of influence in their various dioceses.

During the period of commotion which existed at the time of the Tamil supremacy it is not probable that learning made much progress, nor is there much evidence that Gāmaṇi

[1] *M.V.*, xxvii, v. 23, and xxx, v. 17.
[2] Ibid., xxix, vv. 30 foll.

during the earlier years of his reign had time left for the promotion of intellectual attainment amongst his subjects; for he was completely engrossed in erecting a series of monumental structures. But with the firm establishment of domestic peace and prosperity learning must have proceeded apace, and the arrival of these eminent *theras* from India, from regions as far apart as the Dekkhan and Sāvatthi, together with their followers, must undoubtedly have given a fresh impetus to the study of the religion of which they were the exponents. A hundred years had elapsed between Mahinda's mission and the visit of these holy and learned men, and many things had happened in Ceylon during that period. In India, too, after the expulsion of the dissentient monks from Moggalīputta-Tissa's Council, many developments had probably taken place in the doctrine, and these visitors were able to acquaint the Ceylon Bhikkhus with such occurrences. No records exist of any literary productivity at this period, because the chroniclers were concerned only with accounts of royal munificence in the erection and endowment of religious structures; but chance references to events such as this visit and the circumstances connected with them justify such conclusions as we have arrived at above.

The thirty-second chapter[1] of the *Mahā-vaṃsa* contains also certain references to several of the chief monks of Gāmaṇi's time. Among them we find Mahā-Malaya-Deva of Kālavela, who was in close connexion with the Bhikkhus dwelling on the Samanta-kūṭa (Adam's Peak), Dhammagutta, the Earth-shaker, of the Kaḷyāṇi Vihāra, Bhaggari-vāsin Mahā-Tissa, and Tissa the Short, who dwelt at Maṅgana in the highest mountains of Ceylon. It is interesting to note that some of these names occur in the list of the *thera-paramparā* (succession of Elders) taken from the old Sinhalese *Mahā-vaṃsa* and preserved in the *Parivāra*[2] and also in the list quoted in full by Buddhaghosa in the *Samanta-pāsādikā*.[3] Professor Rhys

[1] *M.V.*, xxxii, vv. 49 foll.
[2] Oldenberg, *Vinaya*, iii, pp. 313–14.
[3] P.T.S. Ed., pp. 32 foll.

Davids has identified some of them with certain *theras* mentioned in the Jātaka commentary,[1] and the conclusions he has drawn are optimistic. "It is evident," says he, "that these Theras are real personages. In the few scraps of the early Ceylon texts that have already been published we have sufficient information as to their opinions and as to their character to warrant the hope that, when the texts are completely before us, we may be able to reconstruct, to a very considerable extent, the literary and intellectual history of Ceylon in the second century B.C."[2] May his hopes be fulfilled!

There is one more fact in Gāmaṇi's career worthy of attention for our purpose, before we pass on. So great was the king's zeal for the propagation of the religion that he even assumed the rôle of preacher himself, his audience being none less than the monks of the Brazen Palace.[3] He seated himself in the preacher's chair in the centre of the spacious hall and made ready to give the august assembly a discourse on some religious topic from the *Maṅgala-Sutta*. But, although he was quite familiar with the Sacred Scriptures, he could not proceed; he descended from the pulpit "perspiring profusely"; he had realized how difficult was the task of the teachers, and his munificence towards them was made greater. From that period he instituted "the preaching of religious discourses to be kept up in the vihāras in various parts of Laṅkā, supporting the ministers of religion who were gifted with the power of preaching". From that day the custom of regular *bana*-preaching at the village temple became an established institution, continued uninterruptedly to the present day. In ancient times the temple was the village school as well; but with the disappearance of state endowments and the decay of old institutions the function of the schoolmaster has been gradually taken away from the village

[1] *JRAS.*, Oct. 1901, pp. 889 foll.
[2] Ibid., pp. 893–4.
[3] *Pūjāvaliya*, Col. Ed., p. 177.

monk. However, at no time in the history of Ceylon was the Sinhalese peasant deprived totally of education in the wider sense of the term. The monk in the village temple continued to relate to him passages from the Scriptures which he stored up in his memory.[1] In every instance stories were adduced to illustrate the subject under discussion, and morals were drawn from such tales. Even to-day, when a large percentage of the population labours under the ban of " illiteracy ", the peasant cannot be considered totally un-educated ; for the traditional lore which he has inherited from the temple teachers continues to furnish him with ideals of sagacity, of loving service and good fellowship, and this is ultimately a real education. To the historian of literature the institution of these temple discourses has another significance. To them may directly be traced the origin of the *Kathā-vatthu* books of religion and folklore, which in later days formed the most cherished possession of the villagers' scanty library. Of this more later.

Gāmaṇi was succeeded by his brother Tissa (Saddhā-Tissa, as he was called, because of his devotion to the religion). His reign of eighteen years was a period of unexampled prosperity. There is one story related of him which illustrates how deep was the interest evinced in Ceylon even by royal personages in the pursuit of wisdom and what great humility marked their acquisition of learning. Whatever literary achievements were accomplished by the Sinhalese were due very largely to the patronage extended to them by men of position and power, kings and queens not excluded. Several of Ceylon's monarchs were themselves distinguished authors, but they all had a love of literature and, what was more, showed it. One day it was announced that the great *Thera*

[1] Parker tells us in one of his interesting volumes on Ceylon that he knew of instances where the villagers used to travel 12 miles up and 12 miles down every full moon day to the nearest temple, carrying with them their meagre provisions for the journey. At the temple under the palm-trees, with the light of the tropical full-moon shining on the sand, they would listen throughout the night to preachers who discoursed to them one after another. The whole-night preaching still continues in certain parts where the bustle of modern life has not penetrated.

Buddharakkhita would preach that night at Mihintale. The king, unannounced and without any ceremony, came to hear the sermon. Having arrived late and being reluctant to disturb the audience, he stood outside the hall, listening with rapt attention. The discourse lasted the whole night, and at dawn the *Thera* concluded the sermon with the usual benedictions. The king's cry of acclamation revealed his identity. The *Thera* asked him when he had come. "When you were just commencing, Sir," said he. "You are king, sire, and not accustomed to such discomfort. How was it possible for you to remain standing outside throughout the night?" "Not one night, Venerable Sir, but many nights in succession would I willingly stand listening to a sermon such as yours. Let me assure you on my honour, I never missed one syllable of your discourse." Then he entered into a discussion with the Elder on the *Dhamma*, at the conclusion of which he offered the throne to the Teaching. But the *Thera* returned it, saying: "Do thou, O King, rule the country on behalf of the *Dhamma*."[1]

For some time after Tissa's death there was internal trouble in the land. The monks made an unfortunate intervention in politics in an attempt to place their favourite on the throne in violation of the law of succession. This attempt ended in failure and brought disaster upon them.[2] The rightful heir, dissatisfied with their conduct, discontinued the various offerings, the cost of which had regularly been borne by the Royal Treasury down to that time, and which had provided the monks with all the necessaries of life, thus enabling them to carry on their work of study and teaching in comfort. This withdrawal of the royal favour greatly inconvenienced the monks, and brought upon them slight and neglect which interfered with the progress of the religion. But a reconciliation was soon effected, and the king, anxious to atone for his erstwhile neglect and remissness, went to the other extreme of lavish expenditure and unbounded munificence. A few

[1] *Saddharmālaṅkāraya*, Colombo Ed., p. 123.

[2] *M.V.*, xxxiii, vv. 17–21.

years later, when his successor was on the throne, a commander of troops in the army raised the standard of revolt and slew the king. But another figure, more powerful than he, appeared on the scene. This was Vaṭṭagāmaṇi, whose reign is of immense interest in the history of Pāli literature. Within twenty-four hours of the revolt, the usurper was no more, and Vaṭṭagāmaṇi had consecrated himself as king. But quite soon the peace of the land was disturbed by rebellion within and invasion without. Taking advantage of the internal troubles, a large army of the Malabars made another of their periodic incursions, their object being plunder and the capture of the throne. In a great battle fought to the north of the capital the Sinhalese were completely defeated, and the king was compelled to mount his chariot and seek safety in flight. During fourteen years the king remained in concealment, befriended by a *Thera*, Mahā-Tissa, and a chieftain, Tanasīva.[1] In the meanwhile the people bowed to the inevitable, and accepted the Tamil domination, confident that soon their own royal line would be restored to them. In the hill-country the remnants of the Sinhalese army stoutly maintained their independence, and after an interval of over fourteen years Vaṭṭagāmaṇi slew the Tamil ruler and liberated the country from its oppressors.

Quite soon after his restoration Vaṭṭagāmaṇi built the Abhayagiri Dāgoba on the site of the Titthārāma, the monastery of the Nigaṇṭhas, whose leader, unmindful of the munificent hospitality which his fraternity had enjoyed at the hand of the Buddhist kings of Ceylon, had gloated over Vaṭṭagāmaṇi's misfortunes and openly expressed his delight at the king's defeat.[2] After the victory the king avenged the ingratitude, and, where the Titthārāma stood, he constructed the Abhayagiri Dāgoba, the mightiest of its kind, which, rising from a square platform of nearly eight acres in extent, exceeded 400 feet in height. The Vihāra attached to

[1] *M.V.*, xxxiii, vv. 50 foll.

[2] Ibid., xxxiii, vv. 44–6 and 81–3.

it he gave over to his benefactor, the *Thera* Mahā-Tissa. This Vihāra was destined later to be the scene of events which were of great consequence both to the religion and to the literature connected with it.

For it happened that the *Thera* Mahā-Tissa, who had accepted the gift of the Abhayagiri Vihāra, but actually lived elsewhere, was credited by general repute with living in domestic intercourse. Thereupon the pious monks of the Mahā-Vihāra, custodians of the purity and the reputation of the faith in Ceylon, assembled together and interdicted him. One of the *Thera's* pupils, who was present, obstructed them, and the tribunal of monks, adjudging the obstructor guilty of misconduct, expelled him from the Order. He, burning with resentment, left with a large body of his followers, and, breaking away from the Mahā-Vihāra fraternity, lived at Abhayagiri Vihāra. Soon their band was strengthened by the arrival in Ceylon of a body of monks from Pallarārāma in India, who, though professedly Buddhist monks, were regarded as heretics by the orthodox monks both of India and Ceylon. They belonged to the Vajjiputta Nikāya, one of the sects descended from those that had refused to recognize Moggaliputta-Tissa's Council. Their teacher was the Ācariya Dhammaruci, and on their arrival in Ceylon, finding no favour with the Mahā-Vihāra, they joined the Abhayagiri fraternity, which quite readily welcomed them and soon accepted also their doctrines and tenets. The dissentient Bhikkhu who had attempted to defend Mahā-Tissa, and who was now living at the head of the Abhayagiri monks, took to himself the name of Dhammaruci Ācariya, and thenceforward the Abhayagiri fraternity became known as the Dhammaruci Nikāya, established in the fifteenth year of Vaṭṭagāmaṇi and 454 years after the Buddha's death.[1] This was the beginning of the first schismatic division among the Saṅgha in Ceylon. It was originally a seceding movement, due purely to personal and disciplinary reasons; but in the course of time doctrinal

[1] *Nikāya-saṅgraha*, pp. 11 and 12.

differences came to be associated with it. For nearly twelve centuries it continued to disturb the peace of the Ceylon monks, and there is no doubt that during its period of existence its adherents produced literary works setting forth their point of view. But, unfortunately for us, kings, in the excess of their zeal for the preservation of the purity of the Dhamma, took it into their heads to persecute the heretics and burn their books, so that none of their doctrinal works have come down to us.[1] It is significant, however, that for quite a long time the Abhayagiri and the Mahā-Vihāra fraternities existed side by side, sometimes on quite friendly terms.

During Vaṭṭagāmaṇi's reign there took place another event which marked an epoch in the history of the Pāli literature not only of Ceylon, but, we may say, of the whole area. The *Mahā-vaṃsa* has but a brief reference to it: "The text of the three *Piṭakas* and the *Atthakathā* thereon did the most wise Bhikkhus hand down in former times orally; but, since they saw the people were falling away (from religion) the Bhikkhus came together, and, in order that the true doctrine might endure, they wrote them down in books." [2]

We gather from other sources, which give more details of this important event, that this solemn act of recording the teaching in books was the result of a council in which 500 Elders participated under the patronage of a certain chieftain. The venue of the Council was Alu-vihāra (Āloka-Vihāra), a rock temple a few miles from the town of Mātale in the Central Province.[3]

During nearly four and a half centuries the Buddha's message had been preserved and propagated mainly by oral tradition. The ancient chronicles of Ceylon give us the names of the elders who formed the most important links in this tradition. At the head of the list appears

[1] Several other works, however, attributed to members of this sect, exist even now. They will be noticed in their places.

[2] *M.V.*, xxxiii, vv. 100–1, also *Dīpavaṃsa*, xx, 20, 21.

[3] See *Nikāya-saṅgraha*, pp. 10 and 11.

Upāli, probably the eminent Nigaṇṭha, but later one of the most prominent of the Buddha's disciples and the chief exponent of the *Vinaya*. Then in succession follow Dāsaka, Soṇaka, Siggava, Moggalīputta-Tissa (President of the 3rd Council), and Mahinda and his fellow-missionaries to Ceylon (Ittiya, Uttiya, Sambala, and Bhaddasāla, all of them Tissa's pupils). First in the line of Sinhalese *theras* is Mahā-Ariṭṭha, Mahinda's pupil. Then follow a number of names whose places in the history of this succession it is difficult to fix with any degree of certainty, the last being Siva, who, perhaps, presided over the Council of Five Hundred responsible for the systematic writing of the *Dhamma* in books. How far the Alu-vihāra redaction agreed with or differed from the canon and commentaries settled by the 3rd Council and introduced into Ceylon by Mahinda's mission, whether after their introduction into the island any passages previously considered unorthodox had crept into the orthodox scriptures and whether the Alu-vihāra council separated such interpolations, and how far the *Tipiṭaka* and its commentary reduced to writing at Alu-vihāra resembled them as they have come down to us now, no one can say. This much, however, is certain, that in the fifth century of the Christian era the present *Piṭakas*, etc., were considered orthodox both on the continent and in Ceylon, as is evidenced by the visits of Buddhaghosa and Fa Hsian; and in view of the great care with which the orthodox monks attempted to preserve the purity of the Word there is not much probability that the canon underwent any material changes in the interval.

There is no reason, however, to believe that the writing of the *Dhamma* was unknown before this time. Mr. Wickremasinghe [1] even goes so far as to say that a written literature existed in Ceylon at least a century earlier than the Alu-vihāra Council. He cites many incidents from the *Mahāvaṃsa* to prove that writing was common long before Vaṭṭagāmani's period. Books are mentioned as early as

[1] Catalogue, p. x.

150 B.C. in the reign of Gāmaṇi. The *Sīhalatthakathā Mahā-vaṃsa,* so often referred to in the *Mahā-vaṃsa-ṭīkā,* must have been, he says, a written document. Elsewhere he asserts, in reference to the Vessagiri Inscription [1] (which he fixes at 161–137 B.C.), that the Sinhalese at the time were acquainted with the Brāhmī alphabet in a form complete enough for writing even Sanskrit. Thus the statement that until Vaṭṭagāmaṇi Abhaya the whole Buddhist canon was transmitted orally, is an exaggeration. Probably, as to some extent even now, the monks as a body knew the whole canon by heart. With regard to the Sinhalese commentaries, said to have been compiled by Mahinda, their very nature precludes the possibility of having been handed down orally. It may be that in Vaṭṭagāmaṇi's time they were still unarranged, rare, imperfect and full of inaccuracies, as even now in manuscripts. At Alu-vihāra the text was rehearsed and commentaries revised and distributed.[2] Writing was known even in the lifetime of the Buddha.[3] There is also the well-known commentarial story of King Pukkusāti, to whom the King of Kosala sent a letter containing an exposition of the *Dhamma.*[4] However, it is safe to assume that writing, save for contracts and probably letters, had not very long been in vogue and was not extensively known or cultivated. And it is very probable that lack of suitable writing material largely restricted its use. And there was also a high degree of sanctity attached to the *saying* of religious truths, so that it was considered most important to receive them direct from a teacher's lips. Even to-day great respect is shown to the man who carries all his learning in his head ; for " who knows whether books may not get lost or destroyed and become not easy to lay hands on ? " And the person who trusts to books for reference is contemptuously referred to as " he who has a big book at

[1] *Ep. Zey.*, i, p. 14.

[2] Wickremasinghe, Catal., p. xi.

[3] *Mahā-vagga,* i, 43, and again ibid., i, 49 (" sace kho Upāli lekhaṃ sikkhissati "). Oldenberg, vol. i, p. 75 and p. 77.

[4] *Papañca-sūdanī,* Col. Ed., p. 234 ; also *JPTS.* 1883, pp. 47–9.

home, but does not know a thing." Anyone visiting a village monastery in Ceylon at the present time will find the *ola* leaf books carefully wrapped up in costly silk cloths and reverently packed in beautifully carved bookcases, that the faithful devotees may offer to them flowers and incense and thus pay honour to the Buddha's word. The monk is expected to carry all his learning in his head.

Such circumstances as these made oral teaching at first the sole, and later the chief, means of preserving and spreading the knowledge of the religion. From the information at our disposal we can form a fair idea of how this was made possible. Buddhaghosa tells us that at the Rājagaha Council, when the *Vinaya-Piṭaka* had been recited, Upāli was entrusted with the work of teaching and preserving it.[1] Similarly other sections of the Teaching were given in charge of other Great Elders and their disciples. These several schools, in their combination, preserved the Teaching in its entirety, so that at any given time there were Bhikkhus who, while conversant with the rest of the Doctrine as well, specialized in the knowledge of a particular section of it. Such were the *Dīgha-bhāṇakas* (reciters of the *Dīgha-Nikāya*), *Majjhima-bhāṇakas*, etc. We also hear of *Vinaya-dharas* and *Tipeṭakis* in the commentaries. This practice of learning up portions of the Scriptures continued quite ordinarily for a very long time. Thus we find at Mihintale in the tenth century an inscription of King Kassapa V, recording that special honour was paid to monks for reciting certain sections of the Scriptures by heart.[2] What the 500 monks of the Alu-vihāra Council did was to arrange systematically the canon and the commentaries, so that what was till then known only to the few might become the possession of the many. Theirs was a definite step forward. Till then each scholar learnt a part of the canon by heart, taught it to his pupils and explained it in Sinhalese. Each was a walking, living edition of a certain text. To assist in

[1] *Sumaṅgala-vilāsinī*, P.T.S. Ed., p. 15.
[2] *Ep. Zey.*, i, pt. ii, p. 56.

remembering the explanation mnemonic verses, often doggerel in nature, were made use of. Books, such as we know now, were not then in existence. But the action of the Alu-vihāra monks changed all this. They systematized the canon and arranged it, so that the study of it became easier and simpler. And this writing down of the literature helped its advance in great measure; for a written literature can develop in a shorter time than one that is handed down by word of mouth, when each single text requires generations of teachers and disciples to be preserved at all. The service done by the Alu-vihāra Council in this respect was invaluable. "For you, as for me," said Sir Robert (now Lord) Chalmers, Governor of Ceylon, speaking in Colombo some years back,[1] "the rocky gorge of Alu-vihāra, impressive though nature has left it, must be always more impressive still as the scene of the fruitful labours of those 500 Bhikkhus—labours that mark an epoch in the history of the scholarship of the world, and that several centuries later drew that very encyclopædic scholar Buddhaghosa to the same venerable scene, there to study the authentic tradition of the Thera-vādins, which writing had safeguarded and preserved amidst wars and the ravages of time in Ceylon."

Manuscripts of the Alu-vihāra edition were soon made and were deposited in the Mahā-vihāra and other principal temples of the island.[2]

[1] Public Hall, Colombo, 27th February, 1915.
[2] *Pūjāvaliya*, Col. Ed., p. 198.

CHAPTER III

The Development of Buddhist Culture

VAṬṬAGĀMAṆI was followed by a series of undistinguished rulers in rapid succession. First came Mahā-Culi Mahā-Tissa, famed for his extreme piety and his ardent devotion to the saintly *Thera* Mahā-Summa. The latter part of his reign was troubled by the lawlessness of his cousin Nāga, known to history as Cora-Nāga (Nāga the rebel or robber). This prince was in all respects the worst of the earlier kings of the Sinhalese dynasty, a man of loose character and of cruel disposition. In spite of the munificence showered on the Buddhist religion by various monarchs and the devotion which most of them showed towards it, its tale is not one of uniform prosperity. And the first of its domestic enemies was Cora-Nāga, who harrassed the monks because they had refused to help him during his marauding career. He spared nothing sacred or profane, and when, after twelve years of oppression, he was poisoned by his Queen Anulā the people heaved a sigh of relief. But Anulā was equally libidinous and licentious, a profligate woman whose passions knew no bounds, of iron will, shrinking from nothing to gain her ends, a firm believer in the efficacy of poison to remove the unfortunates who incurred her disfavour. This " infamous woman ", as the *Mahā-vaṃsa* calls her, the Messalina of Ceylon, was before long put to death by Prince Kūṭakaṇṇa-Tissa, who, seeing the horrified people without a leader, left the monk's life to place himself at the head of the movement against the licentious queen.[1] His son, Bhāṭika Abhaya, succeeded him and reigned during twenty-eight years, a period of uninterrupted happiness to the people. He was a just ruler, truly humane and pious. One of his earliest acts was to remit all the taxes due to himself.[2] His devotion to religion was

[1] *M.V.*, xxxiv, vv. 16 foll.
[2] Ibid., xxxiv, v. 38.

extraordinary, and the chronicles dwell at length on the religious festivals which he held from time to time. His offerings to the Mahā-Thūpa were enormous, and some of them read to us now like fairy tales. Once he ordered, at his own expense of course, the Cetiya to be strewn from the steps to the parasol on the top with jasmine flowers, and thus covered it with a mass of blossoms which he kept from withering by means of water carried by machines from the Abhaya tank.[1] On another occasion he had a net of coral prepared and cast over the Cetiya, and, when he had given orders to fasten in the meshes thereof lotus-flowers of gold as large as wagon-wheels and to hang clusters of pearls to the lotus-flowers beneath, he worshipped the Great Thūpa with this offering. But what is more important, from our point of view, is that in five places in the capital he constantly entertained monks devoted to the acquirement of sacred learning and maintained them with the requisites of life.

The next hundred years was a period of great internal commotion, kings succeeding one another with great rapidity as a result of the varying fortunes of rival claimants to the throne. Sometimes, as in the case of Kanirajāṇu-Tissa,[2] the monks attempted to interfere in these political upheavals with disastrous consequences to themselves. The Lambakaṇṇas (long-eared ones), descended from the princes, who came over from India along with the branch of the sacred Bodhi-tree, had multiplied in numbers and acquired much influence in the country. They became a perpetual source of trouble, ultimately supplanting the ancient line of kings. During the whole of this period the only monarch of any importance was Vasabha, who reigned from about A.D. 65–109. The chronicles describe him as "delighting perpetually in well-doing"; he made lavish gifts to the monks and supported especially those who undertook to go about as preachers and teachers.[3] It is also recorded of him that he restored ruined

[1] *M.V.*, xxxiv, vv. 44 foll.
[2] Ibid., xxxv, vv. 10, 11.
[3] Ibid., xxxv, vv. 92–3.

and dilapidated buildings in various parts of the island where monks carried on their studies, and an inscription informs us of a gift made by him to a *Thera* named Majibvka who lived near Anurādha-pura.[1]

In the reign of the next king a small army of Coḷians invaded Ceylon and carried off much booty and a considerable number of prisoners. This insult was avenged by his son and successor, Gaja-Bāhu (the Elephant-armed), who invaded Tanjore with a large army. The king of Tanjore, intimidated by the sudden attack, acceded to all demands without a single act of hostility.[2] It was the first expedition of the Sinhalese outside their island home, and their success brought about several important and interesting results. Twelve thousand Coḷian prisoners accompanied Gaja-Bāhu on his return home, and they were settled in various parts of the country, where they quite soon became part of the permanent population. Their descendants are scattered in many districts even at the present time, and their language has influenced Sinhalese speech in no small measure. A large number of Coḷian words found their way even into the literary dialect of the Sinhalese. The king of Coḷa also presented Gaja-Bāhu with the jewelled anklets of the Hindu goddess Pattini and the insignia of four Hindu deities, Viṣṇu, Kartikeya, Nātha, and Pattini. The cult of these gods and goddesses was thus introduced into the island; an extensive literature and folklore grew up around these names; special families dedicated themselves to their service, and observances and ceremonies connected with these deities continue to this day. A large number of books dealing with the cult of Pattini are still available.[3]

No event of importance happened till nearly a hundred years later, when Vohāraka-Tissa ascended the throne in A.D. 204. He was so called because of his skill in the law and of his enactments forbidding and abolishing bodily injury as a punitive measure. He was a great patron of learning and

[1] *Ep. Zey.*, vol. i, pt. ii, p. 69.

[2] Pieris, op. cit., p. 9.

[3] *JRAS.* (*C.B.*), vol. viii (29), 462; ix (32), 321; x (34), 43.

helped the monks in all their difficulties.[1] Two *Theras* are mentioned as his special favourites, the *Thera* Deva, a gifted preacher living at Kappukagāma, and Mahātissa of Anurārāma in Rohaṇa. His gifts to the priesthood were immense, but among them is one worthy of special notice. We are told that after his accession he ordered the book called the *Ariya-vaṃsa* to be read frequently, and commanded that on each occasion of such public recital there should be held over the whole island a regular almsgiving of reverence for the true doctrine.[2] Now, this *Ariya-vaṃsa* was, as its name implies, a " book of the holy ones ", probably life-histories of men and women eminent in the Buddhist religion, which were read aloud for the edification of the people. It is obvious from the king's order that the habit existed before his time, and it is interesting to note that this custom has continued down to this day even in the remotest parts of the island. Every full-moon day, when the villagers assemble in the temple precincts to perform their religious observances, the monks relate to them stories of eminent men and women from the books of a bygone age, the chief among them being the *Jātakatthakathā* and the *Dhamma-pada* commentary. We cannot say now whether the *Ariya-vaṃsa* was written in Sinhalese or in Pāli, or perhaps in both, whether the audience were able to follow the stories as they were being read, or whether they had to be explained and expatiated upon by the monks who read them.

In this reign the Buddhist Saṅgha was once more faced with the problem of a violent schism.[3] We have already seen how the formation of the Dhammaruci sect with its headquarters at Abhayagiri in the reign of Vaṭṭagāmaṇi was the first serious blow to the authority of the Thera-vādins in Ceylon, since the establishment of the religion by Mahinda. The division thus originated continued all along, but

[1] *M.V.*, xxxvi, vv. 28 foll.

[2] Ibid., xxxvi, v. 38.

[3] *Nikāya-saṅgraha*, pp. 12–13.

apparently the bitterness of the controversy had disappeared. The two fraternities at Mahā-Vihāra and at Abhayagiri lived independently of each other, and there does not seem to have been any kind of communion between them. Both had become centres of learning, and already in the time of Bhāṭika Abhaya differences of opinion in regard to the text of the canon had begun to manifest themselves. The *Samanta-pāsādikā*[1] gives us an account of a dispute which arose regarding a reading of a certain passage in the Vinaya. When the dispute had dragged on, the king appointed his minister Dīghakārāyaṇa, a man well versed in scriptural lore, to settle the matter. After an exhaustive inquiry, he upheld the view of the Mahā-Vihāra community.

The kings were evidently not quite discriminating in the zeal they exhibited in lavishing gifts on the monks, and the people, too, partly ignorant and partly unconcerned with the individual or general disagreement over particular points of the Doctrine, maintained an attitude of *laisser faire*. The result was that the Dhammarucians, though they had not made much headway in securing adherents to their way of thinking, yet had grown rich in material possessions ; and we find that the monarchs one after another, anxious to maintain the goodwill of both parties, were equally generous to both fraternities. Thus Subha built beautiful rows of cells both at Abhayagiri and at the Mahā-Vihāra.[2] Gajabāhu raised the height of the Abhayuttara Thūpa and caused vestibules to be built at the gates thereof, and constructed the Gāmaṇi-Tissa Tank for the maintenance of the Abhayagiri monks.[3] Kaṇiṭṭha-Tissa caused to be built a splendid structure, named Ratana-pāsāda, at Abhayagiri, for the *Thera* Mahānāga ; he constructed twelve great and remarkably beautiful *pāsādas* at the Mahā-Vihāra, and made a road leading from the grounds to the Dakkhiṇa-Vihāra.[4] The two parties

[1] Colombo Ed., p. 189.
[2] *M.V.*, xxxv, v. 57.
[3] Ibid., xxxv, vv. 119–22.
[4] Ibid., xxxvi, vv. 7–14.

had thus been existing side by side, the Mahā-Vihāra fraternity more or less tolerating their unorthodox rivals. But in the reign of Vohāraka-Tissa the quarrel broke out anew. "In the days of this king," the *Nikāya-saṅgraha* tells us, "the monks of Abhayagiri of the Dhammaruci sect adopted the *Vaitulya-Piṭaka*, which certain infidel Brāhmaṇas called Vaitulyas, who had assumed the garb of monks for the purpose of destroying the religion, had composed in the time of Dhammāsoka Mahārāja, and proclaimed it as the preaching of the Buddha. Thereupon the priests of the *Theriya-Nikāya*, having compared it with the authentic text, rejected the Vaitulya doctrines as being opposed to religion." [1]

It is surmised that the reference here to the events of Asoka's reign relates to the beginning of the form of Buddhism known to us as the Mahāyāna. The close resemblance of the name *Vaitulya* to the *Vaipulya-Sūtras* belonging to that school is very suggestive.[2] The origin of the Mahāyāna sect is generally assigned to the first centuries of the Christian era. It is quite possible, however, that it had a much earlier beginning, but came into prominence only about the time referred to, because of the works of scholars like Aśvaghoṣa, who flourished in that age.

The action of the Mahā-Vihāra resulted in a great controversy, which produced such bitterness that the king himself intervened. He entrusted the investigation of the matter to one of his ministers, named Kapila, "a man who had exhaustively studied all branches of knowledge." Kapila reported in due course that the *Vaitulya-Vāda* was opposed to the strict teaching of the Buddha, whereupon Vohāraka-Tissa burnt all the available Vaitulyan books and disgraced the monks of the Abhayagiri, who had tacitly or overtly adopted the heresy.[3]

[1] p. 12.
[2] See also Geiger, *M.V.*, p. 259, footnote 2.
[3] *Nikāya-saṅgraha*, p. 13.

This was a most unfortunate act of intolerance. Not a single book of the Vaitulyans has come down to us, and we are not able to ascertain the ways wherein their opinions differed from those of the orthodox Thera-vādins.

It is noteworthy that the Buddhist monks, while they were perfectly tolerant with regard to other systems of belief professed by other religionists, were ever vehement in their persecution of schism. In the *Vinaya* an attempt to bring about disunion among the Saṅgha is put in the same category as shedding the blood of the Buddha. Boldly confident in the superiority of their own religion, they bear without impatience the errors, to them glaring, of open antagonists, and even seem to exult in the contiguity of competing systems, as though theirs would derive strength by comparison. To the assaults of open opponents the Buddhist displays the calmest indifference, convinced that in its undiminished strength his faith is firm and inexpugnable ; his vigilance is only excited by the alarm of internal dissent, and all his passions are aroused to stifle the symptoms of schism. The intolerance shown in this instance by the Mahā-Vihāra Bhikkhus brought its own retribution in due time. Like mushrooms that grow by night, the heretics secretly strengthened their numbers and waited for an opportunity to assert themselves. Their chance was not long in its arrival.

Next in our rapid survey of this early period we come to the Saint-King Siri Saṅghabodhi, one of the most revered names in Ceylon history. He embodied the spirit of self-renunciation and self-sacrifice which marked those whose feet were set in the path to *Sambodhi* (Enlightenment). He was a visionary and an idealist, " a man on earth devoted to the skies," and from a worldly point of view his career as king was a disastrous failure. Yet he was loyal to his principles, which he maintained at the cost of his kingdom and his life. The *Hattha-Vanagalla-vaṃsa* (q.v.) gives us a vivid description of the man and his ideals. Born at Mahiyangana, under the shade of the Thūpa, which stands on a spot hallowed by the tradition of the Master's visit, he was trained by his maternal uncle, the *Thera* Mahā-Nanda, who made him an accomplished scholar and a perfect man. Later on he was raised to the throne, and we are told that his piety and compassion were such that they moved the very heavens. But his novel methods of government and administration of justice, amidst a people unaccustomed to such measures, brought about a state of anarchy in the land; and, when one of the ministers, Goṭhābhaya, raised the standard of revolt, he gladly renounced the throne and retired to the forest to lead an ascetic's life. But the usurper felt his position insecure as long as Saṅghabodhi was alive, and he therefore set a price on the head of the fugitive king. Many murders were committed by unscrupulous men who coveted the reward. Meanwhile the king himself, in the course of his wanderings, had come to Attanagalla, where, in a beautiful woodland grove, the eye could linger with delight on the "pillared shades", thick with their dense green foliage and laden with their pendant fruits and flowers. Finding this an ideal spot, he remained there, leading a life of seclusion and meditation. Sometime later he met a peasant travelling through the forest, who on being questioned, not recognizing the king in his disguise, related all that was happening in the land. Being excessively glad at the opportunity of making the supreme sacrifice, the king revealed his identity and pressed upon the peasant to accept his head. This offer met with a positive refusal; but Saṅghabodhi proceeded to immolate himself, and the man, apparently paralysed by this sudden development, could not prevent it. The head was ultimately produced at the court; and when Goṭhābhaya saw it he was struck with sudden remorse. His very first act was to hurry off to Attanagalla, where he found also the dead body of the queen, who had lost her life while searching for her husband. The royal pair were cremated with all the honours due to their rank, and Goṭhābhaya immediately set about making all possible amends for his misdeeds. He built a number of monuments in memory of the departed king, on sites associated in some manner or other with the latter's brief hermit life. The most remarkable of them was the Vaṭa-dāgē ("Circular Relic-house"), a rotunda-shaped building constructed over the king's ashes. His munificence to the monks was great, and by these acts he gradually regained his lost popularity.[1]

This effort on the part of the king to win the people's goodwill was greatly helped by another opportunity of upholding undiminished the purity of the faith, which was to them then, as now, the greatest possession on earth. In the fourth year of his reign the old Vaitulyan heresy raised its head again, the scene of trouble being once more the Abhayagiri Vihāra.[2] The monks launched a campaign of vigorous propaganda. We are told that one of their number, the *Thera* Ussiliya-Tissa, recalling to their minds the disgrace which had befallen the heretical monks in Vohāraka-Tissa's reign, refused to be associated with the new enterprise. Finding dissuasion of no avail, he left Abhayagiri and with some three or four of his followers went over to Dakkhiṇagiri Vihāra. There they accepted as their leader a *Mahā-Thera* named Sāgala, and were thenceforth known as the Sāgaliyas, an offshoot of the Dhammaruci sect, but not wholly believing in the traditions of that community. When reports of these dissentient movements reached the king, he made up his mind to win by one stroke the everlasting gratitude of the true followers of the religion. As patron of the Buddhist church in the island, he assembled the monks of the five chief monasteries which constituted the orthodox Saṅgha of Ceylon—the Mahā-Vihāra, Thūpārāma, Issarasamaṇārāma, Vessagiri Vihāra, and the Cetiya Vihāra. After having satisfied himself by a searching inquiry that the Vaitulyans were heretical in their views, he lost no time in having the books of the *Vaitulya-vāda* collected and burnt. And in order to teach a lesson to the others, he picked out sixty of the principal

[1] *Hatthavanagalla-vaṃsa* (concluding chapters).
[2] *Nikāya-saṅgraha*, p. 13.

offenders, branded them, and expelled them from the country.[1]

For a time all went well. The exiled monks settled down at Kāvīra, in South India, and there they soon made themselves powerful. To them came a young and shrewd adventurer, who, noticing the favours lavished upon them by their followers at Kāvīra, joined the band as a monk. After his ordination he went by the name of Saṅghamitta. It is said that one day, while the monks were changing their clothes preparatory to bathing, Saṅghamitta saw the brand-marks on their bodies and questioned them about it. Having learnt of all that had happened, he offered them his services, if he could be of any use. He was told that, if he could go to Laṅkā and openly and boldly interest himself on their behalf, they might still be able to return thither and wrest power from their enemies, now in triumph. Saṅghamitta had unbounded confidence in his abilities and he gladly entered into the adventure. "I will go and will see that either the monks of the Mahā-Vihāra adopt the Vaitulya doctrines, or that the Vihāra itself is uprooted and destroyed." So said he, and sailed in a few days. On his arrival he took residence at Abhayagiri and began his insidious campaign.

Meanwhile the Sāgaliya sect, which had seceded from the Dhammarucians a few years previously, had not been idle. They had attempted by every means in their power to propagate their views and had met with a certain measure of success. The people were perplexed by these varied views contending for acceptance and were unable to decide for themselves which were the true teachings of the Buddha. The king, wishing to come to some sort of settlement of these disputes, summoned another meeting of the different factions, and a solemn assembly was held, this time at the Thūpārāma. The king himself was present. Here Saṅghamitta denounced the views of the Theriya Nikāya and the practices of the Mahā-

[1] The accounts of these schisms are taken mainly from the *Nikāya-saṅgraha*.

Vihāra fraternity, and he put forward his case with such great force of argument that the king was convinced. The king's uncle, *Thera* Goṭhābhaya, after whom the king had been named, belonged to the orthodox party ; but his attempts to win over the king were of no avail. Saṅghamitta triumphed, and thus began a period of great calamity to the Mahā-Vihāra monks.

It was the first time in the history of Buddhism in Ceylon that a reigning Sinhalese sovereign had accepted and publicly taken the side of a heretical sect in opposition to the orthodox church. For over five and a half centuries the Mahā-Vihāra had been looked upon as the lawful custodian of the purity of the faith, and this secession of the king therefore caused great consternation amongst them. We are told that they held many and frequent meetings of their followers to decide upon a course of action.

Saṅghamitta soon became a great favourite of the king, enjoying his friendship and confidence. He was appointed tutor to the king's two sons, and it is said that when he found the elder son too clever to be deceived by his false doctrines, he paid greater attention to the younger, Mahā-Sena.

Although Goṭhābhaya had thus taken the heretics under his wing, his old attachment to the Mahā-Vihāra was too great to allow him to harm them, as Saṅghamitta desired. On the contrary, he continued to support them, though perhaps not with the same zeal and devotion as before. On his death his elder son, Jeṭṭha-Tissa, came to the throne. He was a proud and arrogant man, and his barbarity towards his nobles, whom he suspected of disloyalty, won for him the surname of "the Cruel". On his accession, Saṅghamitta, realizing that the king was by no means his friend, after consultation with the younger prince, who was his favourite, hurriedly left the country, to wait patiently at Kāvīra for the day of his triumph, when Mahā-Sena should sit on the throne of Ceylon. Jeṭṭha-Tissa proved himself later to be a staunch friend and patron of the orthodox party and showered his favours upon them during the fourteen years of his reign. He was succeeded by his brother Mahā-Sena, one of whose first acts was to send for his erstwhile tutor and friend, Saṅghamitta, who was also asked to preside at his coronation. This act of preference showed quite clearly what the king's disposition was towards the Mahā-Vihāra sect.

From the day of his return Saṅghamitta tried his best to persuade the monks of the Theriya Nikāya to accept the *Vaitulya-Vāda*. But they were loyal to their faith and remained adamant. At last he pointed out to them what their refusal would mean for them, by way of the king's wrath. Such threats were of no influence, and Saṅghamitta was determined to have his revenge. " The dwellers in the Mahā-Vihāra do not teach the true *Vinaya*," he told the king; " we of the Abhayagiri are those who teach the true *Vinaya*." But Mahā-Sena, weak-minded though he was and devotedly attached to his tutor, shrank from the suggestion. The traditions which he had inherited from his ancestors of many centuries proved too strong for him to resist them, and perhaps the fear of the people's indignation at so dastardly a crime as that prompted by Saṅghamitta weighed with him as well. But Saṅghamitta would not be easily baulked. Again and again he pleaded and entreated, he argued, " the Devil quoted scripture for his purpose " and Mahā-Sena yielded at last to his importunities. His reluctance and weak resistance broke down before the ceaseless intriguing of the crafty Saṅghamitta.

Then followed a series of events which formed the darkest chapter in the early history of Buddhism in Ceylon. A Royal Edict went round, " whoever gives alms to a Bhikkhu dwelling in the Mahā-Vihāra is liable to a fine of a hundred pieces of money," and no one dared disobey. Three days the monks went their usual round in the city, begging-bowl in hand, and each day they returned with empty bowls. For the first time in six centuries the Mahā-Vihāra starved. On the fourth day the monks of the Theriya Nikāya assembled in solemn conclave at the Brazen Palace. Their decision was manly: "Even though we starve to death," said they, "we cannot concede that heresy is true doctrine. Should we do so, many others would follow us and suffer evil, and the guilt would be upon us. Let our lives and our asceticism be imperilled, we persist in refusing to adopt the *Vaitulya* doctrines." Thus by their courageous resolve, by their steadfast loyalty to the faith, whose purity they valued more than their very lives, by their self-sacrificing zeal, did they win for Ceylon what has ever remained its proudest boast, that "Laṅkā is the home of a Buddhism whose teachings are pure and unsullied and untainted by heresy". Leaving their vihāras, their abodes of sanctity and their seats of learning, they journeyed out of Anurādhapura, some to the Māyā Province and others to Rohaṇa, there to await the day of their deliverance from persecution.

Saṅghamitta's joy was unbounded; this was the hour of triumph for which he had yearned and planned throughout his life. Things had happened exactly as he desired, and his success was complete. "Ownerless land belongs to the king," he whispered in Mahā-Sena's ear, when the orthodox monks had deserted their vihāras. Thus it happened that all the abandoned monasteries and their possessions were seized in the king's name and appropriated by the Dhammarucians now in power. A campaign was started in dead earnest, led by Saṅghamitta and his friend, a minister named Soṇa, to extirpate the Theriya monks. They carried on apace the work of spoliation and destruction of all that erstwhile belonged to their rivals. Stately structures were demolished and plundered, one after the other; the Mahā-Vihāra, the Brazen Palace, and all such religious edifices, built by the generosity of devout kings and pious noblemen for the use of the orthodox Saṅgha, were razed to the ground. Some three hundred and sixty-four colleges and great temples were uprooted and destroyed, says an ancient chronicle[1]; and the spoils gathered from them

[1] *Nikāya-saṅgraha*, p. 14.

went to enrich and adorn the home of heresy, the Abhayagiri, which, now splendid in ornaments and rich in possessions, stood, pre-eminent over all, as the greatest and the wealthiest monastery in Laṅkā. During nine years Saṅghamitta lived in glory. In the tenth year, however, the popular indignation against the religious activities of the king and his two evil counsellors, came to a head in an open rebellion led by a noble named Meghavaṇṇābhaya, one of the king's own ministers. Mahā-Sena marched with his forces to quell the uprising, and the two armies met near Mahāgāma. There an interesting thing happened. The rebellious minister, anxious to indicate that he bore no personal ill-will against the king, although he was determined to fight and even slay him in defence of the religion, proceeded into the royal camp, taking with him choice food and drink that he might partake of it with the king. He was duly recognized and led before Mahā-Sena. The king, who always bore a great regard, even affection, for Meghavaṇṇābhaya, questioned him as to the motives of his coming. He, setting the food and drink on a table, invited the king to partake of it and talk to him in confidence. In perfect trust Mahā-Sena sat down and, when the meal was over, asked "What has made thee to become a rebel, Meghavaṇṇābhaya?" "Because the Mahā-Vihāra has been destroyed, sire," said he, with tear-filled eyes. "I will make the Vihāra to be dwelt in yet again, Abhaya; forgive me my fault," replied the conscience-stricken king, who evidently was sick himself of the destruction wrought by his evil geniuses. The two were reconciled on the spot, and the two armies marched back to the capital in the friendliest possible intercourse. *Tout comprendre c'est tout pardonner*. At Anurādhapura, meanwhile, the people had taken the law into their own hands, and they broke out into wild demonstrations. The lead for violence was given by one of Mahā-Sena's own queens. She had long and bitterly wept over the destruction of the Mahā-Vihāra, and she had never forgiven the evil-minded Saṅghamitta, who was responsible for this savage act of vandalism and for the expulsion of the Theriya monks. Saṅghamitta was slain by a carpenter, as he attempted to obstruct the building of the Thūpārāma, which this queen had undertaken to restore. The people surrounded Soṇa's house, killed him and flung his body on to a dung-heap. When order was somewhat restored, the angry queen, who had procured Saṅghamitta's death, did what Goṭhabhaya had done thirty-seven years earlier—collected the heretical *Vaitulya* books and made a bonfire of them.

Mahā-Sena, true to his word, began to restore the Mahā-Vihāra, and in a short time the monks of the Theriya fraternity, their nine years' exile ended, returned to the capital. The royal Edict which had necessitated their departure was recalled, and for a time peace and quiet reigned in the land.

But it was not for long. The king was particularly susceptible to heresy. Two years later another dissentient monk, Kohon-Tissa by name, of the Sāgaliya sect, living at Dakkhiṇārāma, succeeded in gaining the king's confidence, and soon began fresh trouble for the Mahā-Vihāra. The king was anxious to construct a stately Vihāra for his new friend, and for this he wished to encroach upon the precincts of the Mahā-Vihāra. Against this the latter strongly protested, and left the Vihāra. But the king was obstinate and he sent men to uproot their boundary marks. Legend has it that a Rākṣasa (demon) with an iron-club uplifted in his hand, appeared on the scene and frightened away the workmen. He then ran amok in the city, and the king, alarmed, undertook to repair the damage done and restore the Vihāra to its rightful owners. Later, however, in spite of strenuous opposition, he built for his friend Kohon-Tissa the majestic Jetavana Vihāra on the Mahā-Vihāra premises. The latter, refusing to be thus inveigled, brought against Kohon-Tissa a charge involving one or more of the extreme offences, punishment for which was expulsion from the Order; and at a full meeting of the Saṅgha Kohon-Tissa was adjudged guilty after a long trial and ordered to be disrobed. The king, apparently dissatisfied with this decision, appointed the Chief Justice of his court, Dhammika, to investigate the charge afresh. In this the king was disappointed; for Dhammika was too upright and fearless to let his decision be influenced by the king's wishes. After a thorough investigation he ordered Kohon-Tissa to be disrobed forthwith and expelled from the Order. Mahā-Sena owned defeat, and sincerely repented of his folly. During twelve years thenceforward he became an ardent friend and supporter of the Theriya Nikāya, and the *Mahā-vaṃsa* mentions that "There is no record of his gifts of food and drink": they were too numerous.[1] He helped all those who wished to devote their lives to learning and literary pursuits and became their great benefactor.

With the death of Mahā-Sena in A.D. 302 ended the "*Mahā-vaṃsa*", or the "Great Dynasty" of Sinhalese kings. The sovereigns of the "*Cūla-vaṃsa*" (or the Lesser Dynasty), says the *Rājāvalī*, were no longer of the unmixed blood, but the offspring of parents only one of whom was descended from the Sun, and the other from those who had brought the Sacred Bodhi-tree or the Sacred Tooth; on that account the fertility of the land was diminished, and the kings who succeeded Mahā-Sena were no longer reverenced as of old.[2]

At the time when the Great Dynasty became extinct the material prosperity of the country was quite sound and auspicious. The people, though occasionally disturbed by minor civil commotions, were able to carry on their pursuits in peace; there was contentment all round. The attention which the kings bestowed on the irrigation of the country had made the food of the people abundant; and the sums expended on the adornment of the city, the multitude of its sacred structures, the splendour of its buildings, and the beauty of its lakes and gardens, bear ample testimony to the wealth of the kingdom. The accounts left to us by the traveller,

[1] *M.V.*, xxxvii, v. 46.
[2] *Rājāvalī* (Upham), p. 239.

Fa Hsien, who visited the island a little while later, fully corroborate the descriptions given in the *Mahā-Vamsa*. It was crowded, he says, with nobles, magistrates, and foreign merchants; the houses were beautiful, the public buildings richly adorned; the streets and the highways were broad and level, and halls for preaching, teaching and reading *bana* were erected in all the thoroughfares. He was assured that the island contained no less than fifty to sixty thousand ecclesiastics, all of whom ate in common, and of whom from five to six thousand were supported by the bounty of the king.[1] In such a community literary genius was bound to sprout in full vigour. Men and women, free from the cares of the material needs of the body, were able to devote their attention to the cultivation of the mind. They studied assiduously not only the text and the commentaries of the Pāli canon, which formed their sacred scriptures, but also all branches of knowledge. There was constant and free intercourse with the mainland of India, and many other parts of Asia as well. Moorish traders from Arabia travelled hither, selling their wares; Pliny records that early in the fourth century A.D. four ambassadors from Ceylon made their way to Rome on a complimentary mission to a state, the intercourse with which is still evidenced by large finds of Roman coins in the island.[2] Along with the intercourse in goods must have existed intercourse in views as well; and the people of Ceylon, then as now, were always prepared to learn and assimilate the culture of other nations. The era of contentment and prosperity gave a fresh impetus to this desire for the development of the intellect. Whatever literary works were produced at this time—and there must have been many such—are unfortunately irretrievably lost, leaving behind them no records at all, and we have to satisfy ourselves with but vague surmises. What such surmises lead us to assume will be more evident in the next chapter.

[1] Giles' translation, pp. 69–70.
[2] Pieris, *Ceylon and the Portuguese*, p. 9.

CHAPTER IV

The Beginnings of Literary Activity

MAHĀ-SENA'S son and successor, Siri Meghavaṇṇa, did all that lay in his power to make amends for the mischief which his father had committed. He assembled all the monks of the Mahā-vihāra, who had been scattered abroad by the measures of Mahā-sena and reverentially asked them how best he could make up for the sacrileges of which his father had been guilty. Acting under their advice, he rebuilt the Brazen Palace, which was the proudest building in the capital; he reconstructed all the *pariveṇas* (the temple-schools) which had been demolished and restored all the lands that had been endowed for their maintenance. Meghavaṇṇa was evidently a student of history, and when he learnt of Mahinda, who had converted the island to Buddhism, he caused an image of the *Thera* to be made and held a great festival in his honour. For the ceremony of dedication he sent messengers and summoned to the city all the monks from the various parts of the country; the *Mahā-vaṃsa* gives a glowing description of the rejoicings that marked the event.[1] He also decreed that a similar festival should be held annually at the conclusion of the rainy season. This order was for a very long time carried out; but, like many another institution, it has now perished.[2] But the most outstanding event of the reign was the bringing over to Ceylon of the Right Eye-Tooth, the Dāṭhādhātu, from Kaliṅga. In the introductory verses of the *Dāṭhā-vaṃsa* the author tells us that his work was based on an ancient poem in Sinhalese (Elu) verse, called the *Daḷadā-vaṃsa*. And this poem appears to have been composed in the ninth year of Meghavaṇṇa's reign—the very year of the arrival of the tooth relic in Ceylon—by the king's express command. It is said to have contained a history of the

[1] *M.V.*, xxxvii, vv. 66 foll.

[2] An attempt, however, has recently been made to revive it.

relic from the death of the Buddha to its arrival in Ceylon. There seems to have been another work, called the *Dāṭhā-dhātu-vaṃsa,* composed either at this time or shortly after and mentioned in *Mahā-vaṃsa* XXXVII. In a footnote to his translation of this chapter Turnour mentions that the work was still extant at the time (1837).[1] In spite of diligent search I have not been able to see a copy. Major Forbes identifies the *Daḷadā-vaṃsa* with this work, but gives no reason for his conclusions.[2]

Whatever information we have at present is based on the *Dāṭhā-vaṃsa,* written by Dhammakitti in the twelfth century A.D. There we learn that the relic was introduced into Ceylon from Dantapura in the ninth year of Siri Meghavaṇṇa's reign by Hemamālā, daughter of Guhasīva, king of Kaliṅga, and her husband, Danta Kumāra, a prince of the Ujjenī royal family. During more than eight centuries the relic had remained undisturbed at Dantapura; but Guhasīva, when he became a convert from Brahmanism to Buddhism, paid homage to the Tooth and thereby incurred the implacable wrath of the Brahman priests. They complained to his suzerain lord of Pāṇḍu at Pāṭaliputra, who ordered it to be brought to his capital, and there by the wonders it exhibited he himself was converted. Shortly afterwards the king of Sāvatthī assembled an army and demanded the relic. War ensued, and Pāṇḍu's army was defeated. The relic was restored to Guhasīva. Sometime later the son of the king of Ujjenī, who was a zealous Buddhist, came to Dantapura, bringing tokens of homage to the relic, and there he married Hemamālā, daughter of the Kaliṅga king. A large army from Sāvatthī appeared at Dantapura, demanding the relic once more, and Guhasīva, apprehensive of the power by which he was assailed, directed his daughter and son-in-law to escape from the city, taking the relic with them. They disguised themselves as members of the Buddhist Order, and after many adventures

[1] Turnour, *Mahā-vaṃsa*, p. 241, footnote.
[2] See *Dāṭhā-vaṃsa* discussion.

came to Ceylon (which is said to have been foretold as its final resting place), and delivered it to the king. There they were received with all the honour due to their exalted rank and the precious object which they escorted. On the arrival of the relic at Anurādhapura the king took charge of it himself and, rendering thereto the greatest homage, deposited it in a casket made of *phalika* (steatite) stone and lodged it in an edifice called the Dhamma-cakka, built by Devānampiya-Tissa. In the height of his felicity the king, so the *Mahā-vāṃsa* tells us,[1] spent 9 lakhs in celebrating the Dāṭhādhātu festival and made proclamation that the relic should be annually honoured by taking it in a procession to the Abhayagiri Vihāra. A century later Fa-Hsien saw the ceremony performed, and he has described it in his memoirs.[2] Dhammakitti[3] mentions in his work a rubric written by Meghavaṇṇa for the observances to be performed before the Tooth (*Caritta-lekhaṃ abhilekhayi*). There is a copy of this ancient ceremonial manual still extant in the Māligāva at Kandy, where the relic is now deposited.

The Tooth Relic from the time of its first arrival in Ceylon obtained among the Sinhalese the position which the Palladium held in ancient Rome, for the sovereignty of the country belonged to the possessor of the venerated object. Even to-day, after the vicissitudes of many centuries, no relic commands more veneration than this. The wealth of the country was freely poured out in its honour. Wherever the palace of the king had to be erected, by reason of the incursions of invading foes, by its side, within the royal precincts, rose the *Daḷadā-Māligāva* (the Palace of the Tooth Relic), smaller but incomparably more beautiful than the royal residence. Entire villages were dedicated to the maintenance of those whose business it was to supply offerings of rice and flowers and incense and oil, and one king at least

[1] *M.V.*, xxxvii, v. 96.
[2] Giles' Translation, pp. 69–70.
[3] *Dāṭhā-vaṃsa*, p. 16.

offered up all his personal ornaments as a mark of humble devotion.[1]

Siri Meghavaṇṇa's contemporary in India was Samudragupta, whose brilliant reign saw the establishment of a mighty Indian empire, second only to that of Asoka. Though a Vaiṣṇavaite himself, he was tolerant towards other faiths, and we are told that in his youth he was a friend of Vasubandhu, the Mahāyānist teacher of great repute. Reference should be made to him here, because of one single event connected with him, which for several reasons is of much interest to us. It is recorded by a Chinese writer that Siri Meghavaṇṇa, king of Ceylon, sent an embassy to Samudragupta and obtained his permission to build a Saṅghārāma near the Mahābodhi Vihāra. Hiuan-Tsang,[2] who saw this monastery two and a half centuries later, gives a full description of it and adds many details about its foundation. According to him, a certain disciple of the Buddha, a monk from Ceylon, went forth to wander through India, but at all the convents he visited he was treated with disdain as a foreigner. He came back, and in great sorrow reported his experiences to the king. The latter, who seems to have held the monk in high esteem, asked what there was that should be done to remedy matters. He was advised to build convents throughout India for the benefit of travelling monks. A minister was accordingly dispatched to the Emperor with costly presents and jewels to ask permission for the purpose. Samudragupta was pleased at this cordiality shown towards him, and granted leave to "take one of the places in which the Tathāgata has left traces of his holy teaching". The Bodhimaṇḍala was chosen as the most suitable spot, and there an imposing edifice was erected to entertain all monks coming over from Ceylon. The king, Meghavaṇṇa, had the following inscription engraved in copper: "To help all without distinction is the highest teaching of all the

[1] Kīrti Srī Rāja-Siṅha, Pieris, op. cit., p. 11.
[2] *Memoirs*, ii, pp. 133 foll. (Beal).

Buddhas; to exercise mercy as occasion offers is the illustrious doctrine of former saints. And now I, unworthy descendant in the royal line, have undertaken to found this Saṅghārāma to enclose the sacred traces, and to hand down their renown to future ages and to spread their benefits among the people. The monks of my country will thus obtain independence and be treated as members of the fraternity of this country. Let this privilege be handed down from generation to generation without interruption."[1] In an inscription of a stone pillar at Allahabad, Samudragupta gives an account of his reign, and among the alliances he formed with foreign powers occurs mention of "the Saimhalakas, who propitiated him with presents".[2]

At the time of Hiuan-Tsang's visit there were over 1,000 monks in this convent, studying the "Great Vehicle" and belonging to the Sthavira (Shang-tso-pu) school. "They carefully observe the Dharma and Vinaya," he wrote, "and their conduct is pure and correct."[3]

The circumstances connected with the founding of this Saṅghārāma allow us to infer that at this time Ceylon monks were not held in high esteem on the continent, the reason being perhaps the ascendancy of Brahmanical power, or more probably because the views of the Ceylon school were not acceptable even to the Buddhist monks of India. The cleavage between Hīna- and Mahā-yāna had grown wider and wider. The disfavour with which Ceylon kings and monks viewed any encroachment by Vaitulya doctrines on the *Thera-vāda* Buddhism of the island had made it impossible for much exchange of scholarship to take place between the two countries. But this establishment of a *Thera-vāda* community near the Bodhimaṇḍala, which was undoubtedly then as now the chief centre of Buddhist pilgrimage, must have facilitated such interchange of views. As far as we know, there do not seem

[1] *The Buddhist*, vol. viii, No. 26, published in Colombo, 1922.
[2] *History of the Sangha*, by D. B. Jayatilaka, in course of publication.
[3] *Memoirs*, vol. ii, p. 133 (Beal).

to have been any restrictions as to who should make use of the convent. Nominally, of course, the chief power was vested in the hands of the Mahā-Vihāra, and we may well assume that monks of the Abhayagiri fraternity, for instance, who wished to study in greater detail and at much closer distance the doctrines which distinguished them from other schools, took advantage of the opportunity thus created for the pursuance of their purpose. I believe also that the familiarity thus brought about with the Mahāyānists, as we may safely call the dissenters from the *Thera-vāda,* was in large measure responsible for the convergence that later seems to have come about between the Mahā-Vihāra and the Abhayagiri fraternities. The Mahā-Vihāra community seems to have treated the Abhayagiri sect with much toleration throughout, and their doings were interfered with only when glaring attempts were made by them to tarnish the purity of the Dhamma. It was also most probably in this Saṅghārāma that the young Brahman Buddhaghosa met Revata *Thera,* who converted him and admitted him into the Order.[1]

Passing over Meghavaṇṇa's brother and successor, Jeṭṭha-Tissa, who was a skilful carver and a clever painter,[2] we next come to Buddhadāsa, according to the *Mahāvaṃsa* "a mine of virtue and an ocean of riches". "This monarch exemplified to the people in his own person the conduct of the Bodhisattas; and he entertained for mankind as large a compassion as a parent feels for his children. The indigent he made happy by distribution of riches amongst them, and he protected the rich in their property and life."[3] In addition to all his other qualifications of wisdom, piety and virtue, he possessed in supreme measure a knowledge of surgery, and many are the miraculous cures attributed to this royal surgeon. One case, for example, was that of a man who had drunk water containing the spawn of frogs in it, and an

[1] See next chapter.
[2] *M.V.*, xxxvii, v. 101.
[3] Ibid., xxxvii, v. 105-110; Geiger's trans., p. xxxix; 267, *n.* 1.

egg entering the nostril, ascended into the head and being hatched there became a frog. There it attained its full growth, and in rainy weather it croaked and gnawed the head of the man. The king, splitting open the head and extracting the frog and re-uniting the several parts, quickly cured the wound.[1] He provided hospitals all over the island, not only for men but also for birds and beasts. To every ten villages a royal physician was appointed, and for their guidance he compiled a work called the *Sārārtha-saṅgraha*, a compendium of medical science.[2] By way of the encouragement of learning, he sought out ministers who could expound the doctrines of the faith, patronized them, devotedly attended to their needs, and provided all facilities for carrying on their work. At the Mahā-Vihāra he built a Pariveṇa called Mora or Mayūra (the remains of which still exist) and made large endowments for its maintenance.

It was during this reign that a certain monk named Mahā-Dhammakathī translated the Suttas of the *Piṭakattaya* into Sinhalese.[3] Who this Dhammakathī was and what was the nature of his translation it is impossible to say, because no records of him or his work exist at the present time. The *Mahā-vaṃsa* gives but the name of the man and the barest account of his work, dismissing the subject with only one verse. Mr. Wickremasinghe[4] identifies him with Dharmagupta mentioned by Fa Hsien in the account of his visit to Ceylon. According to him Dharmagupta lived at Mihintale at the head of about two thousand monks. He was " a Śramaṇa of great virtue, honoured and looked up to by all the kingdom. He has lived for more than forty years in an apartment of stone, constantly showing such gentleness of heart that he brought snakes and rats to stop together in the same room, without doing one another any harm ". The identification, ingenious as it is, has, as far as I am aware, nothing but

[1] *M.V.*, xxxvii, v. 144.
[2] Now published with a translation by a later author, Colombo, 1899.
[3] *M.V.*, xxxvii, v. 175.
[4] *Ep. Zeyl.*, vol. i, pt. iii, p. 83.

conjecture to support it. Legge [1] in his translation of Fa Hsien adds a footnote: "Eitel says (p. 31) a famous ascetic, the founder of a school which flourished in Ceylon, A.D. 400," and adds further: "But Fa-Hsien gives no intimation of Dharmagupta's founding a school." Little as we know of Dhammakathī (and there is hardly any probability of our ever being able to learn much more), his work is of great significance as showing the outcome of a steady tendency on the part of the Sinhalese language to assert itself over the Pāli.

Whatever be the origin of Sinhalese as the language of the people of Ceylon—whether it was brought over by Vijaya and his followers from some part of the Indian peninsula, or whether it was derived from the same source as classical Sanskrit and Pāli,[2] or was, as the *Mahā-vaṃsa* [3] puts it, indigenous (*dīpa-bhāsā*), "the language of the land," and later modified and developed by the Aryan settlers—within two and a half centuries after Vijaya's arrival the language was found sufficiently rich and copious in its terms and regular in its structure to have been capable of the enunciation in it of matter so varied and so abstract as that contained in the commentaries brought over by Mahinda from the Council at Pāṭaliputta. With the advent of Pāli, as the language of the sacred Scriptures, Sinhalese borrowed and derived from it various terms and expressions with all their specific connotations. The steady and constant intercourse kept up with the mainland enabled all the advances made in various branches of knowledge in India to find their way into Ceylon; and the numerous colonies of Brahmanas and others that from time to time settled down in the island contributed to enlarge the vocabulary of Sinhalese by the addition of words from their literatures. The frequent invasions of Tamil marauders—each one of whose attacks is sure to have left behind some of their number as permanent settlers, even

[1] p. 107, footnote 2.
[2] For a discussion of this question see D'Alwis, *Sidat-saṅgarā*, Introduction.
[3] Chap. I, vv. 2–3.

after they had been repelled—provided another source of enrichment for the language. Thus Sinhalese steadily and quickly grew up to be a language capable of expressing the most varied ideas and emotions, rich in its vocabulary and supple in its structure. From the time when Pāli was introduced into Ceylon its study was assiduously cultivated, but, as Sinhalese grew in power, monks and laymen alike tended more and more to use this medium for the exposition of the Buddhist faith. Mahinda gave the lead to this tendency not only by preaching in "the language of the land", but more so by translating into it the commentaries on the *Piṭakas*.[1] The very nature of the *Atthakathās* demanded that they should be compiled in a manner to be easily understood, and the choice of Sinhalese, which was mainly the people's tongue, is therefore no matter for surprise. We shall see later, how eagerly scholars availed themselves of this concession to conduct their expositions in their own language, by the number and variety of the works—histories, poems, etc., commentarial and otherwise—which they produced in that medium, with a line or two of Pāli verse being introduced here and there, at salient points, to emphasize certain things, or to sum up the narrative.

But from the very commencement it seemed to have been agreed upon that the text of the canon itself, the *Piṭaka-ttaya*, was to remain intact in Pāli; that no attempt should be made to have it in any other language. The reason for this was obviously the preservation of the purity of the doctrine, so that whenever doubt arose on some doctrinal matter, as variously expounded by the commentators, there was always the resource of appealing to the Scriptures themselves for the correct interpretation. This understanding seems to have been respected for quite a long time, and the first attempt, as far as we know, to violate it was that made by Mahā-Dhammakathī in Buddhadāsa's reign.

[1] See next chapter on Buddhaghosa's work, which was based on these translations.

The reason for Dhammakathī's enterprise is not difficult to guess. Most probably, as the Sinhalese language, by the accretion it received from many sources, grew in force and in extent, and as writers exercising themselves in its composition acquired greater and greater facility in expressing their ideas in that medium, they began to cultivate it even more assiduously than before, and Pāli soon became of secondary importance, its use being restricted to mnemonic purposes. Fewer and fewer became those who specialized in Pāli, and Dhammakathī probably felt himself justified in the belief that, if the canon were to be made more widely known amongst the people, it should be put into the form most easily intelligible to them. And a beginning was made with the translation of the *Suttas*.

We are not told that the work, thus commenced by Dhammakathī, was continued by others. Probably the conservatism of the monks in this matter stopped any further attempts. Clear evidence of the neglect of Pāli studies at this time is afforded by the fact that when scholars *did* come to write in that language, such as, for instance, in the case of the *Dīpa-vaṃsa*, which, according to Oldenberg,[1] was begun about this period, the language was unnatural, weak and stilted, lacking in subtlety and virility of expression. The reaction against this lamentable state of decline came when Buddhaghosa's works gave fresh impetus to the study of Pāli, and a definite attempt was made to supersede the "language of the land" by means of Pāli.

It is interesting to observe that, side by side with the ascendency of Sinhalese over Pāli, another language was gradually coming into vogue in Ceylon. This was classical Sanskrit, which had rapidly become the medium of expression for learned works on the mainland of India. Scientific and secular works in that language had found their way into Ceylon, and were studied with care. And when the surgeon-

[1] Oldenberg, *Dīpa-vaṃsa*, p. 9.

king, Buddhadāsa, compiled his memorable work, "the *Sārārtha-saṅgraha*"—the first of its kind in Ceylon—it was neither Pāli nor Sinhalese that he used, but Sanskrit. We shall have occasion to refer to the influence of Sanskrit on Ceylon literature later; but the compilation of Buddhadāsa's book in a language so far not used in Ceylon to any large extent is worthy of notice here.

Buddhadāsa's elder son, Upatissa, succeeded him. During his reign the island was afflicted with drought, disease, and distress, and, acting on the advice of the monks, he requested a body of them to walk about in the streets of the city throughout the night, chanting the *Ratana-sutta* and sprinkling water. We are told that, as a result, at sunrise great clouds poured down rain upon the earth; all the sick and crippled disported themselves with joy, and the king issued the following decree: "Should there at any time be another affliction of drought and sickness in the island, do ye observe the like ceremonies."[1]

This account of the ceremony given in the *Mahā-vaṃsa* is interesting, in that it is the first recorded instance of the *Parittaṃ* having been recited for the public weal, the only other occasion being the one on which the Buddha himself is traditionally said to have preached the *Ratana-Sutta* to banish a deadly plague from Vesālī. Ever since this time the ceremony of chanting the *Parittaṃ* has taken fast hold of the imagination of the Sinhalese, and is extensively observed, even at the present day. The *Suttas* most often chanted are the *Maṅgala*, the *Ratana*, and the *Karaṇīya-Metta Suttas* of the *Khuddaka-pātha*; and the *Pirit-pota*, or the book containing the *suttas* for such recital, forms part of the meagre library of every Sinhalese household. Such recital is believed to ward off all evils and danger, and to bring about health and prosperity. Most Sinhalese know some part of these *suttas* by heart, and every child is taught to recite at

[1] *M.V.*, xxxvii, vv. 189–198.

least a portion of them every morning and before retiring to bed.[1]

Several translations of these *Paritta-suttas* have been written in Sinhalese, some of them most elaborate, but, most of them being more difficult of comprehension than the original Pāli, not much use is made of them, and the efficacy of the recital is believed to remain unaffected whether the reciter understands or not the meaning of what he chants !

Upatissa was killed by his queen consort, who was infatuated with his younger brother Mahānāma, at that time a member of the Order. On his brother's death, however, he threw off his robes, became king and married Upatissa's consort. His approval of the queen's treachery was evidently viewed with disfavour by the Mahā-Vihāra fraternity, for we find both him and his queen actively supporting the Abhayagiri establishment of schismatic priests.[2] It was during this reign that there arrived in Ceylon the greatest of the Buddhist commentators, Buddhaghosa, whose works are of monumental importance.

To this period are traditionally ascribed two short works in Pāli, the *Khudda-Sikkhā* and the *Mūla-Sikkhā*, supposed to have been written prior to the advent of Buddhaghosa. Both works are alluded to by name in the great inscription of Parākrama Bāhu at Galvihāra, Polonnaruva (A.D. 1065),[3] and the grammarian Moggallāna, who lived at that time, is said to have written a commentary on the *Khudda-Sikkhā*.[4] This commentary no longer exists, but it was apparently based on an older Sinhalese commentary. The two works are short summaries of Vinaya rules, a kind of *memoria*

[1] It is interesting to recall that, when I left Ceylon for England, among the tokens of remembrance given to me were several editions *de luxe* of such *Pirit-Potas*.

[2] *M.V.*, xxxvii, v. 212.

[3] Müller's *Ancient Inscrip. of Ceylon*, No. 137, 11 (1922).

[4] Fryer's *Subodhālaṅkāra*, p. 4, note on Kaccāyana ; see also under Moggallāna in the present treatise.

technica of the Vinaya. The works are for the greatest part in verse, with only a few passages in prose. The verses are put together in a rough and ready manner, appropriate for the mnemonic purpose they are intended to serve. A colophon at the end of the *Khudda-Sikkhā* ascribes that work to a monk named Dhammasiri, who was "like unto a banner in Tambapaṇṇi" (Ceylon). Though no mention of an author's name is made in the *Mūla-Sikkhā*, tradition agrees to ascribe it to Mahāsāmi. The two, being both monks of Anurādhapura who lived in the same period, were probably confrères.[1] Nothing more is known about these authors and, from the evidence at our disposal, it is very difficult to form any opinion as to the age of the books. Dr. Edward Müller, basing his arguments on the language and certain forms of words used to meet the exigencies of metre, is inclined to think, that they are later than the *Mahā-vaṃsa*, and are not earlier than the sixth or seventh century A.D.[2] D'Alwis, in his Introduction to the *Sidat-saṅgarā*, assigns a rather early date, viz. A.D. 350.[3] The language of both compilations is simple and free from artificiality and all Sanskritisms. Rhys Davids agrees to confirm the traditional date, viz. about A.D. 350, and is convinced that both belong to the memoriter period of Pāli.[4] Most of the extracts given in the works are from the text of the *Vinaya-Piṭaka*, but a few passages remain unidentified. Dr. Müller thinks such passages are quotations from the *Vinaya* commentaries.[5] A Sinhalese *sanne* or translation of the *Khudda-Sikkhā* exists, a work of great scholastic merit, written in very elegant and archaic language, the author of which is not known. It is generally assigned to the eleventh century, and two *ṭīkās* were written in Pāli based on this, the *Porāṇa-ṭīkā*, by Revata or Mahā-Yasa, the author of a *ṭīkā*

[1] *JPTS.*, 1883, pp. 86–7; also De Zoysa, *Catalogue.*
[2] Ibid.
[3] Introduction to *Sidat-saṅgarā*, p. cl.
[4] *JPTS.*, 1883, p. xiii.
[5] *JPTS.*, *loc. cit.*

on Buddhadatta's *Vinaya-vinicchaya*,[1] and the other by Saṅgharakkhita, author of the *Subodhālaṅkāra* and several other valuable works, whose date was the latter half of the twelfth century. The works are used in Ceylon and Burma at the present day by novices of the Order as a handbook of Vinaya rules.

[1] q.v.

CHAPTER V

BUDDHAGHOSA

CONSIDERING that Buddhaghosa ranks in the Buddhist church as its greatest commentator and exegetist, and that the service which he rendered to the cause of the Buddha's religion was of the most useful and enduring kind, the information we have about his life is very meagre. Very little is known about him, except through his own writings; we have nothing to go upon except his commentaries, and a few traditions and legends. And these very traditions and legends are so much coloured by the imagination of their creators that much reliance cannot be placed upon them. Circumstantial details are so interwoven with fictitious elements, that it is difficult to separate strict truth from mere romance. Facts of historical value occupy comparatively little space in these narratives.

The *Buddhaghos'-uppatti* [1] is the longest account of his life and is, in its entirety, a work highly diverting as well as instructive. But its author had evidently little authentic knowledge of the subject of his study, and his collection of legends is mostly valueless from the historical point of view. It reads too much like a romance and does not help us much in elucidating Buddhaghosa's history. Gray, in his translation of the work, gives [2] a list of other sources which contain accounts of the commentator's life—a list of what he considers the most trustworthy Burmese records. Besides these, the earliest connected account of his life is that contained in the *Mahā-vaṃsa* (chapter xxxvii), which, though it is considered by some to be by a later writer of the thirteenth century, is by far the most authentic source of our information, and is itself probably derived from very much older material.

[1] Edited and translated by J. Gray, Luzac & Co., 1892.

[2] Ibid., p. 9 foll.; see also that very valuable book, *The Life and Work of Buddhaghosa*, by Bimala Charan Law, Calcutta, 1923.

The whole narrative bears upon it the impress of truth, and our only regret is that it contains so very little. It fixes for us quite definitely the period of Buddhaghosa's activities, and this fact is in itself most useful.

The following is a translation of the *Mahā-vaṃsa* account: "A Brāhman youth, born in the neighbourhood of the Great Bodhi-tree,[1] accomplished in arts and sciences, one who had mastered the three *Vedas*, was well-versed in knowledge, skilled in all disputes, himself a schismatic wanderer over Jambu-dīpa, assuming the character of a disputant, lived in a certain monastery and was in the habit of rehearsing by day and by night with clasped hands a discourse which he had learnt, perfect in all its parts, and sustained throughout in lofty strain. A certain Elder, Revata by name,[2] becoming acquainted with him, thought 'This being is one of great wisdom; he should be converted'. (So thinking) he inquired: 'Who is this that brays like an ass?' The youth replied: 'Dost thou know, then, the meaning of the ass's braying?' 'I do,' rejoined the Elder, and the youth exhibited the extent of his knowledge. The Elder explained each of his statements and pointed out their fallacies. Being thus refuted, the youth exclaimed, 'Come now and propound thy creed,' and the Elder recited to him a passage from the *Abhidhamma*. The Brāhman could not understand the meaning of that text, and inquired: 'Whose manta (teaching) is this?' 'It is the Buddha's manta.' On his exclaiming 'Impart it to me', the Elder replied: 'Enter the Recluses' Order.' And he, being desirous of acquiring knowledge of the Three *Piṭakas*, and being convinced that 'This is indeed the Way', took the vows of a Recluse.

[1] According to Burmese tradition he was born in North India in the fifth century A.D. in the Magadha country (see Gray, op. cit.). The *Sāsana-vaṃsa* (p. 29) says that he was the son of a *Purohita* named Kesa and that his mother was Kesī.

[2] I have suggested in the preceding chapter that this Revata may have been an Elder of the Saṅghārāma built for Ceylon monks by Kitti Siri Meghavaṇṇa.

"Because he was as profound in his eloquence as the Buddha himself, they called him Buddhaghosa (the voice of the Buddha); and throughout the world he became as renowned as the Buddha. Having there (in Jambu-dīpa) composed an original work called the *Ñāṇodayaṃ*, he at the same time wrote the chapter called '*Attha-sālinī*' on the *Dhamma-saṅgaṇī*. Revata *Thera* then, observing that he was desirous of undertaking the compilation of a *Paritt-atthakathā* (a concise commentary on the *Piṭaka-ttaya*), thus addressed him: 'The text alone (of the *Piṭaka-ttaya*) has been preserved in this land: the *Atthakathā's* are not extant here; nor is there any complete version of the different *vādā* (schools). The Sinhalese *Atthakathā's* are genuine; they were composed in the Sinhalese language by the inspired and profoundly wise Mahinda, who had previously consulted the discourses of the Buddha, confirmed at the three Convocations, and the dissertations and arguments of Sāriputta and others; and they exist among the Sinhalese. Repairing thither, and studying the same, translate them according to the rules of the Māgadhī grammar. It will be an act conducive to the welfare of the whole world'.[1] Having been thus advised, this eminently wise man, rejoicing therein, departed thence, and visited this island in the reign of this monarch, Mahānāma.[2] On reaching the Mahāvihāra he entered the Mahā-Padhāna Hall, the most splendid of the apartments in the Vihāra, and listened to the Sinhalese *Atthakathā* and the *Thera-vāda*, from beginning to end, propounded by the Elder Saṅghapāli. He became thoroughly convinced that they contained the true meaning of the doctrines of the Dhammarāja. Thereupon, paying reverential respect to the priesthood, he thus

[1] The *Sāsana-vaṃsa* (p. 29) says he was sent to make amends for having thought himself cleverer than his teacher.

[2] The *Ceylon Antiquary and Lit. Register* (vol. i, pt. ii, pp. 94 foll.) gives over a score of different dates fixed upon by different scholars; some as early as 543 B.C.! Most of them centre round the name of Mahānāma, king of Ceylon. Sinhalese tradition assigns his arrival to 965 years after the Parinibbāna.

petitioned: 'I am desirous of translating the *Aṭṭhakathā*; give me access to all your books.' The monks, to test his qualifications, gave only two stanzas, saying: 'Hence prove thy ability; having satisfied ourselves on this point, we will then let thee have all our books.' From these stanzas, and consulting the *Piṭaka-ttaya* together with the *Atthakathā*, and condensing them, he composed the commentary, the *Visuddhi-magga*. Thereupon, having assembled at the Bo-tree the monks who had acquired a complete knowledge of the Buddha's doctrines, he commenced to read out his work. The devas, in order to make his wisdom celebrated amongst men, rendered that book invisible. He, however, for a second and a third time, recomposed it. When he was producing his book for the third time the devas restored the other two copies also. The monks then read out the three books simultaneously. In the three versions, neither in a signification nor in a single misplacement by transposition, nay, not even in the *Thera* controversies, or in the text was there, in the measure of a verse or in the letter of a word, the slightest variation. Thereupon the monks, rejoicing again and again, fervently shouted, saying: 'Most assuredly this is Metteyya himself,' and gave him the books where the three *Piṭakas* were recorded, together with the commentaries.

'Taking up his residence in the secluded Ganthakāra-Vihāra,[1] at Anurādhapura, he translated according to the grammatical rules of the Magadhas, the root of all languages, the whole of the Sinhalese *Atthakathā*. This proved

[1] Lord Chalmers says: "I venture on the confident opinion that, although it was probably at the Mahā-Vihāra in Anurādhapura (where he would meet Ceylon's most accomplished scholars) that Buddhaghosa began his work by writing three editions of his own expository *Visuddhi-magga*, it is surely an impeccable tradition that makes him journey for his authentic copy of the *Piṭakas* and *Atthakathās* to Alu-vihāra, renowned as the venerable birthplace and still the faithful custodian of the written records he had come so far to seek. For in these things sentiment counts for much and to none more than to a zealous and reverent scholar such as Buddhaghosa undoubtedly was." (*Ceylon Antiq. and Lit. Reg.*, vol. i, pt. i, p. 2 foll.)

an accomplishment of the utmost benefit to all languages spoken by the human race. All the Theriya teachers held this compilation in the same estimation as the *Tipitaka*. Thereafter, the objects of his mission having been fulfilled, he returned to Jambu-dīpa to worship at the Bo-tree."[1]

So much, then, for Buddhaghosa's life, as far as may be gleaned from the information at our disposal. The monks of the Mahā-Vihāra in Ceylon were by no means slow to recognize his genius, and they provided him with every facility for carrying out his work. One monk after another requested him to enter upon new fields of scholarship, and he responded gladly. Buddhism was at this time on the wane in India. Various new sects had arisen on the continent, each claiming to possess the authentic tradition of the Buddha. We saw in the last chapter that the Ceylon monks were not held in high esteem by members of these dissentient schools. The only place, perhaps, where the *Thera-vāda* yet had a foothold was in the Sinhalese Saṅghārāma at the Bodhi-maṇḍapa. But even there the *Piṭakas* and their commentaries were not being studied in their entirety. It may be that no exegetical works were available to them in a language easily understood by their disciples on the spot. Buddhaghosa evidently felt this keenly himself; for, according to the *Mahā-vaṃsa* account, the desire to compose a concise commentary on the *Piṭakas* (*Piṭakatthakathā*) was expressed by him spontaneously to his teacher, Revata, and the latter was only too glad to encourage this ambitious project and devise ways and means of helping its accomplishment. When

[1] Kern says that after completing his work in Ceylon, Buddhaghosa went over to Burma to propagate the Buddhist faith (*Manual of Buddhism*, p. 125), while Spence Hardy mentions that the Burmese ascribe the new era in their religion to the time when the great exegetist reached their country from Ceylon (*Buddhism*, p. 532). The *Buddhaghosuppatti* states (pp. 65–6) that he was born in the Tusita heaven after his death. The Cambodian Buddhists have a tradition that Buddhaghosa died in their country, in a monastery called after him Buddhaghosa-Vihāra. He was cremated there, his relics collected and *stūpas* built over them (Law, *Life and Work of Buddhaghosa*, p. 42).

Buddhaghosa mentioned his wish to the Mahā-Vihāra monks, they realized well the importance of his works, and the fruitful results that would follow therefrom. Once the commentaries, which contained a full exposition of the *Dhamma*, were available in a language understood by the monks of India, a new impetus would be given to the study of the orthodox teaching, and the glory of the religion would thereby be increased in manifold measure. We find them, therefore, most eager in their encouragement of his work. The king himself, though not very favourably disposed towards the Mahā-Vihāra fraternity, for reasons given in the preceding chapter—extended to Buddhaghosa his royal patronage, and we find this acknowledged by Buddhaghosa himself. Thus in the epilogue to the *Samanta-pāsādikā* he says that he completed his work in the twenty-first year of King Sirinivāsa of Ceylon, who was his benevolent patron.[1]

But the work he undertook was by no means an easy one, and it is no wonder, therefore, that the learned Sinhalese monks, before they gave their consent to his being assigned this Herculean task, thought it prudent to test his talents beforehand by giving him a text from the sacred canon as a subject for a thesis; and it was a natural tradition that armed him with Sakka's iron stylus that he might be possessed thereby of speedier penmanship.

While already in India, according to the *Mahā-vaṃsa*, he had composed a work called "*Ñāṇōdaya*", about which nothing further is known. We may, I think, assume that it was not preserved among his permanent compilations, probably because it was incorporated in his later and more substantial and better-informed works. The name of the book, however, lends colour to the assumption that it was a treatise on some philosophical subject. His first work in Ceylon was the *Visuddhi-magga*, set him, as we saw above, as a test-subject for a disquisition by the Mahā-Vihāra monks. In the *Nidāna-kathā*, or Introduction to the book, he gives in detail the

[1] Also *Dhamma-pada* Commentary, vol. iv, p. 235.

circumstances in which he made this compendium, and again repeats them towards the close of the work.[1] It is an encyclopædia of the Doctrine, containing the whole of the Buddha's teachings in a connected volume, and, as Gray says in his Introduction [2] to the *Buddhaghos'-uppatti*, "If he had written nothing else, it alone would have secured for him undying fame." The *Sāsana-vaṃsa-dīpanī* [3] summarizes it thus: "In short, the work deals with *kusalā, akusalā, avyākata-dhammā, āyatana, dhātu, sati-paṭṭhāna, kamma, pakati*, and many other topics of Buddhist philosophy, and is the only book in which the whole of the Buddha's system is well depicted in an abridged compilation of the three *Piṭakas*, together with quotations from the commentaries on the passages from the *Piṭakas* mentioned therein."

No mention is made in it of any of Buddhaghosa's other works, whence it is concluded that it was the first permanent work of his pen. The work is a masterly production, and Buddhaghosa undoubtedly took great pains over it; for we are told that he made three editions of the work, before it was put into final shape. The work, as we have it, is divided into three parts: Conduct, Concentration (or Mental Training), and Wisdom. The quotations mentioned in it are plentiful and varied, and bestrew the work from beginning to end. They have been taken from nearly every work in the earlier Buddhist literature; the three *Piṭakas*, the Sinhalese commentaries, notably the *Mahā-Atthakathā* of the Māha Vihāra community, the *Milinda-pañha*, and the *Peṭakopadesa*.[4] The result is an extraordinary book, written with admirable judgment as to the general arrangement of the matter and in lucid style (though at times long words are used and the language is difficult to understand), free from argument and discussion—a book of which, according to Mrs. Rhys

[1] Vol. i, p. 2; vol. ii, pp. 711 (Pali Text Soc. ed.).
[2] p. 31.
[3] pp. 30–1.
[4] See *V.M.* (P.T.S.), pp. 753 foll.

Davids,[1] " we might say, within limits, what is said of the *Divina Commedia* and of the Shakespearean plays : in its pages may be found something on everything—i.e. in the earlier Buddhist literature . . . a closely packed microcosm . . . of macrocosmic range."

Mr. Nagai,[2] in a very learned article, draws attention to the extraordinary similarity that exists between the *Visuddhi-magga* and a Chinese Pāli work called the *Vimutti-magga*, and seems inclined to conclude that they are one and the same work appearing in different attire. The *Vimutti-magga* was translated into Chinese in A.D. 505 by a Cambodian (Funan) priest whose name (according to M. Nagai) was Saṅghapāla, and it is an " encyclopædia of Buddhist theology ". Legend says it was composed by Arahā Upatissa, usually identified with Sāriputta ; but Mr. Nagai, basing his conclusions on the internal evidence of the *Dīpa-vaṃsa*, assigns him to the first century A.D. The translator, Saṅghapāla, came from Mid-India, and stayed in China during fifteen years. His master, Guṇa-bhadra, had visited Sīhala-dīpa, and other southern countries, and brought with him copies of various works. We do not know whether the *Vimutti-magga* was among the books so brought, or whether it was of Mid-Indian or even Cambodian origin. The *Vimutti-magga* is an Abhidhamma exegesis, serving as a compendium for that portion of Buddhist literature. A comparison of the two works shows that, though they resemble each other very much in form, inasmuch as both divide the contents according to *Sīla*, *Jhāna*, *Paññā*, and *Vimutti*, yet they differ greatly in the way of explanation, the arrangement of the materials, etc., those portions which are curtailed in one being given fully in the other or vice versa, and in some points the Chinese work seems to have been influenced by the Mahāyāna doctrine.

There is, I feel, no need to conclude, therefore, that "the *Visuddhi-magga*, which has been considered to be entirely

[1] *V.M.*, p. 763.
[2] *JPTS.*, 1917–19, pp. 69 foll.

Buddhaghosa's own work is in reality a revised version of Upatissa's *Vimutti-magga* ". If we suppose that the *Vimutti-maggā* was the result of books brought by Guṇa-bhadra of Mid-India, from his travels in Çeylon and other Hīnayāna countries, the solution of the problem seems clear. Both authors drew their inspiration from the same sources. A close examination of the two works shows that their greatest resemblance lies in the treatment of philosophical (*Abhidhamma*) matter. We saw that, in the school where Buddhaghosa first received his knowledge of Buddhism, the special subject of study was the *Abhidhamma*. It was by the recital of an *Abhidhamma* text that Buddhaghosa's attention was first drawn to the Buddha's teaching, and Buddhaghosa's first work was the *Ñāṇōdaya*, apparently a treatise on that particular aspect of Buddhist lore. Buddhaghosa is sent to Ceylon to get a complete edition of the Commentaries because, as his teacher tells him, " There is no *complete* version of the different schools (*vādā*) with us. *The Sinhalese Atthakathā are genuine*; the text alone (of the *Pitaka-ttaya*) is preserved in this land; the *Atthakathā* are not extant." This does not mean that *some*, at least, of the commentaries were not studied in India, especially in view of the existence of the Sinhalese Saṅghārāma at the Bodhi-maṇḍapa. As long as the text was extant the traditional interpretation thereof, in various degrees of authenticity, at different times, existed as well, handed down through the centuries by a line of teachers who aimed as far as was possible at consistency in doctrinal interpretation. Buddhaghosa makes reference in the *Visuddhi-magga* [1] to the commentaries on the *Aṅguttara*, *Majjhima*, and *Saṃyutta Nikāyas*. This reference may well be, as Maung Tin suggests,[2] not to Buddhaghosa's own commentaries, but to the original Ceylonese Commentary from which he later made his redaction, and in which he was so deeply steeped, even at the time when he wrote the *Visuddhi-magga*. If, then, it is assumed that

[1] See index to the *Visuddhi-magga*.

[2] *Path of Purity*, Preface, pp. v and vi.

the *Vimutti-magga* found its way to China by way of some of the schools which flourished in India at the time, and which studied the canon in the more or less traditional method, it would not be difficult to conclude that the *Visuddhi-magga* and *Vimutti-magga* are more or less independent works, written by men belonging to much the same school of thought —the *Thera-vāda*.

But by far the greatest service rendered by Buddhaghosa to the progress of Buddhist knowledge was his series of masterly commentaries. The *Atthakathā*'s (or "talks about the contents, meaning, or purpose of various parts of the doctrine", as the word itself implies) represented the most ancient, orthodox, and traditional interpretations of the Buddha's teachings. They were not so much creative as explicative and interpretative. Such talks go back to the time of the Buddha himself. Law, in his book on Buddhaghosa,[1] has a very interesting chapter on the origin of these commentaries. He says that the need for an accurate interpretation of the Buddha's words, which formed the guiding principle of life and action of the members of the Saṅgha, was felt from the very earliest days of the Order. When the Master was alive there was always the possibility of referring disputed questions direct to him. But even during the Master's lifetime—at the Buddhist centres formed at various places under the leadership of one or other of the famous disciples—discussions, friendly interviews, and analytical expositions used to take place, and the *raison d'être* of the commentaries is to be traced to these discussions. Sometimes it happened that accounts of these discussions were duly reported to the Teacher, and some of them were approved by him, and he would then ask the monks to bear the particular expositions in mind as the best that could have been given. The utterances of the disciples that won such approbation were treasured by the members of the community, and especially of their respective groups, and held in high esteem, honoured as much as the

[1] Law, op. cit., pp. 48 foll.

words of the Buddha himself. These formed the nucleus of the commentaries. Often, when the Buddha preached a sermon in concise form on some aspect of the doctrine, the monks used to repair to one of the chief disciples and get the points explained in greater detail. Such was Mahā-Kaccā[ya]na, for example, who was foremost in reputation for his power in giving detailed expositions of what the Buddha said in brief. When later the text of the canon came to be compiled, arranged, and edited, some of the expositions found their way into the *Piṭakas* and were given a permanent place therein. Thus we have the *Saṅgīti-suttanta* [1] of the *Dīgha-Nikāya*, ascribed to Sāriputta and forming a complete catechism of terms and passages of exegetical nature. Such was also the *Sacca-vibhaṅga* [2] (an exposition of the Four Noble Truths) of the *Majjhima*, which later found its proper place in the second book of the *Abhidhamma-Piṭaka*, and also the *Madhu-piṇḍika-sutta* of Mahā-Kaccāyana, included in the *Majjhima-Nikāya*.[3] It sometimes happened that for a proper understanding of the text explanations of a commentarial nature were quite essential; and in such cases the commentary was naturally incorporated into the text and formed part of the text itself. Thus we have an old commentary embedded in the *Vinaya* and the *Parivāra* added as a supplementary examination paper to the whole. Then there is the *Niddesa*, a whole book of commentary on texts now included in the *Sutta-nipāta*; and there are passages clearly of a commentarial nature scattered throughout the *Nikāyas*. Lastly, there are the interesting fragments of commentaries, tacked, the one on to the *Dhamma-saṅgaṇī* and the other to the *Vibhaṅga*. We saw in an earlier chapter how the canon, in order to facilitate the learning and the retention of it, was divided into sections and entrusted to various groups of disciples to form their special study. There is a very old

[1] Vol. iii, p. 207 foll.
[2] *Majjh.*, iii, pp. 248 foll.
[3] Ibid., i, pp. 110 foll.

tradition which tells us that the commentaries on all the principal canonical books were handed down by these schools *along with* the texts themselves. This probably explains how it was that parts of the commentaries came later to be attached to the texts which they interpreted, e.g. in the case of the Dhamma-saṅgaṇī. This, however, does not mean, as Mrs. Rhys Davids points out,[1] that all the commentaries were so handed down in all the schools, or that each of them was exactly the same in each of the schools where it was taught. But, where the commentaries were so handed down, tradition tells us that they were compiled and subsequently written in the dialect of the district where the school was situated. They were, therefore, not the work of one single author, but of a community of brethren.

It must be borne in mind that these commentaries were not compiled in the modern sense of the word, nor did any commentaries, such as Buddhaghosa himself wrote later, exist in the Buddha's lifetime or immediately after his death. So that, when Buddhaghosa mentions, in the opening stanzas of the *Sumaṅgala-vilāsinī*, that the commentary to the *Dīgha-Nikāya* was at the first council rehearsed by 500 holy Elders, we may assume that he means, that at this meeting the *meanings* to be attached to the various terms—particularly to those that appear to have been borrowed from Hindu philosophy—were discussed and properly defined. This removes the difficulty of conceiving the contemporaneous existence of the commentaries and the *Piṭakas* from the very earliest times. Such definitions and fixations of meaning formed the nucleus of the later commentaries. The Elders had discussed the important terms at the First Council, and had decided on the method of interpreting and teaching the more recondite doctrines.

Later, when schisms arose within the Buddhist Church, they were caused mainly by differences of opinion as to the correct interpretation of certain rules of the Order, and of

[1] *Bud. Psy. Ethics,* 2nd ed., Introd., p. xxvi.

the meaning to be attached to various points in the Doctrine. With the lapse of time the philosophical notions implicit in the Dhamma had grown, new ideas had developed and earlier conceptions been elaborated; the simpler, archaically expressed *Sutta* teachings had been expanded and widened in their scope, and various schools of thought had arisen within the Order itself. Some of them were obviously heretical in their views. When, at the Second and the Third Councils, the custodians of the orthodox tradition met together to condemn such heresies, we may be sure that they determined with even greater preciseness and clearness than before the connotations and the applications of the Buddha's teachings. By the time of the Third Council such commentarial literature (using the word in the wider sense) had been more or less fully developed; and when, after the conclusion of that Synod, Mahinda came to Ceylon, he brought over with him the expositions of the teaching which had been sanctioned by the Elders at that meeting. Very soon after Mahinda's arrival he translated them into "the language of the land", and there they continued to be studied and pondered upon and further developed by the monks of Ceylon.

At the time when Buddhaghosa arrived in the island—in the early part of the fifth century A.D.—the commentaries so handed down in the schools at various times and places had already been put together into treatises, and books had been made of them, written in the native dialects. And we know, at least, the names of several of those which existed at this period. They are [1]:—

1. The *Mūla*- or *Mahā-Atthakathā*, or simply the *Atthakathā*, of the dwellers of the Mahā-Vihāra at Anurādhapura.
2. The commentary of the dwellers of the Uttara-Vihāra, also at Anurādhapura.
3. The *Mahā-paccarī*, or "Great Raft", so called because it was composed on a raft somewhere in Ceylon.

[1] *Manual of Bud. Psy. Ethics*, pp. xxvii and xxviii, also Vijayasinha, *JRAS.*, 1870, vol. v, pp. 298 foll., N.S.

4. The *Andha-Atthakathā*, handed down at Kāñcīpura (Conjevaram), in South India.

5. The *Kuruṇḍī-Atthakathā*, so named because of its having been written at the Kuruṇḍavelu Vihāra in Ceylon.

6. The *Saṅkhepa-Atthakathā*, or "Short Commentary", which was also, possibly, of South Indian origin.[1]

Buddhaghosa thus found a large mass of material at his disposal. These commentaries doubtless embraced various shades of opinion, and represented different schools of thought. It is difficult to decide whether each one of them dealt with the canon as a whole, or only with separate portions of it, but the former is not probable. The *ṭīkās* themselves give but very imperfect accounts of them, because, judging from the meagre information they contain with regard to them, at the time when the *ṭīkās* came to be compiled, almost all traces of the older commentaries had disappeared. In the *Sammoha-vinodanī* on the *Vibhaṅga*[2] Buddhaghosa tells us that he composed it "by taking the substance of the old commentaries" (*porāṇatthakathānaṃ sāram ādāya*). Thus, it is pretty clear that at least the first three of those mentioned above were separate works on the entire *Ti-piṭaka*, and that

[1] In addition to these Buddhaghosa often quotes the authority of what he calls the *Porāṇā*. Mrs. Rhys Davids suggests (Law, op. cit. Foreword) that these *Porāṇās* represented an evolving school of philosophical thought. It is distinctly stated in the *Gandha-vaṃsa* (pp. 55–9) that the *Porāṇā-cariyā* are also the *Atthakathācariyā*. Law (p. 64) considers that the name refers to eminent and revered teachers of the Order, who were often asked to interpret questions arising among the Saṅgha, and whose interpretations were embodied in the great *Atthakathās*; and he suggests that these were preserved in the Great Sinhalese Commentaries, and distinguished by being quoted in the original Pāli. I am of opinion that the *Porāṇās* merely refer to teachers whose expositions were not necessarily embodied in the Commentaries, but handed down in various schools by oral tradition, sometimes with mnemonic verses to help the memory and that Buddhaghosa refers to such traditional explanations as the anonymous *Porāṇā*. Often in Sinhalese books, when the author quoting from an ancient work either does not know—or does not think it necessary to give—the source, he introduces it merely by *eheyin purātaṇayō kīhu* ("therefore the ancients said").

[2] Vijayasinha, loc. cit., p. 299.

all of them were more or less directed to the elucidation of one or more of the *Piṭakas*, and that they purported to be separate and independent commentaries.

The task before Buddhaghosa was, therefore, by no means an easy one. The very copiousness of the material was an embarrassment. When he set out from India to make his "Concise Commentary", his idea was merely to study the Sinhalese *Atthakathā*'s and translate them into Pāli. But now, faced often with conflicting views, contradictory assertions, and sometimes incompatible doctrines, he had to expunge, abridge, enlarge, and make new a commentary of his own. The author of so systematic and coherent a synopsis as the *Visuddhi-magga* could not rest content with a mere translation; for that no great ability was required, and certainly far less extraordinary talent than he possessed. He wished to collect and systematize the knowledge which the various works contained, to garner the criticism of ancient scholarship for the use of future generations of scholars; and therefore he did not shrink from rewriting them so as to expand what he found into a fuller and richer form, embodying in the old material whatever he found elsewhere, to illuminate and elucidate the text of his comment. He approached his task with no iconoclastic desire to supersede the earlier scholiasts; on the contrary, he studied with great assiduity what his predecessors had written and incorporated with pious care in their works; he had always one great object predominantly in view, namely, to inspire reverence for what he considered supreme authority.

He himself describes what he did in the metrical introduction to the *Samanta-pāsādikā*[1]: "In commencing this commentary—having embodied therein the *Mahā-Atthakathā*, without excluding any proper meaning from the decisions contained in the *Mahā-paccarī*, as also in the famous *Kuruṇḍī* and other commentaries, and including the opinions of the Elders—I shall perform my task well. Let the young and

[1] *PTS.* ed., p. 2, vv. 10–16.

the middle-aged and the elderly monks who entertain a proper regard for the doctrines of the Tathāgata, the Luminary of Truth, listen to my words with pleasure. The *Dhamma*, as well as the *Vinaya*, was declared by the Buddha and his sons understood it in the same sense as it was delivered; and inasmuch as in former times they (the Sinhalese commentators) composed the commentaries without disregarding their (sons') opinions, therefore, excepting any error of transcription, everything contained therein is an authority to the learned in this Order, who respect ecclesiastical discipline. From these commentaries, after casting off the language, condensing detailed accounts, including authoritative decisions, without overstepping any Pāli idiom (I shall proceed to compose my work). And, as this commentary will be explanatory of the meanings of words belonging to the *Suttas* in conformity with the sense attached to them therein, therefore ought it the more diligently to be studied."

Thus Buddhaghosa's work formed a synthetic unity, deliberately planned as a consistent scheme for dealing with the traditions which had come down through the centuries, handed down by distinguished members of the Order and ever growing in the scope of their expositions of the canon. He was a critical scholar in some ways; there is evidence of this in almost every passage of his commentaries; he consulted manuscripts of various schools, and faithfully recorded the variant readings which he found in the same. Often, especially in the case of narratives, he found different versions of the same incident, and preserved them for the information of later generations. Working in this manner, he wrote the following commentaries which have come down to our day: The *Samanta-pāsādikā*, regarded by some as his most important work. It is a voluminous compilation, dealing with the *Vinaya* texts, and he says he wrote it before all others because the *Vinaya* forms the foundation of the Buddhist faith.[1] Apart from its value as a commentary to explain the

[1] P.T.S. Ed., p. 1, v. 5.

rules of morality, etc., embodied in the *Vinaya*, it contains a great mass of social, political, moral, religious, and philosophical history of Ancient India.[1] The work was translated into Chinese quite soon after it was written, and the Chinese translation, made by a monk named Saṅghabhadra in A.D. 489 (according to Nariman),[2] exists to this day. In Ceylon itself several *ṭīkās* have been written on this work at various times, and they will be referred to in their proper places; several of them still survive.

His other commentary on the Vinaya is the *Kaṅkhā-vitaraṇī* on the *Pāṭimokkha*, which forms one of the books of the *Vinaya-Piṭaka*, and contains certain rules of discipline for members of the Order, in such form as could easily be committed to memory by them. There exists a Sinhalese glossary on this work, written several centuries ago.[3]

These books were followed by commentaries on the four *Nikāyas* in succession: the *Sumaṅgala-vilāsinī* on the *Dīgha-Nikāya*, written in three parts, showing us Buddhaghosa's encyclopædic learning at its best, and composed in language less confused than that of his other commentaries, the *Papañca-sūdanī* on the *Majjhima*, the *Sārattha-ppakāsinī* on the *Saṃyutta* and the *Manoratha-pūraṇī* on the *Aṅguttara-Nikāya*. In the introductory verses to each of these books he gives the circumstances in which, and names the scholars at whose instigation, he undertook and carried out the work. In addition to these he is also said to have compiled commentaries on three books of the *Khuddaka-Nikāya*—the *Khuddaka-pāṭha*, the *Sutta-nipāta*, and the *Dhamma-pada*. The commentary on the first two divisions is called the *Paramattha-jotikā*.

Some doubts have been expressed by various scholars as to the authenticity of the tradition which ascribes the *Dhamma-pada-atthakathā* to Buddhaghosa.[4] Not a few scholars

[1] Law, p. 77.
[2] Nariman, *Buddhist Literature*, see Index.
[3] De Zoysa, p. 7.
[4] e.g. Burlingame in his translation (Yale University Series).

are of opinion that the work is modern and that the author was a later Buddhaghosa (Culla-Buddhaghosa), who obtained his materials from the same source as the Sinhalese *Saddhamma-ratanāvalī*, written by *Mahā-Thera* Dhammasena in the thirteenth century.[1] At the end of the commentary we find the following colophon: "*Vipula - visuddha - buddhinā Buddhaghoso' ti garūhi gahita-nāmadheyyena katāyaṃ Dhamma-padassa attha-vaṇṇanā.*" ("This commentary on the *Dhamma-pada* was written by Buddhaghosa of eminent and lustrous knowledge.") This may well refer to the great commentator. In a Sinhalese work, the *Pūjāvaliya*, it is mentioned that he wrote the work at the request of King Sirinivāsa and his minister Mahānigama.[2] This Sirinivāsa was undoubtedly Mahānāma, and the *Samanta-pāsādikā* tells us that Buddhaghosa wrote in the Ganthakāra Pariveṇa built by the great Minister Mahānigama and that on other occasions he lived in the palace built by the king himself, this palace forming part of the monastery at the Mahā-Vihāra where Buddhaghosa came to study the Sinhalese commentaries. At the end of the Dhammapadatthakathā is a stanza:—

"*Vihāre adhirājena kāritamhi kataññunā*
Pāsāde Sirikuḍḍassa rañño viharatā mayā."

("By me residing in the palace of King Sirikuḍḍa in the monastery built by the grateful king.") Sirikuḍḍa is apparently only another name for Sirinivāsa (Mahānāma).[3]

The chief stumbling block is the difference in language and style between this work and the other commentaries which undoubtedly belong to Buddhaghosa. Compared, for instance, with the commentary on the Majjhima Nikāya, the *Dhammapadatthakathā* resembles more the Jātaka commentary than anything else. At best it seems to be the work of a compiler who collected and edited sermons and stories,

[1] Wickremasinghe, p. 11.
[2] Colombo Ed., 1897, p. 16.
[3] Vide D. B. Jayatilaka, Introd. to the *Sikhavalanda* (Colombo Ed., 1923), p. vii.

not inventing new ones, but merely presenting in literary Pāli what existed already as folklore ; and the arrangement is different even from the *Sutta-nipāta* commentary. But this difference may possibly be due to the difference in the subject-matter of the various texts taken up for comment. " The Dhammapada, unlike the great Nikāyas, which consist of prose and gāthās, is entirely made up of gāthās without the prose setting, which, in the Nikāyas, is supplied in the text itself. Here, therefore, was the necessity of bringing it into line with those canonical works." [1] Hugh Nevill in the Introduction to his Catalogue ventures upon the view that this work did not belong to the three great *atthakathās* (*Mahā*, *Paccarī*, and *Kuruṇḍī*) which Buddhaghosa studied, but merely represented the popular legends accepted before the Aluvihāra redaction, and were either not then treated as of canonical value, or accepted by rival sects without dispute, and therefore not found necessary to be specially set down in writing. In Buddhaghosa's time they had acquired considerable authority, and they were translated by him and arranged at his discretion. It may be quite possible, Nevill says, that the legends had their origin in India or elsewhere and that they did not belong to Mahinda's school ; this may account for the different method of treatment. Where different versions are given of the same story,[2] the responsibility belongs not to Buddhaghosa, but to the different accounts from which he obtained his information.

A translation of the *Dhammapadatthakathā*, called the *Saddhamma-ratanāvalī* was made during the thirteenth century A.D. by an Elder named Dhammasena.[3] All the stories,

[1] Law, op. cit., p. 81.

[2] See Hardy, *JRAS.*, 1898, pp. 741–94, for examples of such different versions. That different recensions of even the *Dhamma-pada* existed is shown by a comparison of the Pāli work with the Chinese. See Norman, *Dhamma-pada Commty.*, i, pt. ii, pp. 15–16.

[3] Dhammasena is mentioned in the *Nikāya-saṅgraha* with authors such as Vilgammūla Anuruddha, who lived in the reign of, or just before, Paṇḍita Parākrama Bāhu (A.D. 1236–71). See Wickremasinghe, *Catalogue*, for fuller description, Nos. 13 and 14.

save quite a few, are taken from the *Dhamma-pada* commentary and follow more or less the same order. The greater part is merely a translation of the Pāli original, though, as is stated in the Introduction to the book, it does not follow the text throughout. Unlike the author of the Pāli commentary, the translator does not quote the actual words of the *Dhamma-pada*, but in most instances gives the substance of the aphorisms by way of introductions to each illustrative tale.

Besides these works Buddhaghosa also wrote a series of commentaries on the books of the *Abhidhamma-Piṭaka*. The best known of them is the *Attha-sālinī* on the *Dhamma-saṅgaṇī*, said to have been composed in India.[1] The work contains more than one distinct reference to the *Samanta-pāsādikā*,[2] showing that it was written or at least completed after the *Vinaya* commentary. Mrs. Rhys Davids suggests [3] that, though it was written at Gayā, it was later subjected to a complete revision by the author after his studies in Ceylon. This supposition is strengthened by the fact that in the body of the work he quotes from or refers to many works including, as Mrs. Rhys Davids has shown, the Ceylonese *Atthakathā*'s and the *Visuddhi-magga*. The commentary on the *Vibhaṅga* is named *Sammoha-vinodanī*, and the exegeses on the other five books are collectively called the *Pañca-ppakaraṇ-atthakathā* (sometimes also *Paramattha-dīpanī*).[4]

Such in brief was the nature of Buddhaghosa's vast labours, accomplished single-handed with a talent as wonderful as his industry was extraordinary. The *Buddhaghosuppatti* tells us [5] that when Buddhaghosa had completed his recension of this whole library of books expository of the *Tipiṭaka*, a bonfire "as high as seven average-sized elephants" was

[1] *M.V.*, xxxvi, v. 225, and *Sāsana-vaṃsa* (P.T.S.), p. 31.
[2] pp. 97 and 98.
[3] *Manual Bud. Psy. Eth.*, p. xxvii.
[4] De Zoysa, *Catalogue*, p. 3, and Nevill's *Catalogue*.
[5] p. 7.

made of the Sinhalese translations which Mahinda gave to Ceylon three centuries earlier, and which had later been added to in that land. We need not take this statement as being literally true. All that it probably means is that in his own time, and certainly to-day, they were completely superseded by Buddhaghosa's compilations ; he had eclipsed all others. As a stanza in the *Buddhaghosuppatti* has it : [1]

" *Buddhaghose patiṭṭhante paññavantā pi ye janā*
Tesaṃ paññāpabhā n'atthi Rāhu-mukhe va candimā."

(" When Buddhaghosa is by, even wise men lose the lustre of their wisdom, like the moon in the Dragon's mouth.")

It is a hopeless task to inquire into what has become of the old Sinhalese commentaries ; no trace of them now exists. " The early diffusion of Pāli among the priesthood and the learned laity, and the subsequent introduction of Sanskrit literature and Sanskrit verbiage into the once pure Elu, must have so choked that language that it died out early and its memory was cherished only by the lovers of Parnassus. For all religious and philosophic purposes Pāli and Sanskritized Sinhalese began to be used from a very early period and continue to be used to this day." [2]

So much has been written on the value of Buddhaghosa's labours that very little need be said here. Perhaps Buddhaghosa's greatest value to the modern historian lies in the very limitations of his mental powers, such as originality and independence of thought, which were imposed upon him by his extreme reverence for all that was traditional. For him there was no development in the doctrine and all the texts were the words of the Master himself. For the correct understanding of that doctrine, however, Buddhaghosa's work is indispensable. Many points of Buddhist teaching and many cruces of philosophy would be unintelligible to us but for his

[1] p. 66.
[2] *JRAS.* (N.S.), vol. v, p. 301.

expositions. Though his philology is sometimes crude [1] and often fanciful, yet his notes on rare words are invaluable and often conclusive. "For nearly fifteen centuries," said Sir Robert (now Lord) Chalmers on one occasion, "Buddhaghosa has remained the unchallenged expounder of Buddhism for the *Thera-vādin*, or Southern School. In the evolution of Buddhist thought he marked an epoch; he restated thought for his own day and stereotyped it ever since for the orthodox . . . Viewed as a scholar rather than as a philosopher, there is ample evidence in his writings to show that he was a critical scholar . . . From the point of view of textual criticism his help is invaluable to modern editions of *Piṭaka* texts; for through Buddhaghosa's records they can base their text on the best manuscripts which existed 1,500 years ago; and, where Buddhaghosa's reading is certain, it is an almost unerring guide in these later days. We have to get back through Buddhaghosa's commentary to his text of the canon and beyond this we can never hope to penetrate in restoring the *Piṭaka* texts as first written down at Alu-vihāra." [2]

It is true, no doubt, as Professor Rhys Davids has told us, "that the method adopted in his commentaries follows very closely the method of those much older ones preserved in the canon, but the literary skill with which he uses it is a great advance, more especially in lucidity, over older documents." [3] The stories he gathered together in his writings from various sources and the expositions he gave with the help of his

[1] It is sometimes asked whether Buddhaghosa knew Sanskrit. A *Mahā-kāvya* in Sanskrit on the life of the Buddha, called the *Padya-cūdāmaṇi* is sometimes attributed to the great exegete (Law, p. 85 foll.). Perhaps his reluctance to use Sanskrit in his etymology was due to the suspicion with which that language is viewed in defining terms of Buddhist philosophy and its traditional taboo for scriptural purposes. But the evidence yielded by his etymological exegeses is heavily against his having known, or at least been proficient in it. Cf. Dr. Stede, *Pāli Dictionary*, Afterword.

[2] *Cey. Antiq. and Lit. Reg.*, vol. i, pt. i, p. 2.

[3] *Enc. Rel. Eth.*, vol. ii, p. 887.

very wide, if not profound, erudition constitute a thesaurus, preserving for later generations invaluable information of the social customs, commercial values, folklore, ceremonies, and beliefs of the ancient world. "It may readily be granted," observed Mrs. Rhys Davids, in a critical study of one of his works,[1] "that Buddhaghosa must not be accepted *en bloc* . . . to me his work is not only highly suggestive, but also a mine of historic interest. To put it aside is to lose the historical perspective of the course of the Buddhist philosophy."

But even greater than this, for Ceylon, was the immense influence which his writings exerted on the development of the literary faculty among the Sinhalese Buddhists. The impetus he gave to Pāli learning was very great, and we shall see in our next chapter how it resulted in enriching the literature of the island.

[1] *Op. cit.*, p. xxxi. Cf. her ed. *Visuddhi-magga*, Afterword; and Foreword to Dr. B. C. Law's *Buddhaghosa.*

CHAPTER VI

Buddhaghosa's Successors

THE description, quoted from the *Mahā-vaṃsa* in the last chapter, of the life and work of Buddhaghosa might cause us to think that he wrote commentaries on the whole *Tipiṭaka*; but we know now that this statement is a poetic exaggeration. There is no doubt that Buddhaghosa's ambition was to write a complete recension of Buddhist commentarial literature, but he was unable to achieve his aspirations completely. He was compelled to leave Ceylon before his task could be finished; the reason for his departure we do not know; it may have been failing health; he had laboured ceaselessly for years, engaged in hard, strenuous work, and his spirit, indomitable as it was, had to give way to his weaker body; or it may be that his teacher was dying—Revata, who had shown the young enthusiast the way to a most fruitful life—and Buddhaghosa was summoned to his bedside; or after many years of exile undertaken for a noble cause the motherland may have called to him with a voice that would accept no denial; he was growing old, and he felt it was but right that India should see the fruits of his work before he died; for it was in India's cause that he first went out to Ceylon, that he might make a summary of the Sinhalese *Atthakathā* for the use of Indian monks, who were handicapped for want of such help in understanding the *Dhamma*.

Whatever the reason may have been, Buddhaghosa left Ceylon while some of the commentaries remained yet unedited and untranslated into Pāli. But others were forthcoming to complete the task thus left unfinished. Even in his own time Buddhaghosa was but one, the greatest, it is true, but only one, of several who were labouring, fired by the same purpose, enthusiastic in the same cause—that of writing the commentarial literature in Pāli.

Buddhaghosa's fame spread far and wide, quite soon after the compilation of his monumental *Visuddhi-magga*; in his own lifetime his works were being assiduously studied in more than one country—in mid-India, in Ceylon, in unlettered Thaton, and lastly in Burma, where, as some believe, he spent the latter part of his life. He established the pre-eminence of Ceylon over all other countries in the genuineness of its traditional heritage of the Buddha's religion, and justified her claim to be the home of the orthodox *Thera-vāda* of his day. Scholars were thus attracted to the island for purposes of study in even larger numbers than heretofore, and their visits, as we shall see later, resulted in the production of works of much value.

But above all stands the service which Buddhaghosa rendered to the development of the Pāli language. In place of the archaic, stilted, sometimes halting *Sutta* speech, almost Puritanical in its simplicity, groping about often for want of words to express ideas and conceptions then fresh to the minds of the users of this or that dialect, Buddhaghosa left behind him in his many works a language rich in its vocabulary, flexible in its use, elegant in structure, often intricate in the verbiage of its constructions, and capable of expressing all the ideas that the human mind had then conceived. Sonorous, long-winded sentences took the place of the direct simple composition of the *Suttas*. The Oriental mind, fascinated by the ornamentation of its structure, soon began to use much more extensively than before the Pāli language now grown into adolescence. And we find one author after another beginning his works with the proud boast that he was compiling his works for the benefit of learners in Pāli; in Māgadhī, that language "which is the root of all speech, sweet to the taste, pleasant to the ear, and delightful to the heart".[1] In Ceylon itself, where so far the native writers of the island had contented themselves with composing their books in the language of the land, they now deliberately sought to super-

[1] *Rūpa-siddhi*, Introduction.

sede that language by the cultivation of their new love—Māgadhī or Pāli. They were also undoubtedly attracted by the prospect of appealing to a wider public through Pāli than was possible through Sinhalese. It seems to have caught their fancy: they were like children fascinated by a new and clever toy, in the manipulation of which they had acquired more than average proficiency. Pāli made rapid strides as the cultivated literary language of the wise, and mastery over its form grew with use till it resulted in such limpid, lucid verse as we find in the *Mahā-vaṃsa*.

Material prosperity is the handmaid of literary development, as of all artistic work; and the century that followed Buddhaghosa's arrival was an era of peace and happiness to the people. The Malabar invasions had ceased, at least for the time being, and the islanders were left free to devote themselves to the pursuits of industry and skill. The annals of this period are replete with accounts of Anurādhapura's growth—its rich endowments of temples, lands and gardens, maintained at the nation's cost, of hospitals and playgrounds, of granaries and storehouses, of aqueducts for carrying water into the city, and numerous other works for the public benefit.

The city had grown in strength and power and splendour. Fa Hsien, who visited the island during this period, has left us a graphic account of what he saw and heard during his visit. He tells us of royal residences, monastic edifices and dāgobas, all enclosed within walls of great strength and shut in by massive gates, and of the outer city, set apart for the common people, who carried on the business life of the capital, divided into various quarters, and inhabited by provision dealers and drapers, artisans and goldsmiths, with shops for the sale of every description of goods. The parks were maintained for the growth of innumerable flowers, solely for the decoration of temples and dāgobas, and for the ornamentation of the streets of the great city on festal days, when the entire population gave themselves up to rejoicing and merry-making. They presented a brilliant spectacle, one unbroken vista of holiday-makers in their hundreds and thousands, garbed in festive attire, walking along the long, winding highways bestrewn with black and white sand, and flanked by festoons of bright-hued flowers, while the huge forms of gaily caparisoned elephants passed in slow procession to the chief dāgoba with its myriad garlands of the gayest blossoms, resplendent in the tropical sunshine.[1]

In the presence of such contentment and prosperity, confined to their island-home, and therefore free from endless frontier wars and from the difficulties and anxieties that trade produces upon society in general, the people found in the cultivation of letters not only a necessity, but also their chief delight. Each succeeding sovereign interested in the people's welfare rendered them most valuable service in this respect, and, whilst their own intellectual development was nearest to their hearts, that of their subjects was not neglected. The monasteries served as schools for the growth of Buddhist culture, and the monks and the nuns acted as the religious instructors.

By this time the art of writing had been fully developed ; the difficulty of finding a cheap, easily accessible material, durable enough for writing had been solved by the discovery of the ola-leaf, made of the dry shoots of the talipot palm, and we need therefore not be surprised that a notable array of authors followed in the footsteps of Buddhaghosa, and carried on the work which he had begun and continued in so masterly a manner.

First among them in chronological order was Buddhadatta. The *Gandha-vaṃsa* [2] puts him next in order to Buddhaghosa. There is an interesting account given in the *Buddhaghosuppatti* [3] of a meeting between the two scholars. Buddhadatta was already in Ceylon before Buddhaghosa had made up his mind to make a summary of the Sinhalese commentaries ;

[1] *The Travels of Fa Hsien*, Giles, pp. 66 foll.
[2] *G.V.*, p. 59.
[3] Ed. Gray, pp. 49–51.

but he had to leave the island without accomplishing the object which had brought him there. And on the very day when Buddhadatta left Ceylon Buddhaghosa is said to have taken ship for Anurādhapura. After three days the two ships passed near each other, according to the legend, through the influence of Sakka; the meeting of the monks was, therefore, a dramatic one. They introduced themselves to each other. Buddhaghosa announced the purpose of his journey. "I am returning from there," said Buddhadatta, "after having written the *Jinālaṅkāra*, and the *Danta-dhātu-bodhi-vaṃsa*, but not the *aṭṭhakathā*'s and the *ṭīkā*'s; if you render the teachings of the Master into Māgadhī from Sinhalese, write out the commentaries of the three *Piṭakas*." He also gave Buddhaghosa his iron stylus, myrobalan and a stone, and added: "If you have trouble in the eyes or pain in the back, rub this myrobalan on the stone and apply it and your pain will assuredly disappear." Buddhaghosa had evidently already heard of Buddhadatta; for he is said to have praised the *Jinālaṅkāra*—"Your book is very deep and difficult for the unwise to understand." "I came to the island," replied Buddhadatta, "to write out the teaching of the Master from Sinhalese into Māgadhī; but I shall not live much longer. Do you therefore accomplish the task; and, when your commentaries are finished, send them on to me, that I may summarize your labours." Whatever we may think of this description of the meeting of the two teachers in mid-ocean, there is no reason to disbelieve the statement that a meeting did take place.

The facts known about Buddhadatta are very few. At the end of his book, the *Vinaya-vinicchaya*, we are told that it was written by Buddhadatta of Uragapura (*Uragapurena Buddhadattena racito'yam*), and the same appears at the close of the *Abhidhammāvatāra*. The *Vinaya-vinicchaya* colophon gives us the further information "by the great exegetist of Tambapaṇṇi" (*Tambapaṇṇiyena parama-veyyākaraṇena*). In explaining this the author of the *ṭīkā* tells us that Uragapura was a city in the south of India and that Buddhadatta was born in the Coḷa kingdom situated in the Kāveri[1]; but he entered the Order at the Mahā-Vihāra at Anurādhapura, and therefore belonged to the Mahā-Vihāra fraternity.[2] Both the *Abhidhammāvatāra* and the *Vinaya-vinicchaya*, however, were written in India, probably after his return there; for the colophons tell us that he wrote in the country of Coḷa, at Bhūta-maṅgala-gāma in the monastery built by Veṇhudāsa, and that the author's royal patron was king Accutavikkama.[3] It thus appears that he resided for some time in Ceylon, and longer, perhaps, in South India.

His chief works are the *Abhidhammāvatāra* and the *Vinaya-vinicchaya*. The *Vinaya-vinicchaya ṭīkā* confirms the account given in the *Buddhaghosuppatti* of the meeting of the two scholars and adds that Buddhaghosa kept his promise to send Buddhadatta copies of his commentaries. It also says, further, that Buddhadatta read them and summarized the *Abhidhamma* commentary in the *Abhidhammāvatāra* and the *Vinaya* exposition in the *Vinaya-vinicchaya*.

As its name implies, the *Abhidhammāvatāra* is an introduction to the study of Buddhist philosophy. There is much similarity between it and the *Visuddhi-magga*, and this lends colour to the tradition which makes it a concise summary of Buddhaghosa's works. At any rate, we are quite safe in assuming that they drew their materials from the same sources. "It is probably right to conclude," says Mrs. Rhys Davids, "that they both were but handing on an analytical formula which had evolved between their own time and that of the final closing of the *Abhidhamma-Piṭaka*."[4] They often use the same similes (e.g. the simile of the blind man and the lame helping each other to walk, to define *nāma* and *rūpa*).

In one respect, at least, his exposition of the *Abhidhamma*

[1] Aung (*JPTS.*, 1910, p. 123) puts the Coḷa province in Ceylon, east of Anurādhapura, but gives no reason for doing so.

[2] *Abhidhammāvatāra*, P.T.S. Ed., Introd., pp. xii, foll.

[3] Ibid., colophon and *Vinaya-vicchaya*, colophon.

[4] *Buddhist Psychology*, p. 179.

is better than that of Buddhaghosa. Thus, whereas Buddhaghosa expounds his psychology in terms of the five-aggregate division, Buddhadatta opens his scheme with the fourfold division of the *Compendium*: mind, mental properties, material quality, and Nibbāna. . . . His work is, mostly, in metrical Pāli, but he stops at times to supply his own prose commentary. Already in his works, in place of the usual numerical and often, to us, arid analyses, we detect traces of an advance in synthesis, e.g. the doctrine of function (*kicca*) and of process (*pavatti*).[1]

There is no doubt that Buddhadatta's work marked a further advance in many ways in the study of the *Abhidhamma*. His diction is very often less involved and ambiguous than Buddhaghosa's, his style less discursive and more graphic, his vocabulary is extraordinarily rich, and he obviously profited by the labours of the earlier and yet in many ways the greater commentator. The work has been held in high esteem from ancient times and is extensively used both in Ceylon and in Burma.[2] Two *ṭīkās* on it exist in Ceylon, the older by Vācissara Mahāsāmi, of the Mahā-Vihāra, and the later by Sumaṅgala, pupil of the scholar named Sāriputta.

Buddhadatta's other book on the *Abhidhamma*, the *Rūpārūpa-vibhāga*, does not, at present, exist in Ceylon. His well-known work on the *Vinaya*, the *Vinaya-vinicchaya*, is sometimes (e.g. in the *Saddhamma-saṅgaha*, ix, 30) attributed to an author named Buddha-Sīha. But the colophon to the book definitely states that Buddhadatta was the author and that he dedicated it to his pupil Buddha-Sīha.[3] It is a moderately large work and a glossary has been published in Sinhalese in quite recent years by a monk of the South of Ceylon, Dhīrānanda by name.[4] The *Vinaya-vinicchaya* is now usually found, bound together with its

[1] Cf. *Buddhist Psychology*, p. 179.

[2] This and the *Rūpārūpavibhāga* form two of the nine classical summaries of the *Abhidhamma* in Burma (Little Finger Manuals or *Le-han*).

[3] So does the *Gandha-vaṃsa*, p. 40.

[4] Galle, 1864.

supplementary volume, the *Uttara-vinicchaya* (also a commentary on the *Vinaya*) dedicated (according to the *Gandha-vaṃsa*, p. 40) to another pupil, Saṅkhapāla.[1] Vācissara wrote a commentary to both works in the thirteenth century; but both *Vinicchayas* and their *ṭīkās* have been largely superseded by Sāriputta's monumental work, the *Vinaya-saṅgaha*, written in the twelfth century A.D. (q.v.). An older *ṭīkā* on the *Vinaya-vinicchaya* also exists, by one Revata *Thera*, who wrote a commentary on the Sinhalese *Khuddha-Sikkhā*, and who lived probably towards the end of the eleventh century A.D.

A Ceylon tradition attributes to Buddhadatta the authorship of two other works—the *Madhurattha-vilāsinī*,[2] and the *Jinālaṅkāra*. The former is a commentary on the *Buddha-vaṃsa*, one of the books of the *Khuddaka-Nikāya*, and is a compilation of legends dealing with the lives of Gotama, when he practised the *Pāramitā* during the régimes of twenty-four previous Buddhas. The commentary follows very closely the method of Buddhaghosa's works, showing that the author was quite familiar with the great exegetist's writings. Mr. Wickremasinghe, perhaps struck with this similarity in the method of treatment, seems inclined to believe that the author of the *Buddha-vaṃsa* commentary was distinct from the Buddhadatta under discussion.[3] But we saw above that Buddhadatta's expositions resemble Buddhaghosa's in many ways, and I therefore can see no reason for separating the two authors. The *Pūjāvaliya* of the thirteenth century [4] mentions the *Buddhavaṃsaṭṭhakathā* as among Buddhadatta's works,[5] and the Ceylon tradition is, I find, supported by the Burmese authors as well.[6]

[1] Ed. by Rev. A. P. Buddhadatta, for the P.T.S.

[2] Sometimes also called *Madhurattha-pakāsinī* (De Zoysa, p. 2).

[3] *Catalogue*, p. xii.

[4] Colombo Ed., p. 169.

[5] The *Abhidhammārtha-saṅgraha Artha-kathā* given in the list, evidently refers to the *Rūpārūpa-vibhāga*. See also *Abhidhammāvatāra* (P.T.S.).

[6] Law, *Buddhaghosa*, p. 96, and *Sāsana-vaṃsa*, p. 33.

Even more obscure is the authorship of the *Jinālaṅkāra*. It is a Pāli poem of 250 verses, containing a narrative of the Buddha's life, written in brilliant rhythmical cadences and elegant language, with a large variety of versification. Some of the stanzas show traces of artificiality in construction,[1] with internal rhymes, alliterations and other such rhetorical devices. Gray attributes its authorship to Buddharakkhita, "who is stated to have been born in Ceylon in the 117th year of the Nirvāṇa of the Buddha, i.e. 426 B.C. His birthplace was Rohaṇa, and it appears that he was at the head of a congregation of priests in Coḷikatambaraṭṭha (afterwards Tambamaṇi), the maritime western division of Ceylon . . . With the inducements to missionary work in Vijaya's domain our author must have joined the Church, and, as an outcome of his devotion to Pāli studies, composed the *Jinālaṅkāra*."[2] He further states that a *ṭīkā* on the work exists written by Buddhadatta, "contemporary of Buddhaghosa, the great commentator," with which the text has been embodied, and "which, as a storehouse of much information in connexion with the life and teachings of the Buddha, is held in high appreciation by native scholars". The *Gandha-vaṃsa*, however, attributes the *Jinālaṅkāra* itself to Buddhadatta and its *ṭīkā* to Buddharakkhita.[3] De Zoysa follows the *Gandha-vaṃsa* with regard to the authorship of the work.[4] It is very rare in Ceylon and is not to be found in any of the old Temple Libraries; whatever copies do exist in the island are, in my opinion, importations from Burma. I have not heard whether it is studied to any extent in Ceylon. Nor is it referred to in the passage from the *Pūjāvaliya* mentioned above. The Ceylon tradition regarding Buddhadatta does not seem to make any mention of such a work by him. The language of the book makes the date assigned to it by Gray preposterous. Gray

[1] Gray, *Jinālaṅkāra*, Introd., p. 10.
[2] p. 7 foll.
[3] pp. 69 and 72.
[4] p. 7.

evidently feels so himself; but he tries to explain it away. "It contains," he says, "stanzas in the style of Kālidāsa, Bhāravi, and Māgha." But nothing could destroy his faith in the author's existence four centuries before Christ. "If he (the author) is to be looked upon as an imitator of Sanskrit writers, the authors of *Raghu-vaṃsa* and *Kirātārjunīya* must have flourished, not after the commencement of the Christian era, but at least four centuries before. Several parallels may be noticed between the artificial stanzas in their works and those occurring in the *Jinālaṅkāra*." [1]

Some of the varieties of versification found here are not met with in Pāli books till a quite late period, when the study of Sanskrit had come to influence Pāli to a large extent. Nor is there any justification, except the postscript which Gray found attached to the copy of his *ṭīkā*,[2] for believing that Buddhadatta wrote the *ṭīkā*. Be that as it may, it is quite certain, if the evidence of language and construction be of any value in determining the date of an author, that the *Jinālaṅkāra*, as we have it now, was a work not earlier than the sixth or seventh century A.D. We do not know who wrote it, nor who was the author of its *ṭīkā*. It is quite possible that there was a much earlier work by the same name; the life of the Buddha was a favourite subject for verse (e.g. the *Buddha-vaṃsa* itself); but such a work, if it existed, is now irretrievably lost, and only a traditional reference to it remains. I am inclined to believe that the confusion between Buddhadatta (if that was his name), who wrote the commentary on the *Jinālaṅkāra*, and Buddhadatta, the contemporary of Buddhaghosa, was due to the fact that the latter, too, had written a commentary on the life of the Buddha, namely the *Madhurattha-vilāsinī* on the *Buddha-vaṃsa*.[3] The author of the *Jinālaṅkāra-ṭīkā* was comparatively

[1] pp. 10 and 11.

[2] Mandalay MS.

[3] I am strengthened in this opinion by another fact mentioned by Gray, viz., that the *Jinālaṅkāra* is regarded in Burma as an *atthakathā*, a commentary. Introd., p. 10.

unknown, and his work was grafted on to the more famous scholar. Such instances are not unknown in the history of literature.[1]

To this period also undoubtedly belongs Dhammapāla, author of a large number of commentaries. It has sometimes been suggested that, as the name is a very common one among Buddhists, ancient and modern, there has possibly been confusion of several authors of the same name by writers on Buddhist ecclesiastical history. In the *Gandha-vaṃsa* four scholars of the name of Dhammapāla are enumerated in a chapter entitled " On the native places of the scholars " (pp. 66 seq.). Two of them are mentioned in a series of ten scholars, all natives of India. The first is distinguished by the name of *Ācariya* (the teacher), and is said to have written fourteen books (p. 69). His name follows that of Buddhadatta and that of Ānanda, the author of a *ṭīkā* on Buddhaghosa's *Abhidhamma* commentaries. The second is called Culla-Dhammapāla (Dhammapāla the Lesser) to distinguish him from his greater namesake ; he was the senior pupil of Ānanda, and is the author of *Sacca-saṅkhepa*. A third is mentioned between Sangharakkhita, author of the *Vuttodaya* (*G.V.*, pp. 61, and 70, and *Sās.*, p. 34), and Anuruddha (author of the *Abhidhammattha-saṅgaha*), and therefore belongs to about the twelfth century. A fourth Dhammapāla belongs to a group of scholars who are said to have written at Arimaddana in Burma (*G.V.*, p. 67, and Mrs. Bode's Introd., p. 3). It is the first with whom we are concerned here, distinguished as the Ācariya Dhammapāla. The others will be dealt with, each in his proper place. The *Sāsana-vaṃsa* [2] records that he dwelt at Badaratittha [3] in the

[1] e.g. the *Jātakatthakathā*. It is interesting that in the list of works of Buddhadatta given in *G.V.*, p. 59, no mention is made of the *Jinālaṅkāra* ; on p. 72 occurs the name Buddhadatta, author of a *ṭīkā* to the *Jinālaṅkāra*, also, apparently, called the *Jinālaṅkāra*. I suggest that the confusion in authorship is due to the identity of the two names, and that, what we have now is a text extracted from the *ṭīkā*.

[2] p. 33.

[3] Sometimes spelled *Padaratittha*, e.g., in the *Sāsana-vaṃsa*.

Damila kingdom near Ceylon. He was, therefore, very probably Tamil by birth, and wrote in S. India. Badaratittha is on the south-east coast of India, just a little to the south of Madras. His works show that he was a native of Kāñci-pura (Conjevaram). We cannot be sure as to the time in which he flourished, but it is generally agreed that he was slightly posterior to Buddhaghosa. Neither scholar makes any reference to the other by name [1] or by their works; but considering that Buddhaghosa's works cover the chief portions of the Buddhist scriptures, the Four *Nikāyas*, the *Abhidhamma-Piṭaka*, and the *Vinaya-Piṭaka*, it is most probable that Dhammapāla came later. Else he, by no means of lesser intellect, would surely have attempted the exposition of the more important works of the canon, e.g. the Four *Nikāyas*. The Khuddaka *Nikāya*, which formed the special subject of Dhammapāla's study, was admittedly of minor importance compared with the rest of the *Sutta Piṭaka*. This supposition is further strengthened by the fact that he is credited with having written a *ṭīkā* (called the *Paramattha-mañjūsā*) on Buddhaghosa's *Visuddhi-magga*.[2] He also wrote a sub-commentary on Buddhaghosa's exposition of the four *Nikāyas*.

That he studied at the Mahā-vihāra in Ceylon, whether he wrote his books there or not, is undoubted, because he states in his works (e.g. the Introduction to the commentaries on the *Peta-vatthu*) that he follows the traditional interpretation of texts as handed down in the Mahā-vihāra, and we know from Buddhaghosa's mission to Ceylon that the Thera-vāda commentaries, then studied by the Mahā-vihāra fraternity in Ceylon, were not available in India. It is quite likely that he had the advantage of studying the Tamil commentaries (of which we know that at least two existed) as well. In a

[1] But there are traces in Dhammapāla's works, of several borrowings, evidently from Buddhaghosa—especially the *Attha-sālinī* and the *Dhp.A.*; see Hardy's Introd. to the *Netti*, xv–xvii.

[2] Aung, *JPTS.*, 1910, p. 121. This *ṭīkā* is not much used in Ceylon, but seems to be extensively used in Burma.

translation of a book of travels by the Chinese traveller Hiuan-Tsang,[1] some interesting details are given of Dhammapāla's life. Hiuan-Tsang visited Kāñcī-pura, the capital of the Tamil country, in A.D. 640. The monks then told him that the famous Dhammapāla was born there. "He was a boy of good natural parts, which received great development as he grew up, and when he came of age a daughter of the king was assigned to him as wife. But on the night before the ceremony of marriage was to be performed, being greatly distressed in mind, he prayed before an image of the Buddha. In answer to his prayer a god bore him away to a mountain monastery, some hundreds of *li* from the capital. When the brethren there heard his story, they complied with his request and gave him ordination." There is good reason to believe that this, very probably, refers to our author.[2] The *Gandha-vaṃsa* gives a list of the works ascribed to Dhammapāla.[3] Seven out of his fourteen commentaries are on the principal books of poetry preserved in the canon (*Thera-* and *Therī-gāthā*, *Udāna*, *Vimāna-vatthu*, and *Peta-vatthu*, *Itivuttaka* and *Cariyā-piṭaka*). His other works are a commentary on the *Netti* (with a *ṭīkā* on the same), the *Paramattha-mañjūsā*, referred to above (a commentary on the *Visuddhi-magga*) and the *Līnattha-vaṇṇanā* (also called the *Līnattha-pakāsinī ṭīkā*) on Buddhaghosa's commentaries to the Four *Nikāyas*, and another by the same name on *Jātakatthakathā*.[4] The *Gandha-vaṃsa* also mentions a *ṭīkā* on the *Buddhavaṃsatthakathā* and an *Anu-ṭīkā* on the *Abhidhammatthakathā*.[5] These last two works are very rare; in fact I do not know of any copy existing in Sinhalese

[1] Ed. by Rhys Davids and Watters, London, 1905, vol. ii, p. 226 sq.

[2] See also Hastings' *Encyclopaedia*, vol. v, p. 701.

[3] p. 60.

[4] *G.V.*, 60 and 69. The commentaries on *Udāna*, *Itivuttaka*, *Vimāna-* and *Peta-vatthu*, and *Cariyā-piṭaka* are collectively called *Paramattha-dīpanī*, or sometimes, as in Burma, *Vimala-vilāsinī* (De Zoysa, p. 2, and Law, *Buddhaghosa*, p. 96).

[5] p. 60.

characters; and I am inclined to believe that they are the result of the labours of a later author, probably an Indian or a Burmese Dhammapāla.

Dhammapāla's works show great learning, much exegetical skill, and a good deal of sound judgment. There are many resemblances between him and Buddhaghosa. "It would seem," says Rhys Davids,[1] "that Dhammapāla was educated in the same university as Buddhaghosa . . . the two writers hold very similar views. They refer to the same authorities; they have the same method of exegesis; they have reached the same style in philological and etymological science and they both have the same lack of any knowledge of the simple rules of higher criticism." Yet Dhammapāla shows much individuality in the treatment of his subject. He confines himself rigidly either to questions of meanings of words or discussions of ethical import in his texts; he is, however, not so ethically insistent as Buddhaghosa; his style is simpler, less garrulous, less diffuse, and shows more of the grammarian and the academician than of the exegetical compiler and fanciful etymologist. His explanation of terms is quite clear, and shows an advance over Buddhaghosa; though he was evidently well-read and quite well-informed, Buddhaghosa's knowledge was more widely diffused and more encyclopædic; and the information we derive from his works with regard to the social, religious, philosophical, and moral ideas of his time, though considerable, is far less than that afforded by Buddhaghosa's writings. "Dhammapāla's chronicles are, for the most part, unduplicated in any other extant work, but, not seldom, they run on all fours, not only with parallel chronicles in Buddhaghosa's commentaries, but also with the prose and framework of poems in the *Sutta-nipāta* or the *Saṃyutta-Nikāya*, not to mention the *Jātaka*."[2] Often his explanations of episodes and their characters are, it is true, but legends woven out of legends, yet they represent the most ancient

[1] Hastings' *Encycl. Rel. and Ethics*, vol. iv, pp. 701 foll.

[2] Mrs. Rhys Davids, *Psalms of the Brethren*, Introd., p. xxv.

orthodox tradition, and help us immensely in understanding the more archaic idiom of the original Pāli. Dhammapāla's work was, as he states in the colophon to several of his books, compilations from already existing commentaries, and shows the importance attached at this period, in the history of orthodox Buddhism, to the work of re-writing in Pāli the traditional interpretations so far handed down in local dialects, namely Sinhalese or Tamil.

In his commentaries, especially to the poetic work of the canon, Dhammapāla follows a regular scheme. First [1] comes an introduction to the whole collection of poems, giving the traditional account of how they came to be thus put together as one whole, then each poem is taken separately and the words explained philologically and exegetically. And this presentation of verses in a groundwork of prose-narrative is essentially the historical Buddhist way of imparting canonical poetry. Much of Dhammapāla's work is but a recast, a re-compilation in scholastic Pāli, of the older Sinhalese or Tamil commentarial literature. Thus we need not be surprised if the narratives contain much hagiographical myth; the exegesis is coloured by later developments of doctrine, and twisted by professional exigencies of edification. Yet, as Mrs. Rhys Davids tells us, these commentaries "have a venerableness of their own, bridging over the seas of time between Asoka and the days of the greater scholastics to a greater extent than at first appears".[2] They contain the old "talks on meaning", as they came down to him unbroken, if varied in diction, from the earlier age of his faith, and are, to that extent at least, of immense value. Such defects as he had were but the shortcomings of his age, when higher criticism, as we now know it, was yet unborn, and when faith took the place of historical and scientific investigation.

Mr. Wickremasinghe [3] includes in this period also Upasena,

[1] e.g. *Peta-vatthu* commentary.
[2] *Psalms of the Brethren*, Introd., p. xxv.
[3] *Catalogue*, p. xii.

author of a commentary on the *Mahā-Niddesa* (which is itself a commentary) called *Saddhama-ppajjotikā*. Nothing further is known about him. The *Gandha-vaṃsa* includes him in the list of Ceylon authors,[1] and the *Sāsana-vaṃsa*[2] merely states that he was the author of this volume.

His name does not occur in the list of writers who succeeded Buddhaghosa, given in the *Nikāya-saṅgraha*.[3] A colophon to the *Saddhamma-ppajjotikā* states that it was written by "Mahā Thera Upasena, like unto a banner in Tambapaṇṇi", and that he followed the tradition of the Mahā-vihāra. It is a fairly long work, but distinctly inferior to the achievements of Dhammapāla or Buddhaghosa. The author was merely retranslating into Pāli what he found in the Ceylon commentaries and makes no attempt at originality.

Another work of much importance, which was composed during the period under consideration, is the *Jātakatthakathā* (the commentary on the *Jātakas*). The *Jātakas* belong to the *Ākhyāna* type of Indian literature,[4] out of which the later epic poems evolved. Their chief characteristic was that the entire story was not yet rigidly established in form, but only certain parts were metrically fixed and thereby secured from further departure from the tradition. Such parts were, especially, passages of direct narrative. They were bound together by a framework of prose, where the details of the situation were described, and the names of the characters of the story were told, the secular prose, which held the sacred verses intact, forming with them "a picture, as it were, of wooded slopes of verdant growth, clothing the hills that tower relatively unchanging, above them."[5]

The telling of legends of virtuous monarchs, valorous men and holy hermits was a very early custom in India. It was supposed to remove evil, and in the *Aitareya-Brāhmaṇa*

[1] pp. 66–7.
[2] p. 33.
[3] p. 23, Colombo Ed.
[4] Oldenberg, *JPTS.*, 1910, pp. 19 foll.
[5] Mrs. Rhys Davids, *Brethren*, p. xxv.

we are told that "if those who are longing to have a son born to them will have the legend of Śunaḥśepa related to them, their wishes would be gratified." [1] And the tendency to relate a story in order to inculcate a moral has always been a characteristic trait of the Indian temperament. Tradition tells us, therefore, that, as occasion arose, the Buddha was accustomed throughout his long career of teacher, to explain and comment on events around him by relating similar things that had occurred to him in his own previous births; the experience of many lives was always present to him, and he used this "to point a moral and adorn a tale". The stories so told were treasured by his disciples and later gathered together to form the *Jātaka* book, on which a commentary had been handed down, first in India and then in Ceylon.

Whether we believe these details or not, it is recorded that the *Jātakas* or birth-stories were recognized by the Master himself for purposes of teaching. Several of them occur in the canonical books (e.g. the *Tittira Jātaka* in *Cullavagga*, vi, 6, 3–5, *Mahāsudassana Jātaka* in *Dīgha*, vol. ii, 1). The *Cariyā Piṭaka* is in reality a *Jātaka* book giving in verse accounts of previous births which the Bodhisat had to pass through in order to acquire the ten perfections necessary for the attainment of the Enlightenment. So was the *Apadāna*, another of the *Khuddaka-Nikāya* volumes, containing metrical episodes in the lives of recluses, resembling very closely the introductory tales of the *Jātaka* commentary. So too was the *Buddha-vaṃsa* (the history of the Buddhas), giving an account of the life of Gotama, when, as Bodhisat, he had to receive *vivaraṇa* (the declaration) at the hands of the twenty-four previous Buddhas.

By the third century B.C. most of the *Jātakas* were well known, as we can be sure from the numerous representations of the stories on the bas-reliefs at Sāñchī and Amarāvatī, and especially at Bharhut, which show that at that time the *Jātakas* were widely known and were considered part of the

[1] Winternitz, *Calcutta Review*, Nov., 1923, p. 130.

sacred history of the religion. From India they came over to Ceylon, and there took firm hold of the imagination of the people. When Fa Hsien visited Ceylon in the fifth century,[1] he witnessed the annual procession of the Tooth Relic being carried from Anurādhapura to Mihintale, and he describes how on both sides of the road were hung pictures of the 500 different births of the Buddha, painted in different colours, and "executed with such care as to make them appear living".

Even to-day, among the Sinhalese, the relating of the *Jātaka* stories is a very common practice. In the Sinhalese homes, it is true, the fireside with which those of harsher climes associate story-telling, is absent, but it finds its representative in the little verandah or on the roadside; and often, when the family have retired to rest for the night in the single room or verandah which generally forms the house of the Sinhalese peasant, one member, frequently the grandfather, relates stories from the *Jātaka* book till the dull god of sleep has drawn away his audience. In the night, as the villagers sit guarding the ripening grain of the paddy-fields from the inroads of the elephant or the wild boar, these stories serve to pass pleasantly what, otherwise, would be a weary vigil, and on numerous occasions story-telling plays an important part.[2]

We cannot say how the *Jātakas* were originally handed down. No one who reads them can fail to recognize that the verses constitute the essential element in the form adopted by the compilers of these stories; but they are not verses which are given as quotations, extracted from some treasures of old lore—they are seen to have their home in the

[1] Fa Hsien, Giles' *Travel*, p. 71. The 73rd chap., v. 72, of the *Mahāvaṃsa* states that Parākrama-Bāhu the Great erected at Polonnaruva a circular house, in which he might listen to the recitation of the *Jātakas*.

[2] Most of the existing books of poems in Sinhalese are verse translations of *Jātaka* stories; e.g. *Sasadā-vata*, *Guttila-kāvya*, *Kusa-jātaka*, *Kāvya-śekhara*, and, perhaps the most popular, the *Vessantara-jātaka*.

narrative itself, they have their value because the characters in the story and the Bodhisat are made to say them. But was the prose narrative, too, handed down or was it left to the judgment and the discretion of those who related the story? We cannot say, but certainly the essential points of the story, as well as the verses, were handed down, for most often the latter contain no indication of the persons who figure in the narrative.

The *Jātakas*, as we have them now, consist of 551 stories, in twenty-two *nipātas* or groups, roughly divided according to the number of verses in each story. Each story opens with a quotation of part of a verse, followed by a preface (called *paccuppanna-vatthu*, or story of the present), giving the particular circumstances in which the story was related by the Buddha, and this leads the Buddha to recall some past event (*atīta-vatthu*) in the long series of his previous lives as Bodhisat. It ends always in a short summary where the Buddha identifies the different characters in the story showing the parallelism which runs between the two stories, and which constitutes their connexion (*anusandhi*). Every story is illustrated by one or more *gāthās*,[1] uttered usually by the Bodhisat or sometimes by the Buddha himself, in which case they are called *Abhisambuddha-gāthā* (stanzas after enlightenment). This is followed by a series of short comments on the words of the stanzas.

The whole collection is prefaced by a long introductory essay called the *Nidāna-kathā* (History of the Lineage), giving the Buddha's history before his birth as Siddhattha, and also during his last birth before he became the Awakened One.[2]

Even the most orthodox Buddhist will admit that the

[1] "In the midst of the unmeasured indefiniteness of the prose diction appear formations of another kind, welded, rounded off, and gathering into themselves the essence of the whole." Oldenberg, loc. cit.

[2] For a fuller and more detailed account of the nature of the *Jātakattha kathā* see Rhys Davids' excellent introduction to his *Buddhist Birth Stories*, now re-edited by Mrs. Rhys Davids in Broadway Translation Series, London, 1924.

present collection contains some fables, fairy-tales, "Joe Millers," and records of everyday experience, such as are in no way peculiar to Buddhism, but are the common property of the world, floating down the ages.[1] But not even the most critical scholar will deny that some of the stanzas and all the central stories are genuinely Buddhistic, and that some of the narratives of the *Paccuppanna-vatthu* contain genuine fragments of the life of the Buddha, and that another considerable portion, if not distinctly Buddhistic, is Indian and local, and has its origin and application within a limited range. The stories inculcate pointed, allegorical lessons of morality, most of them specific points of Buddhist teaching, and are fables only in the most general sense of the term; they are full of feeling and genuine admiration for high standards of self-sacrifice, perseverance, justice, and correct valuation of pleasure and sagacity. Some have called them "artistic sermons" ready to hand, and to be preached to mixed audiences. Professor Kunte, in a very interesting paper read before the Ceylon Branch of the Royal Asiatic Society,[2] described how such an artistic sermon is made to work. "A part of a *gāthā* is first recited. Faith in the Buddha is thus awakened, and a good basis for the chant of the *gāthā* in full is thus prepared. Then, in explaining the *gāthā* the preacher shows his power of erudition. The ordinary audience listens on, half-puzzled and half-struck by what the mind considers to be profound and mysterious and, moved by the incomprehensible, it works up into the marvellous and obtains from this a passive intellectual enjoyment. The preacher proceeds with an energy of his own. The strain on the mental power of the audience is now at its height, when abstruse comments upon the *gāthā* are abstrusely but eloquently explained. This is succeeded by the narration of the simple, but popular, *atīta-vatthu*. There is thus a sudden transition

[1] e.g. *The Talkative Tortoise* (Fausböll, 215), and *The Ass in the Lion's Skin* (Fausböll, 189).

[2] C.B.R.A.S. *Journal*, vol. viii, pp. 193 foll.

from the mysterious to the simple, from the more religious to the popular element. Such a transition produces a contrast, and the parallelism which runs between the two stories and which constitutes the *anusandhi* is thus combined with a contrast. And parallelism and contrast are the foundation upon which all æsthetic pleasure, whether intellectual or emotional, is built. The transition from the comments on a *gāthā* affords relief to the minds of the audience." And further on he gives the reasons for such procedure. "An audience cannot be trifled with—pleasure it must have. The number of lay ladies and gentlemen attending a convent gave it importance."

Quite interesting and ingenious, but, I am afraid, rather fanciful.

It is quite uncertain as to when the *Jātakas* were put together into a systematic form. They were probably first handed down orally and disjointedly, but their growing popularity necessitated a more permanent form, at least of the kernel. Rhys Davids has shown quite conclusively that the *Jātaka* book existed at a very early date as a separate compilation,[1] and we have the evidence of the Ceylon tradition of the history of Buddhism that a collection called the *Jātakas* existed at the time of the Council of Vesāli, for that formed one of the portions of the *Tipiṭaka* rejected or altered by the dissentient Vesālian monks.[2] The Ceylon tradition is that the original *Jātaka* book consisted of *gāthās* alone, and a commentary on these, containing the stories with which they were connected, was written in very early times in Sinhalese. This was translated in the fifth century by Buddhaghosa, and the Sinhalese original was afterwards lost. The verses are undoubtedly very much older than the prose narrative, as it has come down to us. Their language is distinctly archaic, and they contain archaic forms and forced constructions, and the corrupt state in which some of the verses are found,

[1] Op. cit., Introd., pp. lv foll.
[2] *Dīpa-vaṃsa*, vv. 35 and foll.

as compared with the regularity and simplicity of the prose parts, shows that the verse was much older. Rhys Davids thinks [1] that the vast majority of the stories were earlier still, that in most cases the verses were added after the stories became current, that the stories—about one-tenth of the collection—without the verses at all (the verses being found only at the conclusion) are probably the oldest, and that they were handed down in Ceylon in Sinhalese while the verses remained intact in Pāli, as they were received. It is probable, however, that the verses form the older kernel of the work, and that in its original form the *Jātaka* book, like the *Cariyā-Piṭaka*, consisted only of verses. But the verses are, most of them, quite unintelligible without the story.

Who was the author of the present *Jātakatthakathā* ? Most Western scholars deny that it was the work of the great commentator, Buddhaghosa,[2] as do also the most advanced of scholars in Ceylon.[3] More direct evidence is necessary before we can come to any definite conclusion. It is very probable that the book is the work of one author ; in the *paccuppanna-vatthu* references are made backwards and forwards, the comments on later *gāthās* are abbreviated, and directions about such abbreviations are given, and the same system is followed of fitting in all the elements of the story and its commentary—part of *gāthā, paccuppanna-vatthu, gāthā* in full, comment, *atīta-vatthu,* and conclusion. And the Pāli work is not necessarily to be considered as a translation of a Sinhalese commentary ; for the author refers several times to a previous *Jātaka* commentary, which, probably, was a Sinhalese work, and in one case (i.e. in discussing the age of Rāhula at the time of Siddhattha's renunciation) mentions what it says only to overrule it.[4] There is no reason to suppose

[1] Op. cit., p. lxxviii.

[2] Childers assigned it to Buddhaghosa (*Dictionary,* Preface, p. ix, note).

[3] e.g. H. Sumaṅgala, the greatest scholar in Ceylon in the last century.

[4] Rhys Davids, op. cit., p. lx.

that it belonged to the three Sinhalese commentaries which Buddhaghosa translated ; it may equally have belonged to the Dhammaruci fraternity of Abhayagiri. A very old glossary to the Pāli commentary, of unknown date, exists in Sinhalese, certainly older than the Sinhalese translation, made in the thirteenth century, and there the work is assigned to the great exegetist.

In the *Sutta-nipāta-atthakathā*, which is, admittedly, Buddhaghosa's, the reader is referred to the *Nidāna-kathā* of the *Jātaka* commentary [1] ; but Buddhaghosa does not say he wrote it. On the other hand, in the commentaries attributed to Buddhaghosa, there appears at the end an eulogy of himself (*parama-visuddha-saddhā-buddhi-viriya-guṇa-patimaṇḍitena . . . Buddhaghoso'ti garu-gahita-nāmadheyyena katā*). No such mention is made in the *Jātaka* commentary ; Buddhaghosa gives a separate name to each of his commentaries—*Samanta-pāsādikā*, *Kaṅkhā-vitaraṇī*, *Sumaṅgala*, etc.—but no such name is given to the *Jātaka*, though it is larger than the above-mentioned. The usual aspirations of Buddhaghosa, expressed at the end of his works ("may all beings enjoy the taste of the Dhamma of the Omniscient One, may the good Dhamma last long"), have in the *Jātakatthakathā* given place to a personal ambition : "May I be born in Tusita heaven, and, when Metteyya comes, may I receive nomination to become a Buddha, and after having perfected the *Pāramitās* may I become Buddha." The adoration of Buddhaghosa of the Buddha, Dhamma, and Saṅgha, and of his scholarly predecessors, etc., given at the beginning of the commentaries which are undoubtedly his, are charming in their style and captivating in their sentiment. The same cannot be said of the verses at the outset of the *Jātaka* commentary, which begin :—

> "*Jāti-koṭi-sahassehi pamāṇa-rahitaṃ hitaṃ*
> *Lokassa loka-nāthena kataṃ yena mahesinā.*"

[1] Colombo Ed. (Mahābodhi Press), p. 2.

In the introduction to Buddhaghosa's commentaries he gives the names of those at whose special request each work was compiled, and in all the other books they are *Theras* of the Mahā-vihāra, distinctly stated as such. Three *Theras*, however—*Atthadassi*, *Buddhamitta*, and *Buddhadeva*—are mentioned in the *Jātaka* commentary, and in introducing one of them it is said that he belonged to the Mahiṃsāsaka sect (*mahiṃsāsaka-vaṃsamhi sambhūtena nayaññunā*), which is one of the unorthodox sects, then separated from the Theravāda.[1] Nothing is said about the others, but we may presume that they belonged to the same school. It is true, nevertheless, that he states his intention of compiling the commentary in conformity with the exposition current among the Mahā-vihāra fraternity. As Rhys Davids points out,[2] it is noteworthy that there is not the slightest allusion, either to Buddhaghosa's conversion, or to his journey from India, or to the high hopes he entertained; there is no mention of Revata, his teacher in India, or Saṅghapāli, his teacher in Ceylon; this silence seems "almost as convincing as such negative evidence can possibly be". After reading a great deal of Buddhaghosa's works one feels that the language of the *Jātaka* commentary and its method of treatment are not characteristically Buddhaghosa's—it is a mere matter of subconscious inference, but it is there all the same.

So much, then, for what might be said both in favour of and against assigning the work to Buddhaghosa. If not by Buddhaghosa, the work must have been composed after his time, and soon after: otherwise his name would not be connected with it. It is significant that the whole of the *Avidūre-Nidāna* up to the conversion of the Sākyas agrees, almost word for word, with the account given in the *Madhurattha-vilāsinī*, Buddhadatta's commentary on the *Buddha-vaṃsa*. Could they have been the work of the same hand? Or were they drawn from one common source?

[1] Cf. *M.V.*, v, vv. 6 foll.

[2] Op. cit., p. xv.

We cannot conclusively say. In the list of Buddhaghosa's works given on page 59 of the *Gandha-vamsa* the *Jātaka* commentary is included. On the other hand, a treatise called the *Jātattagī-nidānaṃ* is attributed to a Culla Buddhaghosācariya (p. 63), a native of Laṅkā (p. 67). Could he have been the author of our work? Nothing more is known about him except the very meagre details given in the *Gandha-vaṃsa*. If Culla Buddhaghosa was reponsible for the present *Jātaka* commentary, he must have lived very soon after the older and greater Buddhaghosa. For it is clear from the *Mahā-vaṃsa*, as Rhys Davids points out,[1] that before Buddhaghosa's arrival no Sinhalese commentaries had been turned into Pāli, and it is certain that his good example was quickly and most enthusiastically followed by others, and it was impossible that so important a work as the *Jātakas* could have been for long left untranslated. Once this proximity of time between the two authors is assumed, it is easy to understand how the lesser author's individuality got merged in that of his greater and more glorified namesake.

We may, however, I think, be quite certain that the *Jātakatthakathā*, as we have it now, is the work of a Ceylonese author. There is no doubt that after the *Jātakas* had been brought to Ceylon certain tales were added to them there. In two of the *Jātakas* (*Hatthipāla*, Fausböll 509, and *Mūgapakkha* 538) occur the names of six Ceylon *Theras* (*Māhāvaṃsaka Tissa, Phussadeva of the Mountain-Side Gloom, Uparimaṇḍalaka Malaya-vāsī Mahā Saṅgharakkhita, Bhaggarī-vāsī Mahātissa, Mahāsiva of Vāmanta Hill,* and *Mahā-Maliyadeva of Kālavela*), famous for their learning and held in high esteem by the monks of the Theravāda-paramparā.[2] As already mentioned, a very old glossary to the *Jātakatthakathā* exists in Sinhalese, written perhaps about

[1] Op. cit., Introd., pp. lxv–lxvi.
[2] For their description see Rhys Davids, *JRAS.*, 1901, pp. 890 foll.

the thirteenth century, and attributed to an author named Rājamurāri, of whom nothing further is known.[1]

The existing Sinhalese version, called the *Pansiya paṇas Jātaka*, is a translation of the Pāli work made in the reign of King Paṇḍita Parākrama-Bāhu IV (*circa* A.D. 1305), according to the *Mahā-vaṃsa*,[2] by the king himself, who had learnt them from a Coḷian monk, but more probably by several compilers at the instigation of the king, and, as the Sinhalese Introduction tells us, at the personal request of the minister Parākrama. Though a faithful translation, it is not servile, and in several instances has avoided the defects of the Pāli commentary. Some of the stories are told in indifferent Sinhalese, and many provincialisms are to be detected; a few Tamil expressions and words are also to be found, as was to be expected. After the translation was completed the king had it read before a learned assembly of monks and distributed copies all over the island. The charge of its preservation was entrusted to a learned Thera, named Medhaṅkara and the pupils who became his successors.[3]

What were the monks of the Abhayagiri fraternity and their confederates doing during this period under review? It is impossible to believe they were idle, for ceaseless activity in the propagation of their views had been their characteristic ever since they gained a foothold in Ceylon. The wave of great literary activity which swept over the island could not have left them unaffected. The Chronicles do not record any attempts on the part of the orthodox Thera-vādins to persecute them or suppress their activities; the glory of the Mahāvihāra had blossomed in all its brilliance; its fame had spread far

[1] It was published (badly edited, unfortunately) in the *JRAS.* (Ceylon Branch), vol. vii, pp. 184 foll.

[2] Chap. xc, vv. 80–6.

[3] For a fuller and more detailed description of the work, see Mr. Wickremasinghe, *Catalogue*, pp. 118 foll. Other independent versions of single Jātakas, in prose as well as in poetry, made both before and after this work, and based probably on the Pāli text, are to be found scattered throughout the island.

and wide ; scholars came to it from many climes in pursuit of wisdom, in their search for the true unadulterated doctrine of the Buddha. In the hour of their triumph we may presume they were content to leave the Dhammarucikas free to go on their way. We saw that both Mahānāma and his queen were lavish in their gifts to the Abhayagiri community, and we may be sure that, thus endowed with material prosperity, they and their followers produced works of merit. In discussing the authorship of the *Jātaka* commentary it was suggested that the work was a compilation of the Abhayagiri school.

Unfortunately for us, such a state of tolerance of heterodoxy did not last long, and in the holocaust of book-burning, which followed a few centuries later, and through the gradual absorption of the dissentient Nikāyas into the State Church, their works were either completely destroyed or gradually fell out of use. There is, however, one incident on record which shows that they were not unmindful of the importance of literary development in the progress of religion. In the account of Fa-Hsien's travels we are told that he lived in Ceylon for two years, and continuing his search for the sacred Scriptures " he obtained a copy of the *Vinaya Piṭaka* according to the school of the Mahīsāsakas. He also obtained a copy of the *Great Āgama* (*Dīrghāgama*), the *Miscellaneous Āgama* (*Samyuktāgama*), and also a collection of the *Miscellaneous Piṭaka* (*Sannipāta* (*Sutta-nipāta* ?))—all being books unknown in the land of Han. Having obtained these Sanskrit works, he took passage in a large merchantman ".[1] From the names of the books we are led to conjecture that they did not belong to the Theravāda school. The late Hugh Nevill, in his Catalogue of his manuscript collections now in the British Museum (No. 115), suggests that the *Sahassa-vatthu-ppakaraṇa*, still extant in Burma, which, in his opinion, formed the basis

[1] Legge, *Travels*, p. 111. See also Beal, *Records of the Western World*, vol. ii, pp. 247 foll., for a description of the Abhayagiri sect in the seventh century.

for the Pāli *Rasa-vāhinī* (q.v.), by Vedeha, in the fourteenth century, was also a work of the Dhammaruci sect. As far as I can see, there is nothing in that work itself to justify our assigning it to the Abhayagiri Nikāya, but a more careful perusal than I have been able to give it might bring forward more definite evidence. The *Mahā-vamsa-ṭīkā* refers to it as an *atthakathā*.[1]

[1] Geiger, *Mahāvaṃsa and Dīpavaṃsa*, p. 48.

CHAPTER VII

The Pāli Chronicles

WHILE Buddhaghosa and his fellow-labourers were exploring the field of commentarial literature, and compiling the result of their researches so that the word of the Buddha might be known in what they held to be its pristine purity, not only by the people of Ceylon—who were specially favoured by the presence in their midst of a genuinely orthodox and traditional interpretation of the *Dhamma*, handed down in their own vernacular—but also by the many millions in other countries, another type of literary effort was slowly evolving in the shape of Pāli chronicles, recording the history of Laṅkā, and, what was much more important to the chroniclers themselves, the vicissitudes and the triumphs of the Buddhist faith. Many centuries later, after the labours of these historians had been almost forgotten and had sunk very largely into oblivion, a great stir was caused among students of historical research, when about the year 1826 the discovery was made and communicated to Europe that, whilst the history of India was only to be conjectured from myths and elaborated from dates on copper grants, or from fading inscriptions on rocks or columns, Ceylon was in possession of continuous and written chronicles, rich in authentic facts, not only presenting a connected history of the island itself, but also yielding valuable materials for elucidating that of India. At the moment when Prinsep was deciphering the then mysterious inscriptions of Hindustan and Western India, and when Csoma de Körös was unrolling the Buddhist records of Thibet, and Hodgson those of Nepal, a fellow-labourer of kindred genius, indefatigable in his energy and distinguished equally by his abilities and by his modest display of the same, was successfully exploring these Pāli chronicles of Ceylon. He was George Turnour of the Ceylon Civil Service, and the annals of historical research in later years bear ample testimony to the remarkable evidence his work furnished in elucidating the earlier history of Southern Asia. Since Turnour's day many scholars of repute, both in the East and in the West, have devoted their time and energies to the task of learning more about these chronicles, testing the accuracy of their statements and trying to unravel with their aid something of the earlier history of the Indian Peninsula. What is attempted here is merely to give a brief outline of the researches of such scholars.[1]

The two chief chronicles of Ceylon are the *Dīpa-vaṃsa* and the *Mahā-vaṃsa,* the former by an unknown author in the fourth century, and the latter by an Elder of the Buddhist Church, Mahānāma by name, and written in the fifth century A.D. We saw, in the second chapter of this treatise, that members of the Saṅgha had been, from the earliest times, in the habit of recording noteworthy events in the Order, and attempting to keep a continuous history of their activities. Such, for example, are the records of the last two chapters of the Cullavagga. When Buddhism was introduced into Ceylon and a branch of the Saṅgha established in the island, the Ceylonese Bhikkhus followed the example of their predecessors in Jambudvīpa and handed down, in succession in the Church, historical accounts of the Order. The zeal for keeping such records of their doings does not seem to have been confined to the Order alone; from time to time archæologists have discovered, amongst the cherished possessions of distinguished families of the Sinhalese gentry, authentic accounts of their doings handed down from father to son, faithfully preserved and brought up to date by each succeeding generation. Thus, in a copy of the *Rājāvalī-saṅgraha* (which is an abridged *Rājāvaliya*) written down to the reign of Kīrti Śrī Rājasiṃha, and now forming part of the library of the late Hugh Nevill,

[1] For fuller details and critical discussion see, especially, Geiger, *Dīpavaṃsa and Mahāvaṃsa*: *Mahā-vaṃsa* (P.T.S.); Oldenberg, *Dīpa-vaṃsa*; *JRAS. passim* and *Indian Antiquary passim.*

there is attached to the end of the book a separate account of the family of one Yaṭihelagala Polvatte Vidāne, in whose possession the copy was found. The Vidāne's family holds descent from the Bodhidhara princes who accompanied the branch of the Sacred Bo-tree to Ceylon, and settled down there. The present account is composed in much later language, but it is clearly based on older records and contains accounts of the doings of the family from quite early times.[1] It is useful as showing the nature of personal records kept by the Sinhalese, from which the various histories were afterwards compiled, suppressing matter of private interest alone.

The *Dīpa-vaṃsa*, as was mentioned above, is not associated with the name of any special author, and represents the earliest of the chronicles now extant. It is, as we shall see presently, the outcome of a fairly large number of previous works, no one of which had any special author, and is the last of the literary works of Ceylon which can be assigned to a period during which no books had special authors. Every ancient country, at the beginning of its literary activity, has such a period, and the *Dīpa-vaṃsa* marks the close of a very important epoch—important for us in settling the literary chronology—an epoch of universal anonymity, when every work was the outcome of the literary industry of a whole school. After the date of the *Dīpa-vaṃsa*, books, as a rule, were written by one man, and his authorship was openly acknowledged.

There is an interesting passage in the introduction of the *Mahā-vaṃsa-ṭīkā*[2] which sheds considerable light on how the chronicles, as we have them now, came to be composed in Pāli verse. The author tells us that up to the time when the

[1] It concludes with an interesting section on a dispute in 1852, when a relation of the Vidāne (headman of the village), one Angoda Saṅghānanda Sāmaṇera, ordained in 1842, preached *bana*. The other worthies of the place objected for an unknown cause, and the matter came up before the Police Magistrate of Madawalatenne, who said that under the English law there was perfect freedom in all such matters, and dismissed the case. The volume is included in the Nevill collection of the British Museum.

[2] Colombo Ed., pp. 22, 31–2 ; see also Geiger, *Dīp. and M.V.*, pp. 43 ff.

Mahā-vamsa was compiled there existed in the Mahāvihāra, written in Sinhalese, a *Sīhala-Mahāvaṃsatthakathā*, beginning from "the visits of the Buddha to Ceylon, accounts of the arrival of the relics of the Bodhi-tree; the histories of the convocations and of the schisms of the *Theras*; the introduction of Buddhism into the island, the colonization by Vijaya and all that was known and recorded by the pious men of old (Porāṇā) connected with the supreme and well-defined history of those unrivalled dynasties". And the *Mahā-vaṃsa* itself was an attempt at "an imitation of the history composed by the Mahāvihāra fraternity . . . In this work the object aimed at is—setting aside the Sinhalese language (in which the former history was written)—to write in Māgadhi. Whatever the matters may be which are contained in the *Atthakatha*, without suppressing any part thereof, rejecting the dialect only, this work is composed in the supreme Māgadhi language, which is thoroughly purified from all imperfections . . . I will celebrate the dynasties (*vaṃsa*) perpetuated from generation to generation; illustrious from the commencement and lauded by many bards; like unto a garland strung with every variety of flowers".[1] The main record on which the *Dīpa-vaṃsa* (and later the *Mahā-vaṃsa*) were based was this *Sīhala Mahāvaṃsatthakathā*, sometimes referred to as the *Sīhalatthakathā* and the *Porāṇatthakathā*, sometimes referred to simply as the *Atthakathā*.[2]

Besides this the *Mahā-vaṃsa-ṭīkā* mentions also the following works which contained historical materials: (1) *Uttaravihāra-atthakathā* and the *Uttaravihāra-mahāvaṃsa*, (2) *Vinayatthakathā*, (3) *Dīpavaṃsatthakathā*, (4) *Sīmā-kathā*, (5) *Cetiya* and *Mahā-cetiya-vaṃsa-atthakathā*, (6) *Mahābodhi-vaṃsakathā*, (7) *Sumedha-kathā*, and (8) *Sahassavatthu-atthakathā*. As far as we know, none of these works are now extant, but their names give some indication of the nature of their contents. The first were the chronicles of

[1] Chap. i, opening stanzas.

[2] Geiger, *Dīpavaṃsa and Mahāvaṃsa*, pp. 45 foll.

the Uttaravihāra fraternity, the third a commentary on the *Dīpa-vaṃsa,* the fourth evidently a description of the boundaries of the Mahāvihāra, the fifth accounts of the dāgobas erected in Ceylon, especially the Mahāthūpa of Duṭṭhagāmaṇī, and the last a collection of legends and folk tales. The *Sumedha-kathā* was, perhaps, a life-history of the Buddha, from the time when he received *vivaraṇa* as the ascetic Sumedha at the hands of the Dīpaṅkara Buddha many, many æons before.

If that surmise be correct, the later *Buddhavaṃsatthakathā* was evidently based on the *Sumedha-kathā.* The presence of an *Uttaravihāra-mahāvaṃsa* in the list is very interesting, because it shows that each of the Saṅgha communities was in the habit of preserving special records of their own community. Judging from the quotations given of it in the *Mahā-vaṃsa-ṭīkā*, the *Uttaravihāra-mahāvaṃsa* seems to have differed from the Mahāvihāra chronicle not so much in its general scheme as in matters of detail, and it also, apparently, contained much historical material not found in the other.[1] The numerous references made in the *Mahā-vamsa-tīkā* to these works lead us to conclude that, even at the time of the composition of the *ṭīkā*, there was still in existence a rich literature of collected works, carefully preserved in the different monasteries, most of them forming part of the *Atthakathā*, the commentaries to the canonical scriptures. And quite early in the literary history of Ceylon a secondary literature had sprung up, where single subjects, such, for example, as the history of the Bodhi-tree or the erection of the *thūpas*, were taken out of the original works, and made the theme of connected, continuous chronicles.

The *Dīpa-vaṃsa* represents the earliest attempt, so far as we know, to treat of these subjects in a compact, concise manner, forming one continuous story. It is a conglomeration of myths, legends, tales, and history, and the further we go

[1] The story of the Nine Nanda princes. *M. ṭīkā*, p. 117, and the romantic history of Paṇḍukābhaya and the Yakkhiṇī Cetiyā, ibid., p. 202.

back in time the more mythical it becomes, put together from various traditional sources, in an unaided struggle to create a composite whole from materials existing scattered in various places. This accounts for the outward form of the *Dīpa-vaṃsa*, its clumsiness and incorrectness of language and metre, its repetitions, omissions and general fragmentary character. And this very incompleteness of its composition, and its want of style help us in fixing the date of its compilation. It contains whole series of verses giving the main parts of the story, arranged as mnemonics and inartistically put together, called by Geiger *Memory Verses* (Memorial verse).[1]

Often different versions are given of the same story,[2] showing that they were derived from different sources and also, possibly, because of a desire to keep the various traditions as they had been, more or less authorized, with due reverence for their antiquity, and to hand them on unaltered to later generations. The *Dīpa-vaṃsa* was not the work of a single author, but of several generations, a succession of rhapsodies, added to by succeeding authors, as the Introduction tells us, "twisted into a garland of history from generation to generation, like flowers of various kinds." It was, perhaps, originally meant for oral recitation, and so arranged that several of the more important subjects came up before the listener again and again, gradually impressing the full facts on his memory. If that were so, what appears inartistic and clumsy in the written work would appear highly natural when it was handed down orally. There was also, evidently, a commentary to the *Dīpa-vaṃsa*, giving details of the points raised in the mnemonic verses, for the *Mahā-vaṃsa-ṭīkā* refers to a *Dīpavaṃsatthakathā*, and mention is made of it by the *Mahā-vaṃsa* author himself, as having been recited for him by order of king Dhātusena at the festival of Mahinda.[3]

Nevill, in his Manuscript Catalogue referred to above,

[1] Geiger, *Dīpavaṃsa and Mahāvaṃsa*, p. 8.

[2] e.g. the First Council in 4, vv. 1–26; and again, 5, vv. 1–15.

[3] *Mahā-vaṃsa*, xxxviii, p. 173.

draws attention to the "unique consequence given to nuns" all throughout the *Dīpa-vaṃsa*, and is of opinion that it seems to afford a clue to its authorship. "It can scarcely be a record of the Theravāda fraternity of the Mahāvihāra, because in the very reign in which it was put forward by royal patronage (Dhātusena's) Mahānāma set about to supersede it by his *Mahā-vaṃsa*. It certainly is not a record of the Dhammaruci sect of the Abhayagiri community, because it passes over the history of that wealthy, royal foundation with a well-calculated but short notice that could offend no one. But it dilates on a third society, the community of Theravādin nuns. It would seem that Mahānāma was jealous of their fame, for he tells us nothing even of the still famous Mahilā, daughter of Kāvaṇtissa and sister of Gemuṇu. . . . In chapter xv there is a detailed account of original missionary nuns coming from India, learned in the *Dhamma* and the *Vinaya*; in chapter xvii unusual stress is laid on previous Bo-trees brought by Rucanandā, Kanakadattā, and Sudhammā, although Mahānāma pays them no attention. In chapter xviii there was evidently a list of Bhikkhus preceding that of the Bhikkhunīs. If this was recited by the monks, it could scarcely have dropped out, while it would naturally be omitted by the nuns who wished to impress on the audience the importance of their Order.

"The poem goes on to describe how the missionaries from India taught Vinaya, Sutta, and Abhidhamma. In the reign of Abhaya, however, Sumanā taught Saddhamma-vaṃsa (religious history), and Mahilā was also learned in it. In Saddhātissa's reign no historian is mentioned among the Bhikkhunīs; but in Vaḷagambā's reign the nuns boasted of Sivalā and Mahāruhā from India, who were both historians. In the reigns of Kuṭikaṇṇa and his son Abhaya they were proud of Nāgamittā, ordained in Laṅkā, and also described as well-versed in religious history. After her and before the conclusion of the poem in Mahāsena's reign there flourished among the nuns Sanhā and Samuddā, distinguished for their knowledge in the *Saddhamma-vaṃsa*. The book *Saddhamma-vaṃsa* gives the names of eight historians and rhapsodists among a list of seventy-two nuns who taught the *Dhamma* and the *Vinaya*. I take it as almost certain that, in the reign of Gemuṇu, Sumanā taught the *vaṃsa* for the first time among the nuns. Princess Mahilā embodied the Sinhalese tradition of her family with other traditions handed down from Sanghamittā and her companions. Sivalā and Mahāruhā from India revised this, and very probably formed it into the unpolished almost aboriginal Pāli we now possess, to which additions were made by Nāgamittā, and later by Sanhā and Samuddā."

This suggestion about the authorship of the *Dīpa-vaṃsa* is very ingenious and deserves careful consideration. I am not aware of its having been published anywhere yet, and hence I have quoted it in full. It is not possible with the information at our disposal to come to any definite conclusion. There are certain minor points—which do not affect the main argument at all—in Nevill's statements which are not strictly correct, e.g. that Mahānāma composed the *Mahā-vaṃsa* out of jealousy of the reputation of the nuns. Mahānāma lived in an age when the clumsy, inartistic diction of the *Dīpa-vaṃsa*, with its faulty arrangement, would not suffice for the edification of the learned, and he set about to compile a work which was more in keeping with the literary development of his time.

The *Dīpa-vaṃsa*, like the *Mahā-vaṃsa*, finished its record with the death of king Mahāsena. Whether this was due to the *Mahā-vaṃsa* having superseded it after that date, or whether, as Oldenberg suggests,[1] the authors stopped at the epoch of Mahāsena's reign, where the past destinies of their spiritual abode, the Mahā-vihāra, were divided from the present by the success of a hostile party in obtaining the king's sanction for destroying the Mahā-vihāra, we cannot say. I am inclined to the former view. The *Mahā-vaṃsa* fulfilled all the purposes of the *Dīpa-vaṃsa*, and better, and there was

[1] *Dīpa-vaṃsa*, p. 8.

no reason for its further continuance in the old form. I agree with Oldenberg[1] in assigning some time between the beginning of the fourth and the first third of the fifth century as the date of the *completion* of the *Dīpa-vaṃsa* in its present form. It could not have been closed before the beginning of the fourth century, because its narrative extends till about A.D. 302. Buddhaghosa quotes several times from the *Dīpa-vamsa*, but his quotations differ in some details from our version.[2] In the *Mahā-vaṃsa* we are told that Dhātusena (459–77) ordered the *Dīpa-vaṃsa* to be recited in public at the annual Mahinda festival, so that by that time the *Dīpa-vaṃsa* had been completed.[3] After that date it fell into disuse, its glory outdone by the more brilliant work of Mahānāma; but it seems to have been studied till much later, because Dhammakitti III of the Āraṇyakavāsi sect, quotes it in his *Saddhamma-saṅgaha* with great respect as a work of much merit and immense importance.[4]

The beginning of the fifth century saw an important development in the literary life of Ceylon through Buddhaghosa's activity. Pāli was once more definitely established as the ecclesiastical and literary language of the Buddhists. Buddhaghosa himself mastered the language fully and wrote in it fluently and voluminously. His works soon found their way into every monastery, where they were assiduously perused, portions of them being learned by heart. Buddhaghosa's works marked the turning point between the ancient and the modern epochs of Pāli literature in Ceylon, and with his compositions as their model his successors were soon able to master Pāli grammar and style with perfect ease, and, with his compilations as their background, even to improve upon them. Many fruitless attempts at Pāli

[1] Ibid., p. 9.

[2] e.g. see Oldenberg, *Dīp.*, xii, note 2; and also note on *Dīp.*, 5, 30.

[3] This would make the interval between the two works about 100–150 years, sufficient for the difference in points of their style, remembering that Buddhaghosa came in between them.

[4] e.g. *Saddhamma-saṅgaha*, pp. 47, v. 7; 49, vv. 8 foll.

composition must have marked the transition from the inartistic stilted metre of the *Dīpa-vaṃsa* to the elegant, literary fluency of the *Mahā-vaṃsa* verses. And once the mastery over literary form had been attained, its possessors were anxious to use it. Materials for the exercise of their powers were at hand in plenty. Pāli had once more gained its ascendency over Sinhalese, and it was their ambition, as so many authors of this period tell us, in the process of their works, to set aside the Sinhalese language, reject the *dīpa-bhāsā*, and compose their works in the "supreme Māgadhi language, which is the mother of all tongues, sweet to the ear and delightful to the heart, and cooling to the senses". They found the works of the old authors full of imperfections; defects as well of prolixity as of brevity and inaccuracies of detail. They had all respect for the old wine, but it was contained in primitive jars, antiquated, out of fashion, and covered with cobwebs, and they desired to put it into new bottles, polished and shining and full of artistic decoration. But it was old wine all the same, and a certain flavour of conservatism remained for quite a long time. Thus, when Mahānāma came to write his work the *Mahā-vaṃsa*, "replete with information on every subject, comprehending the amplest details of all important events, like unto a splendid and dazzling garland strung with every variety of flowers, rich in colour, taste and scent . . . avoiding the defects of the ancients," we find that he could not quite rise above his material. He strove to confine himself to his sources to the best of his power. Often he adopted the Pāli verses of the originals unchanged in his work, especially when they appeared to him to be of an authoritative character. He went to the same sources as the *Dīpa-vaṃsa*, and in many passages the two works agree word for word.[1]

Very little is known of the author of the *Mahā-vaṃsa*. In the concluding passage of the *Mahā-vaṃsa-ṭīkā*,[2] he is named Mahānāma, and it is said of him that he lived in a cell built

[1] See Geiger, op. cit., pp. 14 foll.
[2] p. 502.

by the General Dīghasaṇḍa who was the commander of the army in Devānaṃpiya-Tissa's reign,[1] and the vihāra founded by him bore the name of Dīghasaṇḍa-senāpati-pariveṇa, and belonged to the Mahāvihāra. Ceylon tradition assumes that this Mahānāma was the uncle of king Dhātusena, who is said to have lived in the habitation of Dīghasaṇḍa.[2] Turnour (Introduction, liv) accepts this tradition, but Geiger[3] is convinced that Turnour was mistaken. "I am fully convinced," says he, "that we must entirely separate the Mahānāma, author of *Mahā-vaṃsa*, from the uncle of Dhātusena."

I am not so "fully convinced ". Geiger's chief argument is chronological. Dhātusena entered the monastic life under the protection of his uncle (Mahānāma) in the reign of Damiḷa Paṇḍu. The uncle was "*at that time a Thera*" (italics are mine), and "thus in all probability considerably older than his nephew ". Dhātusena came to the throne in 436. The transference of Sīhagiri Vihāra to Mahānāma, presbyter of the Dīghasaṇḍa Vihāra (*M.V.*, xxxix, 42) was early in the reign of Moggallāna I (497–515). Geiger's objection is that the reign Mahānāma to whom the Sīhagiri Vihāra was transferred, and who was our author, cannot be the same as Dhātusena's uncle, because the latter could not have lived so long. Why ? Because he was already a Thera when Dhātusena entered the Order somewhere between A.D. 436 and 441, and must therefore have been comparatively old. I believe that this inference is unjustified, for, though Dhātusena's uncle is *referred to* as *Thera*, that does not prove he was *then* a Thera. When the verses came to be written he had come to the *Thera* age and was naturally referred to as such. (If we say that when King George was five years old he was a boy of sweet temper, it does not necessarily mean that he was king at the age of five.) If Mahānāma had been, say, thirty years old at the

[1] *M.V.*, xv, vv. 212–13.
[2] *M.V.*, xxxviii, v. 16, and xxxix, v. 42.
[3] *Dīpavaṃsa and Mahāvaṃsa*, pp. 41 foll.

time of Dhātusena's Ordination, he would have been about ninety, at the most, when Sīhagiri Vihāra was transferred to him, an age by no means impossible. So, while I agree, therefore, that the evidence at our disposal is not sufficient to establish the identity, I hold that the Ceylon tradition has not yet been proved false.

Nothing further is known about the *Mahā-vaṃsa* author. An inscription at Buddhagaya [1] mentions a Mahānāma among Ceylon teachers in the following succession : Bhara, Rāhula, Upasena, Mahānāma, Upasena (II), Mahānāma (II). The first Upasena may well refer to the author of the *Mahā-Niddesa-Atthakathā*, and the first Mahānāma to our author. The date of this inscription is not, however, definitely known.[2] Of Mahānāma's work Geiger says : [3] "The *Mahā-vaṃsa* is already worthy the name of a true epic. It is the recognized work of a poet, and we are able to watch this poet at work in his workshop. Although he is quite dependent on his materials, which he is bound to follow as closely as possible, he deals with them critically, perceives their shortcomings and irregularities, and seeks to improve and to eliminate." But though the level of epic poetry was reached with the *Mahā-vaṃsa*, the process of literary development had not yet come to its highest attainment. It was still too early for that to be possible, so soon after Buddhaghosa's work had given fresh impetus to Pāli studies. Even the materials of the old chronicles yet remained unexhausted, and later authors seized upon them and continued what Mahānāma had begun so well. Mahānāma was no genius, he was too much hide-bound by tradition, and his work cannot rank as a literary performance of the first order ; yet his services to the cause of Pāli literature, and to historical studies of later generations, were immense, and to us invaluable.

After Mahānāma's death the chronicle was continued by

[1] Fleet, *Gupta Inscriptions*, pp. 274 foll.
[2] Rājendralal Mitra, *Buddha-gaya*. pp. 190 sq.
[3] *Dīpavaṃsa and Mahāvaṃsa*, p. 2.

later authors. The history of the island from the reign of Mahāsena, A.D. 302, to the time of Paṇḍita Parākramabāhu of Dambadeniya (1240–75) was compiled by Dhammakitti II under royal patronage.[1] Rhys Davids questions the accuracy of this statement.[2] "Each new chronicler hurried over the kings preceding the one under whom he wrote, and then enlarged at length on the events of that monarch's reign. There seems to be a break at the eventful chapter of Parākrama the Great's reign, while the following kings are hurried over until Parākrama of Dambadeṇiya, who occupies seven chapters. Perhaps there is some confusion between the two Dhammakittis, the one the author of *Dāṭhā-vaṃsa* in Parākrama the Great's reign, and the other the author of a part of the *Mahā-vaṃsa* in the reign of Parākrama of Dambadeṇiya. The latter seems evidently later in style." There is no evidence to support this contention, and until such evidence is forthcoming, we shall have to rest content with tradition. The name of the author by whom the history of Ceylon was written from the reign of the Dambadeṇiya king to that of Paṇḍita Parākrama-Bāhu of Hastisailapura (modern Kurunegala) has not yet been ascertained.[3] The chronicle from that date until A.D. 1758 to the death of Kīrti Śrī Rājasiṃha was compiled by Tibbotuvāve Sumangala Thera, and it has since been continued to 1815 (the date of the cession of Ceylon to the British) by the late Hikkaduvē Śri Sumaṅgala and Baṭuvantudāve Paṇḍita.[4]

There is extant a *ṭīkā* [5] on the *Mahā-vaṃsa*, written by an author of whom we know nothing. In the closing words of his work he calls it the *Vaṃsattha-ppakāsinī*. The Ceylon tradition assigns it to Mahānāma, author of the *Mahā-vaṃsa*

[1] Wijesinha, *Mahā-vaṃsa*, p. 284, and Wickremasinghe, *JRAS.*, 1896, pp. 202 foll.

[2] *JRAS.*, vii, p. 354 and footnote.

[3] De Zoysa, p. 18.

[4] Colombo, 1877.

[5] Printed in Colombo and edited by Sumaṅgala and Baṭuvantudāve.

itself.[1] But it is improbable that the two authors were identical. On the other hand, Geiger assigns it to the tenth century.[2] The author of the *ṭīkā* distinguishes himself quite clearly from the older writer by calling the latter *ācariya*.[3] It is clear that many years had elapsed between the original work and its *ṭīkā*, sufficiently long to allow the name of a village to have undergone change.[4] The *ṭīkā* also mentions the king Dāṭhopatissa II ("the nephew" to distinguish him from the older king of the same name),[5] and it cannot, therefore, have been composed earlier than, roughly speaking, A.D. 670. But I cannot agree with Geiger in saying that the *Mahā-vaṃsa-ṭīkā* belongs to the period between the years 1000 and 1250.[6] In my opinion the date is far too late. Geiger's one argument for so late a date is a quotation from the *Mahābodhi-vaṃsatthakathā* (the only one so far traced) found in the *Mahā-vaṃsa-ṭīkā*.[7] He identifies this *atthakathā*- with the *Mahābodhi-vaṃsa* of Upatissa, which he assigns to the tenth century. Now the *Mahābodhi-vaṃsa*, as we have it, is admittedly a translation of an original work. Upatissa says so definitely in his proem,[8] and there is no means of ascertaining whether the Sīhala *Mahābodhi-vaṃsa* referred to there was identical with the *atthakathā* mentioned in the *M.V. ṭīkā*, or whether it was not itself a later compilation in Sinhalese of an earlier *Mahābodhi-vaṃsa-atthakathā*. There is no need to deny that the Pāli *Mahābodhi-vaṃsa* is a later work, written, perhaps, as late as the tenth century, and the language certainly points to some such date, as we shall see later. It is quite possible that both the quotation in the *M.V. ṭīkā* and the passage in the *Mahābodhi-vaṃsa* were drawn from the

[1] De Zoysa, p. 18.

[2] Geiger, *Dīpavaṃsa and Mahāvaṃsa*, pp. 32 foll.

[3] e.g. p. 25, line 1 and ll. 34–5 ; p. 28, line 18.

[4] Sāmagalla in the *M.V.* became Moragalla at the time of the *ṭīkā*, *M.T.* p. 427, line 26.

[5] 456, 27.

[6] *Dip. and M.V.*, p. 34.

[7] *M.T.*, 294, 8.

[8] P.T.S. Ed., p. 2.

same source directly or indirectly (if indirectly, through the Sinhalese *Mahābodhi-vaṃsa*). I think, therefore, that the date assigned to the *M.V. ṭīkā* by Geiger rests on very slender evidence.

And not this alone. A perusal of the *M.V. ṭīkā* shows that it adds to the *Mahā-vaṃsa* a not inconsiderable amount of material of legends, as well as of folklore, and these were drawn, as we saw in our discussion of the *Mahā-vaṃsa* originals, not only from the sources whence the author of the *Mahā-vaṃsa* derived his materials, but from others equally old [1]—like the *Mahāvaṃsatthakathā*, *Dīpavaṃsatthakathā*, and the *Uttaravihāratthakathā*. We saw how very soon after Buddhaghosa compiled his commentaries in Pāli from the materials he gathered out of the exegetical works written in Sinhalese the original Sinhalese commentaries fell into disuse, and, before long, completely disappeared, because it was found that they no longer served any useful purpose, their function having been taken up by Buddhaghosa's works. Now the *Mahā-vaṃsa* bore to the Sinhalese *vaṃsatthakathā* exactly the same relation as Buddhaghosa's commentaries did to the scriptural *atthakathā*. It was a concise and relatively accurate compilation from various sources, avoiding their imperfections and containing practically all their details.

We may, I think, legitimately presume, therefore, that the Sinhalese *vaṃsatthakathās* did not long survive Mahānāma's work. And in view of the fact that at the time the author of the *ṭīkā* compiled his work the original sources were still being studied, or, at least, were extant, his period could not have been as much as five centuries later than Mahānāma's. Since Mahānāma lived in the sixth century A.D., I would assign the author of the *ṭīkā* to the seventh or eighth century. I am also supported in this by the name of a second Mahānāma appearing in the Buddhagaya inscription referred to above, in the succession Upasena I, Mahānāma I, Upasena II, Mahānāma II; I believe, also, that the later Mahānāma was

[1] See also Geiger, op. cit., pp. 47 and 48.

identical with the author of the *Paṭisambhidā-maggatthakathā*.[1] The identity of the name, and the proximity in time, of the two authors would account for the Ceylon tradition which regards the *Vaṃsattha-ppakāsinī* (*M.V. ṭīkā*) as a work of the *Mahā-vaṃsa* author himself.

Much has been written on the value of the *Dīpa-vaṃsa* and the *Mahā-vaṃsa* as works of historical accuracy and on their usefulness in unravelling the history of Southern Asia. The greater the care and the attention that have been given to the statements in these works the more evident has it become to students of historical research, that they are of immense importance in arriving at a correct understanding of the mysterious mazes of Indian chronology. Vincent Smith early in his career called both works "silly fictions of mendacious monks", and wrote of them: "I reject absolutely the Ceylonese chronology prior to the reign of Duṭṭhagāmiṇi in about 160 B.C. The undeserved credit given to the statements of the monks of Ceylon has been a great hindrance to the right understanding of ancient Indian history."[2] But he was sufficiently convinced before his death to write about the date of the Buddha's death, which forms one of the most important cruces of Indian chronology: "The new reading of the Khāravela inscription . . . if correct, obliges us to move back all the Saisunāga dates more than fifty years, and therefore supports the Ceylon date for the death of the Buddha, viz. 544 or 543 B.C. It may be argued that traditions preserved in Magadha should be more trustworthy than those recorded at a later date by monks in distant Ceylon; but there is ample evidence of the fact that Gautama Buddha was contemporary with both Bimbisāra or Sreṇika and his son Ajātasatru or Kūṇika, and, this being so, I feel compelled, until further light is thrown on the subject, to accept, tentatively, the earlier date, 543 B.C."[3]

[1] q.v.
[2] *Aśoka*, preface, p. 6.
[3] *Early History of India*, p. 50, 1924 ed.

Geiger, in his invaluable Introduction to his translation of the *Mahā-vaṃsa*, has brought together ample evidence from external sources to justify the faith which later-day scholars have been induced to place in the Ceylonese chronicles.[1] In their details, it is true, they manifest the same love of the marvellous, the same credulity and superstition, the same exaggeration in description, the same adulation of kings and princes, as is met with in the annals and religious history of nations called civilized, Christian and non-Christian, of ancient and modern Europe. Their chief defect, in my opinion, is that, while they inform us of the history of monarchs and their deeds, and their endowments for the glorification of the religion, they make no mention of the everyday lives of the people, the many millions who made history in those ancient times. But that would not permit us "to throw away the child with the bath". With all their drawbacks, common, however, to annals and religious histories of all nations, their chronology is admirably accurate,[2] and neither Brāhmanism nor even the Sanskrit language can show any work of an unquestionable date with the shadow of a claim to their honesty of intention and their accuracy of chronological record.

[1] *Mahāv.*, Introd., pp. xv foll. Also Norman, *JRAS.*, 1908, pp. 1 foll.

[2] See Geiger, Introd., pp. xx foll.

CHAPTER VIII

THE DAWN OF THE GOLDEN ERA

THE history of Ceylon from the end of the fifth century to about the beginning of the eleventh, is but a narrative of the decline of the power and prosperity which had been matured under the old dynasty of kings and of the rise of the Malabar marauders, whose ceaseless forays and incursions eventually reduced authority to feebleness and the island to desolation. The accounts given of the royal imbeciles who filled the throne during this period contain hardly any events of sufficient importance to relieve the monotonous repetitions of temples founded, and dāgobas repaired, of tanks constructed, and monks endowed with lands for their maintenance. Civil dissensions, religious schisms, royal intrigues and assassinations contributed equally with foreign invasions to diminish the influence of the monarchy and exhaust the strength of the kingdom.

Intimate relations existed between the Tamils of the Dekkhan and the Sinhalese settlers from quite an early period. Vijaya's second wife was the daughter of a Pāṇḍyan king and her companions were married to Vijaya's ministers and other officials. Similar alliances are frequent, and the Sinhalese annalists allude on more than one occasion to the Damiḷa (Tamil) consorts of their sovereigns. Intimate intercourse and consanguinity were thus established from the remotest times; high employments were given to the Tamils, their services made use of, and privileges given to them. Thus encouraged, the Malabars first came over to Ceylon as settlers and later as invaders. As early as 237 B.C. Sena and Guttika seized the throne, and, as they ruled righteously, the people seem to have acquiesced in their sovereignty.[1] The first regular invasion, however, was under Elāḷa, who ruled for forty-three years, with characteristic justice and impartiality. These earlier bands of immigrants brought with them a certain amount of civilizing

[1] *M.V.*, xxi, vv. 10–12.

influence in the form of Hindu culture, which, as we have already seen, the Sinhalese were quick to assimilate. The Tamils of South India, then as now, were earnest students of Sanskrit literature, and we may well presume that their presence in the island helped much in encouraging the study of Sanskrit in Ceylon. The Tamil colonists became one with the people; they settled down peacefully, pursuing their different vocations unmolested in the observance of their religious rites, because of the broad-mindedness of the Sinhalese rulers.

Settlement and intermarriages had all along been encouraged,[1] and many Sinhalese families of rank had formed connexions with the Tamils. The schisms among the Buddhists themselves, tending as they did to engraft Brahmanical rites upon the doctrines of the purer faith, seemed to have matured the intimacy that existed between the two peoples; some of the Sinhalese kings erected temples for the Hindu gods,[2] and the promoters of the Vaitulyan heresies found refuge from persecution among their sympathizers in the Dekkhan.[3]

But the majority of the subsequent invasions by the Malabars were not regular conquests nor were they, by any means, attempts at peaceful penetration. They were of a predatory character, periodic forays made by a restless and energetic race, into a fertile and defenceless country. From time to time successive bands of marauders would swoop down upon some place of debarcation, gather together as much spoils as they could from the unwarlike Sinhalese of the coast, and retire into their fortified strongholds on the continent. Once, in A.D. 113,[4] Gaja-Bāhu avenged their outrages by means of a punitive expedition into the Coḷa country and inflicted upon them so severe a defeat, that the lesson was long remembered, and from that time till about the middle of the fifth century there was an interval of respite from their

[1] Turnour's Epitome, p. 19.
[2] *Rāja-ratnākara*, p. 78.
[3] *M.V.*, xxxvii, and Epitome, p. 25.
[4] Tennent, i, p. 397.

depredations. In A.D. 433, however, a large army landed in Ceylon and seized the capital,[1] and for twenty-seven years, till Dhātusena recovered possession of the north of the island, five Tamil rulers in succession administered the government of the country north of the Mahāväligaṅga. But Dhātusena was followed by his son Kāsyapa,[2] and the country was thrown into a state of chaos once more. In the succession of assassinations, conspiracies and civil wars, which distracted the kingdom during the next several centuries, and during the struggles of the rival branches of the royal house, each claimant, in his adversity, betook himself to the Indian continent, and Malabar mercenaries from Pāṇḍiya and Coḷa enrolled themselves indifferently under any leader, and deposed or restored kings at their pleasure. The *Rājāvalī* in a single passage, enumerates fourteen sovereigns who were murdered, each by his successor, between A.D. 523 and 648.[3] For nearly four hundred years, till the beginning of the eleventh century, the Sinhalese annals are filled with these exploits and escapades of the Malabars; they filled every office,[4] and it was they who decided the claims of competing candidates for the crown. At last the island became so infested with them that the feeble kings, finding it impracticable to oust them from the capital city of Anurādha-pura, began to move southwards to escape their attentions and transferred their residence to Polonnaruva, which eventually became the capital. It is remarkable that these later-day Malabars never identified themselves with any plan for promoting the prosperity, and for the embellishment of Ceylon; they aspired not to beautify or enrich, but to impoverish and to deface; their influence tended not to exalt and civilize, but to ruin and debase all that was worthy in the culture of Ceylon.

The Sinhalese were either paralysed by dread, and made

[1] *M.V.*, xxxviii, vv. 11 ff.
[2] Ibid., vv. 85 ff.
[3] *Rājāvalī*, p. 244.
[4] Epitome, p. 33.

but feeble efforts to rid themselves of their invaders, or were fascinated by their military pomp, and endeavoured to conciliate them by alliances, or sometimes purchased the evacuation of the island by paying huge ransoms. Every now and then the more patriotic among the Sinhalese (especially the sturdy mountaineers of Rohaṇa), impatient of foreign domination, made determined efforts to resist the encroachments of the hated Malabar oppressors, but the brave highlanders were helpless against the numerical superiority of their foe. In the reign of Mahinda III (*circa* A.D. 997), the king married a Kaliṅga princess, and in a civil war that followed during the régime of his son and successor the island was reduced to extremes of anarchy and oppression, and finally in 1023, when the Coḷians again invaded Ceylon, they succeeded in establishing a Malabar viceroy at Polonnaruva (the capital city), who held sway over the kingdom for nearly thirty years, protected by a foreign army of mercenary soldiers. The rightful sovereign had been taken captive and cast on the coast of India, where he died in exile.[1]

Meanwhile in Rohaṇa, stern and rugged mother of many of Ceylon's noblest sons, a brave and heroic band had striven to maintain their sturdy independence in the only remnant of free territory left unmolested by the oppressors. From out of the gloom and despondency of anarchy and intrigue, and amidst the terrible confusion of these conflicts, there suddenly arose in Rohaṇa's mountain fastnesses the hero destined to rescue the kingdom from alien domination, deliver it from the hated sway of the Malabars and bring it back to its ancient wealth and tranquillity. It was a stupendous task, this restoration of national independence, but the new leader was equal to it. Kitti was his name. With indomitable courage and aided by the steadfast loyalty of his mountaineers, he achieved victory after victory over all his enemies, and re-united the severed kingdom of Ceylon under one national banner. When his position was thus consolidated, he

[1] *Rāja rat.*, pp. 84–5, and *M.V.*, lv, vv. 18–33.

proclaimed himself king under the name of Sirisaṅghabodhi Vijaya-Bāhu. Thus was peace given once more to the stricken land.

During the troublous times that intervened between Dhātusena and Vijaya-Bāhu, the study of the *Dhamma*, as well as of the secular branches of learning that had been cultivated to a high degree in earlier times, had perforce to be abandoned, owing to the alien occupation. But during these four hundred years, of bitter gloom and despondency, it was their common religion that held the people together and sustained them in their adversity. Their rulers recognized this fact, and, whenever a chance arose, the rival claimants to the throne attempted to earn the goodwill of the populace by munificent gifts to the Saṅgha.

A few of them—indifferent to, or happily unembarrassed by, any questions of external policy or foreign expeditions, and limited to the narrow range of internal administration—devoted themselves to intellectual pursuits. The accounts of their reigns refresh the records of this period like oases in a desert tract. Some of them were ardent lovers of literature. Such was Culla Moggallāna : "There was no one like to him as a poet," says the *Mahā-vaṃsa*,[1] and, "being a man of great talent, he composed many sacred songs, which he caused to be recited by men seated on elephants at the end of discourses at the temple services ". He made " unusual " offerings to those that preached the Doctrine and caused them to read the *Tipiṭaka* with its commentaries. So was also Kumāra-Dhātusena, also called Kumāradāsa, author of a melodious Sanskrit poem, the *Jānakī-haraṇa*,[2] and so passionately attached to his bosom friend Kālidāsa, that, in despair at his death, he flung himself into the flames of the poet's funeral pyre.[3] Another was Aggabodhi I, patron of the arts,

[1] Ch. xli, vv. 55–61. (Wijesinha's transl.)

[2] Wickremasinghe, p. xiii.

[3] Alwis, *Sidat-saṅgarā*, p. cliv. This Kālidāsa was not the Sanskrit dramatist, but apparently a Sinhalese poet, one or two of whose verses have been preserved.

surrounded by twelve talented poets,[1] of whose works, unfortunately, we know nothing, and Silāmēgha Sena or Matvala Sen, author of the *Siyabas-lakara*, the standard work on Sinhalese prosody. Others patronized the Saṅgha, the repository of all religious and secular learning, by providing them with alms, and dwelling places and extensive lands for the maintenance of their monasteries. Some of them were actuated in their generosity by a desire to make amends for their misdeeds,[2] and we find the orthodox monks of the Theriya Nikāya more than once disgraced because of their reluctance to accept gifts from those of whose actions they could not approve.[3]

The annals of this period are full of records of gifts to the heretic sects, possibly because of their connivance at the crimes of their patrons.[4] The Abhayagiri fraternity seems to have benefited most by such royal favours; but even they suffered from the capriciousness of their benefactors, who would not hesitate to undo all the good they had done, pull down their monasteries, and remove from them all objects of value.[5] The activities of the schismatics in carrying on their propaganda were much in abeyance during this period, and we hear of only one attempt to spread heresy, which, however, proved abortive,[6] being put down with a firm hand by the ruling prince of the district where it reared its head. Some of the more broad-minded among the rulers attempted to bring about a reconciliation between the various sects by making them endowments to be held in common. Thus Aggabodhi I gave the Saṅghikagiri Vihāra with 200 fields to all members of the Order and dedicated the Kuruṇḍa Vihāra to all the

1 *Nikāya-saṅgraha*, p. 17.

2 e.g. the parricide Kāsyapa. *M.V.*, xxxix, vv. 8 foll.; chap. xliii, vv. 28 foll.

3 Ibid., xxxix, vv. 11 foll.

4 Ibid., *passim.*

5 Ibid., xliv, vv. 139–42.

6 Ibid., xlii, vv. 35–40.

fraternities.[1] Perhaps the repeated invasions of the island by the fierce Tamils did much to foster the feeling of brotherhood among the monks, who, in spite of all their dissensions, were yet patriotic Sinhalese and faithful sons of the Buddha. But the old feud between the Mahāvihāra and the Abhayagiri Vihāra continued, and, when Silāmeghavaṇṇa requested the two communities to observe the *uposatha* ceremony together, the former promptly refused, and thereby earned the wrath of the king.[2] And later, when Dāṭhopatissa II built the Kappura Pariveṇa for the Abhayagiri monks on land which encroached upon the sacred boundary of the Theriya brethren, the latter showed their great disapproval by performing towards him the *patta-nikkujjana-kamma* [3] (inversion of the alms bowl on their begging rounds, thus indicating their refusal to accept his alms, a kind of excommunication).

The gifts thus indiscriminately given to members of the Saṅgha and the want of proper supervision brought disorganization within the Order itself, and attracted into its fold many undesirables who were actuated merely by desire for gain. So low was the degeneracy into which the monks had fallen when Vijaya-Bāhu came to the throne that, as we shall see later, he had to obtain help from Rāmaññadesa in re-establishing ordination in Ceylon.

But even before Vijaya-Bāhu two attempts were made to prevent moral worthlessness among the Saṅgha. The first was by Dalla Moggallāna (A.D. 608–14), who proclaimed a *Dhamma-kamma*.[4] The second was by Silā Meghavaṇṇa (614–23), who was a staunch adherent of the Abhayagiri

[1] *M.V.*, chap. xlii, vv. 9–22.

[2] Ibid., xliv, vv. 80–2.

[3] Ibid., xlv, vv. 32 ff.

[4] The expression often occurs in the *M.V.* to denote the manner in which the earlier kings interfered to carry out reforms in the Buddhist Church. It means literally a *legal act*. The act seems to have consisted in the promulgation by the king of a decree enforcing the observance of discipline among the priesthood, and, in some cases, empowering one or more of its Order to carry the decree into effect by means of an ecclesiastical court. Wijesinha, *M.V.*, ii, p. 25, footnote.

fraternity. This Nikāya had become quite degenerate; prosperity had corrupted the members of the community, whose lives were now unworthy of their high calling. A young and zealous bhikkhu, Bodhi by name, realizing the immediate necessity for reform, approached the king personally and requested him to issue a decree for enforcing discipline in the Order. The king readily acceded and entrusted the execution of it to the young reformer himself. The latter, armed with the royal authority, proceeded to hold a thorough investigation, as a result of which a large number of bhikkhus were expelled. This zeal for reform, however, cost him his life. The men who were thus driven out of the Order conspired together and murdered him. The king, in righteous indignation, had all the leading conspirators arrested, cut off their hands and made them tank-keepers.[1] Many others were banished. And, appreciating the zealous efforts of the murdered bhikkhu, he carried out the reforms which had been initiated, and purified the Order. His attempts, however, to unite the Mahā-Vihāra and Abhayagiri fraternities ended, as we saw earlier, in complete failure.

And every now and then some of the monarchs, more enlightened than others and more anxious for the welfare of the religion, strove to keep alive the study of the *Dhamma*. Thus Dāṭhopa-Tissa I (*circa* 640–52) gave a special *pariveṇa* to the Elder Nāgasāla at Maricavatti and prevailed upon him to teach the *Abhidhamma* with the *Atthakathā*,[2] and his successor Kassapa II made great offerings to the holy monk Mahādhammakathī, and made him teach the *Dhamma*. For the monk, who dwelt at Kaṭandhakāra in the monastery built by the king's brother, he caused the whole Pāli scripture to be written, together with the lesser books or "epitomes" (*Sa-saṅgahaṃ*).

The extant inscriptions of this period reveal to us

[1] *M.V.*, xliv, vv. 75–83.
[2] Ibid., vv. 149 ff.

the great care with which the monastic rules were drawn up with a view to securing the independence, the exalted prestige, and, above all, the purity of the Buddhist Church. No kind of corruption was tolerated in the management of temple property, no slackness in the observance of religious ceremonies. No monk of questionable character was allowed to remain in the Vihāra, and for anyone who desired to enter the Order a minimum knowledge of the *Dhamma* was insisted upon. Thus from an inscription of Kassapa V (929–39), who, it is interesting to note, expounded the Abhidhamma himself and caused it to be written on plates of gold (*M.V.*, lii, vv. 49–50), we learn that no one was allowed to join the Order unless he knew (probably by heart) at least four sections (*bhāṇavāra*) of the *Paritta.*[1]

Mahinda IV (*circa* 975–91) encouraged the study of the *Dhamma* by decreeing, in an inscription which is still preserved, that the monks who read aloud and explained to an audience the *Vinaya-piṭaka* should be assigned five *vasag* [2] of food and raiment, for the *Sutta-piṭaka* seven *vasag*, and for the *Abhidhamma-piṭaka* twelve *vasag.*[3] He, moreover, caused Dhammamitta to expound the *Abhidhamma*, and Dāṭhānāga, "who dwelt as a recluse in the forest and was like an ornament unto Laṅkā, to discourse thereon."[4] Sena IV (*c.* 972), on one occasion sat in the Lohapāsāda and expounded the *Suttanta* to the brethren of all the three fraternities assembled therein.[5] The great attention paid to the *Abhidhamma* is significant. As a result of these activities of enlightened rulers, the torch of learning was prevented from being totally extinguished, and even this dark chapter of Ceylon's history is not completely barren of literary productions concerned with Pāli literature.

To this period may be assigned the *Khema-ppakaraṇa*

[1] *Ep. Zey.*, vol. i, pt. ii, pp. 42–3.

[2] *Vasag*, a vasag is five cells with food and raiment. *Ep. Zey.*, vol. i, p. 100, n. 4.

[3] Ibid., vol. i, pt. iii, p. 100.

[4] *M.V.*, liv, vv. 35–7.

[5] Ibid., liv, v. 4.

(also called the *Paramattha-dīpa*[1] by the Elder Khema). The book is now not widely known in Ceylon, and whatever copies there are at present have been introduced from Burma. The *Gandha-vaṃsa* ascribes it to a Khema Thera of Ceylon.[2] According to the *Saddhamma-saṅgaha*,[3] it is a work expository of the *Abhidhamma*, and it is extensively studied in Burma as one of the nine mediaeval compendia of *Abhidhamma*, known as *Let-Than* or "little finger manuals".[4] It is more often called in Ceylon *Nāma-rūpa-samāsa*, and this title is more appropriate to the contents of the work. It contains short descriptions of the *citta*, a discourse on *citta-cetasikā*, defining *kusalā* and *akusalā dhammā*, and concludes with a list of twenty-eight mnemonic verses, giving in brief the meanings of such terms as *mahābhūta*, *indriya*, etc., which occur in *Abhidhamma* literature. That the book was held in high esteem in Ceylon from ancient times is evident from the references to its author in the *Nikāya-saṅgraha* and the *Saddhamma-ratnākāra*,[5] and in the latter he is spoken of as *Tipiṭaka-pariyatti-dhara* (versed in the text of the *Tipiṭaka*). There is a commentary on it by Vācissara Mahāsāmi of Ceylon (q.v.), written in the twelfth century.[6] Both text and commentary were published in Sinhalese characters by a monk named Baṭapola Dhammapāla in Ceylon in 1908, and an English transliteration of the text alone has appeared in the *Journal of the Pāli Text Society*.[7] The short disquisitions on the various subjects are concisely written in simple, easy style and the whole work forms a little handbook for the study of mediaeval *Abhidhamma*.

Mr. Wickremasinghe agrees with Professor Geiger in accepting the tenth century as the date of the compilation of

[1] *Sāsana-vaṁsa--dīpa*, v. 1222.
[2] *G.V.*, p. 61 and 71.
[3] p. 63, *JPTS*. Ed.
[4] Aung, Compendium, pref., p. viii.
[5] p. 367, Colombo Ed.
[6] De Zoysa ascribed the *Khema-ppakaraṇa* itself to Vācissara. *Catalogue*, p. 8.
[7] 1915, pp. 1 foll.

the Pāli *Mahābodhi-vaṃsa.*[1] S. Arthur Strong, who edited it for the Pāli Text Society (1891), assigned the author to the same period as Buddhaghosa, his reason being that the *Gandha-vaṃsa* mentions it as having been written at the instigation of one Dāṭhānāga, whom he identified with another named Dāṭṭha, who is said (in the *Gandha-vaṃsa*) to have requested Buddhaghosa to write the *Sumaṅgala-vilāsini.* Strong was wrong in assuming that Dāṭṭha and Dāṭṭhānāga were one and the same. Besides the *Gandha-vaṃsa,* the Sinhalese version of the Pāli work, written by Saranaṅkara Saṅgharāja in the eighteenth century, and named the *Madhurārtha-prakāśini,*[2] mentions that the *Bodhi-vaṃsa* was written at the instigation of a Dāṭhānāga.[3] Both Wickremasinghe and Geiger identify Dāṭhānāga with the *thera* of the same name, whom Mahinda IV (975–91) appointed to discourse on the *Abhidhamma.*[4] If that supposition be correct, the *Mahābodhi-vaṃsa* must have been written in the last quarter of the tenth century.

It begins with a history of the Buddha Dīpaṅkara, gives in a short summary an account of the existence of the Bodhisatta under previous Buddhas, the life of Gotama, his enlightenment at the foot of the Bodhi-tree, the planting of the Bodhi-tree at Jetavana by Ānanda, providing the occasion for the Buddha to preach the Kaliṅga-bodhi-jātaka,[5] the Parinibbāna, the Three Councils, Mahinda's mission, the establishment of Buddhism in Ceylon, the introduction there of the relics and a branch of the Bodhi-tree, the planting of the sacred tree and the establishment of the Bodhi-pūjā, or ceremonies in connexion with it.

The book itself says nothing about its authorship, except that it was a translation from a Sinhalese original. The

[1] *Catal.*, p. xiv, and Geiger, *D.V.* and *M.V.*, p. 79.
[2] Wickremasinghe, p. xxi.
[3] De Zoysa, p. 16.
[4] *M.V.*, liv, v. 36,
[5] Fausböll, iv, p. 288 foll.

Gandha-vaṃsa (p. 61) mentions the work by name, but in a group of five works assigned vaguely to unnamed authors. The *Sāsana-vaṃsa-dīpa* (v. 1262) calls Upa-Tissa the author of the *Bodhi-vaṃsa*, but says nothing more about him. The *Elu-Bodhi-vaṃsa*,[1] which is an enlarged Sinhalese translation of the Pāli work, done by Vilgammūla Mahāthera, in the beginning of the fourteenth century, ascribes the Pāli *Bodhi-vaṃsa* to Upatissa and so does Saranaṅkara's later translation referred to above, written at the beginning of the eighteenth century. Guruḷugōmi, who lived about the latter half of the twelfth century,[2] author of the *Amāvatura*, wrote a masterly commentary in the Sinhalese of his period on the Pāli *Bodhi-vaṃsa*, called the *Bodhi-vaṃsa-parikathā*, but better known as the *Dharma-pradīpikā*, and there, too, the work is assigned to Upatissa. An Upatissa of Ceylon is mentioned in the *Gandha-vaṃsa* (p. 67), but we know nothing more about him.

In the whole of the first chapter the close dependence on the *Nidāna-kathā* is unmistakable. Even verbal identity is not rare.[3] Usually the *Mahābodhi-vaṃsa* account is shorter and more like an epitome. It is interesting, however, to note that the story of the Kaliṅga-bodhi-jātaka as given in the *Bodhi-vaṃsa* differs from Fausböll's version of it ; among other peculiarities in the former version, being a long description of *dibba-cakkhu* (clairvoyance) and the seven gems of a *cakkavatti* king. The later chapters show direct dependence on the *Samanta-pāsādikā* and the *Mahā-vaṃsa*, chiefly the former. Thus the description of Mahinda's activities after his arrival in Ceylon agrees almost word for word with that in the *Samanta-pāsādikā*, so much so that we are led to the conclusion that the whole passage was directly borrowed from Buddhaghosa's commentary. The concluding verses of some of the chapters are the same as the closing chapters of the

[1] Wickremasinghe, p. 22.
[2] Wickremasinghe, p. 31.
[3] Cf. *M.B.V.*, 31–4, with *J.N.K.*, 17, 82.

Mahā-vaṃsa.[1] In our discussion in a previous chapter of the date of the *Mahā-vaṃsa-ṭīkā,* we presumed that the *Bodhi-vaṃsatthakathā* referred to there was different from Upatissa's work, and was more probably the earlier Sinhalese source of our *Mahābodhi-vaṃsa.* But the quotations from later works such as the *Mahā-vaṃsa* and the *Samanta-pāsādikā* would lead us to believe that Upatissa did not merely *translate* the Sinhalese text directly, but also improved upon it in the translation, supplementing it with quotations from works, which, in the meantime, had attained great authority. We shall see later that this was the case with other historical works of a similar type, e.g. the *Thūpa-vaṃsa.*

Even where the *Mahābodhi-vaṃsa* borrows from other works its style is different from theirs, more artificial and affected ; the stanzas are written in sonorous Pāli, the ornamental epithets are plentiful and the author is fond of long periods. There are distinct traces in the language of the influences of Sanskrit on the Pāli, and we may regard this book as marking the beginning of the period of Sanskritized Pāli. Sometimes Pāli words are used in their Sanskrit sense, sometimes Sanskrit words not found perhaps elsewhere at all in the old Pāli literature,[2] and long compounds, possibly derived from an acquaintance with Sanskrit Kāvyas, are employed ; the whole tone and manner of his work betray a tendency to use a kind of Sanskritized Pāli.

Somewhere about A.D. 1300 an amplified Sinhalese version of the Pāli *Mahābodhi-vaṃsa* was made by Vilgammūla Mahāthera, chief monk of the Kitsirimevan Kälaṇi Temple, at the request of Paṇḍita Parākrama-Bāhu of Kurunegala (*c.* 1295–1347). The author is probably the one mentioned in the *Nikāya-saṅgraha* (p. 24) as having made a Sinhalese paraphrase of Mayūra's Sanskrit poem *Śūrya-śataka* in the

[1] e.g. *M.V.*, xiv, 65 ; *M.B.V.*, p. 122 ; *M.V.*, xvi, 18 ; *M.B.V.*, p. 139 ; *M.V.*, xviii, 68 ; *M.B.V.*, p. 153. See Geiger, *M.V.* and *D.V.*, p. 77.

[2] e.g. *udite bhuvana-sekhara*, p. 5 ; *pārāpata-caraṇa-pāṭala-rāge*, p. 61, to give but two. See also Rhys Davids, *JRAS.*, 1905, p. 393.

reign of Dam̃badeṇiya Parākrama-Bāhu (*c.* 1236–71).[1] This is written in almost pure Elu, which evidently made it difficult to be understood in later years, when Elu had come to be regarded as too archaic for ordinary usage ; for we find that early in the eighteenth century Saranaṅkara Saṅgharāja compiled an interverbal paraphrase of the Pāli work into the Sinhalese of his own period.[2] It is curious that Saranaṅkara makes no mention of Vilgammūla's translation. There also exists a Sinhalese glossary of the Pāli terms, of extreme philological value, judging from the language, written about the fourteenth century by a scholar of unusual attainments of whom nothing is known. Both this and the other less famous work on the Bodhi-tree—the *Sulu-bodhi-vaṃsa* (the lesser *Bodhi-vaṃsa*) are still in manuscript form.[3]

The *Gandha-vaṃsa* [4] also mentions an Upatissa, a native of Ceylon, as author of the *Anāgata-vaṃsa-atthakathā.* According to the *Gandha-vaṃsa,* the original *Anāgata-vaṃsa* was the work of an Elder named Kassapa,[5] who also wrote *Moha-vicchedanī, Vimati-cchedanī,* and the *Buddha-vaṃsa.* The *Sāsana-vaṃsa-dīpa* (v. 1204) says that he was a poet who lived in the Coḷa country, but we know nothing either of his date or of his other works. It is certain that the *Buddha-vaṃsa,* which he is supposed to have written, was different from the canonical work of the same name. Ceylon tradition supports the *Gandha-vaṃsa* in ascribing the *ṭīkā* on the *Anāgata-vaṃsa* to an Upatissa, but nothing more is known about him. A copy of this which is in the library of the Daḷadā Māligāva at Kandy in Ceylon, quotes the *Anāgata-vaṃsa* in full, and then proceeds to explain it. The style of the *ṭīkā* inclines me to the view that we may be justified in identifying its author with Upatissa of the *Bodhi-vaṃsa,* but I would not venture any opinion until more definite evidence is forthcoming.

[1] Wickremasinghe, p. 23.
[2] Ibid., p. 109.
[3] See De Zoysa, p. 20.
[4] p. 72 and p. 67.
[5] p. 61.

The *Anāgata-vaṃsa* [1] itself is a poem of about 150 stanzas (the number varies in different copies) on the future Buddha Metteyya. It is remarkable that, so far as we know, there does not seem to be any mention of Metteyya's name in the *Nikāya's* except in the *Cakkavatti-Sīhanāda-sutta* of the *Dīgha* (vol. iii, p. 76), quoted also in the *Milinda* (p. 159), where the Buddha speaks of the glorious spread of the *Dhamma* under Metteyya's regime. The name occurs also in the last stanza of the *Buddha-vaṃsa*. By the time of the *Mahā-vastu* the legend is in full vogue,[2] but it is in the *Anāgata-vaṃsa* that we find the fullest and most complete account of the tradition. That it is a late work there is not the slightest doubt; many in Ceylon regard it as a spurious work altogether.[3] It is regrettable, however, that we cannot get any definite information as to the date of the origin and the subsequent growth of the belief held by the Buddhists in their future Buddha, Metteyya. In earlier times it was enough to say that many future Buddhas would come to be born in the world, and then a few details, one after the other, were added about the Buddha who was to come immediately after the last Gotama, until the legend grew as we have it now. There are several points of analogy between the belief in Metteyya and the Western idea of a Messiah, though they are not the same. Mrs. Rhys Davids has found one reference to the *Anāgata-vaṃsa* in Buddhaghosa's *Visuddhi-magga*,[4] but whether the work referred to there is the same as ours, there is no possibility of saying.

Personally, I am inclined to the view that Upatissa's commentary is based on a much older work, just as the *Bodhi-vaṃsa* goes back to an earlier *Bodhi-vaṃsatthakathā* referred to in the *Mahā-vaṃsa-ṭīkā*. Both works are now lost, and we shall

[1] For the text with extracts from the commentary see *JPTS.*, 1886, pp. 33 foll.

[2] Rhys Davids, *Hastings Encyclopædia*, i, p. 414.

[3] e.g. De Zoysa, p. 5.

[4] *Visuddhi-magga*, ii, p. 761.

probably never have a chance of knowing more about them. The introductory verses of the present *Anāgata-vaṃsa* mention that it was preached by the Buddha at the request of Sāriputta,[1] who wished to know about the future of the Buddha's religion. There is no doubt that this statement goes back to an old tradition. To the tenth century or the earlier part of the eleventh also belongs the small but delightful Pāli poem of ninety-eight stanzas, known as the *Tela-kaṭāha gāthā*—the stanzas of the Oil Cauldron. They purport to be the religious exhortations of a great Elder named Kaḷyāṇiya Thera, who was condemned to be cast into a cauldron of boiling oil on suspicion of his having been accessory to an intrigue with the Queen Consort of king Kälaṇi-Tissa, who reigned at Kelaṇiya (306–207 B.C.). The story is related in brief in the 22nd chapter of the *Mahā-vaṃsa*,[2] but it omits the fact that the *thera* was killed by being placed in a cauldron of boiling oil. We are told, instead, that both the *thera* and his attendant were slain and thrown into the sea. The *Rasa-vāhinī*, written by Vedeha in the first half of the fourteenth century, gives us greater details of the story.[3] There we are informed that the kings' attendants placed a cauldron of oil on the hearth and, when the oil was boiling, hurled the *thera* into it. The *thera* at that instant attained *vipassanā*, and, becoming an Arahat, rose up in the boiling oil and remained unhurt, " like a royal haṃsa in an emerald vase," and, in that position reciting a hundred stanzas, looked into the past to ascertain of what sin this was the result. He found that once upon a time, when he was a shepherd, he cast a fly into boiling milk, and this was the punishment for his former misdeed. He then expired, and the king had his body cast into the sea. A *vihāra* seems to have been built later on the spot where the *thera* was put to death, for the *Säḷalihiṇi-sandeśa*, written in A.D. 1462, refers to it as still existing.

[1] *JPTS.*, 1886, p. 41, vv. 1–5.
[2] *M.V.*, xxii, vv. 13–20.
[3] See Alwis, *Sidat-saṅgarā*, pp. clxxx and cclxxi.

"The decorated hall, which in their zeal
The merit-seeking people built upon
The spot where stood the cauldron of hot oil
Into which King Kelaṇi-Tissa threw
The guileless sage, a mere suspect of crime."[1]

The present text purports to contain the stanzas uttered by the Elder in the boiling cauldron, but their language and style most definitely point to a very much later date. The verses as we have them now are only ninety-eight in number;[2] possibly the "hundred" mentioned in the *Rasa-vāhinī* is only a round figure. Neither the author of our version nor his date is known. There is no doubt, however, that he was a member of the Order, well versed in the *Piṭakas* and commentarial literature.

The stanzas show great depth of religious and metaphysical learning. The verses embody in them the fundamental tenets of Buddhism and are an earnest exhortation to men to lead the good life. They open with a blessing upon the king, apt beginning for the utterances of a holy man before his murderer. Their setting is exquisite, and the style of the poem clearly shows that it was written by a man who also knew Sanskrit quite well. Only such a man could have constructed in the elaborate and beautiful metre of the poem, so delicate a specimen of mosaic work in Sanskritized Pāli. Yet the Pāli is not overladen with Sanskritisms, which shows that the work is earlier than the twelfth century. It is a fine specimen of the literature of what might be called the Pāli Renascence period, before the language became contaminated by Sanskrit influences and lost its pristine purity of diction and simplicity. I give below the first verse, which is a good example of the style of the poem:—

Laṅkissaro jayatu vāraṇarājagāmī
Bhogindabhogarucirāyatapīnabāhu
Sādhūpacāranirato guṇasannivāso
Dhamme ṭhito vigatakodhamadāvalepo.

[1] Macready's version, verse 70.

[2] See the text in *JPTS.*, 1884, p. 55 foll.

Such, then, are the Pāli works of which we have any knowledge that were written during the four centuries previous to the accession of Vijaya-Bāhu. Vijaya-Bāhu succeeded to a kingdom torn by strife and completely overrun by foreign enemies. Just previous to him Sena V had reigned (*c.* 991), a lad of 12 years at the time of his coronation. Because of his evil companions his ministers rebelled, and the young king in despair handed over his capital to the Tamils and fled south. In his adversity he took to drink and became so addicted to the vice that he was nicknamed Matvala Sen (the mad tiger). When he died after ten years, he was succeeded by his brother Mahinda V, who was fitted neither by character nor by capability to rule a kingdom. Sena's misrule had plunged the country into confusion. Strangers from across the seas, belonging to diverse races, had become so numerous and powerful in Anurādhapura, that the king found it difficult to maintain his position there. The weakness of his administration led to insubordination; the people refused to pay taxes, and the king had not the wherewithal to pay his army. The Coḷa king, seizing the opportunity, sent over a large army and conquered the country north of the Mahāväligaṅga. In a few years the Tamil domination extended even beyond the river. The Coḷas became masters of both Anurādhapura and Polonnaruva. This was the last of the glory of Anurādha-pura, which for twelve centuries had been the centre of all the activities of the Sinhalese, religious, social, and intellectual. Robbed of its ancient splendour, this noble city ceased henceforward to be the pride of Laṅkā and gradually fell into decay and ruin.

In the thirty-sixth year of his reign Mahinda himself and his queen were captured and taken away. The Tamils were masters of all Ceylon. They sacked all the Vihāras and the Dāgobas, and destroyed whatever they could not carry away. They had been taught by the earlier Sinhalese royal imbeciles who hired them[1] that wealth was to be found in plenty in

[1] e.g. by Kassapa II and Dāṭhopa-Tissa I.

the monasteries. "The Tamils, like unto Rakkhasas (demons)," says the *Mahā-vaṃsa*,[1] "began to oppress the country and take by force whatever belonged to the people." Mahinda's capture was in A.D. 1001. Till Vijaya-Bāhu was crowned as king of all Ceylon in A.D. 1065 there was no peace in the land. The interval was one long period of war and persecution. "Thus did these kings war with one another," bemoans the *Mahā-vaṃsa*; and "drive each other away from the throne; and by reason of this continual warfare the people were sore oppressed and suffered greatly, and the country was brought to great poverty." [2]

When he had driven out the enemy who had been completely tyrannizing over the island for over a century, Vijaya-Bāhu turned his mind to the task, equally colossal, of repairing the fearful damage that had been inflicted upon the national life during that period of alien domination. He resided at Polonnaruva, which now became the capital of the kingdom. The century of Coḷa supremacy was much more than a political evil. Its devastating effects were felt in every fibre of the national being, but nowhere so disastrously as in that of religion. The destruction of the great religious edifices, the Vihāras, pariveṇas, and monasteries, resulted in the dissolution of the great fraternities that formed the Saṅgha, and the consequent decay of that high-souled institution and of the national learning, of which it had been the faithful custodian. The most significant evidence of the complete disorganization of the Saṅgha under the Tamil rule lies in the total disappearance of the Bhikkhunī Order during this period. Henceforward we find no reference to nunneries in the *Mahā-vaṃsa*. Up to this time they had continued to flourish unaffected by persecutions consequent on schisms, though there is evidence that among the Bhikkhunīs, too, there were heretical schools [3];

[1] *M.V.*, liv, vv. 66–8.

[2] Ibid., vv. 34 foll.

[3] Thus, e.g. Moggallāna I (497–515) is said to have built a special convent called Rājinī and given it to the Sāgalikā sisterhood, *M.V.*, xxxix, v. 43.

but we do not hear of their having been persecuted at any time. The Bhikkhunī Order had been fostered and cherished by successive rulers for over twelve centuries, and why it was now allowed to die out completely without any attempt at resuscitation, it is difficult to understand.

Vijaya-Bāhu found that no ordination of bhikkhus had been held for long years, because the whole island could not muster five ordained monks. He therefore sent an embassy to his friend and ally, King Anuruddha of Rāmañña-desa, soliciting his help in restoring the Sāsana in Ceylon. A number of eminent *Theras*, masters of the *Tipiṭaka*, were sent over, who re-established the ordination in the island and helped in the resuscitation of learning by instructing a large number of bhikkhus in the three *Piṭakas* and the commentaries.[1] King Anuruddha was then fresh from vigorous measures against heresy in his own country, and it is said that he consulted Vijaya-Bāhu and came to an agreement with him as to the Pāli texts which were to be accepted as representing the true teaching of the Buddha. (Mrs. Bode, *Pāli Lit. in Burma*, p. 11.) The three fraternities were restored to their ancient homes, and, although they reappear as distinct bodies, they seem to have lost much of the sectarian spirit which had kept them disunited. A Tamil inscription of Vijaya-Bāhu records that he brought about a reconciliation of the three Nikāyas,[2] and we find that they consented to accept in common a Vihāra he built for them at Polonnaruva.[3]

This religious revival was, as might be expected, accompanied by a great intellectual re-awakening. The king himself was a scholar and a poet of no mean order ; the pursuits of literature had a great attraction for him. Amidst his multifarious duties, he found time every morning to seclude himself for a few hours in his religious library (*dhamma-mandira*) and there he composed a Sinhalese translation of the *Dhamma-saṅgaṇī*.[4]

[1] *M.V.*, lx, v. 5–7.
[2] *Epy. Zeyl.*, vol. ii, pt. vi, p. 254.
[3] *M.V.*, lx, v. 13.
[4] Ibid., v. 17.

Unfortunately, this work, as well as the Sinhalese poems which the *Mahā-vaṃsa* says he composed, are now lost. He was a generous patron of learning; the young noblemen attached to his court were encouraged by suitable presents to engage themselves in literary pursuits, and the king himself acted as judge of them. He caused the three *Piṭakas* to be written and given to the monks who desired copies. Scholars from abroad, especially from India, brought Ceylon once more into touch with the culture and the intellectual movements of other lands. Sanskrit and Tamil were assiduously studied, and several works of merit in Pāli too were produced.

Chief among these was the *Abhidhammattha-saṅgaha* of Anuruddha. Earlier in this chapter attention was drawn to the fact that during this period (seventh–eleventh century) much care was bestowed on the study of the *Abhidhamma*. Special teachers were appointed to give instruction in the subject. Generous endowments were made to those who devoted themselves to *Abhidhamma* learning and recitals. More than one king studied it himself, and we now find Vijaya-Bāhu translating the *Dhamma-saṅgaṇī*. We need not be surprised, therefore, that the works of this time deal mostly with the *Abhidhamma Piṭaka*.[1]

It was mentioned earlier that one of the influences of the migration into Ceylon of large numbers of Tamils from South India was the greater attention devoted to the study of Sanskrit. Already in the fourth century Buddhadāsa had composed a medical treatise (the *Sārārtha-saṅgraha*) in that language. At the beginning of the sixth century Kumāradāsa had written an exquisite Sanskrit poem, the *Jānakī-haraṇa*, and in the *Siyabas-lakara*, a work on Sinhalese prosody,

[1] When King Jeṭṭha-Tissa (A.D. 623) was losing ground in his fight with the Tamils, the message he sent to his queen was that she should betake herself into a convent, learn the Doctrine and, having preached the *Abhidhamma*, give him the merits thereof; and we are told that the queen did as she was asked, and perfected herself in the *Abhidhamma* and the *Atthakathā*—a striking illustration of the great veneration in which the *Abhidhamma* was held (*M.V.*, xliv, vv. 107–17).

already noticed, written by Silāmegha Sena (846–66), the influence of the Sanskrit rhetoric is clearly to be seen. Somewhere about the tenth or eleventh century lived an Elder named Ratnaśrijñāna, also called Ratnamatipāda, author of two works on Sanskrit grammar, the *Cāndragomi-vyākaraṇa-pañjikā*, and the *Śabdārtha-cintā*.[1] The Pāli language, which had reached the height of its development with Buddhaghosa and his successors, Dhammapāla, Mahānāma, and others, remained as the cultivated literary language of Ceylon, used by those who had a clear mastery over it, for about three centuries. With the incursions of the Tamils and the consequent general disorder in the kingdom circumstances were incompatible with much literary effort and the cultivation of Pāli generally dwindled. More attention began to be given to secular subjects than heretofore, and Sanskrit came to be regarded as being of the first importance for that purpose. Already in the *Mahābodhi-vaṃsa* the influence of Sanskrit studies was plainly perceptible in the loss of the simplicity of its Pāli, in the restriction of its freedom, in its long compounds, and its intricate versification. Mention was made of the fact that Vijaya-Bāhu I encouraged learned men from other lands to come and settle down in Ceylon. They were *par excellence* Sanskritists, and set up a faction for Sanskrit modes of literature. Sanskrit forms of expression became the vogue. This process, however, did not reach its culmination till about a century or two after Vijaya-Bāhu; but we see its clear workings even in the literature of the period now under review.

The author of the *Abhidhammattha-saṅgaha* was an Elder named Anuruddha. His name is mentioned in the colophon of that work, and there he is stated to have been an incumbent of the Mūlasōma Vihāra. The style of his language shows that he did not live before the tenth or eleventh century, most probably the latter, and the fact that Sāriputta, who lived in the reign of Parākrama-Bāhu the Great (1164–97), compiled a

[1] Wickremasinghe, p. xiii.

paraphrase to the *Abhidhammattha-saṅgaha*—coupled with the fact that no mention is made in Anuruddha's work of the exploits of Parākrama, whose greatness was extolled by all the writers of his period—would lead us to place the author before that monarch. Scholars agree in ascribing him to the beginning of the twelfth century.[1] Not much more is known about him. According to the Burmese tradition Anuruddha was an Elder of Ceylon and wrote the compendium at the (Mūlasōma) Vihāra founded by Sōmadevī, Queen of Vaṭṭagāmaṇi (88–76 B.C.) and the minister Mūla, at Polonnaruva.[2] The statement that he lived at Mūlasōma Vihāra is supported by the Colophon to the Compendium mentioned above.

The *Sāsana-vaṃsa* merely calls him "Anuruddha Ācariya of Ceylon".[3] The *Saddhamma-saṅgaha* of the fourteenth century gives him as the author of the *Abhidhammattha-saṅgaha*, and states also that Anuruddha (most probably identical with our author) also wrote another work on Abhidhamma, the *Paramattha-vinicchaya*; but he is there mentioned as having lived at Kāñcī-pura (Conjevaram), reputed as the abode of the commentator Dhammapāla.[4]

In his edition of the *Buddhaghosuppatti* J. Gray gives a chronological list of saintly and learned men of Southern India, taken from the Talaing records, and there we find Anuruddha mentioned [5] after authors who are supposed to have lived later than the seventh or eighth century. The *Gandha-vaṃsa* (p. 61) gives him as author of three treatises on the *Abhidhamma*, the Compendium, *Paramattha-vinicchaya*, and *Nāma-rūpa-pariccheda*, and mentions him among the Ceylon authors (p. 67). The evidence before us would lead to the conclusion, therefore, that Anuruddha lived about the beginning of the twelfth century, that he was a native of

[1] *Comp. of Phil.*, p. vii and footnote.

[2] Compendium, p. vii.

[3] p. 34.

[4] P.T.S. Ed., p. 62.

[5] p. 26.

Ceylon, but spent part of his time at Kāñcī-pura, in South India, and that he was the author of three works on the Abhidhamma. Such is also the universal belief in Ceylon.[1] In the printed edition of the *Anuruddha-śataka*, a Buddhist devotional poem of 101 stanzas, in elegant Sanskrit—one of the few Sanskrit works now extant in Ceylon—Paṇḍita Batuvantudāve, one of the most erudite of Oriental scholars in Ceylon in the last century, states that the *Saddhamma-saṅgaha* mentions the *Anuruddha-śataka* and the *Abhidhammattha-saṅgaha* as works of the same author, Anuruddha.[2] D'Alwis, in his catalogue, reiterates the same statement.[3] The Pāli Text Society edition of the *Saddhamma-saṅgaha*, however, makes no such mention. The statements of these two responsible scholars show that they had a variant reading of the passage before them. At any rate, that both the *Śataka* and the Compendium are the works of the same author is universally believed in Ceylon.[4] Now the *Śataka* tells us in its concluding stanzas :—

> " *idaṃ vyadhattottaramūlanātha-*
> *ratnāṅkuropasthavirānuruddhaḥ* "

that " it was done by Anuruddha, Upasthavira (or Anunāyaka), who was like unto a gem in the necklace of the Uttaramūla (Nikāya) ". This is the first time, as far as we know, that this new Nikāya comes into sufficient prominence for notice to be taken of it. There is no doubt, to my mind, that the Uttarōla monastery referred to in the *Mahā-vaṃsa*[5] was the headquarters of the new fraternity. It was built by King Mānavamma, son of Kāsyapa II, who ascended the throne in 691, and ruled at Anurādha-pura, according to the *Pūjāvaliya*, for thirty-five years.[6] It was an offering of gratitude by him to the monks of the Abhayagiri Vihāra

[1] De Zoysa, p. iv.
[2] Colombo Ed., 1866, p. ii.
[3] p. 170.
[4] See also Wickremasinghe, p. xiv.
[5] Chap. lvii, v. 20.
[6] Wijesinha, *Mahā-vaṃsa*, pt. II, p. xx (table).

for having consented to take into the Order his elder brother in spite of the loss of one eye, which he had suffered in some yoga practices.[1] The first chief of the Uttarōla was the king's brother himself, and he was in charge of 600 monks ; he was granted great honours and privileges together with five classes of servants to minister unto him. He was appointed to supervise the guardians of the tooth relic, and from that time the monks of the Abhayagiri became the king's counsellors, and we are told that " hearkening unto their counsel he governed righteously ".[2] Mānavamma was Vijaya-Bāhu's paternal ancestor, according to the *Mahā-vaṃsa*, and from a Tamil inscription of this king we find that he kept up his patronage of the Uttaramūla Nikāya, for it is recorded that he himself gave over the custodianship of the tooth relic, which was the most precious heritage of a Ceylon king, to a monk named Moggallāna, of this fraternity.[3] Probably this same Moggallāna was the Mahā-Nāyaka of the Nikāya during Anuruddha's time, for we find Anuruddha describing himself as Upasthavira (the second chief). In later times the Uttaramūla Nikāya gave birth to many an illustrious star in Ceylon's literary firmament, Moggallāna, Vilgammūla, and Śrī Rāhula, to mention but three. Successive kings extended to them their patronage and made munificent endowments for the maintenance of the Nikāya. Of these, each in its proper place.

For nearly nine centuries the *Abhidhammatha-saṅgaha* has stood at the head of works on Abhidhamma, held in the highest esteem by all Buddhists of the Southern school. It gives in outline what the teaching of this part of the Doctrine meant to the ancient Buddhists, but it is no systematic digest of the Abhidhamma Canon. Its style is unattractive, with its dry, terse categories, elliptical mnemonic summaries, its endless catalogues and analyses. " Compared with the older

[1] *M.V.*, lvii, vv. 7–11.
[2] Ibid., vv. 16–26.
[3] *Epigraphia Zeylanica*, vol. ii, p. vi, pp. 250

and the more famous classic, Buddhaghosa's *Visuddhi-magga*, the Compendium covers very largely the same range of subject-matter as that work, though without the same amplitude of treatment. But the object of each work, and hence, to some extent, the order and emphasis of treatment in each, is different. The Compendium is a concise statement of a view of things, with purely theoretical analysis. The *Way of Purity* is ethical in its end, and is psychological only in order the better to teach ethics, and the way to saintship. The two works are thus to some extent mutually complementary."[1] The curt and dry method of its treatment, and the numerical characters of its psychological analyses, required a great deal of patient study before they could be mastered. But here we have a " famous and venerable digest of that mere abstract, analytical teaching which the Buddhists called Abhidhamma, or ' ultra-doctrine ', wherever the narrative and the homily of the Suttanta discourses found no place ",[2] and the very nature of the work made perhaps, a simpler, more attractive treatment of the subject very difficult. Words were yet wanting to express certain ideas ; the crystallized experience of the ages had not yet become sufficiently familiarized with the fundamental question of philosophy, for such subjects as mental phenomena to be talked of, except in crude and bizarre numerical analyses. Anuruddha's work, however, was in great measure an advance on what had gone before him[3] ; yet the subjects he treated of were abstruse and difficult to understand. Everyone had not the high gifts to unravel the cobwebbed structure of this little manual, these subtle psychological analyses. Hence grew up around it a mass of exegetical literature, explanatory of its difficulties.[4] In

[1] Mrs. Rhys Davids, Compendium, p. x.

[2] Ibid., p. xvii.

[3] e.g. in the treatment of the *bhavaṅga* and the *cittas* ; the methods of introspection employed with regard to the theory of *cetasikas*. For a fuller description see Compendium, preface, pp. xix foll., and Mrs. Rhys Davids, *Bud. Psy.*, 2nd ed., 1924.

[4] The *Piṭakattha-main* (a Burmese bibliography of Burmese Buddhist works) mentions twenty-three different Burmese *nissayas* on this work.

Ceylon itself Sāriputta Mahāsāmi (also, apparently, called in Burma Navavimalabuddhi) and his pupil, Sumaṅgala, wrote *ṭīkās* on the work, the first of which is now hardly ever used. Sumaṅgala's *ṭīkā*, *Abhidhammattha-vibhāvanī*, still remains in favour both in Burma and in Ceylon. Sāriputta also wrote an interverbal paraphrase in Sinhalese.[1] Several commentaries on the book have been written in Burma, some in Pāli and others in Burmese, and the Compendium continues to be studied with great zeal and earnestness in Burma even to-day.[2]

Two other works of Anuruddha, the *Nāma-rūpa-pariccheda* and the *Paramattha-vinicchaya*, are included among the nine Little Finger Manuals (*Let-than*) of the Burmese.[3] Both works were written while the author was residing at Kāñcī-pura, in the Tambaraṭṭha, as he says in the colophon or *nigamana* of the *Paramattha-vinicchaya*. They are composed in *gāthā* verse, and show him as a poet of much ability, with more scope for his metrical gifts than was possible when he was composing the analyses of the Compendium. It is interesting to note what he says, in the *Nāma-rūpa-pariccheda*, that he composed the work according to the commentaries of the Mahāvihāra[4]; in the colophon he makes affectionate reference to Ceylon, showing his connexion with the island (vv. 1849–55). The treatment of the subject in the *Nāma-rūpa-pariccheda* is much simpler than in the Compendium ; it is meant to be an introduction to the study of the Abhidhamma, divided into thirteen chapters, giving a general idea of the subjects that would come before the student as he reads the Abhidhamma books, and thus familiarizing his mind with the chief lines of

All the Burmese authors of the seventeenth century took it in hand, and it has been carefully edited by modern Hsayās (Mrs. Bode, *Pāli Lit. in Burma*, pp. 61–2).

[1] De Zoysa, p. iv.

[2] Compendium, pp. ix–x.

[3] The others being Buddhadatta's *Abhidhammāvatāra* and *Rūpārūpa-vibhāga*, Dhammapāla's *Sacca-saṅkhepa*, Kassapa's *Moha-vicchedanī*, Khema's *Khema-ppakaraṇa*, and Chapaṭa's *Nāmācāra-dīpaka*.

[4] *JPTS.*, 1923, p. 5, v. 2.

thought he would have to follow out later in greater detail. Two *ṭīkās* exist on the work, one by Vācissara (thirteenth century) and the other by Sumaṅgala, author of the *Vibhāvanī-ṭīkā* on the Compendium.

The *Paramattha-vinicchaya* is a much shorter work in twenty-nine sections, dealing with *citta, cetasika, rūpa,* and *nibbāna,* by no means so comprehensive as the *Nāma-rūpa-pariccheda*; nor is it as extensively used. A commentary exists, written by a Mahā-Bodhi *Thera,* of whom nothing more is known except that he was an incumbent of the Mahā-vihāra at Anurādha-pura.[1] Both works are notable specimens of mediaeval Pāli verse.

[1] Aung, *JPTS.*, 1910, p. 126. The *Saddhamma-saṅgaha* also mentions him as the author of a *Sacca-saṅkhepa-vaṇṇaña* on Dhammapāla's *Sacca-saṅkhepa* (q.v.).

CHAPTER IX

THE AUGUSTAN AGE

VIJAYA-BĀHU'S death in A.D. 1120 was again the signal for internal discord, which threatened to dissever the unity of the kingdom. But in this emergency a mighty figure appeared on the stage and all other claimants to the throne were overruled in favour of Parākrama, a prince of great accomplishments and of energy so unrivalled as to secure for him the goodwill of his kindred and the admiration and loyalty of the people. High thoughts welled within his breast. "If I, who am born of a princely race, should not do a deed worthy of the heroism of kings, my life would be of no avail,"[1] he had said while yet a child, and it had been his ambition to rescue his motherland from foreign dominion and consolidate the monarchy in his own person. He completed by foreign travel an education which, according to the *Mahā-vaṃsa*,[2] comprised every science and accomplishment of the age in which he lived, including theology, medicine and logic, grammar, poetry and music, the training of the elephant and the management of the horse. With consummate skill and unsurpassed power of organization, with an originality which always stood him in good stead and with unremitting care for details, he soon became master of the kingdom and in A.D. 1164 crowned himself "sole king of Laṅkā".

There is no name in all the annals of Sinhalese history which commands the veneration of the people in such measure as that of this prince of the "mighty arm", Parākramạ Bāhu, since he united in his person the piety of Devānampiya-Tissa and the chivalry of Duṭṭhagāmaṇi. Once peace was assured within his dominions, he would not rest content with the inglorious ease of his predecessors. His was the ambition to combine the renown of foreign conquests with the triumphs of domestic policy. In pursuance of the former he carried his arms even

[1] *M.V.*, lxiv, v. 48.
[2] Ibid., lxiv, vv. 30 ff.

into such distant countries as Cambodia and Arammana, which had offered him insult or inflicted injury on his subjects.[1] To secure the prosperity of the land he devoted himself most earnestly to agriculture as his first task and constructed as many as fourteen hundred and seventy tanks, three of them of such vast dimensions that they were known as the " seas of Parākrama ".[2] By a careful organization of a splendid civic service he suppressed all lawlessness with a firm hand, and in one of his inscriptions it is recorded, that " the security which he established as well in the wilderness as in the inhabited places was such that even a woman might traverse the island with a precious jewel in her hand and not be asked what it was." [3]

But all his energies he made subservient to the restoration and the embellishment of his religion, and the encouragement of the fine arts. In spite of Vijaya-Bāhu's efforts to purge the Buddhist Saṅgha of undesirables there still remained within its fold members who were unfit to lead the monastic life, fattening on the endowments given to various monasteries by monarchs whose zeal for generosity was not tempered by any discrimination. " In the villages that were given to the Order," says the *Mahā-vaṃsa* with scathing sarcasm, " purity of conduct among monks consisted only in that they supported their wives and children. Verily of purity there was none other than this. Neither was there any unity in the performance of the office of the Church ; and those monks that walked the blameless life cared not even to see each other." [4]

The king determined to end this lamentable state of affairs, and, being a just man, impartial and, resolute withal, he proceeded with great tact and skill. He decided to hold a council of the Elders of the three fraternities and appointed Mahā Kassapa of Udumbaragiri Vihāra, a man learned in the

[1] *M.V.*, lxxvi, vv. 12 foll.
[2] *Rāja-ratnācarī*, p. 88.
[3] Tennent, i, p. 409.
[4] *M.V.*, lxxviii, vv. 3–4.

three *Piṭakas*, who knew the *Vinaya* wholly, as the head of the assembly. He first invited the leaders of the dissentient schools, who lived in various parts of the country, to Polonnaruva and then requested the Mahāvihāra monks to be reconciled to them. But they were unwilling, "inasmuch as the lewd brethren prevailed in the church and the breach was from old time." [1] Some departed to countries over the seas, others took off their robes and many wished not even to sit in the same judgment hall. Then began the great trial to see whose teachings were correct, and very hard were the questions that had to be determined. "Verily, it seemed as if the endeavour to accomplish this unity was like unto the effort to raise Mount Meru." But the king was not to be baffled in his purpose. He secured the assistance of great doctors learned in the three *Piṭakas*, and with their help solved the questions that arose for judgment. He was convinced of the righteousness of the claims of the Mahāvihāra, and ended by becoming their patron. He upheld their decisions and decreed that their teachings should be accepted. With great care and patience he made investigation into the members of the schismatic schools; many of them he caused to return to the life of novices, others he persuaded to leave the Order, giving them lands and offices for their maintenance.[2] Where persuasion was of no avail, he used force and compelled them to disrobe themselves. The triumph of the Mahāvihāra was complete, the three fraternities [3] were united and from this time we hear no more of the power of dissentient bodies. This unification of religion was succeeded by the erection of numerous buildings for the benefit of its votaries. Dāgobas and statues of the Buddha were multiplied without end, temples of every form erected in Polonnaruva and elsewhere throughout the country. Halls for the reading of *bana*,

[1] *M.V.*, lxxviii, v. 12.
[2] Ibid., chap. lxxviii, vv. 17-20.
[3] The Abhayagiri, the Jetavana, and the Mahāvihāra.

image-rooms, residences for the priesthood, ambulance halls and rest-houses for their accommodation when on journeys were built in every district, and rocks were hollowed out as dwellings for those more inclined to solitude.[1]

The *Mahā-vaṃsa* devotes several chapters to describing the various activities of the king. Even now the ruins of Polonnaruva, the most picturesque city in Ceylon, attest to the care which he lavished on his capital. Ramparts were built and fortresses erected; palaces for his own use, schools and libraries, magnificent halls for music and dancing and drama, tanks for public baths, parks and flower-gardens.

The bare enumeration of such works conveys an idea of the immense prosperity which must have made their performance possible. With this perfect internal tranquillity, undisturbed by oppression, encouraged in their activities by the great and devout interest taken by the head of the State himself, and working amidst congenial and beautiful surroundings, there arose during this period a band of scholars, who made this epoch the Augustan age of Ceylon literature.

Oldest among them was Mahā Kassapa of Dimbulāgala (Udumbaragiri) Vihāra, who, as we saw above, was appointed by the king to preside over the great council of Elders in order to decide the Vinaya rules. He was especially proficient in the Vinaya Law, and his services were of great use at the Assembly.[2] He was the author of a Sinhalese *sanne*, a paraphrase, to the *Samanta-pāsādikā*, which is no longer extant. He was a Sanskrit scholar as well, and wrote a grammar in that language, called *Bālāvabodhana*, on the lines of the *Cāndra-vyākaraṇa*.[3] He is also reputed to have written a *porāṇā ṭīkā* on the *Abhidhammattha-saṅgaha*. Whether he is identical with the Elder Kassapa, whom the *Sāsana-vaṃsa-dīpa*[4] calls a poet of the Coḷa country, but who is regarded in Burma

[1] *M.V.*, chap. lxxviii, vv. 31 ff.
[2] *M.V.*, lxxviii, v. 7.
[3] Wickremasinghe, p. xv.
[4] v. 1204.

as a native of Ceylon [1] and author of a treatise on the *Abhidhamma* called the *Moha-vicchedanī* (which forms one of the little-finger manuals), a *ṭīkā* on the same, a Vinaya commentary called the *Vimati-vinodanī*, and also according to the *Gandha-vaṃsa*,[2] of two other treatises called *Buddha-vaṃsa* and *Anāgata-vaṃsa*, we cannot say. Of these the *Vimati-vinodanī* commentary on the *Vinaya*, though now hardly known in Ceylon itself, has been held in great esteem in Burma. It was one of the authorities appealed to when Dhammaceti carried out his reforms in the fifteenth century, and is mentioned in the Kaḷyāṇi inscriptions. It was largely used by the Pārupaṇas in their debate with the Ekaṃsikas, which ended in the defeat of the latter by the clever Ñāṇābhivaṃsa at the end of the eighteenth century.[3]

Contemporaneous with Kassapa was the Elder named Moggāllana, author of the *Moggāllana-Vyākaraṇa*. He is, perhaps, to be separated from the lexicographer of the same name, who also lived at this time and wrote the *Abhidhānappadīpikā*. But of this more presently. Moggallāna's work was an attempt to start a new school of Pāli grammar in Ceylon. The influence of extensive Sanskrit studies during this period undoubtedly had something to do with it, as we shall see later on. Up to this time the *vade mecum* of Pāli writers in determining their grammatical form had been *Kaccāyana-vyākaraṇa*, which was held in very high esteem. This work consisted of eight divisions, each division comprising *suttas* or rules expressed with sententious brevity; *vutti* or supplementary comments to explain the deficiencies in the *suttas* and render them intelligible; *payoga* or grammatical analyses with examples, and the *nyāsa* or scholia, giving explanatory notes on some of the principal grammatical forms in the shape of questions and answers. The *Nyāsa* often exists as a separate book called *Mukha-matta-dīpanī*.[4] Tradition has it that all the

[1] Aung, *JPTS.*, 1910, p. 126, and Bode, op. cit., p. 33, note.
[2] *Gandha-vaṃsa*, p. 61.
[3] Bode, op. cit., p. 76.
[4] Bode, op. cit., p. 37

suttas or aphorisms were written by one and the same person—Mahā-Kaccāyana. In the *Kaccāyana-bheda*, written by Mahāyasa Thera of Thatōn about the thirteenth century,[1] there occurs a memorial verse : "The aphorisms were made by Kaccāyana, the Vutti by Saṅghānandi. The illustrations by Brahmadatta. And the Nyāsa by Vimalabuddhi." From the distinct mention of different names for the authors of the different parts, it would seem that Saṅghānandi was different from Kaccāyana. In the *ṭīkā* to his work, written by Mahāyasa himself, he tries to justify the tradition that both rules and supplements were written by Kaccāyana, on the hypothesis that Kaccāyana may also have been called Saṅghānandi. That the tradition continued to be accepted as being authoritative, however, is shown by the fact that, in the *Kaccāyana-vaṇṇanā* or commentary on the *Sandhi-kappa* (section treating of euphonic combination of letters) of Kaccāyana, Mahāvijitāvi of the Abhayagiri Parvata at Panyā (Vijaya-pura), who lived about the sixteenth century,[2] still assigns the whole of the grammar and the *Mahā-Nirutti* and the *Netti-ppakkaraṇa* to Mahā-Kaccāyana. In the commentary to Buddhappiya's *Rūpa-siddhi*,[3] a grammar based on the Kaccāyana, the author of the older grammar is identified with the Great Elder Mahā-Kaccāna, one of the eighty chief disciples of the Buddha. "Who is this Kaccāyana ? Whence his name ? It is he who was selected for the important office (of compiling the first Pāli Grammar) by the Buddha himself, saying 'Bhikkhus, amongst my disciples capable of elucidating in detail what is expressed in the abstract, the most eminent is Mahā-Kaccāna'." According to the *Rūpa-siddhi*, Kaccāyana's purpose was that "men of various nations and tongues, rejecting the dialects which have become confused by its disorderly mixture with Sanskrit and other languages, may with facility acquire, by conformity to the rules of grammar

[1] Bode, p. 37.
[2] p. 46, Bode.
[3] q.v.

propounded by the *Tathāgata*, the knowledge of the word of the Buddha ".[1] In the *Anguttara Atthakathā*, Kaccāyana is represented as " a thera who was able to amplify the concise words of the Buddha both by means of letters and by showing their sense. Others could do it only one way or the other. Therefore was he called the chief ".

It is quite possible that the great Elder Mahā-Kaccāna, a chief disciple of the Buddha, did compile a set of rules in the languages in which the Canon was handed down. There is evidence to show that Mahā-Kaccāna was the head of a school at Avantī. The *Mahā-vastu* [2] says that he was the nephew of Asita or Kāladevala, seer of Vindhyācala. Acting under the seer's advice, he, together with his companions, visited the Buddha and there, impressed by the Buddha's erudition, they became monks and later attained Arahatship. Kaccāna (or Nalaka, as he was called, Kaccāna being the gotta or gotra or *gens* name), is said to have been the son of the minister of Caṇḍappajjota of Avantī. He returned with his followers from Sāvatthī and founded *āśramas* in the Avantī country at Kururaghara-papāta and Makkara-kata. The *Thera-* and *Therī-gāthā* contain several names of monks and nuns of this Avantī fraternity, e.g. Nanda Kumāraputta, Isidatta son of a caravan-guide, Dhammapāla, and Soṇakuṭikaṇṇa.[3]

Though the Avantī school never grew to be large in numbers, yet they had an important voice in matters of dispute with regard to changes of doctrine and in the rules of discipline, for we find that in the Council of Vesālī they had to be called in to take part in discussing the questions raised by the Vajjian monks.[4] The *Vinaya*, in the 5th book (13) of the *Mahā-vagga*, mentions Avantī as a place difficult of access, and in the *Sutta-nipāta* the names of the halting stations are given from

[1] Turnour, *Mahā-vaṃsa*, introd., p. xxvii.
[2] *Mahā-vastu*, vol. ii, p. 382.
[3] See *Psalms of the Brethren*, under these names.
[4] Kern, *Manual of Buddhism*, p. 107.

Patiṭṭhāna to Sāvatthī through Avantī, in describing the journey of Bāvari's ten disciples when they came to see the Buddha. In the *Culla-vagga* (ii, p. 299) it is said that the Avantī Bhikkhus laid special stress on ascetic practices allowed in the Buddhist code which are known as the *dhuta-vāda* practices. It is significant that the *Netti-ppakaraṇa*, which is a special work of doctrinal interpretation by way of exegetical analysis, should also be ascribed to Mahā-Kaccāna, who was reputed to be the greatest analytical exponent in the Buddha's time. Living in comparative isolation, the school at Avantī may quite possibly have developed a system of analysis and of grammar—two more or less related subjects—and the traditional assertion that Mahā-Kaccāna himself was the author of the terse aphorisms would therefore be justified to this extent that he was the founder of the school in whose *paramparā* the subject was handed down and further developed. And, just as in sanctioning the Vinaya rules as authoritative declarations, the words "anujānāmi bhikkhave" were put into the mouth of the Buddha, so quite possibly the grammatical rules were upheld by directly attributing them to the founder of the school himself.

That the Grammar was the work of a south Indian school is further supported by the fact that when, after Moggallāna's grammar had superseded Kaccāyana's authority, the reaction set in a century later in favour of the elder author, it was led by a south Indian, Buddhappiya or Dīpaṅkara, with his grammar, the *Rūpa-siddhi*. It seems, therefore, reasonable to conclude that there existed a set of grammatical rules going back possibly to Mahā-Kaccāna himself, and quoted on his authority, and that they were developed apparently in India, probably by members of the Avantī school, Saṅghānandi, Brahmadatta, and lastly by Vimalabuddhi. The text now known to us may be considered a revised edition of what were traditionally known as the *Mahā-Kaccāyana Suttas*, arranged and enlarged by Saṅghānandi. This would also account for Mahāyasa's surmise, mentioned earlier, that

Kaccāna and Saṅghānandi were one and the same. It is the generally accepted theory in Ceylon that the *Kaccāyana-vyākaraṇa* has extensively borrowed its terminology from Sanskrit grammar and that there is much resemblance between the works of Kaccāyana and those of the Kātantrics rather than those of Pāṇini and his school. The Kātantric grammars do not labour under the studied brevity and obscurity of the Pāniṇians, and this perspicuity and method of treatment bear close affinity to those adopted in Kaccāyana's work. It is clear however that, except in the examples drawn from Buddhist canon and texts, most of the others are adapted from the well-known and common examples of all Sanskrit grammarians.[1]

D'Alwis, in the scholarly Introduction to his edition of the *Kaccāyana*,[2] has shown that either Buddhaghosa was not familiar with the work of Kaccāyana, or the grammar had not in his time acquired the authority which it certainly exercised a few centuries later. Since, however, Buddhaghosa does make reference to Kaccāyana in his *Aṅguttara Atthakathā* as the chief of the Neruttikas and mentions the *Kaccāyana-pakaraṇa* in the *Sutta-Niddesa*, the first supposition falls to the ground. If in Buddhaghosa's time Kaccāyana's work had been widely-known and accepted as the chief authority, he certainly would have used Kaccāyana's terminology. That Buddhaghosa's terms were different from Kaccāyana's will be clear from the following tabulated list of cases[3] :—

Buddhaghosa	*Kaccāyana*
Paccattaṃ	Paṭhama
Upayogaṃ	Dutiyā
Karaṇaṃ	Tatiyā

[1] For details see D'Alwis' Introduction to his edition of the grammar, Colombo, 1864.

[2] pp. xxv foll.

[3] There is, however, a Burmese tradition that Kaccāyana's grammar was brought to Burma by Buddhaghosa, and the Burmese translation and commentary are ascribed to him (*Pāli Grammar*, by Francis Mason, introd., p. v).

Buddhaghosa	*Kaccāyana*
Sampadāna	Catutthī
Nissakka	Pañcamī
Sāmi	Chaṭṭhī
Bhumma	Sattamī
Ālapana	Ālapana

When, however, we come to the author of the *ṭīkās* written during and soon after the reign of Parākrama Bāhu I (A.D. 1164), we find that their terminology tallies with that of Kaccāyana.[1] We may, therefore, reasonably conclude that the Kaccāyana came to be put into its present form and recognized in Ceylon as an authority on Pāli grammar somewhere between the century after Buddhaghosa and the eleventh century. Edmund Hardy has shown us in his introduction to the *Netti-ppakaraṇa* [2] that that work, too, does not seem to have been well known to Buddhaghosa. Possibly both works were introduced to Ceylon during the time when scholars from South India migrated to Ceylon in large numbers to study at the Mahā-vihāra and other centres of learning in Anurādha-pura, soon after Buddhaghosa's works proved to them the richness and the genuineness of the Ceylon *Thera-vāda* tradition. It is now generally accepted that the Kaccāyana came into vogue in Ceylon about the seventh century of the Christian era.[3]

In the eleventh century, when Vijaya-Bāhu of Ceylon appealed to Anuruddha, king of Burma, for help in re-establishing the Saṅgha ordination in the island, the intercourse between the two countries became closer and more intimate. We saw in the last chapter how the two monarchs co-operated in arranging a common authoritative canon for both countries, and how Anuruddha obtained from Ceylon

[1] D'Alwis, loc. cit.

[2] P.T.S. Ed., pp. xiv–xv.

[3] Thus Mrs. Rhys Davids, *Compendium*, Preface, p. viii. See, however, *Pāli Grammar*, by Vidyābhūsaṇa, published by the Mahā Bodhi Society, Calcutta, where Kaccāyana's period is given as third century A.D. at Mathurā (Introd., p. xxviii).

copies of the Pāli *Tipiṭaka*, which he examined and compared with the Thatôn collection, aided by the Talaing monk Arahanta. Anuruddha died in 1057 without being able to see the firstfruits of his husbandry, but during the reigns of his immediate successors Pāli learning took firm root at Pagan, and the works of this period show that the Burmese monks specialized in the study of Abhidhamma and Nirutti (grammar). In 1154 the monk Aggavaṃsa completed the *Sadda-nīti*, a grammar based on the *Tipiṭaka*, and described it as the most comprehensive in existence.[1] It established the reputation of Burmese scholarship in that age, and of the author to the present day, for the *Sadda-nīti* is still regarded in Burma as a classic. The *Sadda-nīti* formed the first return gift of Burma to Ceylon. A few years after its completion, the *Thera* Uttarajīva left Pagan for the Mahāvihāra, taking with him a copy of the work, which immediately evoked enthusiastic admiration and was declared superior to any work of the kind written by Sinhalese scholars.[2] Uttarajīva was accompanied by his pupil, the novice Chapaṭa, who lived amidst the Ceylon Saṅgha for several years, received ordination at their hands, and later became one of the most famous of the Burmese *literati* under the name of Saddhammajotipāla, author of many books, including several grammatical treatises based on the Kaccāyana, to which we shall refer later.[3]

The intimate association with grammarians of such eminence as these was bound to inspire their colleagues in Ceylon with a zeal for the study of the *nirutti-sattha* (grammatical science). A new zest was given to the perusal of such works as they had already with them. Chief amongst such was undoubtedly the Kaccāyana, which they regarded as their manual. But since Kaccāyana's day other influences had been at work, shaping and moulding Pāli grammatical

[1] Bode, "*Early Pāli Grammarians in Burma*," *JPTS.*, 1908. An edition by Mr. Helmer Smith is now being published.

[2] *Sāsana-vaṃsa*, p. 74.

[3] Bode, op. cit., p. 89.

forms. In Ceylon the great attention given to Sanskrit by the learned monks had brought about the birth of a Sanskritized Pāli, which was recognized as good literature. The need was therefore felt for a more up-to-date treatise on Pāli grammar, and an Elder named Moggallāna came forward to supply that need.

Of the man himself, apart from his work, we know little. He was a pupil of Mahā-Kassapa of Udumbaragiri, and it is stated in the colophon of the grammar that he wrote it in the reign of Parākramabāhu the Great, after the king had purged the Saṅgha of all heretical and sinful Bhikkhus, i.e. after A.D. 1165. Śri Rāhula, author of the *Pañjikā-pradīpa* on *Moggallāna-vyākaraṇa* states that Moggallāna was an incumbent of the Thūpārāma Vihāra at Anurādha-pura.[1] He was perhaps identical with the Moggallāna *Thera* mentioned in the Tamil inscription of Vijaya-Bāhu,[2] as having been entrusted with the custodianship of the Tooth-relic, in which case he was the head of the Uttaramūla Nikāya, of which fraternity the author of the *Abhidhammattha-saṅgaha* was *anunāyaka.* He was doubtless a distinguished scholar, for he is very highly spoken of by his contemporary, the learned Medhaṅkara [3] of Udumbaragiri Vihāra, a pupil of Sāriputta and author of several works of note. He is also mentioned as one of his teachers in most eulogistic terms by Saṅgharakkhita,[4] another of Sāriputta's pupils, who wrote no less than five comprehensive works on Pāli grammar and prosody.

As has been already mentioned, there are several points of difference between Moggallāna's grammar and those of the Kaccāyana school. Aggavaṃsa's *Sadda-nīti,* introduced into Ceylon from Burma, had followed the terminology of Kaccāyana. Moggallāna differs from them both. His aphorisms are differently worded. He disputes the correct-

[1] See also De Zoysa, p. 24.
[2] *Ep. Zeyl.*, vol. ii, pt. vi, pp. 246 foll.
[3] In the *Vinayārtha-samuccaya* (q.v.).
[4] In his *Sambandha-cintā* (q.v.).

ness of the very first sutta in the Kaccāyana—that there are forty-one letters in the Pāli alphabet—and contends that the number is forty-three, including short *e* and *o*. Kaccāyana, in his second chapter, mentions that the three inflexions, *āya*, *ā*, and *ē*, are used optionally with nouns for *sa* (dat. sing.), *smā* (abl. sing.), and *smiṃ* (loc. sing.) respectively, and that they are never used with pronouns. Moggallāna denies this, and quotes examples from the *Tipiṭaka* to support his contention. He takes exception to the Kaccāyana definition of the dative case as " that which expresses a wish to give, that which pleases or holds ", and states that, though words of giving govern a dative case, and though the forms of the two cases are identical, yet words expressing pleasure and bidding govern a genitive.[1] The work is divided into six chapters : terminology and *sandhi*, declensions, compounds, nominal derivations, verbal derivatives, and verbs. Moggallāna himself calls his work *Sadda-sattha* (work on verbal science), and mentions in the colophon that not only did he write the aphorisms, but also composed to them a *Vutti* explanatory of the rules in detail. He also wrote a *pañcikā* or commentary on his *Vutti*, and called it the *Vutti-vaṇṇanā-pañcikā* dealing with the *kāraka* (syntax) only. This work is well known because of the *Pañcikā-pradīpa* written on it, by Śri Rāhula Saṅgharāja, mentioned above. Moggallāna's work started a new school of Pāli grammar in Ceylon, which included such luminaries of learning as Saṅgharakkhita, Piyadassi, author of the *Pada-sādhana*, Ānanda, Vanaratana Medhaṅkara, and Śri Rāhula. Their works will be dealt with in their respective places.

A Moggallāna was also the author of the *Abhidhānap-padīpikā*, written at the same time as the above, in the reign of Parākrama the Great. Whether he was identical with the grammarian or with the Moggallāna referred to in Vijaya-Bāhu's inscription, it is at present impossible to say. A Sinhalese *sanne* or interverbal paraphrase of the work says that it

[1] Also D'Alwis, *Catalogue*, p. 184.

was composed by the author of the *Vyākaraṇa*, but, though the *sanne* is undoubtedly an ancient and a valuable work, we know neither its author, nor the date of its compilation. The same statement is made in a *ṭīkā* or commentary which is certainly later than the *sanne*, for reference is made there to the latter work. The tradition in Ceylon is that the author of the *Abhidhāna-ppadīpikā* is different from the grammarian.[1] The work belongs to the latter part of Parākrama's reign, for the author speaks in high praise of the king and of the works done by him for the adornment of his capital and as " having *long* extended his protection to the united Saṅgha of the Three Nikāyas ". Moggallāna calls himself " the special object of the King's wish-conferring patronage and a dweller amongst the Sarō-gāma fraternity ". He composed his work at the Mahā Jetavana Vihāra in Pulasti-pura (Polonnaruva).[2] The seventy-eighth chapter of the *Mahā-vaṃsa* speaks of Moggallāna as having attended the Convocation of Mahā-Kassapa from the country of the Upa-rāja or sub-king.[3] The headquarters of the Sarō-gāma fraternity were at Seruvāvila near Trincomali, and this community came into prominence in the thirteenth and fourteenth centuries, when one of its members became head of the Kitsirimevan Kälaṇi Temple and compiled several works of merit.[4] Even in the twelfth century they must have constituted an important body of monks; otherwise they would not have been represented in the Convocation. The Jetavana Vihāra was built by Parākrama to rival in splendour Anāthapiṇḍika's gift to the Buddha. We are told that it consisted of 520 dwelling-houses, apart from other buildings, and was replete with every means of comfort.[5]

The *Abhidhāna-ppadīpikā* is the only ancient Pāli Dictionary in Ceylon, and it follows the style and method of the Sanskrit

[1] See Subhūti's edition, Colombo, 1865, and also see De Zoysa, p. 21.
[2] Subhūti's edition : colophon.
[3] *M.V.*, lxxviii, v. 9.
[4] Wickremasinghe, p. 23.
[5] *M.V.*, loc. cit., vv. 31–48.

Amara-koṣa. As the name implies, it is meant to throw light (*padīpa*) on the meanings of nouns (*Abhidhāna*). In the opening stanzas Moggallāna tells us that his work was written because "an intimate acquaintance with nouns and their genders is essential for those desiring to learn the correct significance of words and is a help to those wishing to master the word of the Buddha". In the colophon he says that the lexicon "interprets the names of all objects in the Deva, Mānuṣa, and Nāga worlds". The work is divided into three parts, dealing with celestial, terrestrial, and miscellaneous objects respectively, and each part is subdivided into several sections, which are by no means mutually exclusive. The whole book is a Dictionary of Synonyms, all the names given to one particular thing being grouped together and put into verse to facilitate memorizing them. The last two sections of the last part are devoted to homonyms and indeclinable particles. The work is held in the highest esteem both in Burma and Ceylon. In Burma an important officer of state under King Kittisīhasūra (A.D. 1351) wrote a *Saṃvaṇṇanā* on it and the Elder Ñāṇavara of Pagān translated the Lexicon into Burmese in the eighteenth century, thus completing a task which had been begun by his predecessors in the seventeenth century.[1] In Ceylon itself a *sanne* and a *ṭīkā* were written, to which reference has already been made.

Mrs. Bode mentions[2] that in the Ekaṃsika-Pārupaṇa controversy in the last quarter of the eighteenth century, the Ekaṃsikas quoted in support of their arguments a treatise called *Cūḷa-gaṇṭhi-pada*, which they attributed to the Arahat Moggallāna, one of the two chief disciples of the Buddha. They explained that it was embodied in a text known as the *Piṭaka-ttaya-lakkhaṇa-gandha*, brought to Burma by Buddhaghosa. But the Pārupaṇas maintained that the text on which the Ekaṃsikas depended was a treatise called the *Vinaya-gaṇṭhi-pada*, of the twelfth century, and was written

[1] Bode, *Pāli Lit. in Burma*, p. 67.
[2] Ibid., p. 76.

in Ceylon by the *thera* Moggallāna in Parākrama-Bāhu's reign. The title of the book would suggest that it was a dissertation on the *Vinaya*, but no such book is known in Ceylon at the present day, and, so far as I am aware, Moggallāna did not write any compilation on the *Vinaya* and the only work bearing the name of *Vinaya-gaṇṭhi-pada* extant at present in Burma is ascribed to a Sinhalese monk named Joti, of whom nothing more is known.[1]

Perhaps brightest among the constellations that adorned Ceylon's literary firmament during Parākrama-Bāhu's reign was Sāriputta, called also Sāgaramati,[2] "like to the ocean in wisdom." He was one of the prominent members of Parākrama-Bāhu's convocation, and we are told that the king built for him "a mansion of great splendour containing many halls and chambers", attached to the Great Jetavana Vihāra at Polonnaruva.[3] Like all the other learned men of his period, he was a clever Sanskrit scholar as well, and wrote a *ṭīkā* on Ratnasrijñāna's *pañjikā* to the *Cāndragomi-vyākraṇa.* This was called the *Ratnamati-pañjikā-ṭīkā* or *Pañjikālaṅkāra.* He is also credited with having written a concise grammar in Sanskrit, called the *Padāvatāra,* dealing mainly with words, their forms and meanings, but this work is now apparently lost.[4]

Another of his works is the *Vinaya-saṅgaha*, a summary of the *Vinaya Piṭaka*, divided into various sections, giving concise explanations of *Vinaya* rules. Thus: *divāseyyā ti divānibbajjanaṃ, tatrāyaṃ vinicchayo : anujānāmi, bhikkhave, divāpaṭisalliyantena dvāraṃ saṃvaritvā paṭisallayitun ti vacanato divā nippajjante dvāraṃ saṃvaritvā nibbajjitabbaṃ.* (*Divāseyya* means "sleeping by day". This is the decision with regard to it, "Bhikkhus, I rule that he who rests in sleep by day should have his door closed," from this, "if one

[1] Dr. Forchhammer's List published by the Government of India, 1879.
[2] *S.-saṅgaha*, p. 63.
[3] *M.V.*, lxxviii, v. 34.
[4] See preface, p. xvi, printed ed. of *Moggallāna-pañjikā-pradīpa.*

sleeps by day the door should be closed.") In the colophon Sāriputta mentions that it was written by him at the request of King Parākrama. The work seems to have been known under various titles. The Mandalay MS. in the India Office Library has the title *Mahāvinaya-saṅgaha-pakaraṇa*, by Sāriputta, and in the colophon the work is called *Pālimuttaka-Vinaya-vinicchaya*. The MS. in the Colombo Museum Library bears the title *Pālimuttaka-Vinaya*; D'Alwis in his Catalogue (p. 170) gives a Pāli *Muttaka-Vinaya-vinicchaya* as one of Sāriputta's works, and Westergaard has the same in his Catalogue (p. 48). Forchhammer's list contains *Vinaya-mahā-saṅgaha*, by Sāriputta. The *Gandha-vaṃsa* calls it *Vinaya-saṅgaha* (p. 61), and so does the *Sāsana-vaṃsa* (p. 33). In Burma the work is known as the *Vinaya-saṅgaha* and *Vinaya-saṅgaha-pakaraṇa*,[1] and is mentioned in the Kalyāṇi inscription,[2] among several works of Sinhalese authorship. It formed one of the chief works consulted by King Dhammaceti of Pegu in the fifteenth century, when he instituted his reforms for the Saṅgha,[3] and the *Piṭaka ttha-main* (p. 43) mentions a commentary on it by the *Ācariya* of King Sin-gu of Ava. It has been suggested in view of the variety of the titles under which the book is known that *Vinaya-saṅgaha*, or, to give it its full name, *Pālimuttaka-Vinaya-vinicchaya-saṅgaha*, was only part of a much larger *Mahā-Vinaya-saṅgaha-pakaraṇa*,[4] but I see no reason to accept this suggestion. It is only too well known that the work of ancient authors often bore more than one title—sometimes confusedly so—and it is quite likely that Sāriputta's work was no exception to this custom and that whatever its full and original name was, it was generally called the *Vinaya-saṅgaha*. Two *ṭīkās* [5] are extant on it in Ceylon, one old (*porāṇa*) and the other new (*nava*), but the author and the date of neither is known. The *Gandha-vaṃsa* (p. 61) says

[1] Bode, p. 38, and p. 39, footnotes.
[2] *Ind. Antiquary*, vol. xxii.
[3] Bode, p. 38.
[4] e.g. Fausböll, *JPTS.*, 1896, p. 18.
[5] De Zoysa, p. 15.

that Sāriputta wrote a *ṭīkā* on it himself. He also wrote a Sinhalese *sanne* to the *Abhidhammattha-saṅgaha.*

Sāriputta's most comprehensive work, however, is the *Sārattha-dīpani*, his masterly sub-commentary on Buddhaghosa's *Samanta-pāsādikā* on the *Vinaya-Piṭaka.* The immense amount of valuable information he has collected therein shows that his knowledge was extensive and profound, and that he was not second to the great commentator himself in exegetical ability. The language betrays the influence of Sanskrit learning on the author's Pāli. Many of the illustrative stories given are of Ceylonese *Theras* and laymen, and the work contains a very valuable historical account of the eighteen schools into which the Buddhist Saṅgha were divided at the time of the Third Council, and gives much information not available at present anywhere else. The work is divided into two sections—*Cūḷa* and *Mahā*, and follows closely the lines laid down by Buddhaghosa, thus suffering from the same weakness of being tied down too much to orthodox interpretations. Sāriputta is also sometimes credited with having written two other *ṭīkās*, the *Sārattha-mañjūsā* on the *Aṅguttara*, based on Buddhaghosa's *Manoratha-pūraṇī*, and the *Līnattha-ppakāsinī* on the *Papañca-sūdanī* of the Majjhima.[1] To this time, most probably, also belong the *ṭīkās* on the other three *Nikāyas* of the *Sutta-Piṭaka* collectively known as the *Sārattha-mañjūsā ṭīkā.*[2]

The *ṭīkās* were sub-commentaries, that is to say, works containing expositions of points in the *Atthakathā* or commentaries which needed further elucidation for their correct interpretation; or sometimes they merely gave additional information regarding the discussions in the commentaries, e.g. more illustrative stories. The *ṭīkās*, unlike the commentaries, were purely of Ceylonese origin, compiled and written by Ceylonese scholars, and the *ṭīkās* on the Canonical texts and commentaries were composed soon after the Convocation held under the patronage of Paṛākrama-Bāhu

[1] Wickremasinghe, p. xv.
[2] De Zoysa, p. 3.

with Mahā-Kassapa as President. The *Saddhamma-saṅgaha* [1] has an interesting chapter on how they came to be written. Thus :—

" After the three fraternities of Ceylon monks had been reconciled and monasteries and places of learning had been built for their use, Mahā-Kassapa, head of many thousand monks at Jetavana Vihāra, assembled there and made the following declaration : " Whatever commentaries have been compiled by teachers of old on the *Atthakathā* of the three *Piṭakas* are now of no use to monks living in the various countries. Many of them are written in the Sinhalese language, and the others in Māgadhi mixed with various languages (*ākulaṃ*) and unintelligible. Let us therefore remove such faults and compose exegetical commentaries, complete and clear in exposition." The Bhikkhus agreed and requested him to obtain the royal sanction. That having been secured, they reassembled in the hall (at Jetavana) built by the king, and composed *ṭīkās* (*līnattha-vaṇṇanā*) on the *Vinaya-Piṭaka* (*Sārattha-dīpanī*), the four chief *Nikāyas* of the *Sutta-Piṭaka* (the *Sārattha-mañjūsā* divided into four parts) and on the *Abhidhamma-Piṭaka* (*Paramattha-dīpanī* in three parts)."

To the *Abhidhamma ṭīkās* more detailed reference will be made later. It is significant that Sāriputta's name is not mentioned in this connexion, and that no special works are assigned to him by the author of the *Saddhamma-saṅgaha*. Unreliable as the information of the *Saddhamma-saṅgaha* is in many respects, as we shall see when we discuss it later, there is no doubt that the account of the *ṭīkā* compilation, as given here, contains more than a germ of truth. It has to be remembered that for several centuries preceding Parākrama's reconciliation of the communities the Saṅgha had been torn by various schisms. The different sects, while they accepted the authority of the common canon and of Buddhaghosa's commentaries, interpreted various points of teaching in their own way, to support each in their claims to orthodoxy. These

[1] *JPTS.* Ed., pp. 58 foll.

interpretations were written and handed down in *ṭīkās* or additional commentaries, and, as the author of the *Saddhamma-saṅgaha* puts into the mouth of Kassapa, they were variously written, some in Sinhalese, others in Pāli, others in a mixture of dialects, due to the conglomeration of the many elements that constituted the Saṅgha. The *ṭīkās* contained much valuable information and often the correct traditional interpretations that would be of great assistance in a correct understanding of various points of the *Dhamma* teaching. Much matter must have accumulated since Buddhaghosa compiled his works, especially after scholars began to come over to Ceylon from Burma and China, South India and Cambodia. And, just as Buddhaghosa felt the necessity of making a concise compilation of the different *atthakathās* that had come down to his day, the need was realized of bringing these various *ṭīkās* together and making a synthetic summary of them all. It was impossible, however, to accept all or even most of what they contained, nor was it politic that the works of any particular school should supersede those of the others. There were yet in the Saṅgha those who were not quite wholeheartedly reconciled to the victory of the Mahāvihāra over the other schools; thus unity of the fraternities had been secured only with great tact and patience and labour, and a wise man, such as Kassapa undoubtedly was, would have shrunk from doing anything fresh to rekindle dissatisfaction. We may well believe, therefore, that he consulted his colleagues at Jetavana and obtained their help in settling the *ṭīkās*. These *ṭīkās* may be regarded, therefore, as the work of a school, rather than of single individuals; they were rehearsed in solemn conclave and completed after discussion.

What, then, about Sāriputta's part in this task? He was an important member of the Jetavana monastery and undoubtedly took a prominent part in the proceedings. He may possibly have been appointed to supervise certain sections of the work—the *Vinaya*, *Aṅguttara*, and the *Majjhima* portions. It may even be that after consultation with his *saddhi-vihārikas* he was authorized by them to write those sections which now bear his name. The custom of single authors making compilations was then quite well-established, and, as long as the matter which they contained won their approval, the *ṭīkā* compilers would have had no objection to any one of their number—and Sāriputta was certainly one of the most eminent amongst them—writing the work. This supposition would account also for Sāriputta having written a *Vinaya-saṅgaha*, apart from the *ṭīkā* on the *Vinaya* associated with his name. The first was purely his, the second the work of an assembly (or a committee, we may call it), of which he was the head. The *ṭīkās* on the *Vinaya Piṭaka* and on the *Aṅguttara* and the *Majjhima Nikāyas* of the *Sutta Piṭaka* are definitely attributed to Sāriputta. As to the authorship of the *ṭīkās* on the other two portions of the *Sutta Nikāya*, nothing is known. The common name borne by all the *ṭīkās* of each *Piṭaka* would seem to strengthen the hypothesis that they were the work either of one person or of a whole community, and we know that Sāriputta is not credited with having written them all himself. In this connexion it is significant that Dhammakitti, author of the *Dāṭhā-vaṃsa,* who was one of Sāriputta's immediate disciples, also mentions only the *Samanta-pāsādikā ṭīkā* and the *Aṅguttara-ṭīkā* as his teacher's works.[1]

[1] Colophon *JPTS.* Edition, p. 151, i.e. in addition to the *ṭīkā* on *Cāndragomi-pañjikā* and the *Vinaya-saṅgaha.*

CHAPTER X

Sāriputta's Circle

WHILE Mahā-Kassapa, assisted by Sāriputta and others of equal eminence, was labouring for the glory of the religion in Ceylon, an event took place which drew Burma and Ceylon together, even more intimately than before, and which had far-reaching consequences in the later history of the Buddhist Saṅgha in both countries. Ever since the time of Buddhaghosa, Burmese monks were in the habit of coming over to the Mahāvihāra that they might there imbibe the orthodox Theravāda tradition and bring it back with them to their own land. The intercourse between the two countries was undoubtedly interrupted to some extent during the foreign invasions of Ceylon, and its internal discords; but after Vijaya-Bāhu obtained the help of King Anuruddha in re-establishing the ordination in his own country it revived, and, in the prosperous reign of Parākrama the Great, increased to a very large extent. It was about this time, somewhere about the beginning of Parākrama's regime in A.D. 1165, that the Elder Uttarajīva left Pagān to visit the celebrated Mahāvihāra, taking with him, as we saw, a copy of Aggavaṃsa's great work, the Pāli Grammar, *Sadda-nīti*. Uttarajīva was accompanied by his pupil, the novice Chapaṭa, known in religion as Saddhammajōtipāla,[1] whose fame surpassed, for a time, at least, even that of Aggavaṃsa. He received the *upasampadā* from the Saṅgha in Ceylon, and lived with them for several years, studiously learning the *Dhamma* as handed down in the Mahāvihāra, and perhaps mastering many texts which were as yet unknown in Burma. He was a man of great skill and ability, and his stay in the sacred island was of great importance to the literary history of Burma. He returned to his country deeply imbued with the conviction, that the Mahāvihāra alone had preserved the legitimate line of

[1] *Sāsana-vaṃsa*, p. 74.

thera-succession from the time of the Buddha, and that the *upasampadā* would be valid only if it were conferred by the Mahāvihāra fraternity. He, therefore, brought with him into Burma four Siṅhalese monks,[1] and this little group formed the nucleus of a Sīhala Saṅgha in Burma, the rightful heirs of the legitimate tradition. We are not concerned here with following the vicissitudes of that community. It was well that the Sīhala Saṅgha *did* gain a foothold in Burma and rise into eminence there, for, in later years, when the *upasampadā* was again lost in Ceylon, during a period of great adversity, it was the Burmese Saṅgha who helped in large measure to make good the loss and re-establish the ordination.[2]

Chapaṭa was the author of several works, eight in all, according to the *Gandha-vaṃsa*,[3] only one of which was written in Ceylon, the *Saṅkhepa-vaṇṇanā*, a commentary on the *Abhidhammattha-saṅgaha*, divided into nine chapters, closely following Anuruddha's work.[4] Meanwhile Sāriputta was head of a large school at Jetavana, in a splendid monastery built by the king for his special use. He was, perhaps, more responsible than anyone else of this period for the spread of learning in Ceylon. Famed far and wide as Sāgara-mati, "like to the ocean in wisdom," he left behind him several disciples of profound learning and great abilities, at least six of whom have come down to posterity as authors possessed of high literary erudition.

Among them was Saṅgharakkhita, who specialized in *nirutti* (grammar), rhetoric, and prosody. In the *Vuttodaya* he speaks with great respect of the grammarian Moggallāna, and calls him one of his teachers. He also mentions among his preceptors a certain Selantarāyatana (Galaturu-mūla) *Thera*, and in the colophon to the *Sambandha-cintā* calls himself a pupil of Medhaṅkara "who purified the religion", evidently

[1] *Sās.*, p. 65.
[2] Bode, op. cit., pp. 16–20.
[3] *G.V.*, p. 74.
[4] Fausböll, *India Office Catalogue*, *JPTS.*, 1896, p. 39.

Udumbaragiri Medhaṅkara, pupil of Kassapa and Sāriputta. Perhaps the Selantarāyatana *Thera* and Medhaṅkara were one and the same. In the *Canda-sārattha ṭīkā*[1] to his *Sambandha-cintā* he is called a grandson of King Dāṭhōpatissa, which is undoubtedly a mistake, because Dāṭhōpatissa lived about three centuries earlier. Perhaps the author was mistaken for another earlier writer of the same name of whom nothing is known. In the colophon to the *Sambandha-cintā* Saṅgharakkhita tells us that he also wrote the *Vuttodaya, Susadda-siddhi, Yoga-vinicchaya, Subodhālaṅkāra*, and a *Khudda-sikkhā-ṭīkā*. Chief among his works ranks the *Vuttodaya*, the only original work, so far as we know, extant on Pāli prosody; it is of moderate length, divided into six chapters and written partly in prose and partly in verse. The author tells us in his introductory stanza, that "the works on prosody composed in earlier times by Piṅgala and others are not in a manner satisfactory to those studying pure Māgadhi. Therefore for their easy comprehension do I now commence in the Māgadhi language this *Vuttodaya* adapted to popular prosody and divided into Mattā and Vaṇṇa, composed in language pleasing and abounding in sense and embodying both rule and example".[2] It is wholly based on works dealing with Sanskrit prosody, the terms of which it has borrowed and adopted and, in some instances, whole sentences are incorporated from Piṅgala and other authorities with no more alterations than are necessary when Sanskrit is turned into Pāli.[3] It is divided into six chapters dealing with prosodial feet (8 *gaṇas*) and technical terms, metre (different types of metre and their rules, chiefly the Ariyā), Samavutta or verses where every line is alike, Aḍḍha-samavutta (where every half-gāthā is alike), Visama-vutta (the four lines of a gāthā are unequal), and the last, on the

[1] By Saddhamañāna of Pagān, in the fourteenth century (*Piṭakattha-maiṇ*, p. 74).

[2] Colombo Ed., p. 7.

[3] e.g. the last ten verses of the first chapter on Pada-ccheda (caesura), which are taken directly from Halāyudha.

six kinds of knowledge essential to good poetry (e.g. spreading of rhythm, ascertaining the tune, symbols of rhythm, etc.). There is a Sinhalese *Sanne*, written, probably, by the author himself, and a Pāli *ṭīkā* by an unknown hand.[1] It has been made the subject of several commentaries and glosses in Burma, notably the *Vuttodaya-pañcikā* of Saddhammañāṇa and the *ṭīkā* of Vepullabuddhi of Pagān.[2]

Another of Saṅgharakkhita's works is the *Sambandha-cintā*, dealing with the Pāli verb and its use in syntax. It also gives a description of the six Kārakas or Cases used with the verb in the sentence. This treatise is based on the grammar of Moggallāna, whom he mentions as his teacher, along with Medhaṅkara, both of whom he eulogizes in the opening stanzas as having assisted in the suppression of heresy. There exist a Pāli *ṭīkā* by an unknown author (see below), and a Sinhalese *Sanne* by Gotama Thera,[3] both of whom, judging from their comments, were undoubtedly well-versed in the principles of Pāli grammar. Mahāyasa's *Kaccāyana-sāra* of the thirteenth century quotes extensively from the *Sambandha-cintā*, showing that Saṅgharakkhita's work became famous after it was written. Abhaya, a Burmese author of Pagān of the fourteenth century, also wrote a *ṭīkā*,[4] which is probably the one extant in Ceylon at present.

The *Subodhālaṅkāra* is a work on the art of poetry, as the following table of contents shows, apart from the technique of prosody, which is dealt with in the *Vuttodaya*. It is a learned and important work, and treats chiefly of the Gāthā verse. It is divided into five chapters : (1) Incongruity of sense and tautology ; (2) the art of avoiding such faults ; (3) elegance of words and phrases ; (4) the elegance of sense and how it can be acquired ; (5) the elegance of sound and the art of making verse pleasant to the listener. The work is much used in Ceylon and in Burma, where a *Nissaya* or

[1] Wickremasinghe, p. xviii.
[2] Fausböll, *Cat. Mandalay MSS.*, p. 50.
[3] De Zoysa, p. 29.
[4] Bode, p. 22, and *G.V.*, 64–74. pp.

scholiast has been written on it as late as 1880 called the *Alaṅkāra-nissaya*.[1]

Of Saṅgharakkhita's two other known words: (1) *Susaddasiddhi* or *Sārattha-vilāsinī*, a *ṭīkā* on the *Moggallāna-pañjikā*, and (2) the *Khudda-sikkhā-ṭīkā*, mention has already been made in connexion with the works on which they are based.

Contemporary with Saṅgharakkhita was Sumaṅgala, another of Sāriputta's pupils. He specialized in the study of Abhidhamma, and wrote *ṭīkās* on several Abhidhamma works. His *ṭīkā* on Buddhadatta's *Abhidhammāvatāra* is entitled *Abhidhammattha-vikāsinī* (the Blossoms of Philosophy). He also wrote a *Nava-ṭīkā* on Dhammapāla's *Sacca-saṅkhepa*, called *Sārattha-sālinī* (the Essence of Meanings). But by far the best known work is the *Abhidhammattha-vibhāvanī* (Philosophy made clear), on the Compendium. It was once known in Burma as the *Ṭīkā hla* (the Beautiful *Ṭīkā*), because the comments in it are so very apt to the subject of discussion. But when, in the fifteenth century, Ariyavaṃsa of Ava became proficient in the Buddhist Scriptures, the *Ṭīkā hla* changed its name to *Ṭīkā gyau* (the Famous *Ṭīkā*).

The *Sāsana-vaṃsa* [2] gives us some interesting details of this change of name. Ariyavaṃsa was a member of Chapaṭa's Sīhala-saṅgha, and went to Sagaing to study grammar under a learned Thera called Ye-din (the water-carrier). Either to restrain his own inclination for talk, or because he found his companions too talkative, this monk was in the habit of keeping his mouth filled with water. When Ariyavaṃsa first came to him, there seemed little hope that the silent water-carrier would discourse to him on any subject. But he was not discouraged. He came daily to the Vihāra, performing all the services of a pupil to Ye-din, till the latter asked him his reasons for these visits. Ariyavaṃsa begged permission to study with the famous Ācariya because, though he had

[1] Bode, p. 95.
[2] pp. 95 foll.

studied texts, he had not grasped their meaning, and till then, the expositions of his teachers had not been of help to him. Ye-din consented to give him some instruction and explained this *Abhidhammattha-vibhāvanī*. In a short time Ariyavaṃsa had grasped all the knowledge he had missed till then. The Ācariya charged him to help other students of the subject by writing a commentary on the text he felt fitted best to expound, and the result was the *Maṇisāra-mañjūsā*, his *ṭīkā* on the *Abhidhammattha-vibhāvanī*. We are told that, while writing it, Ariyavaṃsa submitted his work chapter by chapter to the criticism of his fellow-monks, reading it aloud to them as they assembled on *uposatha* days at the Vihāra.[1] Because of Ariyavaṃsa's masterly exposition of the book Sumaṅgala's work henceforth came to be known as the Famous *Ṭīkā*, and now forms part of the regular course of Abhidhamma studies in Burma. Chapaṭa, who also wrote a *ṭīkā* on the Compendium (the *Saṅkhepa-vaṇṇanā*), in referring to the earlier *ṭīkās*, compares Sumaṅgala's work to "the moon which cannot shine within bamboos", and his own work to the "firefly which can". A pretty and modest simile, but by no means flattering to those who read his book.

To the group of Sāriputta's disciples also belongs Buddhanāga, who wrote the *Vinayattha-mañjūsā*, a *ṭīkā* on Buddhaghosa's *Kaṅkhā-vitaraṇī*. He mentions in the colophon that he wrote the work at the request of an Elder named Sumedha, "wise and clever and anxious for the furtherance of the Religion."

Another was Medhaṅkara of Udumbaragiri, first of four Medhaṅkaras[2] famous in Ceylon literature. Perhaps there was a fifth, oldest of them all, whom Saṅgharakkhita refers to by name as one of his teachers. Our Medhaṅkara mentions both Sāriputta and Moggallāna as his preceptors; but, though he belongs to the Udumbaragiri fraternity, no mention is made

[1] Bode, pp. 41–2 and 61.

[2] The other three were: (1) Araññaka Medhaṅkara; (2) the translator of the Jātakas into Sinhalese; (3) author of the *Jina-carita*.

of Kassapa. He does not appear to have written any works in Pāli, or, if he did, they were later superseded by other works, for the only one of his compilations which has come down to us is a work in Sinhalese prose. It is called the *Vinayārtha-saṃuccaya*, a compendium of Vinaya rules translated into Sinhalese from the original Pāli with explanatory notes taken from the Commentaries.

Sāriputta had another pupil named Vācissara. I agree with Mr. Wickremasinghe in his suggestion [1] that there were two Vācissaras, both of whom lived before the end of the thirteenth century, the one slightly senior to the other. Considering the number of works assigned to Vācissara in the *Gandha-vaṃsa*,[2] one would almost be inclined to the belief that there were even more than two, not all of them from Ceylon, but living about the same period.

The *Gandha-vaṃsa* attributes even the *Bālāvatāra* to Vācissara, but we know now that the author lived after the thirteenth century. It was the younger Vācissara that describes himself as the pupil of Sāriputta. The elder I would consider to have been either a contemporary of Sāriputta, or, more probably, slightly anterior to him. To the senior monk, I would attribute the *Khema-ppakaraṇa-ṭīkā*, two *ṭīkās* on Buddhadatta's works (one called simply the *Uttara-vinicchaya-ṭīkā* on the *Uttara-vinicchaya*, and the other on the *Vinaya-vinicchaya* called *Yoga-vinicchaya*), and an original work on the Abhidhamma called *Rūpārūpa-vibhāga*. He also wrote a treatise called the *Sīmālaṅkāra* on boundaries and sites for religious ceremonies, to which Chapaṭa compiled a *ṭīkā*.[3] A *porāṇa-ṭīkā* on Anuruddha's *Nāma-rūpa-pariccheda* is likewise to be assigned to him, together with a *ṭīka* on the *Sacca-saṅkhepa*. There seems to be some uncertainty as to the authorship and the date of the *Sacca-saṅkhepa*. The *Saddhamma-saṅgaha* [4] assigns it to Ānanda, but we know that

[1] Cat., p. xvi.
[2] p. 62.
[3] Bode, p. 18.
[4] Chap. 9.

the *Saddhamma-saṅgaha* is not always reliable in its information. The *Gandha-vaṃsa*[1] ascribes it to Culla-Dhammapāla, and the colophon of the work agrees with this.

The author of the *Sacca-saṅkhepa* is to be distinguished from the commentator of the same name, who is usually called Ācariya to differentiate him from his less illustrious namesake, Culladhammapāla. The *Gandha-vaṃsa* calls him the eldest pupil of Ānanda. Nevill, in his Manuscript Catalogue, takes this Ānanda to be the same as the teacher of Vedeha and Buddhappiya, and fixes his date as early as the seventh century. But Buddhappiya and Vedeha certainly lived very much later, as we shall see when we come to consider those authors.

The Ānanda who was Culla-dhammapāla's teacher was undoubtedly older than Buddhappiya's teacher, for Culla-dhammapāla lived before the twelfth century at the latest. Chapaṭa[2] mentions the *Sacca-saṅkhepa* in his *Saṅkhepa-vaṇṇanā* commentary on the *Abhidhammattha-saṅgaha*, and, if Mr. Aung[3] is right in his information, Dhammapāla lived even earlier than Anuruddha, for we are told that, when Anuruddha wrote his work, the *Sacca-saṅkhepa* was as a *vade mecum* superseded by it in the twelfth century. The work—*Summary or Outline of Truth,* as its name implies—is a short treatise in five chapters, dealing with such Abhidhamma matters as Rūpa, Vedanā, Citta, Khandha, and Nibbāna. It forms one of the Let-Than or Little Finger Manuals, and, as such, is extensively studied in Burma. In his commentary on the Compendium, Chapaṭa points out certain differences between that work and the *Sacca-saṅkhepa*, and acts as an apologist for the former, going into very minute details. "Thus, while the *Sacca-saṅkhepa* begins with an exposition on the body, Anuruddha sets out with an inquiry into the mind. Why? Because he had the *Dhamma-saṅgaṇī* instead of

[1] pp. 60, 70.
[2] *JPTS.*, 1910, p. 125.
[3] Ibid., 1917, p. 2.

the *Vibhaṅga* in his mind when he wrote the Compendium."[1] There is no doubt, I feel, that it was the elder Vācissara who wrote the first or *Porāṇa-ṭīkā* to the *Sacca-saṅkhepa*, and not the younger, who describes himself in the *Sambandha-cintā-ṭīkā* as a pupil of Sāriputta. For we find that another of Sāriputta's pupils, Sumaṅgala, also wrote a *ṭīkā* on the same work, called the *Abhinava-ṭīkā*, and it is not probable that two pupils of the same teacher would have written on the same work.

If the elder Vācissara specialized in the *Abhidhamma* and the *Vinaya*, the younger gave most of his attention to the study of grammar. He was, evidently, one of Sāriputta's youngest pupils, for among his works several are *ṭīkās* on books written by Saṅgharakkhita, one of Sāriputta's chief disciples. They are the *Sambandha-cintā-ṭīkā*, *Subodhālaṅkāra-ṭīkā*, and *Vuttodaya-vivaraṇa*. He also wrote, at the request of Sumaṅgala,[2] a *Nava-ṭīkā* on the *Khudda-sikkhā*, to which Saṅgharakkhita had already written a sub-commentary. Vācissara called his work the *Sumaṅgala-pasādanī*, as a compliment to his colleague who incited him to write it. Another of his compilations was a *Moggallāna-vyākaraṇa-ṭīkā*. Perhaps it was this same Vācissara who, according to the *Mahā-vaṃsa*, left Polonnaruva during the invasion of Māgha and went over to the Paṇḍu and Coḷa countries, to seek for protection for Laṅkā.[3] The authorship of the *Thūpa-vaṃsa* is also ascribed to him (see below).

Apparently contemporary with the elder Vācissara was a *Thera* named Vimalabuddhi, author of the oldest *ṭīkā* on the Compendium.[4] His work was quite recent during the time of the senior Vācissara, and that was why the latter wrote his *ṭīkā* only on Anuruddha's *Nāma-rūpa-pariccheda*, and why, a few years later, Sāriputta contented himself with writing

[1] *JPTS.*, 1910, p. 125.
[2] Colophon to that work.
[3] Ch. lxxxi, vv. 17–21.
[4] De Zoysa, p. 4

only a Sinhalese *sanne* on the Compendium. But, some time afterwards Sumaṅgala felt himself at liberty to write a *Nava-ṭīkā*. Vimalabuddhi's work is now unknown in Ceylon, and considered quite superannuated even in Burma,[1] where it has been completely replaced by Sumaṅgala's "famous *ṭīkā*" (*Ṭīkā-gyau*). To Sāriputta's period also belongs Piyadassi, pupil of the grammarian Moggallāna.

He wrote the *Pada-sādhana*, an abridged Pāli grammar based on Moggallāna's work. He tells us in his colophon that he was a pupil of the great Nirutti-ācariya, and that he wrote, at the request of a village chieftain named Kappinna. The author of the Sinhalese *sanne* tells us that Piyadassi was incumbent of the Devarāja Vihāra in Dolosdās-rata (Girivapattu) on the Valave River in Ruhuṇa, South Ceylon. Kappinna was his maternal uncle, and was in charge of the Rambhā Vihāra lands of which Devarāja Vihāra formed a part.

The work is divided into six sections dealing with Saññā, Sandhi, Samāsa, Prefixes, Suffixes, and Verbs. The author called it *Pada-sādhana* or *Moggallāna-Saddattha-ratnākara*, but posterity has refused to accept the longer name! Vanaratana Ānanda wrote a Sinhalese *sanne* on it, which we shall notice presently, and there also exists a Pāli *ṭīkā* called the *Buddhi-ppasādaṇi* by Śrī Rāhula of the fifteenth century.

Possibly to the same period belongs Mahābodhi, author of a *Porāṇa-ṭīkā* (*Mukha-mattakā*) on Anuruddha's *Paramattha-vinicchaya*.[2] He seems to have written a *ṭīkā* on the *Khema-ppakaraṇa* as well and also according to the *Saddhamma-saṅgaha*,[3] a *Sacca-saṅkhepa-vaṇṇanā*, entitled *Nissayattha-kathā*.

Parākrama-Bāhu the Great died in A.D. 1197. He was a noble king, just and tolerant and a scholar of deep learning

[1] *Compendium*, p.ix.
[2] *JPTS.*, 1910, p. 125.
[3] Chap. ix, v. 25.

withal, the greatest figure in the annals of the island. Ceylon was never to produce his like. His death was the signal for fresh internal strife ; his family were unable to sustain the honours which he had won for the land of his birth. After several conspiracies and assassinations among his heirs and relations, his widowed queen ascended the throne under the name of Lilāvatī, only to be deposed in less than three years. Within a short time, however, she was restored, and for a while all went well. But the ignominious and selfish schemings of rival aspirants to the throne brought disruption, discontent and disunion in the land, and within thirty years after Parākrama's death the kingdom had been reduced to such an extremity of weakness by their contentions, that the Malabars, ever vigilant for an opportunity to carry out their projects, landed in Ceylon in a large band of 24,000, led by Māgha, and in a short time reconquered the whole island. Māgha was crowned king and his reign was marked by extreme cruelty. His merciless brigands swept through the country, plundering, ravishing, mutilating and slaughtering. Not even the modest-looking yellow robe of the pious bhikkhu would afford any protection from the cruelties of the Malabar Mercenaries. The holiest shrines were violated and overthrown. The *Mahā-vaṃsa* [1] and the *Rāja-ratnākarī* describe with painful elaboration the gradual extinction of Buddhism, the plundering of the temples, the expulsion of the monks, and the desecration of all that was holy. No outrage appeared too heinous to the plunderers, no torture too cruel ; with sheer wantoness they broke the cords that held together the valuable and rare palm-leaf books and scattered the leaves to the winds. All books and literary records such as fell into their hands were piled up and burnt, and the whole island resembled a dwelling in flames or a house darkened by funeral rites.[2]

After an interval of twenty years Vijaya-Bāhu III collected

[1] *M.V.*, Ch. lxxx, vv. 54 ff., and *Rājarat.*, pp. 93 foll.

[2] *Rājāvalī*, p. 256 (Upham).

as many Sinhalese soldiers as he could and with their aid succeeded in winning for himself a portion of the kingdom. While the Malabars were holding sway over the rest of the island from the capital city at Polonnaruva, Vijaya-Bāhu established himself at Dam̃badeniya, 50 miles to the north of the present Colombo. From there he governed the Province of Māyā; but it was not till the time of his son and successor, Paṇḍita Parākrama Bāhu, that the people succeeded in compelling the invaders to abandon Polonnaruva and retreat towards the mainland of India.

During the earlier part of these internal conflicts and foreign invasions, the generality of the people were left free to follow their own pursuits, and the monks, supported by a generous laity, devoted their energies to the service of literature. Thus except when Māgha's ruthless campaign completely destroyed the peace of the land, the period that intervened between the death of Parākrama the Great and the accession of Paṇḍita Parākrama, was not wholly devoid of literary productions.

Vijaya-Bāhu, who succeeded Parākrama the Great, was himself a man of some education, and we are told that he wrote with his own hand, in the Pāli tongue, a letter of great merit and sent it to the Burmese king at Arimaddana.[1] The contents of the letter we do not know, nor did the king live long enough to achieve any work of literary importance. When Lilāvatī was restored to the throne with the help of her faithful minister, Parākrama, she became a generous patron of art; she had, also, a minister Kittisenāpati, mentioned in a Sinhalese poem of this period,[2] who evinced a deep interest in literary work.

During her reign was compiled the Pāli poem *Dāṭhā-vaṃsa*. The author was Dhammakitti, the first of four scholars bearing the same name and famous in Ceylon literature.[3] He was a pupil of the celebrated Sāriputta, and he speaks most respect-

[1] *M.V.*, lxxx, v. 6.
[2] *Sasadāva Colophon.*
[3] For the other three see Index.

fully of his teacher in the colophon to the present work. We are told that the *Dāṭhā-vaṃsa* was composed at the request of the minister Parākrama of the Kālanagara race, for whom the author seems to have entertained the highest regard, because of his exertions on behalf of the religion.[1] Dhammakitti speaks highly also of Lilāvatī, "spotless as the moon . . . sweet-worded, just, like a mother unto her subjects, possessed of great intelligence, giving whatever was asked of her." He tells us that the Pāli *Dāṭhā-vaṃsa* is based on an older *Daḷadā-vaṃsa*, "written in the language of the land by the poets of Sīhala," and that it was composed in Māgadhi for the benefit of those living in other lands. We can infer from the *Mahā-vaṃsa*[2] that this *Daḷadā-vaṃsa* was written in Elu verse in the ninth year of Kitti Siri Meghavaṇṇa by his orders soon after the tooth relic was brought over to Ceylon. It is said to have given the history of the relic from the death of the Buddha, to the time of its arrival in Ceylon, as predicted by the Buddha. By the time of Dhammakitti the Sinhalese poem had become almost unintelligible. Turnour, in his translation of the *Mahā-vaṃsa*,[3] remarks that the original Sinhalese poem was still extant in 1837, but I have not been able to see it.

The *Dāṭhā-vaṃsa* is a very elaborate work, and rightly ranks among the Pāli classical poems. It is written in sonorous language, and gives vivid descriptions, in the manner of Sanskrit poets. The earlier chapters give a minute account of the great struggle between the Buddhists and the Brahmans of India for religious supremacy (in the third century), and may, perhaps, have been taken from a very old and almost contemporary record of the events described therein. Except where the author attempts vivid descriptions, the poem presents one of the finest specimens of the stern simplicity, chasteness, and beauty of rhythm of Pāli poetry, clothed in elegant diction, free from high-flown metaphors and ornately

[1] vv. 5–6.
[2] Chap. xxxvii.
[3] p. 241, footnote.

elaborated ideas. Coomāraswāmy, who has translated it into English prose,[1] compares it to the *Nalopākhyāna* in its sweetness of rhythm and unaffected flow of words. The *Dāṭhā-vaṃsa* does not contain the history of the relic beyond the period of its arrival and reception in Ceylon. Turnour mentions that the *Dāṭhā-dhātu-vaṃsa*, referred to above, had two more chapters than are found in our work, relating the vicissitudes of the relic up to the eighteenth century. A Sinhalese paraphrase was written by Dhammakitti himself for the benefit, as he tells us, "of less educated and local readers." In the Introduction to the Sinhalese *sanne* he calls himself a *rājaguru* (royal preceptor) in addition to his other titles. There are several works in Sinhalese on the history of the tooth relic, to which reference will be made in so far as they come within the purview of this dissertation.[2]

After Vijaya-Bāhu III established his capital at Dambadeniya, he helped, as much as lay in his power, those who were labouring in the cause of religion and literature. Thus, the *Nikāya-saṅgraha* tells us [3] that under his auspices two of Sāriputta's pupils, Saṅgharakkhita, the head of the Church of his day, and Udumbaragiri Medhaṅkara, held a synod at the Vijayasundarārāma built by Vijaya-Bāhu, and there, after much effort, settled various disputes which had arisen amongst the priesthood, formulated a new code of Vinaya rules, and "did great service to religion". The king also gave shelter to all the monks who were fleeing from Polonnaruva, "leaving their books and other necessaries wherever they chanced to be," and provided them with such comforts as were possible to obtain.[4] But the country was too distracted for peaceful pursuits to be possible. Māgha was carrying on his campaign of destruction "like unto a wild fire that consumeth the tender plants of the forest of charity,

[1] Publ. Trübner, 1874, Introd., p. ix.
[2] See Wickremasinghe, *Catalogue*, *passim*, for further particulars.
[3] p. 22.
[4] *M.V.*, lxxxi, vv. 41–63.

like unto the sun when he closeth up the petals of the sacred lily of justice, and the moon when she obscureth the splendour of the lotus-pond of patient endurance ".[1]

At this time, however, there existed in Ceylon a school of monks who were left undisturbed by any political upheavals. They belonged to the Vanavāsī or Araññavāsī fraternity and owed allegiance to the Mahāvihāra. They differed from each other, perhaps, only in the degree of rigour of their religious life, while they agreed on all doctrinal matters. Thus we find them acting together quite harmoniously at the Council of Paṇḍita Parākrama. We hear of this sect first, at the beginning of the sixth century, when during the reign of Aggabodhi II (A.D. 598–608) the King of Kaliṅga, having resolved to lead the life of a recluse, came over to Ceylon and joined the Order under the famous Elder Jotipāla. Vedeha, author of the *Rasa-vāhinī*, has given us, in the colophon to that work, an account of the beginnings of the Vanavāsī school to which he belonged.[2] It had once at its head an elder named Ānanda, who, according to the *Gandha-vaṃsa* (p. 66), was a native of India. We do not know the date of his reign, but he probably lived about the eighth or the ninth century. He it was that composed, at the request of Buddhamitta,[3] the *Mūla-ṭīkā* to the seven books of the *Abhidhamma*, which, according to the *Saddhamma-saṅgaha* account mentioned in the preceding chapter, was revised by Mahā Kassapa and his colleagues. This work now exists in three sections, one each for the *Attha-sālinī* and the *Sammoha-vinodanī* and the other for the *Pañca-ppakaraṇa*. Probably the original edition was in one volume—the *Satta-ppakaraṇa*, as it is still in Burma. He was also known as Vanaratana-Tissa, because of his connexion with the Vanavāsī school. The *Mūla-ṭīkā* were based on Buddhaghosa's commentaries, but their author occasionally dissents from the great exegetist. Thus, in

[1] *M.V.*, lxxx, v. 59.
[2] Printed Ed., Colombo, end.
[3] *G.V.*, p. 69.

discussing the life-term of matter he disputes the existence of a static phase of thought, and regarded it as merely hypothetical.[1] The Vanavāsī sect seems to have been closely associated with the Buddhists of Kaliṅga, for we find even at the end of the thirteenth century Vedeha mentioning the name of a Kaliṅga *Mahā-Thera*, an Elder of great eminence, who acted as sponsor at Vedeha's Ordination by Ānanda; and later, Buddhappiya of Coḷa belonged to the same fraternity. This connexion with Coḷa and Kaliṅga may possibly also account for the special attention members of the school devoted to the study of the *Abhidhamma*.

I am inclined to believe that it was the same Ānanda that had as his pupil Culla Dhammapāla, author of the *Sacca-saṅkhepa*, noticed earlier in this chapter, and also of an *Anu-ṭīkā* on Ānanda's *Mūla-ṭīkā*, called *Līnattha-vaṇṇanā*. Whether he was the author of several other *ṭīkās* mentioned in the *Gandha-vaṃsa* (p. 60) as well, we cannot say with any degree of definiteness.

The Araññavāsī sect continued to flourish even during the troublous times of the twelfth and the thirteenth centuries, and when Vijaya-Bāhu was reigning at Dambadeniya it was presided over by another Elder named Ānanda, who was a disciple of Udumbaragiri Medhaṅkara, pupil of Sāriputta.[2] One of his pupils, Buddhappiya, speaks of him as "Tambapaṇṇi-ddhajānaṃ" (a banner unto the island of Ceylon).[3] He and his school lived in seclusion and were able to carry on their pursuits undisturbed. Ānanda himself wrote a Sinhalese interverbal translation to Piyadassi's Pāli grammar the *Pada-sādhana*, and another to the *Khudda-sikkhā*.

The authorship of the Abhidhamma *Mūla-ṭīkā* is also generally ascribed to him,[4] but, as I have endeavoured to show above, that work was evidently composed prior to the Council

[1] *Compendium*, p. 26.
[2] *Pada-sādhana-sanne* colophon.
[3] *Rūpa-siddhi* colophon.
[4] Wickremasinghe's Catal., p. xvii.

of Kassapa in A.D. 1165; for we find that Culla Dhammapāla, who certainly lived before the twelfth century, wrote an *Anu-tīkā* on it.

Probably to the same period, but not, perhaps, to the same author, belongs the religious poem *Saddhammopāyana*. In the colophon to the Sinhalese paraphrase and in the introduction to a commentary on it called the *Saddhammopāyana-viggaha*, the work is assigned to a great Elder of the Order, named Abhaya-giri Kavi-cakravarti Ānanda *Mahā-Thera*.[1] Whether he is in any way connected with Vanaratana Ānanda, we have no means of finding out. The *Saddhammopāyana* itself gives no clue to its authorship, except in the introductory stanzas, where we are told that it was composed to be sent as a religious gift to the author's friend and companion Buddhasoma.[2] Nevill, in his manuscript Catalogue, has recorded a tradition that Vanaratana Ānanda and Buddhasoma were contemporaries and great friends, and that the *Saddhammopāyana* was written to dissuade the latter from renouncing his life as a monk. It is a treatise in nineteen chapters, dealing with such subjects as the difficulties of obtaining birth as a human being, a tendency to sin and the severe penalty attending it, the misery of existence as Pretas and lower animals, the advantages of being righteous, and the rewards it brings (such as birth in the Deva worlds), the merits of charity, chastity, piety, meditation, listening to the Doctrine, preaching it, etc. In one of the concluding stanzas the author expresses the wish that he might himself, one day, become a Buddha. It is written in simple and beautiful language, and parts of it are very frequently quoted by monks in the course of their sermons. It is held in very high estimation in Ceylon up to the present time.

There is a Sinhalese paraphrase by a later writer, also called Ānanda, and a commentary, the *Saddhammopāyana-viggaha*, by an anonymous writer.

[1] Colombo Ed., 1874.

[2] *JPTS.*, 1887, p. 36, v. 3.

Parākrama-Bāhu II. came to the throne in A.D. 1235; he was a mighty prince, endowed with all the qualities of leadership, and he soon succeeded in ridding the country of its foreign invaders. Once more the Sinhalese flag floated over the whole of Ceylon, and the king set himself vigorously to create order out of the chaos which the Malabars had left behind them. With its wonderful elasticity and richness of natural resources, the island soon recovered from the effects of the Tamil occupation, and the people were once more free to follow their pursuits of peace. It was a miracle exhibited by the tooth relic that had given Parākrama confidence in his ability to overthrow his enemies, and had shown him that he was destined to advance the welfare of the Religion and the land of its adoption,[1] and as soon, therefore, as the country had settled down, he devoted all his energies to the glorification of the Faith. The *Daṁbadeni-asana* and the *Rāja-ratnākara* are full of glowing accounts of his numerous accomplishments, and because of his extensive and profound knowledge of religious and secular subjects he was styled Kalikāla Sāhitya Sarvajña Paṇḍita—"the all-knowing sage of the dark (*kali*) age of literature." He was of an intensely religious disposition, and, hearing that there prevailed much misconduct in the Saṅgha calculated to damage the religion among those who entered the Order to lead lives of idleness and impurity, he called together a synod under the leadership of Araññaka Medhaṅkara[2] of the Udumbaragiri succession, chief pupil of Buddhavaṃsa Vanaratana Ānanda. With their help, he held an inquisition and expelled those who were found guilty of misconduct and unsuited to the office of monkhood. He also drew up a Katikāvata (code of monastic law) formulating rules for the monks who devoted themselves to study or to meditation, so that their religious observances might be maintained in strict conformity with Vinaya

[1] *M.V.*, lxxxii, vv. 16–40.

[2] The second Medhaṅkara in our list. The Elder Buddhavaṃsa was evidently also a member of the Vanavāsi fraternity.

regulations.[1] We are also told that he obtained from the Coḷa country monks of great eminence, learned in the *Tipiṭaka*, endued with piety and great purity of life.[2] The Araññavāsī sect came in for his special favour, and he built for their use, on a mountain in the forest, the Puṭabhatta-sela (Paḷābatgala) monastery,[3] which later became famous as the abode of many monks of great learning and severe austerities. He obtained teachers from India to teach the Ceylon bhikkhus such secular subjects as logic and grammar and the various sciences, and he persuaded his younger brother, the sub-king Bhuvaneka-Bāhu, to acquire much wealth of knowledge and become a teacher to many thousands of Elders.[4] Several authors of this period, including Vedeha, speak most highly of the patronage extended to them by the king's minister Devapatirāja, who, according to the *Mahā-vaṃsa* (chapter 86), was a man of great wisdom and devotion.

Such encouragement given to learning could not fail to be productive of great literary achievement, and Parākrama's reign is renowned as a period of numerous scholars of high repute. The king himself, towards the latter part of his life, handed over the reins of government to his son Vijaya-Bāhu who, to judge from the *Mahā-vaṃsa* account, was a prince extremely well-beloved of his subjects. The leisure thus obtained Parākrama used in prosecuting such studies as were not possible to him amidst the responsibilities of government, and he also wrote several works of merit: Sinhalese translations to the *Visuddhi-magga* and the *Vinaya-vinicchaya* (the latter of which he called Nissandeha), and a Sinhalese poem, *Kav-siḷumiṇa*, which is a masterpiece of beautiful Elu, melodious in its strains and sublime in its ideas. The Sinhalese *Daḷadā-sirita* (*History of the Tooth Relic*). is also attributed to him.[5]

[1] *Nikāya-saṅgraha*, p. 23.
[2] *M.V.*, lxxxiv, v. 10.
[3] Ibid., v. 24.
[4] Ibid., vv. 26–31.
[5] Wickremasinghe, p. xvii.

At his request Dhammakitti compiled the *Mahā-vaṃsa* from the date at which Mahānāma left off down to his own times. This Dhammakitti is usually identified with the author of the *Dāṭhā-vaṃsa*.[1] If this identification be correct, then Dhammakitti must have lived in retirement at Tambaraṭṭha in South India, when he was invited by Parākrama. The king had heard that a lotus had once sprung up in the path of the Elder as he went on his alms-rounds, and, being greatly astonished, sent gifts and offerings to the Tamba country, and persuaded him to come back to Ceylon, where he was held in the highest esteem.[2]

An author whose name we do not know, but who is referred to as the Pañca-pariveṇa-adhipati (Pas muḷa Mahāsāmi) composed in Pāli a medical work—the only one, so far as we know, of its kind extant—called the *Bhesajja-mañjūsā* (the Casket of Medicine). The *Mahā-vaṃsa* [3] says it was written in the time of Parākrama-Bāhu of Dambadeniya, by "the learned and benevolent Elder, chief of the monks at the Pañca-pariveṇa, to the intent that all who strive to fulfil their religious duties, may thereby become free from disease. Of the author nothing more is known. In a Sinhalese medical work, *Yoga-ratnākara*,[4] compiled about the end of the fourteenth century, a verse in the colophon states that that work was arranged on the plan, "of the *Mañjūsā*, a medical work in Pāli stanzas, composed by Atthadassi Thera about the year A.D. 1267." [5] If this information be correct, the author is undoubtedly our Pañca-mūla-pariveṇa-Adhipati. The *Bhesajja-mañjūsā* is mentioned in a Burmese inscription in Pagān, dated A.D. 1442.[6] Saraṇaṅkara Saṅgharāja wrote a Sinhalese paraphrase to it in the eighteenth century, and it is stated there that, having found his original defective, he added

[1] Wickremasinghe, p. xvii and footnote 4.
[2] *M.V.*, lxxxiv, vv. 12–16.
[3] xcvii, vv. 59–62.
[4] Wickremasinghe, p. 58.
[5] Dr. Kynsey's report on Parangi, Ceylon Sessional Paper, 1881.
[6] Bode, p. 108.

eighteen sections, making them sixty. The author of the *Mañjūsā* also wrote a *ṭīkā* on his work, but copies of it are rare. The *Mañjūsā* once enjoyed great repute, but it has later been superseded by Sanskrit works on the subject and is now hardly ever consulted.

To the same *Thera* is also generally ascribed the authorship of the *Sikkhā-pada-valañjanī*, the Pāli translation of the Sinhalese *Sikha-valañda*.[1] It is a code of monastic rules, drawn up for the guidance of monks by an unknown author, who also wrote a commentary on it, called the *Sikha-vaḷañda-vinisa* (the exegesis of the *Sikha-vaḷañda*). Both works contain quotations from the *Samanta-pāsādikā* and other works on the Vinaya.[2] In an inscription of Mahinda IV (*circa* A.D. 947) mention is made of a chapter—the *Sikha-karaṇī*—of the *Sikha-vaḷañda*, a fact which proves that the work was in existence prior to that date. On linguistic evidence the Sinhalese *Sikha-vaḷañda* is assigned to the earlier part of the tenth century. The author of the Pāli *Sikkhā-pada-valañjanī* tells us in his introductory verses that it was a translation of the Sinhalese original, but an examination of his work shows that it is an abridged compilation made from the two Sinhalese texts rather than a literal translation. The author gives no clue to his identity, but in copies of his work, made by latter-day scribes, is usually found the subscription : "The *Sikkhā-pada-valañjanī* of Pañca-mūla-pariveṇādhipati Mahā Thera."

About this time was composed the Pāli *Thūpa-vaṃsa*. It resembles the *Mahābodhi-vaṃsa* rather closely and follows the conventional form of the Pāli epic tradition in beginning with the history of the earlier Buddhas, passing on to that of Gotama, the story of the missions, the collecting of the relics, the arrival of the Bodhi-tree, and then on to its special subject, the erection of Thūpas in the island. The last eight chapters (there are sixteen in all) are devoted to a description of the

[1] *Sikha-vaḷañda*, Ed. Jayatilaka, Colombo, Preface, 1923.
[2] Ibid., p. 116.

activities of king Duṭṭhagāmaṇi, and of these two whole chapters deal with the erection of the Mahā-Thūpa at Anurādha-pura. In the colophon to the work[1] the author calls himself Vācissara, and says that he was a relation of king Parākrama, employed by him to supervise the Dhammāgāra. He professes to have been well-versed in the *Tipiṭaka* (*Piṭaka-ttaya-pāragu*), and mentions that he was the author of several other works which he had written in Sinhalese: A *Līnattha-dīpanī ṭīkā* on the *Paṭisambhidā-magga*, two glossaries, one called *Attha-dīpanā* on the *Sacca-saṅkhepa*, and the other *Attha-ppakāsanā*, on the *Visuddhi-magga*. It is now generally agreed that this Vācissara is identical with the younger Vācissara, referred to earlier in this chapter, pupil of Sāriputta.[2] He was one of the heads of the Church under Vijaya-Bāhu III, and there is nothing improbable in that he should still have been working under his successor. The *Rāja-ratnākara*[3] enumerates a list of learned monks and laymen who flourished between Buddhaghosa and the year 1809, after the Buddha (A.D. 1266). It mentions a Vāhīsvara third from the end, who, evidently, is our author.

In the introductory verses to his work Vācissara acknowledges obligation to two older compilations of the history of the Thūpas. One was written in Sinhalese, and, therefore, was of use only to the inhabitants of Ceylon; and the other, though in Pāli, showed many defects which made a revision very necessary. The old Pāli work referred to is perhaps the *Cetiya-vaṃsa-Atthakathā* mentioned in the *Mahā-vaṃsa ṭīkā*.[4] The author has also borrowed extensively from the usual sources: the *Jātaka-Nidāna-kathā*, the *Samanta-pāsādikā*, the *Mahā-vaṃsa*, and the *M.V. ṭīkā*. The language of the poem is the Sanskritized Pāli of this period.

A Sinhalese version of the *Thūpa-vaṃsa* also exists, written

[1] Ed. Dhammaratana, Colombo, 1896.

[2] Wickremasinghe, p. xvi, Geiger, *Dīp.* and *M.V.*, p. 84, and Pref. Colombo Ed.

[3] p. 46, Colombo Ed.

[4] Geiger, op. cit., p. 49.

by a " Sakala Vidyā Cakravarti ", Parākrama Paṇḍita. Some maintain that this was the Sinhalese original to which Vācissara refers in his introductory verses,[1] and that its author was a nephew of Parākrama-Bāhu the Great, who later came to the throne as Vijaya-Bāhu, and whom the *Mahā-vaṃsa* (chap. 80, v. 1) describes as a great scholar and a poet of much renown. Mr. Wickremasinghe has shown this statement to be inaccurate.[2] Besides the language of the Sinhalese version, which is certainly later than the twelfth century, and therefore would not agree with the date of Parākrama-Bāhu's nephew, there are other objections. Parākrama Paṇḍita evidently wrote his Sinhalese version very soon after Vācissara wrote in Pāli. In the *Rāja-ratnākara* list mentioned above his name appears last among the learned laymen, showing that he lived before A.D. 1266.[3]

The Sinhalese version is not a translation of the Pāli; it is, on the whole, broader and contains more details than the Pāli,[4] showing that it was a later expansion of the Pāli text.[5]

Another historical treatise belonging to the same period is the *Hattha-vanagalla-vihāra-vaṃsa*. It is a history of the Vihāra erected at Attanagalla on the spot where the ex-king, the pious Siri Saṅghabodhi, decapitated himself, lest others should be compelled to suffer on his account. The story of Siri Saṅghabodhi has already been related in brief in an earlier chapter. Attanagalla is a village situated a few miles away from Colombo. The remains of the temple and some of the other religious edifices erected by Goṭhābhaya, in repentance for the death of the good Saṅghabodhi, are still to be seen on a hill at the confluence of two rivulets amidst some of the most beautiful scenery that could be imagined. The work itself is divided into eleven chapters, mostly in verse, but interspersed with prose narrative. Eight of them are devoted to

[1] e.g. Dhammaratana, Colombo Ed., 1889.

[2] *Catalogue*, p. 141.

[3] Also *Nikāya-saṅgraha*, p. 24.

[4] e.g. the history of the Pāramitā, which is not found at all in the Pāli.

[5] For a fuller description see Wickremasinghe, pp. 139 foll.

a history of Saṅghabodhi, the remaining three dealing with accounts of the erection of the various monumental and religious edifices on the spot where the king had died, and the endowments made for their maintenance by successive rulers of Ceylon. It resembles more or less a historical novel into which the author has interwoven much material of varying interest—graphic descriptions of forest scenes, nearly a whole chapter (chapter 2) on the art of good government, a comprehensive moral code and a great deal of matter of historical importance. It is written in elegant, but simple Pāli, and is one of the first works in Pāli to which a student is introduced in Ceylon monasteries with a view to familiarizing him with Pāli grammatical forms and constructions. It is generally assigned to a pupil of Anomadassi Saṅgharāja, who lived in the reign of Paṇḍita Parākrama Bāhu. The author states in his introductory verses (stanza 3) that it was written at the request of his teacher Anomadassi, who was the author of a Sinhalese work on astrology, the *Daivajña-kāma-dhenu.*[1] The events which the history records are brought down to this period, and the writer concludes his work abruptly by expressing the hope that "the annals of Attanagalla may thenceforward be continued by later historians". The Anomadassi mentioned here is identified with the Elder for whom, according to the *Mahā-vaṃsa,*[2] the minister Patirājadeva, following the king's orders, built a temple of three stories and a lofty pinnacle, during the latter part of Parākrama's reign. A Sinhalese paraphrase was written by an anonymous author during the reign of Bhuvaneka-Bāhu V (*c.* 1378–98) by a pupil of Maitrī Mahāsāmi.[3] In the eleventh century Ñānaratana, abbot of the Attanagalla Vihāra, wrote a Sinhalese poem[4] based on this work. In 1866 that indefatigable scholar, James D'Alwis, published in Colombo an English translation of the original Pāli, prefaced with a very valuable Introductory Essay.

[1] D'Alwis, *Attanagalu-vaṃsa*, p. 7, note 6.
[2] *M.V.*, lxxxvi, vv. 37–9.
[3] De Zoysa, p. 17.
[4] Wickremasinghe, p. xxii.

CHAPTER XI

The Age of Paṇḍita Parākrama

VANARATANA ĀNANDA, of the Araññavāsī sect mentioned in the last chapter and pupil of Dimbulāgala Medhaṅkara, left behind him several disciples who were scholars of note and authors of important compilations. One of them, Gotama Thera, wrote a Sinhalese translation of Saṅgharakkhita's Pāli grammar, the *Sambandha-cintā*, on syntax. Two others are much better known as distinguished writers—Coḷiya Dīpaṅkara and Vedeha Thera. The first, Coḷiya Dīpaṅkara, more commonly called Buddhappiya, was, as his name implies, a native of the Coḷa country in south India. He probably formed a member of the community of monks whom Paṇḍita Parākrama-Bāhu persuaded to come over from the Coḷa country to re-establish the Sāsana firmly in Ceylon.[1] Buddhappiya was the author of two books—*Rūpa-siddhi* and the *Pajja-madhu*. In the *Rūpa-siddhi* colophon[2] he describes himself as follows: "This perfect *Rūpa-siddhi* was composed by that monk who received the title of Buddhappiya and was named Dīpaṅkara—a disciple of Ānanda, the eminent preceptor who was like unto a standard in Tambapaṇṇi—he (Dīpaṅkara) was renowned like a lamp in the Damiḷa country, and, being the resident Superior there of two monasteries including Bālādicca,[3] caused the Religion to shine forth." At the conclusion of the *Pajja-madhu*[4] he gives his name and pupilage: "May they drink deeply of these nectar-like verses (*Pajja-madhu*)—made by the bee Buddhappiya, delighted with the Buddha's virtues—who constantly attends upon that lotus, the Venerable Elder

[1] *M.V.*, lxxxiv, v. 10.

[2] Colombo Ed., end.

[3] The commentary says that the other monastery was called Cūḍāmāṇikya.

[4] *JPTS.*, 1887, p. 16, v. 103.

Ānanda Vanaratana (Jewel of the Forest), heavy-laden with the perfume of his virtues and always in bloom."

Both works were evidently written while the author was residing in the Coḷa country, where, at this period, Buddhism was flourishing and where Buddhappiya, as we learn from the *Rūpa-siddhi* verse, held the incumbency of two monasteries and had achieved eminent renown for his abilities.

The *Rūpa-siddhi* is a Pāli grammar on the model of the Kaccāyana. Its proper designation, as the author tells us in the opening stanzas, is *Pada-rūpa-siddhi—Etymology of the Parts of Speech.* Although it follows the *Kaccāyana Sandhi-kappa* in his general outlines, the *Rūpa-siddhi* is a much fuller and more exhaustive work, supplying many deficiencies in the *Kaccāyana*; and even the division of sections differs in some degree from that adopted in the older grammar, as will be seen from the following list of contents. It is divided into seven chapters: *Sandhi* (five classes *saññā, sara, pakati, vyañjana, niggahīta*), declension (masculine, feminine, neuter, pronominals, and numerals, personal pronouns having no gender, indeclinables, and inseparable particles), *kāraka* (syntax), *samāsa, taddhita* (nominal derivatives), *ākhyāta* (verbs), and *kitaka-uṇādi* (verbal derivatives and particles). The book and its divisions were subjected to very strong criticism by Medhaṅkara in his *Payoga-siddhi*, written a little while after, and because of its great length and the abstruse nature of its treatment was later superseded by Dhammakitti's *Bālāvatāra*, written in the fourteenth century. It is, however, much studied in Ceylon even at the present day, and retains its former prestige to some extent. The Burmese grammarian, Māha Yasa, in his *Kaccāyana-sāra*, written about the fourteenth century,[1] quotes with approval many extracts, from the *Rūpa-siddhi*. A *ṭīkā* on it is usually assigned to Buddhappiya himself,[2] and an old Sinhalese paraphrase exists, written by an anonymous author, but

[1] Bode, p. 37.
[2] *G.V.*, pp. 60 and 70.

evidently compiled soon after the *Rūpa-siddhi* itself, because it is quoted in Rāhula's *Pañjikā-pradīpa* (A.D. 1457).

Buddhappiya's other work, the *Pajja-madhu*, is a beautiful Pāli poem of Sanskritized Pāli, couched in ornate language; it contains 104 stanzas. The first sixty-nine verses describe the beauties of the Buddha's person, dwelling on each detail, from the nails of his toes to the *ketu-mālā*, or garland of rays over his head. Every feature is extolled with a wealth of poetical imagery: thus, the single curled hair between the Buddha's eyebrows is like the moon in its circuit from which fall drops of ambrosia upon the lotus-blossoms of his toes, the nails of which are their petals. The rest of the poem is taken up with praising the "unfathomable wisdom" of the Buddha, a panegyric upon his disciples the Saṅgha, and several verses describing the glories of Nibbāna. There is a Sinhalese paraphrase by an anonymous writer, which is of very little use, being more intricate in its explanations than the original Pāli.

The *Gandha-vaṃsa* [1] ascribes to Buddhappiya another book called the *Sārattha-saṅgaha*. Mr. Wickremasinghe [2] calls it "a religious work", but I do not know of any copies existing in Ceylon.

A *Sārattha-saṅgaha* is included in the list of books in the Pagān Inscription [3] (A.D. 1442). Mrs. Bode thinks it refers to Buddhadāsa's medical work of the same name written in the fourth century.

There is a Sinhalese work on Buddhism, the *Sārārtha-saṅgraha*,[4] but the author makes no mention of its being a translation from the Pāli original. There are extensive quotations from various Pāli works, and the nature of its contents suggests that it was an original work by Saraṇaṅkara.

Ānanda's other pupil was Vedeha, of the Araññavāsi fraternity, author of two Pāli works, the *Rasa-vāhinī* and the

[1] pp. 60 and 70.
[2] *Catalogue*, p. xviii.
[3] Govt. Printing Press, Rangoon, 1899, and Bode, p. 109.
[4] q.v.

Samanta-kūṭa-vaṇṇanā, the first in prose and the second in verse. He is also generally credited with having written the most authoritative Sinhalese grammar extant—the *Sidat-saṅgarā*.[1] Vedeha gives us some account of himself in the Colophon to the *Rasa-vāhinī*, where he says: "The *Rasa-vāhinī* was composed by Vedeha Thera, author of the beautiful *Samanta-kūṭa-vaṇṇanā*, and the Sinhalese Grammar, who, born of the Brāhmaṇa caste, was a banner to the three divisions of Ceylon. His tutor was the Venerable Ānanda of the Forest Hermitage, leader of a large Chapter of monks, and one who has crossed over the Ocean of Knowledge. His preceptor was the Great Elder Maṅgala, skilled in all learning, chief supervisor of boundaries (*Sīmā*) and the Great Kaliṅga Thera." In the *Samanta-kūṭa-vaṇṇanā* Colophon he mentions only the *Sīhala-sadda-lakkhaṇa* as his work, so that the order in which his books were written was: first, the *Sīhala-sadda-lakkhaṇa* (said to be the same as the *Sidat-saṅgarā*), second the *Samanta-kūṭa-vaṇṇanā*, and lastly the *Rasa-vāhinī*. In the *Sidat-saṅgarā*—which was composed at the request of the minister Pratirājadeva Paṇḍita, identified with the minister of that name dispatched by Parākarama-Bāhu to South Ceylon to repair dilapidated religious edifices[2]—the author describes himself as head of the Pratirāja-pariveṇa in south Ceylon.[3]

Of Vedeha's works the *Samanta-kūṭa-vaṇṇanā* is a Pāli poem of about 800 verses, written at the request of a monk named Rāhula, belonging to the same Vanavāsi fraternity as the author himself. As the name implies, the poem purports to be a description of the beautiful peak on which the Buddha is said to have imprinted the mark of his left foot on his third visit to Ceylon. The story is related in the first chapter of the *Mahā-vaṃsa*. But the account of this particular event occupies

[1] D'Alwis, *Sidat-saṅgarā* preface, and *Catalogue*, p. 22. De Zoysa, p. 28, Wickremasinghe, p. 92.

[2] D'Alwis, *Catalogue*, p. 225.

[3] *Sidat-saṅgarā*, p. 43.

only a few verses of the book. The rest of it contains the life of the Buddha from the time of his birth in the Tusita deva-world, prior to his being born in the world of men, and continues down to his third visit to Ceylon after having attained Enlightenment. Vedeha has described in great detail many incidents of the Buddha's life, and in the course of the narrative of the Master's journeyings to Laṅkā the poet makes use of the opportunity to describe in language at once graceful and elegant, and replete with chaste and beautiful imagery, many parts of the island, little known or explored at that time—its hills and dales, mountains and rivers, especially the Kelaṇi and the Mahāväligaṅga, the exquisite splendour of their scenery, the beauty of the landscape and the matchless variety of its forests, with their delicately tinted foliage of luxuriant verdure, apt abode for woodland nymphs paying homage to the Holy Shrine. His vivid pen pictures of cities and their inhabitants, show that Vedeha was deeply imbued with the lore of Sanskrit writers, but there is no trace of slavish imitation. On the contrary, the *Samanta-kūṭa-vaṇṇanā* is undoubtedly the work of a poet, rich in his gifts and inspired with love and reverence for the subject of his poem. The opening verses of adoration, enchantingly sweet in their beautiful cadences, are sung even to-day, by many thousands who have never heard his name and know nothing of his work. A Sinhalese paraphrase of the Pāli poem has been published,[1] in 1890, by two Buddhist monks, Dhammānanda and Ñāṇissara, two of the greatest Oriental scholars of their day.

The *Rasa-vāhinī* is a collection of stories in easy Pāli prose, embodying legends historical and otherwise. In the opening stanza the author tells us that his work is a revision of an old Pāli translation, made from an original compilation, by Raṭṭhapāla Thera of the *Taṅgutta-Vaṅka Pariveṇa* of the Mahāvihāra. We do not know anything more about Raṭṭhapāla, except that he is supposed to have made his

[1] Printed at the Government Press, Colombo, 1890.

translation from a number of legends then extant in the "language of the land" and said to have been related by Arahats. Vedeha found Raṭṭhapāla's translation confused in its constructions and corrupted by repetitions, and he therefore revised it and put it into a new form, naming it the *Rasa-vāhinī*. Perhaps Raṭṭhapāla's translation was drawn from the ancient *Sahassa-vatthu-atthakathā* (*Commentary of the Thousand Stories*), quoted four times in *Mahā-vaṃsa-ṭīkā*, which Geiger considers to be a collection of legends and folk-tales.[1] It contained among others tales of the former lives of the heroes who fought under king Duṭṭhagāmaṇi, and also the romantic tale of the love of prince Sāli, Duṭṭhagāmaṇi's son, for the Caṇḍāla maiden.

Raṭṭhapāla evidently selected a number of sacred legends which had acquired sanctity from the belief that they had been handed down by Arahats. He naturally would not tamper with them and prune them into an elegant work, because each story had its own self-centred and venerated existence either at his time or before. The legends were never made to form a series, but each grew up of itself. Sometimes certain widespread myths, such as the inexhaustible rice-pot and the wishing gem, had clusters of stories which had grown round them as local legends, and they were written down consecutively, containing clumsy repetitions. Vedeha, who was of a poetic temperament, and, therefore, loved beauty of diction, was not satisfied with such an inartistic presentation of these homely stories, and he proceeded to clothe them in a new garb. The result is the *Rasa-vāhinī*, exquisite in its simplicity, charming in its naïveté, and delightful in its innocence. It is worth noticing that a large number of the stories are grouped round the days of Vaḷagam-abā, in whose reign the *Tipiṭaka* and their commentaries were committed to writing in Ceylon. Were they accretions to an old nucleus, or do they show that the original collection was made soon after that date ?

[1] *Dīp.* and *M.V.*, p. 48.

The stories are 103 in number, the first forty relating to incidents which happened in Jambu-dvīpa and the rest in Ceylon. They illustrate the benefits that accrue to those who do good deeds, chiefly by making offerings to the Saṅgha. They are useful to us now, in that they throw new and interesting light on the manners, customs and social conditions of ancient India and Ceylon. Perhaps some of them contain materials of historical importance hidden in their half-mythical tales.

The book is very widely used as an elementary Pāli reader in temple-schools even to this day. The free and easy flow of language makes it pleasant reading, while the wealth of its descriptions furnishes the student with a copious vocabulary.

In the fourteenth century a monk named Dhammakitti, belonging to the Gaḍalādeṇi Vihāra, made a compilation in Sinhalese of Indian and Ceylon Buddhist legends. His work is called the *Saddharmālaṅkāra*, and the last twenty-one of its twenty-four chapters contain all the stories of the *Rasa-vāhinī*. To them are subjoined two other stories, one of which, the *Metteyya-vastu*, is evidently derived from the *Cariyā-piṭaka*; the source of the other, *Padmāvatī-vastu*, is not known. The greater part of the book is undoubtedly a translation of the *Rasa-vāhinī*, though Dhammakitti does not say so. In the colophon, however, he takes his pupillage back to the Chief Elder of the Araññavāsī sect, showing that he belonged to the same fraternity as Vedeha.[1] In Burma the work is known as *Madhura-Rasa-vāhinī*, perhaps by a misconception of the words in one of the opening stanzas: *vakkhām' ahaṃ sumadhuraṃ rasavāhinintam.* Sometimes the section dealing with Ceylon stories is copied separately and called the *Sīhala-dīpa-vatthu*. The *Rasa-vāhinī*, however, forms only one part of a much larger collection, called the *Sahassa-vatthu-ppakaraṇa*,[2] which seems to have been lost in Ceylon.

[1] For a fuller description see Wickremasinghe, *Catl.*, pp. 126 foll.
[2] British Museum Or., 4674. See also Bode, p. 105.

There is a tradition in Ceylon that a pupil of Ānanda Vanaratana also wrote a commentary on four Bhānavāras of the *Tipiṭaka* in Sinhalese at the request of another monk named Anomadassi.[1]

To about this time, or perhaps to a slightly earlier period, I would also assign the *Kesa-dhātu-vaṃsa*, by an anonymous author. Dhammakitti, who, in the reign of Paṇḍita Parākrama, wrote a continuation of the *Mahā-vaṃsa*, mentions it by name. It relates the story of the Buddha's hair relic (*kesa-dhātu*), which was brought to Ceylon in the reign of Moggallāna I (A.D. 497–515) by a novice named Amba Sāmaṇera. He was a man of the Lambakaṇṇa race, Silākāla by name, and had fled to India with Moggallāna through fear of the patricide Kassapa. There he became a recluse at the Bodhimaṇḍa Vihāra, and because of his having served a mango to the Elders he was given the nickname of Amba Sāmaṇera (Mango-novice). When Moggallāna ascended the throne a few years later, Silākāla, now no longer a monk, returned to Ceylon with the *Kesa-dhātu*. Moggallāna received it with great honour, and kept it in the Dīpaṅkara Image-house, in a special casket, beside the statues of the two chief disciples of the Buddha. Silākāla was appointed guardian of the relic, and made sword-bearer—hence his name Asiggaha Silākāla (Silākāla the Sword-Bearer). Later he married the king's sister. Such is the account given in the 39th chapter of the *Mahā-vaṃsa*. Of the later history of the Relic, we know nothing at all. The *Kesa-dhātu-vaṃsa* itself is extremely rare, and I have heard of only one copy in Ceylon. De Zoysa does not mention it in his *Catalogue*, and Mr. Wickremasinghe makes but a passing reference to it.[2]

Paṇḍita Parākrama's eldest son and successor, Vijaya-Bāhu, who was entrusted with the supervision of the state during the very lifetime of the king, was an enlightened prince, extremely

[1] Medhānanda, *Jina-vaṃsa-dīpanī*, 1917, p. 17. A *bhānavāra* is equal to 250 verses of thirty-two syllables each.

[2] p. xviii.

devoted to the cultivation of the arts. He was a man of great religious fervour, and was called Bodhisatta (Buddha-Aspirant) by the people. The *Mahā-vaṃsa*[1] gives glowing descriptions of the measures he adopted to beautify the capital city of Polonnaruva, and we see there evidence of an ascetic mind belonging to a wise statesman, a just ruler and a man of broad views. We are told that he made the city of Pulatthi "like unto the city of Indra, so that by the magnificence thereof it surpassed Mithilā, discomfited Kāñcī, laughed at Sāvatthī, vanquished Madhurā, despoiled Bārānasī, robbed even Vesālī, and made the city of Campā tremble". It was this that perhaps gave Vedeha his material for the picturesque description of cities in the *Samanta-kūṭa-vaṇṇanā*. He encouraged learning among the monks by conferring dignities and offices on such of them as brought glory to the Order. They were given titles of Mahā-sāmi-pāda, Mūla-pāda, Mahā-Thera-pāda, Pariveṇa-Thera-pāda, etc. He held a great ceremony of Ordination at Sahassatittha, the Mahāväli-gaṅga, lasting for a fortnight, to which monks came from every monastery, leaving none behind them, "not even a monk in charge of the stores."[2] He sent gifts to the monks of Coḷa and Paṇḍu as well. The influence of an enlightened ruler is bound to be reflected in the life of his subjects, and the large number of literary works, mostly in Sinhalese, written during this period, are an index to the prosperity and the contentment which he, acting under his great father, achieved.

His brother, Bhuvaneka-Bāhu, who succeeded him (A.D. 1277–88), was no less a patron of learning. He "caused all the Three *Piṭakas* to be written by learned scribes of the Scriptures, rewarded them liberally and placed copies in the diverse Vihāras of Laṅkā, and thus spread the Pāli scriptures throughout the land".[3] During his reign Siddhattha

[1] *M.V.*, lxxxix.
[2] Ibid, vv. 47–59.
[3] *M.V.*, 90, vv. 37–8.

Thera compiled the *Sārattha-saṅgaha.* The author describes himself as a member of the Vanavāsī fraternity, and pupil of Buddhappiya, author of *Rūpa-siddhi,* "famed throughout Coḷī and Laṅkā for his vast learning and great piety." He also has a panegyric on Bhuvaneka-Bāhu, whose patronage he seems to have enjoyed.[1]

The work is divided into forty sections, written partly in prose and partly in verse. The first chapter deals with the Buddhābhinihāra, the preliminaries necessary for aspiring to Buddhahood, and several verses are quoted from the *Sutta-nipāta* commentary; it then passes on to the wonderful features of the Buddha's life, quoting extensively from the commentaries accounts of such Suttas as the *Mahā-Sīhanāda,* and the *Culla-Hatthi-padopama.* This is followed by a description of the gradual disappearance of the Buddha's teaching, the appearance of cakkavatti kings, the enshrinement of the relics of Holy Men, the protection of such shrines, illustrated with stories of men who reached salvation thereby, a discourse on the threefold *Sāsana* (*Pariyatti, Paṭipatti,* and *Paṭivedha*), and a condemnation of heresies and of heretics who entered the order in Asoka's reign attracted by gain. Many stories are given of the virtues of piety and devotedness of heart and self-denial, especially in the matter of giving alms.

One instance is given of a man who sold firewood and prepared alms for some novices (Sāmaṇeras), which they refused to accept because it was not well prepared. He then pawned his daughter, bought a cow, and prepared alms with milk. Later he worked at a sugar mill to get money for his daughter's release, but, as he was coming home with it, he met Piṇḍapātika Tissa *Thera,* whom he found starving for want of food. Paying an exorbitant price to the only man who had food in the place, he gave it to the *Thera* who thereby became an Arahat. To this is added a chapter on dreams—

[1] Preface to printed edition of the first eight chapters: Colombo, 1891, ed. Dhammaratana.

Siddhattha's dream on the day of Enlightenment, the dream of king Kosala, etc., the efficacy of the Refuges, the various kinds of Sīla, methods of meditation, foods suitable for various classes of beings, the reproduction of living things, including a story of how two eggs laid by Ambapāla Gaṇikā gave birth to two Theras. The author says that this is contained in the *Apadāna*, but no such story is found there. The book also has a very ungallant chapter on the nature of woman, and the concluding chapter deals with cosmology.

As will be seen from the above brief list of its contents, it is a curious medley of matter of diverse interest, jumbled together anyhow, with no attempt at arrangement. I am inclined to believe that the book, as we have it now, has been greatly tampered with by later editors, and many spurious additions have been made to it. Else it would be difficult to account for its admixture of religion and demonology and medicine. Copies of it are rare, and though an attempt was made in 1891 to have the book printed, only a few chapters have so far been published.

The Rev. Medhānanda in his recent work the *Jina-vaṃsa-dīpanī* says that it was this same Siddhattha who wrote a *Mahā-nipāta-vaṇṇanā*, the *Dampiyā-sanne*, and the *Rasavāhinī-ṭīkā*.[1]

Another author of the same period was Vanaratana Medhaṅkara (the third of that name famous in the Buddhist Church of Ceylon), who wrote the *Jina-carita* and the *Payoga-siddhi*. In the colophon to the latter work he tells us that he was the pupil of Sumaṅgala Mahā Thera of the Jambuddoṇi Vihāra and was Niyāmaka or director there. The *Jina-carita*, however, is said to have been written at the Vijaya-Bāhu Pariveṇa, built by Vijaya-Bāhu, of which the author was incumbent at the time.[2] This probably refers to the Vihāra built at Yattālagāma by Vijaya-Bāhu III, who ruled at Dambadeṇiya.[3] The *Jina-carita* is a short Pāli poem of

[1] Medhānanda, *Jina-vaṃsa-dīpanī* (Colombo, 1917), Preface, p. 19.
[2] *JPTS.*, 1904, p. 31.
[3] *M.V.*, lxxxi, v. 58.

472 stanzas dealing with the life of the Buddha. The first hundred verses describe briefly his birth as Sumedha in the time of the Buddha Dīpaṅkara, and tells us how in one birth after another he strove to fulfil the Ten Pāramitā necessary for Buddhahood. The greater part of the work deals with the Renunciation and with the visit paid by Gotama to his relations after he had attained Enlightenment. The author gives vivid descriptions of Suddhodana's city, and the Twin Miracle which the Buddha performed at the foot of the Gaṇḍabba Tree to convince his relations and win their confidence. He then proceeds to paint little cameos about the various spots where the Buddha lived during his long ministry of service to his fellow-men.

The poem concludes with the author's aspirations to become a Buddha himself, "Giving my flesh, blood, and eyes with calm mind, fulfilling all the Pāramitā (Perfections) and Virtues, all self-abnegation and wisdom, attaining to the highest pinnacle of Perfection, may I become Buddha incomparable; having preached the sweet doctrine which brings happiness to men, and having freed all the world of men and devas from the fetters of Saṃsāra, may I reach the noble city of Peace and Joy."

There is an old Sinhalese paraphrase to the *Jina-carita*, which is usually ascribed to Medhaṅkara himself. Towards the end of last century the Rev. Dhammānanda, Principal of the Paramadhammacetiya Pariveṇa at Ratmalāna, published a new paraphrase written by himself. An English translation of it has been published in the *Pāli Text Society Journal* (1904–7) by Dr. W. H. D. Rouse, of Perse School, Cambridge.

Medhaṅkara's other work, the *Payoga-siddhi*, is a grammar written on the lines of the Moggallāna school. It bears the same relation to *Moggāllana-vyākaraṇa* as the *Rūpa-siddhi* does to the *Kaccāyana*. The author follows Moggallāna closely, while supplying the deficiencies of that work which are criticized by Buddhappiya in his *Rūpa-siddhi*. The scope of the *Moggallāna* is thereby greatly increased, and Medhaṅkara makes some caustic remarks on Buddhappiya's criticisms. "Many of his rules are mere figments of imagination," he says in one place.

The *Payoga-siddhi* is not now much used in Ceylon. It does not seem to have found its way to Burma at all, for no mention is made of it in any history of Burmese literature. The *Gandha-vaṃsa* and the *Sāsana-vaṃsa* are both silent about it. A Sinhalese paraphrase exists by a later anonymous writer, but neither paraphrase nor original has found much favour.

A few years later, in 1295, Parākrama-Bāhu IV ascended the throne at Kurunegala. He was a wise and mighty prince, and after he had obtained a semblance of peace in the kingdom (for the Malabar peril was ever present like Damocles' sword) he assembled the monks together and caused the ceremony of ordination to be performed many times.[1] He was imbued with a great love for learning, and the books written during his reign are profuse in their admiration for his accomplishments, which were varied and numerous. He was specially devoted in his attentions to the tooth relic, and made to it many offerings and held many feasts in its honour. In order that similar ceremonies may be performed daily, we are told that he, of his own free will, wrote a book in Sinhalese called *Daḷadā-sirita* (the Ceremonial of the tooth relic), according to the tenets of which the rites were to be held daily.[2]

The *Mahā-vaṃsa* (90, vv. 80–4) also tells us that he appointed as his teacher a certain Great Elder from the Coḷa country, a self-denying man, conversant with many languages and skilled in the science of logic and in religion. The king read all the *Jātakas* with him, and constantly heard them expounded, learnt them all, and kept in mind their meaning also. Thereafter he translated in due order the entire collection, 551 in number, from Pāli into Sinhalese. He caused them to be read in an assembly of Elders who were well versed in the

[1] *M.V.*, xc, vv. 64–5.

[2] Ibid, vv. 76–8. But see Wickremasinghe, p. xvii, *re* authorship of *Daḷadā-sirita.* I believe that here we have to do with two different works, one of which evidently has been lost in later years.

Tipiṭaka, and having purified his translations of their faults, he caused them to be transcribed and spread them throughout the whole of Laṅkā. Later he visited an Elder of great eminence called Medhaṅkara, and gave these *Jātakas* into his charge, so that they might be preserved in the line of succession of his pupils.

This Medhaṅkara probably refers to the author of the *Jina-carita* noticed above.

According to the *Mahā-vaṃsa* account the translation of the *Jātakatthakathā* was done by King Parākrama himself. The introduction to the existing Sinhalese version is silent as to its authorship. It merely states that the work was accomplished by the exertions of the minister Vīrasiṃha Pratirāja. The translation does not always follow the Pāli text : sometimes whole sentences being left out, which may perhaps be due to the carelessness of later-day scribes. Sometimes attempts have been made to add embellishments to the Pāli version.[1]

The late Ven. H. Siri Sumangala, Nāyaka Thera, stated in the course of an article to the *Journal of the Ceylon Branch of the Royal Asiatic Society* (vol. viii, No. 28), that " provincialisms are to be detected in the *Jātakas*. Some of them are written in indifferent Sinhalese, some contain a few Tamil expressions and words." From these facts he concluded that the Sinhalese version must have been made by several persons. The language of the translations is certainly not worthy of the king, if the *Mahā-vaṃsa* account of his having been the author of the *Daḷadā-sirita* is correct. It is interspersed with many Sanskrit and Pāli words, and is decidedly colloquial in style. On the other hand, could the colloquialisms have been due to a deliberate desire to make the translation comprehensible to the ordinary layman ? The *Jātakas* formed his chief spiritual sustenance, as they do to this day,

[1] See also Wickremasinghe, p. 119. D'Alwis, *Sidat-saṅgarā*, Introd., p. xxx.

and it was necessary that he should understand as clearly as possible the lessons they inculcated.

From this period a distinct tendency is to be observed among the authors of books towards using Sinhalese as their medium of expression in preference to any other language then used for literary purposes in Ceylon. This was due to several reasons; greater attention than ever before was being paid to subjects of secular interest. Pāli was pre-eminently the language of sacred literature or, at least, of literature having some definite connexion with the religion—the history of religious movements, the chronicles of the doings of the Order, the measures adopted by various sovereigns and distinguished members of the community, for the maintenance of the national faith.

It is true that Sanskrit was there, available for use where Pāli would not suffice; but Sanskrit never became the favourite language in Ceylon at any time to the extent that Pāli did. Perhaps there was a prejudice against it from very early ages because of its having been the language of the Ṭīrthakas (unbelievers) and of the Vaitulya-vādins, who sought through their writings to interpret the doctrines of Buddhism in a manner contrary to the traditions of the Theravāda monks. Besides, Sanskrit was *par excellence* a literary dialect, not to be easily understood, nor to be used with any degree of proficiency except by the very learned. Any work written in it would find circulation only within a narrow circle, for not even all the monks knew Sanskrit, while they were all acquainted with Pāli, and there was not much chance of its gaining currency in the neighbouring continent, unless it should prove to be of remarkable merit, such as was Kumāradāsa's *Jānakī-haraṇa.*

There is no doubt that Vedeha's comprehensive Sinhalese grammar, the *Sidat-saṅgarā*, gave great impetus to the attention paid to Sinhalese studies. There he had made an attempt to keep Sinhalese as a special language apart from Pāli and Sanskrit, though it contained many words derived from them. In such grammatical factors as gender, for instance, he showed how Sinhalese differed from its ancestors. But it was too late to stem the tide. The influence of other languages, especially of Sanskrit, had already proceeded apace.

We saw how the sweet, soft rhythm of old Pāli gradually gave place to a more sonorous, vigorous Sanskritized Pāli; it was the same with Sinhalese. The language was enriched first on the side of its religious vocabulary by words derived from Pāli, while words and phrases and turns of expression now began to be borrowed bodily from Sanskrit. The contiguity of Tamil, too, for several centuries has had its effect. Sinhalese thus once more came back to its own, though it was a language in many ways different from that used prior to the eleventh century. Hitherto Ceylon authors had written their most important works in Pāli; henceforward Sinhalese comes to assume that position; most of the important compositions are in the "language of the land"[1]; no attempts are made now (such as the authors of the *Mahā-vaṃsa* and the *Dāṭhā-vaṃsa* made) to supersede it by any other medium of expression; occasionally an author is found using Pāli, ambitious perhaps to reach a wider audience than that confined to Ceylon, or because the very nature of his treatise was such that Pāli seemed its pre-eminently fitting garb.

From the fourteenth century onwards until the nineteenth the island never enjoyed perfect peace for any length of time; the Malabar hordes were ever waiting to swoop down upon it, and later came enemies from countries further away. Rival claimants to the throne were constantly at war with each other, and it was only on rare occasions that a sovereign was found sufficiently strong and powerful to hold them in check.

[1] For information about them reference should be made to such works as D'Alwis' *Sidat-saṅgarā*, Introduction; Wickremasinghe's *Catalogue of Sinhalese MSS. in the British Museum*, and De Zoysa's *Catalogue* among others. In the present treatise mention will be made of Sinhalese works only in so far as they are translations or commentaries of Pāli books or are in some way connected with them.

Alarmed by this want of security, the influx of scholars from other lands gradually diminished and finally ceased, or perhaps they felt they had now obtained all the learning that Ceylon could give them. This diminution in the traffic of learning also may have been in some measure responsible for the adoption of Sinhalese in preference to Pāli, and it is worth noticing that very few of the books written in Ceylon after the fourteenth century have gained currency in other lands. The golden age of Pāli literature in Ceylon had ended perhaps never more to come back.

Several authors of eminence flourished during the time of Parākrama-Bāhu IV, chief among whom was Śri Parākrama-Bāhu, Mahā Thera of the Vilgammūla fraternity, chief incumbent of the Kitsirimevan Kälaṇi Temple. He made a Sinhalese translation of the *Mahā-Bodhi-vaṃsa* in twelve chapters. It is an amplified version of the Pāli original, interspersed with numerous quotations from Pāli works, both canonical and otherwise, and from Sanskrit works such as Kālidāsa's *Raghu-vaṃsa*.[1] In the colophon the author tells us that the translation was made at the request of the king himself. He was a Sanskrit scholar as well, and made a Sinhalese paraphrase of Mayūra's *Sūrya-śataka*.[2] In the preface to the *Bodhi-vaṃsa* translation mention is made also of the following works in Sinhalese, composed during the same period: a translation of the *Dhamma-padatthakathā* and the *Pēta-vat* (*Peta-vatthu*), the *Viman-vat* (*Vimāna-vatthu*) and the *Buddha-vaṃsa*, which, judging from their titles, were either translations or compilations from the Pāli works of the same names.

Turnour[3] makes out that a portion of the *Mahā-vaṃsa* was written during the reign of this king, bringing the history down to his own times.

Mr. Wickremasinghe assigns also to this period a Pāli

[1] For a fuller description Wickremasinghe, pp. 22 and 23.
[2] Ibid.
[3] Epitome of the *History of Ceylon*, p. 47.

work called the *Dhātu-mañjūsā* (casket of radicals), or the *Kaccāyana Dhātu-mañjūsā*, as it is more often called, a compilation of verbal roots in Pāli and founded on the *Kaccāyana*. It is a kind of metrical vocabulary on the same lines as the *Abhidhāna-ppadīpikā*, but, unlike the latter, it contains only lists of verbal roots. The *Abhidhāna-ppadīpikā* did not contain any lists of verbs at all. The author of the *Mañjūsā* was a monk named Sīlavaṃsa. In the colophon he says: "The *Dhātu-mañjūsā*, rendered clear and easy by its alphabetical arrangement (*vaṇṇa-kkamā*, arranged according to letters), has been compiled for the edification of the uninitiated by the learned Sīlavaṃsa, a monk, who like a swan to the lotus of the Scriptures, resided in the Temple of Yakkhaddi Lena,[1] with aspirations that Buddhism may continue long." In the introductory stanzas he acknowledges his obligation to various Pāli grammars and lists of roots (*Dhātu-pāṭha*) which had been compiled earlier. No date of composition is given and as yet we have no clue which will enable us to determine the period with any definiteness. Sīlavaṃsa divided radicals into seven classes, each class typified by a single word (*bhū*, *rudha*, *diva*, *sū*, *ki*, *tanu*, and *cura*). The 148 stanzas contain over 400 radicals arranged in alphabetical order. Usually only one meaning is assigned to each root. Thus "*kuṭa* = *chedana* (cutting)" (under the *bhvādi*).

The late Don A. de S. Baṭuvantudāve Paṇḍita, of Colombo, one of the foremost of Orientalists in Ceylon in the last century, prepared and published a scholarly edition of the work with a Sinhalese and an English translation, giving an alphabetical list of the radicals, the class to which each belongs and the number of the stanza in which the particular radical occurs in the Pāli original.[2]

[1] Probably Yakdessāgala in Kurunegala District (Wickremasinghe, p. xviii).

[2] Colombo, 1872, pp. 1, 68.

CHAPTER XII

The Twilight Glow

FROM the end of the thirteenth century up to the extinction of the Sinhalese dynasty in the eighteenth Ceylon passed through one long period of unrest punctuated only by very short intervals of peace. During the whole of this time the island cannot be said to have been ever entirely freed from the presence of the Malabars. Even when temporarily subdued by some strong Sinhalese monarch, they continued to exercise their influence in divers ways, and by frequent intermarriages the royal line was almost as closely allied to the ruling princes of South India as it was to the blood of the Sinhalese kings of old. The effects of their ever-present influence are to be seen to-day in every department of life among the Sinhalese, in their language, their domestic and social observances, and in their very national religion, so much so that to this day the *Devālas* for Hindu worship are found either within the precincts of the Buddhist religious edifices (*vihāras*) themselves or in close contiguity with them. The Malabars now exercised undisputed dominion over the northern coasts on both sides of the island. The two ancient capitals, Anurādhapura and Polannaruva, with the rich fertile and well-watered plains surrounding them, fell into their hands; the country from Chilaw in the West to Batticaloa on the East owed allegiance to the foreigners, even adopting their language as the vernacular. In the thirteenth century, with the establishment of a Tamil colony in the sandy plains of Jaffnā-paṭṭanam at the northernmost extremity of the island, their power became firmly rooted, and it irresistibly extended itself. One after another, each capital city in the kingdom had to be abandoned to them, and the seat of government carried further and further south; from Anurādhapura it moved to Polonnaruva, thence to Dambadeṇiya in the thirteenth century; from there to Yāpahuva, Kurunegala, and Gampola, thence to the lofty plateau of the Hill country, with its little town of Senkaḍagala and to lovely Peradeṇiya on the banks of the Mahāvāligaṅga, and finally in the fifteenth century to Jayavardhana-pura, now known as Kōtte, 6 miles away from modern Colombo.

Occasionally the Sinhalese would make desperate attempts to regain their lost independence, with casual successes; but the odds were greatly against them; the Tamils could always rely for help on the bands of marauding allies from the neighbouring continent and the Sinhalese were unable to offer effectual resistance to their overwhelming numbers. Whilst the north of the island was thus almost entirely abandoned to the Tamils, the Sinhalese provinces were subdivided into several petty kingdoms, the chiefs of which often acknowledged nominal supremacy to someone who held sway over the capital city; but they were almost always involved in internecine struggles, because of their rivalry and jealousy and hostilities provoked by the withholding of tribute.[1]

Amidst such conditions of alarm and despondency, when the power of the people was being steadily destroyed and foreign influence was gaining the ascendancy at the Court, there was little to fire the enthusiasm of men of letters. They depended for their encouragement not so much on the meritorious praise of their reading public as on the patronage extended to them by their rulers, who themselves were scholars and lovers of literature. The monks, who because of their dissociation from worldly interests had so far been able to devote their attention to literary pursuits, had to depend for their maintenance on the generosity of the lay community; that support was not always forthcoming; the people were too much engrossed in the protection of their property and persons to have time for anything else. Literature thus fell into decay: the fraternities of monks were disorganized, yet it was they who amidst all adversity kept alive the torch of learning in Ceylon—all honour to them, therefore—and, whenever a patron of

[1] Tennent, *History of Ceylon*, vol. i, p. 416.

letters arose in the ranks of the princes or of their ministers, willing to extend to them a helping hand, they once more roused themselves to activity and produced works of merit, worthy of holding rank alongside with the productions of their predecessors.

One such prince was Bhuvanēka-Bāhu IV (*circa* A.D. 1347), "a man of great wisdom and faith and a mine of excellent virtues," who ruled at Gaṅgasiripura (now Gampola). He had an enlightened minister, Senālaṅkādhikāra Senerat, born of the Meheṇavara-vaṃsa (the descendants of those who had accompanied Saṅghamittā and the branch of the sacred Bodhi-tree). With the consent of the king, he armed himself with royal authority and, in order to purge the Order of the misconduct among its members, held a council of monks under the leadership of the Great Elder Vanaratana of Amaragiri, and caused an inquisition to be held into the characters of those suspected of wrong living.[1]

At this time a monk named Dhammakitti was Saṅgharāja (Primate). He lived in a monastery called Saddhamma-tilaka, in the village of Gadalādeṇiya.[2] According to the *Saddharmālaṅkāra* colophon,[3] he was the pupil of another Dhammakitti, who seems to have flourished during the latter part of the thirteenth century. He was a member of the Puṭabhatta-seḷa (Paḷābatgala) fraternity and lived at Gangasiri-pura. Dhammakitti Saṅgharāja was evidently a man of great learning, considered quite worthy, as later events show, of the high office he held at the head of the Buddhist Church.

Bhuvaneka-Bāhu was succeeded by Parākrama-Bāhu V, and the latter (*circa* 1356) by Vikrama-Bāhu III. His minister was Nissaṅka Alakeśvara, or Alagakkonār, as he is often called, who perhaps forms the most noteworthy figure in the days of the decline of the Sinhalese monarchy. He

[1] *Nikāya-saṅgraha*, p. 24.
[2] Ibid., p. 31, and Wickremasinghe, p. xix.
[3] Wickremasinghe, *JRAS.*, 1896, p. 202.

belonged to a noble family in the hill tribes of South India, and was allied by marriage to Senālaṅkādhikāra Senarat mentioned above. He rose from power to power; a governor of the province of which Peradeniya formed the capital, he had already distinguished himself as a capable administrator; later in the reign of the next king we find him as the Viceroy of the Low Country, with his seat of government at Rayi-gama. Making that his headquarters, he built a fortification at Jayavardhana-pura, so that he might attack the Tamils when the time was ripe for such an enterprise. His noble patriotism would not brook allegiance to a foreigner, and as soon as his plans were ready he challenged the authority of the Tamil king at Jaffna by hanging his officers. War was immediately declared, and under the competent generalship of Alakeśvara the Tamil strongholds one after another fell before the onslaught of the mighty Sinhalese warriors. At the close of the campaign the Tamils, in spite of the aid they had received from India, were thoroughly beaten, and Alakeśvara, his triumph complete, was the hero of the day. He had dared to cross swords with the dreaded foe, and, what was more, had won in the fight. His achievement fired the imagination of his subjects as no other event had done for many a long year. Panegyrics were sung in his honour: "There flourishes that valiant lion, Alakeśvara, very strong in breaking open the frontal knobs of elephants, represented in the person of his enemies, and ever in his place on the grand, beauteous, golden rock of Laṅkā, the home of untold and fascinating wealth." [1] The *Nikāya-saṅgraha*, written soon after this date, devotes several pages to a description of his exploits, and other works of the period bear witness to the importance of the place he occupied in the nation's esteem.

Alakeśvara was not only a great warrior, but also a wise statesman, and an enlightened ruler, devoted to the arts of peace. He was a devout Buddhist as well, and his attention was soon occupied by measures to be adopted for thorough

[1] *Nikāya-saṅgraha*, pp. 26 foll.

reform of the Saṅgha. " In the manner of the cultivators of paddy, who protect the corn by rooting out the tares and the weeds from amongst the corn blades," [1] he held a synod of the church and empowered the pious monks to inquire into the state of religion in the land and disrobe all sinful members of the Order. The work of holding the inquiry was entrusted to the Saṅgharāja Dhammakitti, mentioned above, lineal representative of the Vanavāsi fraternity at Puṭabhatta-sela, "whose fame and glory were spread over the ten directions, and who was possessed of great virtue and influence, the home and abiding-place of a mountain of moral precepts." [2] Thus was tranquillity obtained, at least for a short while.

Dhammakitti composed a Pāli poem called the *Pāra-mī-mahā-sataka*, and in the colophon he pays well-deserved tribute to the high-mindedness of Nissaṅka Alakeśvara of Amara-giri. The poem itself consists of a hundred verses, divided into ten sections, dealing with the ten *Pāramitā* (Perfections), which the Bodhisatta had fulfilled before he attained Enlightenment. The material for the poem is derived from the *Jātakas* and from the *Cariyā-piṭaka*, and the verses are well-written in chaste and elegant language. Copies of the poem are rare in Ceylon.

Dhammakitti had a pupil and successor of the same name, who held the office of Saṅgharāja in the reigns of Bhuvaneka-Bāhu V and Vīra-Bāhu II (*circa* 1372–1410). In the reign of the latter king, in collaboration with his colleague Galaturumūla Maitri *Mahā-Thera*, he held a synod of Buddhist monks, and, by suppressing unorthodox doctrines, is said to have rendered great service to the purification of the religion.[3] He was a man of great literary achievements, and is the celebrated author of several works in Pāli and Sinhalese. In the colophon of his own *Nikāya-saṅgraha* he tells us that " This brief history of the religion was composed by the

1 Nikāya-sangraha, p. 27.
2 Ibid., p. 27.
3 Ibid., p. 29.

learned monk, Devarakkhita, known and renowned over the world as Jaya-Bāhu and celebrated as the Mahā Thera Dhammakitti, who attained the rank of Saṅgharāja and glorified the religion". A set of Pāli verses in the *Saddharmālaṅkāra* [1] gives some more particulars: "Dhammakitti compiled this *Saddharmālaṅkarā*. He was the *atijāta* (more renowned) pupil of Dhammakitti; of the fraternity of monks at Puṭabhatta-seḷa, who lived in the reign of Bhuvaneka-Bāhu. He was also the *anujāta* (taking exactly after his master) pupil of the Saṅgharāja Dhammakitti the author of *Pāramī-mahā-sataka*, who resided at Gadalādeṇi Vihāra. He composed the works *Saṅkhepa*, *Nikāya-saṅgaha*, *Bālāvatāra*, and *Jina-bodhāvalī*."

No information is available as to the nature and contents of two of these compilations, the *Saṅkhepa* and the *Jina-bodhāvalī*. The *Nikāya-saṅgraha* is a very important work, written in Sinhalese, containing the history of Buddhism from the time of its founder to the twentieth century of its existence. It gives much valuable information about schisms in the Buddhist church, and is an authentic record, specially of events which took place in the thirteenth and fourteenth centuries, where the *Mahā-vaṃsa* accounts are often unreliable and seem to want supplementation.[2]

Dhammakitti's *Bālāvatāra* is a work on Pāli grammar, and is the most extensively used handbook in Ceylon on the subject. It is the smallest grammatical work extant, based on the *Kaccāyana*, and forms an extremely good summary of the older grammar. Though it closely follows the *Kaccāyana* in its method of treatment, yet the arrangement is somewhat different. The book is divided into seven chapters, dealing with *Sandhi*, *Nāma*, *Samāsa*, *Taddhita*, *Ākhyāta*, *Kitaka*, and *Kāraka* (in two sections *Uttānutta* and *Vibhatti-bheda*) respectively. The section on *Kāraka* or syntax, especially,

[1] The *Saddharmālaṅkāra* has already been noticed in the discussion of Vedeha Thera's *Rasa-vāhinī*, of which it is a translation.

[2] For a fuller description see Wickremasinghe, pp. 72–3.

is here more clearly and comprehensively dealt with than in any other grammar, and the work thus forms an important addition to the *Sandhi-kappa* of the *Kaccāyana-vyākaraṇa*. D'Alwis says [1] that the author seems to have been familiar with the Sanskrit grammar *Laghu-Kaumudī*, as the arrangement of both works is largely similar. Neither the name of the author nor the date of its compilation is given in the book itself, but the *Saddharmālaṅkāra* colophon, quoted above, helps us to fix both with certainty. The Mandalay MSS. in the India Office Library and the *Gandha-vaṃsa* assign its authorship to Vācissara,[2] but Forchhammer's List [3] agrees with the *Saddharmālaṅkāra* colophon in calling its author Dhammakitti. In 1824 the Rev. B. Clough, of the Wesleyan Mission in Ceylon, published an English translation, copies of which are unobtainable at present. Later, in 1892, L. Lee published an English translation with copious notes in the *Orientalist*, vol. ii.

The *Bālavatāra* forms the nucleus for a cluster of Sinhalese grammatical works on Pāli.[4] Best known amongst them is the *Gaḍalādeṇi Sanne* (paraphrase), so called because it was compiled by an incumbent of the Gadalādeṇi Vihāra, who is usually identified with the author of the *Bālāvatāra* himself.[5]

It is a very large work, and is held in the same high esteem as the original of which it forms a paraphrase, adding many detailed explanations and examples, so that the short aphorisms of the *Bālāvatāra* may be more thoroughly understood. Another well-known paraphrase is the *Liyana-sanne* or *Okandapala-sanne*, or *Pada-siddhi-sanne*, composed at Okandapala Vihāra by Sitināmaluvé Dhammajoti, pupil of Saṅgharāja Saraṇaṅkara, in the eighteenth century. It contains explanations in Sinhalese of the examples given in the *Bālāvatāra*, chiefly in the chapter on compounds (*samāsa*).

[1] *Catalogue*, p. 78.
[2] Fausböll, *JPTS.*, 1896, pp. 45–6, and *G.V.*, p. 62.
[3] Bode, p. 22, footnote.
[4] De Zoysa, p. 22.
[5] *Bālāvatāra*, printed ed., Colombo, 1885, preface.

In 1894 Hikkaduve Siri Sumaṅgala published a scholarly edition of the *Bālāvatāra*, complete with a *ṭīkā* in Pāli, which forms one of the most important works of that distinguished Orientalist.[1]

To Dhammakitti is usually assigned the authorship of another important work in Pāli, the *Saddhamma-saṅgaha.*[2] I cannot agree to this ascription; the colophon of the *S.-saṅgaha* is against it. There[3] the author tells us: "There is a Thera named Dhammakitti, who shines like the moon in Sīhala in the sky of religion, causing to blossom by his rays of wisdom the lotuses, the people of Ceylon. He is a mine of good conduct and virtue and is famed in the land of the Sīhalas like the moon in the sky; thoroughly versed in the *Piṭakas* and in all sciences, a man of wisdom, delighting the Island of Laṅkā. His pupil, known as the Dhammakitti Mahāsāmi, desirous of coming to Laṅkā, having come to that beautiful country, amassed much merit. After receiving the higher Ordination of an Elder he went back to his own land and there, having reached the city of Yodaya (Ayodhya ?), while living in the great abode of Laṅkārāma, built by the King named Paramarāja, by him, Dhammakitti Mahāsāmi, well controlled and wise, was composed this *Saddhamma-saṅgaha*, complete in every way." We are, I think, right in conjecturing that the work belongs to some time within or about the period under consideration. The Dhammakitti referred to as the author's teacher[4] is very probably one of the two Saṅgharāja's mentioned above, but the author is obviously a native of India and wrote his work in that country.

It contains an account of Buddhism, its history and development in eleven chapters, commencing with the history of the three convocations. A fourth convocation is mentioned, it is interesting to note, where Mahinda held a synod

[1] Colombo, 1894.
[2] Wickremasinghe, p. xix, and De Zoysa, 20.
[3] *JPTS.*, 1890–3, p. 90.
[4] De Zoysa says that Dhammadinna was the teacher's name (p. 20).

under the presidency of the first Sinhalese Thera, Mahāriṭṭha, on which occasion the latter recited the Vinaya [1] with great solemnity. We then pass on to the reign of Dutugāmuṇu and the writing of the scriptures under the patronage of Vaḷagam-abā. The author gives a long description of Buddhaghosa's labours and continues to the time of Parākrama-Bāhu the Great, when the *ṭīkās* were written by Kassapa and his colleagues. The ninth chapter is devoted to a notice of some of the principal works then known, giving the names of authors and their compilations. The next two chapters deal with the merits that accrue from setting down the *Piṭakas* in writing and from listening to the Doctrine. The author quotes from the *Kosala-Bimba-vaṇṇanā* the merits of making images, and in his last chapter gives several illustrative stories, some of which are from Ceylon. The work is partly in prose and partly in verse, and is profusely interspersed with quotations from older compilations. The last chapter especially is a sort of anthology of odds and ends of old verses, of rare excellence and beauty. The historical sections, particularly the chapter (ix) on books and their authors, contain many imperfections,[2] and the accounts given are not always reliable. Some of these have already been dealt with; but on the whole they aid us to some extent in our attempts to put together whatever little information we have at present on the history of the religion and of the literature of Ceylon. The fact that the author was away from Ceylon when he wrote the work might possibly account for the deficiencies to be found therein. The chapter on Dhammānisaṃsa has been the source of inspiration for several later-day works in Sinhalese on the same subject. The stanzas which it contains are frequently quoted, and the illustrative stories are quite well known.

[1] *JPTS.* Ed., p. 44.

[2] e.g. the *Abhidhammattha-saṅgaha* is attributed to Sāriputta and the *Sacca-saṅkhepa* to Ānanda; the list given of Dhammapāla's work is incomplete. The names of authors follow no chronological order.

Two other works which probably belong to this period are the *Sādhu-caritodaya* and the *Anāpatti-dīpanī*. The first is a short work, written in Pāli verse, containing selections of stories of pious Buddhists who obtained merit by worshipping and making offerings to the Buddha, the Cetiyas, relics, etc. The author gives his name as Sumedha Thera, of Cūtaggāṁa (Ambagamuva ?).[1] The stories are taken from various sources, and some of them from the *Rasa-vāhinī*. Several of them are included in a Sinhalese didactic poem, *Lōväda-saṅgarā*, composed by Vīdāgama *Thera*, in the fifteenth century.

The *Anāpatti-dīpanī* is a little tract, very rare, which, as its name implies, discusses cases where the infringement of *Pāṭimokkha* rules does not result in sin, because the actions are unintentional. The author does not give his name, but calls himself a pupil of Bhuvaneka-Bāhu *Thera* of the Paṃsu-pabbata Vihāra in Ceylon. There is a Bhuvaneka-Bāhu *Thera* mentioned in the *Vutta-mālā* (q.v.) written in the fifteenth century. He comes in a list of Buddhist monks of eminence whom the author praises for their learning and their services to the cause of religion, and his name appears between Dhammakitti and Saṅgharāja (possibly the Saṅgharāja Dhammakitti III).

About the year A.D. 1412 Parākrama-Bāhu VI came to the throne. He was the son of Sunetrā Devī of the Giri-vaṃsa, and in his earlier years was befriended by an Elder named Vīdāgama Mahā Sāmi, who dwelt in a monastery at Rayi-gama. Legend has cast a halo round the youth of this hero-king, and many stories are told of his miraculous escapes from death at the hands of the Dictator Alakeśvara, who was reigning at Jayavardhana-pura (Kōtte),[2] and who sought to strengthen

[1] De Zoysa, p. 20.

[2] The history of the few years preceding the accession of Parākrama-Bāhu VI is a tangled web, difficult to unravel. Speculation is rife as to his ancestry and the identities of the Alakeśvara here referred to and the Elder Vīdāgama Mahāsāmi. There seems to have been a Chinese invasion of Ceylon at this time, after which, for several years at least, the king of Ceylon paid tribute to China. For further detailed discussion see *JRAS.* (Ceylon Branch), vol. xxii, Nos. 63 and 65.

his position by extirpating all possible claimants to the throne, When he was sixteen years old, the prince slew Alakeśvara and was crowned king at Kotte. His long and glorious reign, covering over half a century (1412–67 ?) was the brightest period in the national annals nearest to the advent of the Portuguese ; he was the last great monarch of a single Laṅkā ; and his reign marks an epoch in Ceylon's island story ; it was the last gleam before the darkness, which saw the Sinhalese engaged in a death struggle for their independent national existence, only to succumb to the sword of their invaders and bend their knee in subjection to foreign domination.

Alakeśvara had made of Kotte a magnificent city, with stone baths, spacious streets, and beautiful buildings. Parākrama embellished it with fine edifices of solid blue-stone, five-storied palaces and temples, shrine rooms and monasteries. He appointed as his Saṅgharāja Mahā Sāmī Vanaratana, and built for him a spacious monastery and a large ordination hall (*pōyagē*).[1] In memory of his mother he built a magnificent shrine and a college for monks as Päpiḷiyāna, called after her the Sunetrā Devī Pariveṇa. Here, by royal command, the *Tipiṭaka* with the *Atthakathā* and *ṭīkā* were inscribed, and lands allotted to the scribes who were daily engaged in the work. He made endowments for other educational establishments as well, and we hear of several ecclesiastical colleges during this period, the Padmāvatī Pariveṇa at Kāragala, under the presidency of Rājaguru Vanaratana Sangharāja, the Woodland Cloister (Aranyaka) at Paḷābatgaḷa, the Vijaya-Bāhu Pariveṇa at Toṭagamuva under Śrī Rāhula, the Irugalkula Pariveṇa at Mulgirigala, the Śrī Gaṇānanda Pariveṇa at Rayi-gama under the Great Elder Maittreya Mahā Thera of the Mahā Netra Vihara, and the Sunetra Devī Pariveṇa, already mentioned, presided over by Maṅgala Saṅgharāja, learned in the *Tipiṭaka*.[2] With the help of his foster son, Sapumal-kumāra, he was able to

[1] *Rājāvaliya* (*Gunasekara*), p. 68.
[2] E. W. Perera, *JRAS*. (C.B.), No. 63, p. 18.

drive the Tamils under Ārya Cakravarti away from the island and to consolidate the kingdom. Soon afterwards we find him successfully organizing a punitive expedition against an insolent Malabar prince of South India in retaliation of an act of wanton aggression upon some Sinhalese merchants.[1] By means of his skilful generalship, combined with rare administrative ability, by his far-reaching statemanship and great genius and capacity for organization, he made of Ceylon once more a united island, respected by her neighbours and inhabited by a people enjoying peace and tranquillity and well-earned prosperity.

Inspired by this feeling of security and contentment, men again turned their attention to the cultivation of the finer arts, and nowhere else do we see the benefits of his mild and beneficent sway more than in the great literary activity which he called forth among the people. They began to sing of the dawn of a new golden age, when the world would be ruled by righteousness and justice; they loved to dwell on the achievements of the king and extolled the beauties of the country over which he ruled; they told of the splendour of his court and the blessings the Gods had showered down upon them because of the piety of the rulers. The poems of Śrī Rāhula, for example, glow with an intense patriotism and a deep affection for the royal family whose patronage he enjoyed. It was an age of much literary productivity, and, fortunately for us, in spite of the Portuguese invasion and the fanatical vandalism which came along with it, much of that literature has come down to us undestroyed. The king himself was imbued with a deep scholarship and a great love for culture in all its variety. He possessed a wide knowledge of Sanskrit, and was probably much struck by the sacred works of the Hindus which he had read. These are unmistakable traces of the great influence which Hinduism exercised during this period, chiefly due no doubt to the close connexion which existed between the courts of Ceylon and South India.

[1] *Rājāvaliya*, p. 69.

Brahmans came thither in large numbers, and we find them studying under the monks and sometimes being converted to the Buddhist faith.[1] Temples were erected in the capital to Hindu Gods such as Nātha, Sumana, Viṣṇu, and Śiva, rivalling in excellence the Buddhist shrines. Srī Rāhula Saṅgharāja was deeply skilled in all the lore of the Hindus and seems to have entertained very liberal notions on the question of religion. This epoch shows in a marked degree the compromise between Hinduism and Buddhism which existed from very early times.

Parākrama-Bāhu was patron of a brilliant band of men who shed the lustre of their learning upon this period. So were his daughter Ulakuḍaya Devī and her husband Nallūrutun. Unfortunately, little is known about their lives, except what we can gather from the records in their own works, and in the compilations of other contemporary writers. The king was the author of a Sinhalese metrical vocabulary, the *Ruvan-mala*, composed on the model of the *Amarasinha*. His son-in-law Nallūrutun Minisanhas also made a similar compilation, the *Nāmāvaliya*, but not so complete as the king's work. But brightest in this constellation was Śrī Rāhula Vacissara, Saṅgharāja and President of the Vijaya-Bāhu Pariveṇa at Toṭagamuva, and probably a member of the royal family. He belonged to the Uttaramūla Nikāya, and tells us that at the age of 15 he received a boon at the hands of the God Kārttikeya, which enabled him to become *Ṣaḍ-bhāṣā-parameśvara* (Master of six languages),[2] in addition to his own, Sinhalese. All his works are in Sinhalese, and he ranks among the highest of the poets of Ceylon. His *Kāvya-śekhara*, appropriately so-called ("Crown of Song"), brought him immortality, and to this day he is regarded as the chief exponent of rhymed verse, and his works are adopted by all Sinhalese poets as their model. It was during this time that the

[1] e.g. Srī Rāmacandra Bhārati, author of the *Bhakti-śataka*.

[2] *Sāḷa-lihiṇi Sandesa* colophon; the six languages being Sanskṛit, Māgadhī (Pāli), Apabhraṃsa, Paiśācī, Śaurasenī, and Tamil.

Sinhalese *Sandesa* (message) poem came to the forefront as a work of art. Such a poem, as its name implies, is based on Kālidāsa's *Megha-dūta* (Cloud Messenger), and embodies a message to be conveyed by some bird to the shrine of a *deva*, invoking his blessings on the king or on some member of the royal family, or imploring the help of the divinity for the victory of the royal arms. The route taken by such a messenger-bird is described in the poem and the description affords ample opportunity for the poet to display his genius. Śrī Rāhula wrote two such *Sandesa* poems: the *Säḷalihiṇi-* and the *Paravi-sandeśa*, and probably also the *Pärākumbā-sirita*, a panegyric on the king. Other works ascribed to him are the *Sīmā-saṅkara-chedanī*, on the choice of boundaries for the performance of *Uposatha* ceremonies, the *Toṭagamu-nimitta*, a work similar to Napoleon's *Book of Fate*, and the *Catur-ārya-satya-kāvya*, a religious poem. He is also credited with having written several works on Demonology.[1]

To students of Pāli literature, however, interest in Śrī Rāhula's works lies chiefly in two very elaborate and important treatises which he wrote on Pāli grammar, viz. the *Moggallāna-pañjikā-pradīpa* and the *Pada-sādhana-ṭīkā*.

The first of these, the *Pañjikā-pradīpa*, is one of the most comprehensive works on Pāli grammar extant in Ceylon, or anywhere else. It is written partly in Pāli and partly in Sinhalese, and is a commentary to the *Pañjikā* written by Moggallāna himself on the Pāli grammar, which bears his name. The author of the *Pradīpa* has made use of his extensive reading and profound scholarship to enrich the volume with detailed expositions of all Moggallāna's rules. It bristles with references to and quotations from numerous Sanskrit, Pāli, Sinhalese, and Tamil works, many of which are no longer to be found in Ceylon. When the Moggāllana school differs from the older Kaccāyana and his commentators, Śrī Rāhula examines their claims to accuracy, and the conclusions he

[1] Hugh Nevill's MS. *Catalogue* and *JRAS.* (C.B.), *passim.*

arrives at show a great deal of critical acumen, unhampered by tradition and free from prejudices.

Subhūti, in his *Nāma-māla*,[1] has drawn up a list of the works quoted by Rāhula, which I give below, because of its interest in enabling us to know at least the names of some of the works studied during this period. Subhūti's list includes: *Kaccāyana*, *Nyāsa*, *Nyāsa-pradīpa*, *Nirutti-mañjūsā*, *Rūpa-siddhi* and its *sanne* (paraphrase) and *gāṭapada* (glossary), *Bālāvatāra* and *sanne*, *Sadda-nīti*, *Cūla-nirutti*, *Nirutti-piṭaka*, *Sutta-niddesa*, *Sambandha-cintā*, *Pada-sādhana* and *sanne*, *Pañjikā-ṭīkā*, *Payoga-siddhi*, *Dik-saṅgi-ṭīkā* (*ṭīkā* on the *Dīgha-Nikāya*), *Bhesajja-mañjūsā* and *sanne*, *Abhidhāna-ppadīpikā*, *Cāndra-vyā-karaṇa*, *Mahā-bhāṣya*, *Bhāṣya-pradīpa*, *Laghu-vṛtti*, *Durgasiṃha - vṛtti - pañjikā*, *Pañjikālaṅkāra*, *Kātantra*, *Śabdārtha-cintā*, *Sārasvata*, *Kāśikā*, *Kāśikā-vṛtti*, *Vārtikā*, *Bhāgavitti*, *Sāra-saṅgraha*, *Padāvatāra*, *Śrīdhara*, *Vaijayantī*, *Abhidharma-koṣa*, *Prākṛta-prakāśa*, *Veda*, *Rāmāyaṇa*, *Bāhaṭa*, *Bharata-śāstra*, *Amara-koṣa*, *Medinī-koṣa*, *Jātaka-sanne*, *Umandā-gāṭapada*, *Ratana-sutta-gāṭapada*, *Demala-jātaka-gāṭapada*, and *Virita-sanne*. This list gives some idea of the vast amount of trouble which the author must have spent in the production of his voluminous work, and the result has been a compilation in every way worthy of the active intellect of Śrī Rāhula.

For many years the work had been sadly neglected for want of authentic copies, and, when the late Siri Dhammārāma, Principal of the Vidyālaṅkāra Pariveṇa, Colombo, brought out his scholarly edition in 1896, he thereby did a distinct service to Pāli learning in Ceylon.

Śrī Rāhula's other grammatical work, the *Pada-sādhana ṭīkā*, is, as its name implies, a commentary on Piyadassi's *Pada-sādhana*. The *ṭīkā* is also called *Buddhi-ppasādanī*, and copies of it are very rare in Ceylon, the work having been, in fact, unknown to Pāli scholars for many years until De Zoysa, in 1873, discovered a MS. in the Ridī Vihāra.[2] The

[1] Subhūti, *Nāma-mālā*, Colombo, 1876.

[2] De Zoysa, *Catalogue*, p. 26.

Buddhi-ppasādanī was evidently a production of the latter part of Rāhula's life, because here he calls himself Saṅgharāja, while in the other works his name is mentioned only as the Head of the Vijayabāhu Pariveṇa. The work suffers very much by comparison with his masterpiece, the *Pañcikā-pradīpa,* and that may have been the reason for its having gradually fallen into disuse at the hands of Pāli students—the greater light had dimmed the less, and made it hide its head in shame.

Other authors who lived during this period or slightly posterior to it and composed work in Sinhalese, besides those mentioned above, are the President of the Irugalkula Pariveṇa at Mulgirigala, author of the *Kovul-sandesa* ; Vättäva *Thera,* author of the *Guttila-jātakaya* ; the anonymous writers of the *Girā-sandesa* and *Tisara-sandesa*—both evidently poets of Jayavardhana-pura (Kotte)—an anonymous pupil of Śrī Maitri Mahāsāmi of Rayi-gama, who made a Sinhalese paraphrase of the *Attanagalu-vaṃsa* at the king's request ; Dhammadinna Vimalakitti *Thera* (also called Siddhattha), author of the *Saddharma-ratnākara* ; Mahā-Netra-prasāda-mūla-Vīdagama *Thera,* a monk renowned for his piety, and a poet in the excellence of his composition almost equal to Śrī Rāhula, and author of the *Budu-guṇālaṅkāra* (a poem in praise of the Buddha, composed in 2015 of the Buddhist Era), the didactic poem *Lōväda-saṅgarā,* and of the *Kivilakuṇumiṇi-mālā,* a treatise on Sinhalese prosody ; and Ranasgallé *Thera* of Toṭagamuvihāra, author of an ethical poem, the *Lōkōpakāraya.*[1]

To the Pāli compilations of this time belongs the *Vutta-mālā*—or, to give it its full name—the *Vutta-mālā-sandesa-sataka,* a Pāli poem of 102 stanzas in various elegant metres, composed by a monk named Gatārā Pariveṇa Upatapassi. In the colophon the author calls himself the nephew of Sarasi-gāma-Mūla-Mahā-Sāmi, incumbent of

[1] For further description of these writers and their works see Wickremasinghe's *Catalogue, passim.*

the Jāti-gāma Monastery (*Sarasi-gāma-mūla-mahā-sāmino bhāgineyya-bhūtena racitāyaṃ*).

The *Sarasi-gāma-mūla* is the Sinhalese *Vilgam-mūla*, the *Vilgam* being *Seruvāvila*, the modern *Thōpur*. The author, therefore, undoubtedly belonged to the Saro-gāma fraternity, which counted many scholars of repute amongst its members. The work was evidently composed in the reign of Parākrama-Bāhu VI (1415–67 ?), for the writer first describes the beauty of a city styled Jāti-gāma,[1] and then extols King Parākrama and his mother Sunetrā Devī. This is followed by a description of the chief Buddhist monastery, and encomiums on several monks, all of whom are scholars and probably belong to the same Ācariya-paramparā as the author. The monks so lauded are: (1) Upalantara-mūla-Thera (Selantara- or Galaturu-mūla); (2) Senāpati-mūla-; (3) Mahā Netta-pāsāda-mūla-; (4) Saro-gāma-mūla; (5) Vanaratna-; (6) Dhammakitti-; (7) Bhuvaneka-Bāhu *Thera* (probably the teacher of the author of the *Anāpatti-dīpanī*); (8) the Saṅgha-rāja or Primate of the time; and (9) Gatārā-upatapassi-Thera, pupil of the Saṅgha-rāja who, both Nevill and Wickremasinghe think, is probably identical with the author himself. Nevill takes Upatapassi to mean the same as Anu-Nāyaka.

These laudatory verses are followed by a description of Kälaṇiya and its presiding deity Vibhīṣaṇa, whose blessings the author asks for Parākrama and his kingdom. The *Vutta-mālā* is supposed to have been composed for the purpose of teaching students the right pronunciation of sounds and the proper modulation of the voice in reciting verse,[2] and, as such, is largely used in temple schools. There exists an inter-verbal paraphrase in Sinhalese by an anonymous writer, who perhaps is identical with the author of the poem itself. Both the poem and the paraphrase have been published.[3]

[1] Probably Dedigama in Beligal-Korale, though the king is not known to have reigned there. See Bell's *Archæological Report on the Kegalle District*, pp. 81–5.

[2] D'Alwis, *Sidat-saṅgarā*, p. 225.

[3] Colombo, 1871–96.

Wickremasinghe assigns to this period the Sinhalese *Dhātu-vaṃsa.*[1] The author, in the last strophe to his work, gives his name as the Thera Kakusandha, but no further particulars are available about him, nor does he say whether the Sinhalese version is an original composition or a translation from the Pāli. I am inclined, however, to agree with Professor Geiger [2] in considering that the *Dhātu-vaṃsa* is only a Sinhalese translation like the *Mahā-Bodhi-vaṃsa* and the *Thūpa-vaṃsa,* and that its Pāli counterpart, to which, curiously enough, is given the fuller title of the *Laḷāṭa-* (or *Naḷāṭa-*) *dhātu-vaṃsa-*, or simply the *Laḷāṭa-vaṃsa,* is an older compilation. The author of the Pāli work and its date are unknown,[3] and copies of it are difficult to obtain. There seems to have been a commentary on it, called the *Lalāṭa-dhātu-vaṃsa-vaṇṇanā,* but I do not know of any copies of it extant in Ceylon. Rhys Davids tells us that the Bibliothèque Nationale at Paris possesses a copy written on twenty-seven ola-leaves.[4] The *Laḷāṭa-dhātu-vaṃsa* is a history, in five chapters, of the frontal bone relic of the Buddha. It is a work, undoubtedly, of great antiquity, and evidently belongs to the cycle of sagas and legends of Rohaṇa and Malaya. It therefore contains many popular traditions not found elsewhere, especially grouped round the family and the contemporaries of the Kākavaṇṇa-Tissa, father of Dutugämuṇu. The work was unknown to the authors of the *Mahā-vaṃsa* and its *ṭīkā,* for we find no reference to it in their compilations. It follows the general outline of all *vaṃsa* books in its mode of treatment, beginning with Dīpaṅkara, and passing on to the three visits of the Buddha, the Parinibbāna, and the distribution of the relics. The third chapter gives the history of the frontal bone relic, from the time of its falling to the share of the Mallas at the distribution to its arrival in Ceylon when Mahānāga reigned in Mahā-gāma. It was first honoured by a wealthy

[1] p. xx.

[2] *Dīpa-vaṃsa* and *Mahā-vaṃsa,* p. 91.

[3] The *G.V.*, p. 62, mentions the *Naḷāta-dhātu-vaṇṇanā,* but gives no author.

[4] *JRAS.,* N.S., vol. vii, p. 171.

man named Mahākāla, and then, later, by the king, when he heard of it. It seemed to have remained for a long time in the hands of the Rohaṇa princes who did honour to it in succession. The last two chapters contain accounts of Kākavaṇṇa-Tissa's family, the history of the erection of a special Dāgoba at Sēruvila for the reception of the relic and its dedication and the enshrinement of the relics. The accounts in these two chapters were undoubtedly derived from popular sources and local traditions, and were, therefore, unknown to the *Mahā-vaṃsa* author, else he surely would have made mention of them. The descriptions of the erection of the dāgoba, etc., are entirely based on the *Mahā-vaṃsa,* and follow them almost word for word. The similarity of treatment between the *Laḷāṭa-vaṃsa* and the *Mahā-Bodhi-vaṃsa* leads me to assign both works to the same period of Pāli literature, namely to the tenth or the eleventh century A.D.

The Sinhalese version of *Kakusandha* is more or less a translation of the Pāli, but contains several details not found in the Pāli compilation, e.g. in the description of the third visit of the Buddha to Ceylon.[1] The Sinhalese work has already been published in Ceylon, edited by Gintoṭa Dhammakkhanda (Dodandūva, 1890), and I understand that the Pāli version is in course of publication.

It was about this time, in the reign of King Bhuvaneka-Bāhu VI (A.D. 1464–71 ?) that Dhammaceti, or Rāmādhipati, King of Pegu, brought about a great religious revival in his own land. Dhammaceti reigned from 1460–91,[2] and his régime was a memorable one for Burma. His fame for wise statesmanship and munificence has spread far beyond the confines of his own country, and he is renowned throughout the Buddhist world for his extreme piety. He was an ex-monk, and for some time was the minister of the famous Queen Shin-sau-bu. Later he became her son-in-law and successor. He was not only a high-minded monarch and a

[1] For fuller description see Geiger, op. cit., pp. 91–3.
[2] Phayre, *History of Burma*, p. 290.

protector of the Order he had quitted, but was an enthusiastic reformer as well. Emulating the example of such kings as Asoka and Parākrama-Bāhu, he made the purity of Buddhism one of the objects of his earnest solicitude. During the four centuries that preceded his accession, Burma had scarcely enjoyed peace for any length of time, and matters pertaining to religion had been greatly neglected. He found that, because of the violent political convulsions which the country had suffered, the succession of teachers (*Thera-vāda-paramparā*) had been interrupted in Rāmañña. In order, therefore, to secure for the Burmese monks direct continuity of apostolic succession from the spiritual descendants of Mahinda, and also to establish for the monks of Rāmañña a duly consecrated place for the performance of their ecclesiastical ceremonies, he sent a mission to Ceylon, consisting of two ministers and twenty-two monks and their pupils, with costly presents to the king of Ceylon and the chief monks and with a letter inscribed on a tablet of gold. They were welcomed with every mark of friendship and civility, and their request was granted. They received their *upasampadā* ordination at the hands of the Mahāvihāra fraternity within the consecrated boundaries (*sīmā*) of the Kaḷyāṇi river, near Colombo. On their return they consecrated the enclosure in Pegu, henceforth known as Kaḷyāṇi-sīmā. Dhammaceti, in the celebrated Kaḷyāṇi inscriptions at Zaingganaing, near Pegu, set forth in detail the account of this mission and laid down for the use of future generations the proper ceremonial of consecrating a *Sīmā* The stone slabs containing the inscriptions were broken up by the vandalism of Portuguese adventurers, but have later been restored to some extent. The records in the inscriptions had been compiled in book form, copies of which are to be met with in many of the monasteries in Ceylon—especially those belonging to the Amara-pura Sect, under the title of " Kaḷyāṇi-ppakaraṇa ". One point of literary interest in the Kaḷyāṇi-ppakaraṇa lies in the mention made in it of the standard authorities on Vinaya subjects at the time, such as the *Vinayatthakathā*, *Sārattha-dīpanī*, *Vimati-vinodanī*, *Vinaya-vinicchaya*, *Vinaya-saṅgaha*, *Sīmālaṅkāra-saṅgaha*, and *Vajirabuddhi-ṭīkā*, practically all of them of Sinhalese authorship.[1] The Kaḷyāṇi-ppakaraṇa is noteworthy because of its significance in showing us to what degree a religious superiority over the rest of the community was claimed by those who had received their ordination direct from the monks of Ceylon. In spite of the many vicissitudes which the Saṅgha in Ceylon had passed through in their chequered career their claim to be the guardians of the genuine Thera-vāda was still recognized in the fifteenth century.

1 For more information about the Kalyāṇī Inscriptions see *Preliminary Study* by Taw Sein Ko in the *Indian Antiquary*, vol. xxii.

CHAPTER XIII

THE DARK AGE

THE two centuries following the death of Parākrama-Bāhu VI constitute the darkest chapter in the history of Ceylon. The political condition of the country was at its lowest ebb, the whole of the sea coast was virtually in the hands of foreigners, chiefly Moors; the interior regions, including the remains of the ancient capitals, were divided into a number of petty fiefs uncontrolled by any paramount central authority and governed by chieftains holding mimic courts at various centres. These petty tyrants, even more degenerate in their character than they were humiliated in station, no longer manifested the patriotism and the zeal for the public welfare which had so significantly characterized the former sovereigns of Ceylon. They had ceased to occupy their attention with the advancement of religion or with the development of institutions calculated to benefit the people. The history of the period contains very little besides accounts of their feuds and jealousies, their ceaseless intrigues and insurrections. Even the food supply of the country, to the maintenance of which the earlier and more enlightened princes had devoted the greater part of their energies, had now failed, and Ceylon had become dependent on India for the very necessaries of life. Such was the sad plight of the country when, at the beginning of the sixteenth century, in the course of their discoveries and conquests in the East, and in the pursuit of their Eastern trade, the Portuguese came upon Ceylon.[1] Dharma Parākrama IX was then reigning at Kotte, a weak and irresolute prince, at the head of an insignificantly small extent of territory. By promising him military aid against any assaults by his ambitious relatives, and by holding out to him hopes of great riches to be derived

[1] For further particulars of the Portuguese period in Ceylon see Emerson Tennent, *Ceylon*, vol. ii, chap. 1, and that excellent book, Pieris, *Ceylon and the Portuguese* (1920), *passim*.

from the trade which they proposed to establish, the Portuguese first gained a foothold in Colombo and erected a fortress on the rocky beach. Once their guns were thus set up, and their formidable galleons had found shelter in the adjoining natural harbour, they were able to overawe the Sinhalese king, whose capital now lay almost within range of the Portuguese cannon. On the other hand, his own subjects, dissatisfied with the favour he had extended to the foreigners, threatened him with revolt and invasion. The Portuguese, with characteristic duplicity, persevered in maintaining an internecine warfare in the country, which enabled them at last to make the king their vassal, and, finding him incapable of refusing any of their arrogant demands, they wrung from him every sort of concession. Within a short time after their arrival they had established permanent trading settlements in various parts of the island, and for one hundred and fifty years, till they were driven away by the Dutch, they carried on a ceaseless warfare against the Sinhalese people, who were now perforce compelled to abandon the maritime provinces to the hated foreigner. The capital of the Sinhalese king was kept in a state of almost incessant siege ; to the minor chiefs who owed him allegiance were held out every inducement to break themselves off from their rightful sovereign ; it was part of the Portuguese policy to inflame their apprehensions one against the other, and excite their jealousy. Thus for many years the maritime provinces were devastated by civil war in its most revolting form. By A.D. 1540 their treachery had so far succeeded in estranging the Sinhalese monarch from the sympathies of his own countrymen, that he found himself now entirely at the mercy of his foreign allies and appealed to them to ensure the succession of his family to the throne. To give solemnity to their acquiescence, an image of his grandson, Dharmapāla—who was the only male representative of the royal household—was made of ivory and gold and silver, and this statue was dispatched, with a jewelled crown studded with Ceylon's finest gems, to Lisbon, where a coronation of the effigy was held by the Portuguese Emperor. In return for this recognition of Dharmapāla as heir to the Sinhalese kingdom, the prince himself eventually abjured the national faith and professed himself a baptized convert to Christianity under the name of Dom Joas Periya Bandāra. The King of Portugal, who was a pronounced fanatic, controlled by peculiarly aggressive ecclesiastical advisers, exacted a further concession. A party of Franciscans accompanied the Sinhalese ambassadors back to Colombo from Lisbon, licence was claimed to preach the Gospel of Christ in all parts of the island, and the first Christian communities were organized in various places in the maritime districts.[1] Thus began the gradual destruction of Buddhism, the "only organization which existed for the spiritual and intellectual education of the people".[2] Meanwhile the Portuguese had been busy extending their power as far inland as possible; and by the beginning of the seventeenth century the territory under their direct government embraced the whole of the maritime circuit of the island, including the Peninsula of Jaffna, and extended inland right up to the base of the lofty zone which encircled the little kingdom of Kandy.[3]

Every stage of their progress was marked by a rapacity, bigotry, cruelty, and an inhumanity unparalleled in the annals of any other European colonial power. Their ferocity and their utter indifference to all suffering increased with the success of their army; their inhuman barbarities were accompanied by a callousness which knew no distinction between man, woman, and child; no feeling of compassion was strong enough to stay their savage hands in their fell work. To terrify their subjects and to bring home to them the might of the Portuguese power, they committed atrocities which, had they not been found recorded in the decades of their own friendly historians, seem too revolting to be true. Babes were

[1] Tennent, *Christianity in Ceylon*, chap. i.
[2] Pieris, op. cit, p. 78.
[3] Tennent, *Ceylon*, vol. ii, p. 26.

spitted on the soldiers' pikes and held up that their parents might "hear the young cocks crow". Sometimes they were mashed to pulp between millstones, while their mothers were compelled to witness the pitiful sight before they themselves were tortured to death. Men were thrown over bridges for the amusement of the troops to feed the crocodiles in the river, which eventually grew so tame that at a whistle they would raise their heads above the water in anticipation of the welcome feast.[1] The officials who acted as administrators had almost absolute power, and the people were ground down by oppressive taxation, and laws of terrible severity. The Sinhalese who remained loyal to their rightful sovereign were deprived of all their possessions, if they escaped with their lives, and refugees who by necessity or by choice joined the Portuguese ranks were received with open arms; wealth and rank and lands were conferred on them, and they were placed in positions of command over the rest. They thus obtained an undesirable influence over their countrymen, who became only too ready to rise in revolt at the bidding of every renegade. The success of any one chieftain only served to arouse intense jealousy among his fellows; war to them was only an excuse for peculation; they were guilty of all manner of excesses, abuse of authority and exactions. The tenants of village lands were so oppressed that they were frequently obliged to sell their children to procure the necessaries of life. The Portuguese officials themselves were never better than brigands, bent on their own aggrandisement during their tenure of office, and their administration was a colossal failure. The whole of the country under their control suffered from their cruel oppression; whatever produce their soil was made to yield was misappropriated; the kingdom was thus depopulated, and the lands mostly left uncultivated; the Sinhalese were left entirely disorganized and decadent, without a proper king and without leaders of ability. But

[1] Faria Y Souza, *Asia Portuguesa* (Lisbon, 1666–75), Stevens' translation, vol. iii, pt. iii, chap. xv, p. 279.

worse than these were the results of the measures the Portuguese adopted to destroy the national religion of Ceylon.

Dom Joao III, who was Emperor of Portugal at this time, was a staunch supporter of the church, fanatical in his zeal for the conversion of his heathen subjects. The Church itself was in a particularly aggressive mood. In 1534 Ignatius of Loyola had founded the Society of Jesus at Paris, and two years later the Inquisition was established. The first *Auto da Fé* was held in Portugal, presided over by the king, in the very year when Bhuvaneka-Bāhu had sent the effigy of his grandson to be crowned at Lisbon. When Bhuvaneka-Bāhu's application for recognition of Dharmapāla as heir to the Sinhalese throne was granted, one of the conditions laid down was, as we saw above, that permission should be given to preach the Christian gospel anywhere in the Sinhalese king's dominions. A band of Franciscan monks accompanied the Ceylon ambassadors on their return from Lisbon to Colombo. They immediately set about their work of converting the Sinhalese, who had so far found consolation in Buddhism. The Portuguese had as their ostensible motto "Amity, Commerce, and Religion", and nowhere were they more zealous than in the propagation of the gospel. Their instructions were "to begin by preaching, but, that failing, to proceed to the decision of the sword".[1] In 1546 the King of Portugal sent a remarkable letter to his Viceroy in India: "We charge you to discover all idols by means of diligent officers, to reduce them to fragments and utterly to consume them, in whatever place they may be found, proclaiming rigorous penalties against such persons as shall dare to engrave, cast, sculpture, limn, paint, or bring to light any figure in metal, bronze, wood, clay, or any other substance, or shall introduce them from foreign parts; and against those who shall celebrate in public or in private any festivities which have any Gentile taint, or shall abet them . . ."[2] His instructions were carried

[1] Faria V Souza, op. cit., vol. i, pt. i, ch. v, p. 53.
[2] Pieris, op. cit., p. 58.

out to the very letter. Whosoever dared to interfere with the work of proselytization, action was to be taken against him without delay, so that the displeasure of the Emperor of Portugal upon those who had the impudence to hinder the conversion of the heathen might be made plain to all. The success of the Franciscans reached its climax when Dharmapāla was baptized as a Christian along with his queen, who took the name of Donna Caterina, after the Queen of Portugal. Even the Pope found time to send the royal convert his Apostolic benediction, and to recommend him to the special protection of the King of Portugal.[1] Dharmapāla's thank-offering to the missionaries who had led him from out of the darkness into the light was a *sannas* (deed of gift) transferring to them the Daḷadā Māligāva (the holiest possession of the Ceylon kings), the two great shrines at Käḷaṇiya, and all the temple revenues in the island for the maintenance of the missionary establishments. The strongest inducements were held out to the people to embrace the new religion; no office could be held by anyone who did not profess Christianity, and all civil rights were denied to the heathen. In the letter of the King of Portugal to the Viceroy mentioned above, he had added: "And, because the Gentiles submit themselves to the yoke of the Gospel, not alone through their conviction of the purity of the Faith and for that they are sustained by the hope of Eternal Life, they should also be encouraged to with some temporal favours, such as greatly mollify the hearts of those who receive them; and therefore you should earnestly set yourself to see that the new Christians from this time forward do obtain and enjoy all exemptions and freedom from tribute, and moreover that they hold the privileges and offices of honour which up till now the Gentiles have been wont to possess."[2] This appeal to the baser side of human nature was eminently successful; it became the fashion to profess Christianity; the example set by the King Dharmapāla

[1] Pieris, op. cit., p. 77.
[2] Ibid., pp. 58–9.

was soon taken up; biblical names began to abound in the Sinhalese Court and outside it, while the language and manners of the Portuguese were rapidly adopted by those who wished to earn the goodwill of those in power. When the Portuguese gradually gained complete ascendancy over the country below the Kandyan Hills, they replaced the gentler means of persuasion, inducement, temptation, and blandishments by more rigorous methods. The missionaries now applied themselves with reckless ardour to the task of pulling down the structure which it had taken twenty centuries to build. "The missionary could see in Buddhism nothing but the abhorrent creation of the devil; he did not stop to inquire what were the principles which were taught by its sages, nor what the ideals after which its lofty philosophy struggled. Buddhism was not Christianity, and, since by Christianity alone could souls escape damnation and hell fire, it was his duty to God to destroy Buddhism by every means in this power. He did not ask whether the people were prepared to receive his new wine or whether the destruction of the ancient beliefs might not mean the destruction of all spiritual life; his every idea was centred on the one thought that Buddhism must be wiped out of existence."[1] No trouble was spared to achieve that object; monasteries were razed to the ground, and their priceless treasures looted; libraries were set fire to, or the leaves of the books they contained scattered to the winds; whosoever dared to worship in public or wear the yellow robe of the ascetic was visited with death; the great institutions at Toṭagamuva and Kāragala, which had long carried on the traditions of Taxilā and Nālanda, were destroyed and their incumbents put to the sword. The land groaned in agony as one after another there fell, before the fierce onslaughts of the fanatic missionaries and their dastardly colleagues, the Buddhist religious edifices, those lovely structures which the piety of generations had strewn broadcast over the country. Never was a glorious civilization and a noble culture more

[1] Pieris, op. cit., p. 80.

brutally destroyed. The work of centuries was undone in a few years—all that was noblest and best in the heritage of Ceylon was lost, and the damage thus wrought was irreparable.

But it was not to be expected that the Sinhalese would accept tamely this subserviency to a hateful foreign domination. More than once they made a stern struggle to win back their lost freedom and stem the tide of destruction that was sweeping over the land. The apostacy of Dharmapāla, who was a traitor alike to his country and to his faith, aroused the indignation of the people as no other single event of this period, and the first to organize armed obstruction to the intrusion of the European adventurers were the inhabitants of the forest-clad heights of Senkaḍagala (Kandy) and the neighbouring villages, who from the earliest times have been distinguished by their sturdy patriotism and ardent resistance to every foreign invader. Their determination to be rid of the enemy in their midst was such as no blandishments could divert and no reverses quench, and their efforts were never relaxed or suspended till the Portuguese were driven away from Ceylon, one hundred and fifty years after their first landing. Exasperated by the pusillanimity of their kings and their faithlessness to their country and the national religion, gallant leaders were forthcoming to guide the people in their insurrections of protest. Such was Māyādunne of Sītavaka, himself of royal blood, and his youngest son, Tikiri Baṇḍāra, who first joined the forces at the age of thirteen. The exploits of the young prince soon won him fame, and his ability as a leader enabled him to gain the confidence of his followers, who saluted him on the field of battle with the title of Rāja-Siṃha (the Lion King), a name which for many years to come caused the blood of the Portuguese in Ceylon to run cold.[1] His fiery audacity and his iron will, coupled with the devoted courage of his men, won for him one victory after another, and by 1586 he was not only master of the lowlands, but was able to invade successfully the territory of Kandy, whose

[1] *Rājāvalī* (upham), p. 297.

king, Jayavīra, had invited Franciscan monks in his dominions, permitted a church in his capital and even expressed a desire openly to embrace Christianity.[1] But Rāja-Siṃha's triumph was brief. The *Mahā-vaṃsa* [2] tells us that "being puffed up with victory, this great fool, in the wickedness of his heart, slew his father with his own hand, and took possession of the kingdom." Later, being seized with the fear of his crime, he inquired of the great Buddhist Elders how he could absolve himself of his sin. When they explained to him that patricide was too great a sin for absolution, "he was provoked to anger, like unto a serpent full of poison, when it is beaten with a stick." Other accounts make no mention of the patricide:[3] according to them some of the Buddhist monks were involved in a conspiracy against the king, whereby they sought to set up another in his place. The fact remains, however, that Rāja-Siṃha visited his anger in terrible measure against the priesthood. He abjured the Buddhist faith and became a follower of the Śaivites. The Chief Buddhist Elder was stoned to death, many of the monks were buried up to their necks in the earth and their heads ploughed off; many others were put to the sword; a large number of sacred edifices were pulled down; and he burnt whatever sacred books fell into his hands. Many valuable works were thus irretrievably lost. Just before this time Vīra Vikkama (in 1542) had caused copies to be made of religious books at great expense:[4] they were now reduced to ashes. Most of the monks who escaped death disrobed themselves and fled from the king's wrath. The lands which had been endowed in ancient times for the maintenance of the temples were taken away from them, and the king, to crown all his acts of impiety, deprived the Buddhists of all control of their most venerated spot, the graceful Pinnacle of the Sacred Foot Print of the Buddha, and placed it in the hands of ash-daubed Indian fakirs.

[1] Tennent, *Ceylon*, ii, pp. 20–1.
[2] Chapter xciii.
[3] See *JRAS. C.B.* vol. xviii, No. 56, pp. 382 foll. and Pieris, op. cit., p. 94.
[4] *M.V.* xcii, vv. 14–15.

Rāja-Siṃha died in 1592, deserted by all authority and success; the last part of his life was a series of reverses, where he lost all that he had gained for himself before.

In the hour of Rāja-Siṃha's triumph patriotism and the pride of their race once more revived in the hearts of the Sinhalese, and there was a brief interval of literary activity. From the king's capital at Sītāvaka arose the national poet Alagiyavanna Mohoṭṭāla (or Mukavāṭi), son of the learned Dharmadhvaja Paṇḍita, a man of great scholarly attainments. He wrote (in Sinhalese) of the glory of Rāja-Siṃha's Court, and fired the imagination of his country in their fervour to rally round the monarch in his conquest of the Paraṅgis (foreigners). Alagiyavanna still remains one of Ceylon's most popular poets; his *Kusa-jātaka* and the *Subhāṣitaya* (a didactic poem) are recited wherever the Sinhalese language is known, while his *Sävul-sandesa*, in spite of its lack of originality, ranks in its elegance of diction along with the work of Śrī Rāhula. Others composed poems dealing with the exploits of the Sinhalese in their struggles with the Portuguese—*haṭana* poems, or poems of war, the language of which is a curious admixture of Sanskrit and Sinhalese. Most of them were panegyrics on Rāja-Siṃha. This period also saw the development of the erotic poem, its chief exponent being the half-Portuguese courtier and gallant Gascon Adigār.[1] Shortly before this period, at the beginning of the sixteenth century, a monk named Dhammaratana wrote a Sinhalese interverbal paraphrase to the *Mahāsudassana-sutta* of the *Dīgha-Nikāya*. In the colophon he tells that he completed it in the year 2048 after the death of the Buddha (A.D. 1505–6).[2]

Rāja-siṃha's successor at Kandy was Vimala-dharma-sūriya, who reigned for twelve years till 1604. He was originally known as Dom Joao, and had been a Christian, who lived amongst the Portuguese. When the hour for action came,

[1] See D'Alwis, *Sidat-saṅgarā*, Introduction, and Wickremasinghe's *Catalogue* for details about these works.

[2] Wickremasinghe, p. 4.

he discarded the faith, which never seems to have appealed to him, and ascended the throne at Kandy under the name of Vimala-dharma-sūriya. Both he and his queen had strong European sympathies,[1] the influence of which soon began to be felt even in the court. Portuguese names were common among the nobility, and their manners soon prevailed over the simpler customs of the Sinhalese. The Portuguese language was freely used in all matters of state, the Portuguese jacket and the *barrette* (or cap) were adopted as the ceremonial dress, and still obtain as such in the Kandy and provinces; Portuguese ideas moulded the fashions at the Kandyan Court and their influence—not always for the best—has come down as a legacy even to the present day. But Vimala-dharma did not allow these external manifestations of sympathy to cloud his vision; he was ever responsive to the call of country and carried on an incessant warfare against her enemies. Whatever leisure was left to him he employed in repairing the damage done by Rāja-Siṃha. The attitude of hostility which the latter had adopted towards the Buddhist priesthood had resulted in there being hardly a single monk left in the country who had been properly ordained. Much grieved thereat, Vimala Dharma sent an embassy to the country of Rahkhaṅga (Arakkan) to bring a Chapter of monks ordained in the sacerdotal succession. The mission was successful and several monks led by the Elder Nandicakka came over to the island.[2]

In 1597 in the Udakukkhepa Sīmā at Gātambē on the Mahavāligañga, near Kandy, an ordination was held and many men of good family entered the Order, to the delight of the people. The Tooth-relic, which had suffered many vicissitudes, was once more installed at the capital in a three-storied edifice, and the control of Śrīpāda (Mount of the Sacred Foot Print) handed over to the Buddhists, its legitimate custodians.

[1] Pieris, op. cit., p. 152.
[2] *M.V.*, xciv, vv. 15–21.

On the death of Vimala-dharma his wife, Donna Caterina, as queen in her own right, assumed the sovereignty, but she was soon set aside by a shrewd man zealous in religious works and beloved by his followers, Senerat by name, who killed rival aspirants to the throne and married Donna Caterina. He was a ruler of strong personality, and under his régime the country enjoyed a brief interval of comparative tranquillity. But he did not cease to wage continual warfare against the Portuguese, and in August, 1630, dealt a crushing blow to their forces, which resulted in the death of the Portuguese general, Don Constantine de Say Noroña, and in the slaughter of his army. Senerat's son and successor was Rāja-Siṃha II, who was destined for the last time to kindle the smouldering fires of Sinhalese patriotism into a blaze. Portentous omens had attended his birth, which took place at Mahiyangana, close to the spot where the Buddha had first touched ground in his visit to Ceylon. On the very night when he was born the commander of the Portuguese fort at Colombo had dreamed that he saw a tiny spark no bigger than a glow-worm, travelling towards him from the West and increasing in size as it reached him, until it flamed into a great fire over the fort of Colombo, destroying everything that lay there. Nor were these portents unjustified; for it was during his reign that the Portuguese were eventually driven from Ceylon, and the people were enabled to breathe a sigh of relief that the bloodstained land was entirely rid of their presence. On the 28th March, 1638, amongst the mountain fortresses of Gannoruva, by the edge of the Mahāveligañga, was fought the last great battle of the Sinhalese race. An anonymous poet has left us a Sinhalese description of the fight, as given by an eyewitness. This work, the *Parangī-haṭane* (the fight with the Parangīs or Portuguese), is the greatest martial poem in the Sinhalese language extant, the most spirited piece of literary composition. "It is no mere medley of tinkling bells and scented flowers, of lovely women and precious gems. It rings with the passion of Pindar; it is Miltonic in its resounding roll of names; it laughs with the glee of Chevy-Chase."[1] The destruction of the Portuguese army was complete, and their power to menace the dominions of the Sinhalese King was finally taken away from them. From this time onwards till their expulsion from the island in June, 1658, they made but feeble attempts to win back their lost glory. The ensuing period of peace was a great comfort to the people, who were utterly weary of devastation and slaughter. They settled down once more to cultivate their fields and reconstruct the villages which had been destroyed during the war. Rāja-Siṃha himself was more a man of martial prowess than a hero of peace. Of overbearing demeanour and haughty disposition, fastidious in his habits and studied in disdain, he spent his leisure hours in the wilds of Bintenna, delighting in the chase, hawking being one of his favourite forms of amusement.[2] His popularity among his subjects was due solely to his achievements on the field of battle; beyond confirming the grants of land made to the temples by his predecessors he did nothing else for the promotion of the national faith[3]; his thank-offering after the victory at Gannoruva was a gift to the god of war, who presided over Doḍanvala Devāla, of his headdress of gold and his sword of steel.[4] His rule often savoured of harshness. When (in 1664)[5] the Kandyans, their endurance giving way, attempted a revolt and proclaimed as his successor his son, a lad of 12 years of age, he had no scruples in having the boy poisoned to prevent a recurrence of such treason.[6] It is not surprising therefore that his reign was not productive of any literary works.

In order to effect the final expulsion of the Portuguese from the island, Rāja-Siṃha had invited to his aid the Dutch,

[1] Pieris, op. cit., p. 223.
[2] Tennet, *Ceylon*, vol. ii, pp. 47 foll.
[3] *Mahā-vaṃsa*, xcvi, v. 41.
[4] Pieris, op. cit., p. 225.
[5] Tennent, op. cit., p. 49.
[6] Knox, *History of Ceylon*, p. ii, ch. 6, p. 58.

who were then cruising near the shores of Ceylon.[1] It was in 1595 that they had formed their "Het Maatschappy Van Verre Landes" (company for distant lands), and in the same year Cornelius Houtman conducted the first fleet of merchantmen round the Cape of Good Hope, in order to capture the Portuguese monopoly of trade in the East. Other expeditions followed in rapid succession, and in the course of their travels, on the 30th May, 1602, the first Dutch ship commanded by Admiral Spilberg touched the Port of Batticaloa on the east coast of Ceylon. Vimala Dharma Sūriya was reigning at Kandy at this time. At first the strangers were given but a jealous and reluctant reception; but when Spilberg produced his credentials from the Prince of Orange, which contained the offer of an alliance, offensive and defensive, Vimala Dharma received him with a guard of honour of a thousand men. The proposal of an alliance was accepted with great ardour and alacrity, and permission was given to the Dutch to erect a fortress in any part of the king's dominions. But it was not till 1612, when Senerat and Donna Caterina were on the throne of Kandy, that the terms of the treaty were fully agreed upon. Marcellus de Boschouwer brought a letter from Prince Maurice of Nassau, then King of the Low Countries, sending his friendship to the "Emperor of Ceylon". The result was a treaty, whereby the Dutch undertook to assist the Sinhalese king with ships, forces, and munitions of war, in case of a renewal of Portuguese aggression by land or by sea. In return for the promised military aid they were given permission to erect a fort at Cottiar, on the Bay of Trincomali, and the monopoly of the trade in cinnamon, gems and pearls was secured for them. It was in pursuance of this agreement that Rāja-Siṃha, in his attempt to expel the Portuguese from Ceylon, addressed himself to the Dutch at Batavia and solicited their active co-operation. The invitation was promptly accepted, and in 1638 began the

[1] The following account of the Dutch is taken from various sources, chief among them being Tennent's *Ceylon*, vol. ii, chap. ii.

conflict between the two European nations, which terminated, as we have already seen, twenty years later, in the complete retirement of the Portuguese from the island, and in the installation of the Dutch in the parts formerly occupied by the Portuguese.

The policy of the Dutch in Ceylon was in marked contrast to that of their predecessors. Throughout their régime their possession of the island was a military tenure, and not a civil colonization. They regarded it as an entrepôt in East Indian trade ; no attempts were made to leave a permanent impress of their influence on the people ; they had no lust for conquest ; the fanatical zeal of the Portuguese for the propagation of their faith gave way to the earnest efforts of the Dutch traders to secure their trading monopolies ; extension of commerce was their only aim, and for this purpose peace was essential at any cost. Even when provocation was caused to them, as happened more than once by outrages on the part of the Sinhalese rulers, or by their bad faith, they attempted no retaliation ; by blandishments and presents they allayed the irritation of their ally and endured with subdued humbleness and meek patience whatever insults and contumely were hurled at them, so long as they were able to extract the utmost possible amount of profit from their trade. The Sinhalese in the dominions of the King of Kandy were therefore left unmolested, and were free to follow their own pursuits in peace.

Rāja-Siṃha II was followed by his son Vimala Dharma Sūriya, who ascended the throne in 1679 (?), and reigned for over twenty years. The *Mahā-vaṃsa* [1] tells us that " he was adorned with faith and the like virtues and regarded the Three Sacred Gems as his own ". In addition to the manifold honours paid to the Tooth-Relic he made a pilgrimmage *on foot* to Samanta-kūṭa (the Srīpāda mountain), an act considered to be of great merit, even at the present day. Finding that the condition of the priesthood was very unsatisfactory,

[1] *M.V.*, xcvii, v, 1.

he determined to hold a festival of ordination (*upasampadā*). And indeed the need was very pressing, for it was discovered that not more than five *upasampadā* monks were to be found in the whole of the island. He accordingly sent an embassy of his ministers to Rakkhaṅga (Arakkan), and obtained thence thirty-three monks, led by the Elder Santāna. The ordination ceremony was duly held, at which thirty-three persons of "good families" were ordained, and we are told also that he persuaded one hundred and twenty persons to be invested with the robe of the novitiate [1]—a significant contrast to the thousands who (under previous sovereigns) entered the order on such occasions.

This pious king was succeeded on his death by his son, Srī Vīra Parākrama Narendra-Siṃha, surnamed Kuṇḍasāla, after the suburb of the city of Kandy which he built in a large coconut grove by the beautiful bank of the Mahāväligaṅga. He ruled twenty-three years. Among his numerous acts of piety was the construction of a two-storeyed building for the Tooth-relic, on the walls of which were painted scenes from well-known *Jātakas*. But he was lukewarm in his supervision of the priesthood, and in his reign their old scandalous practices revived. "So far from begging from door to door, as they were expected to do," says a chronicler who wrote a short while after this period,[2] "they regarded even the eating out of their alms-bowl a disgrace. Their food was cooked in the same fashion as that of the great nobles amongst the laity, and it was eaten out of plates! In fact, they were monks in nothing but the use of the name." Narendra-Simha's successor was Srī Vijaya Rāja-Siṃha, a man "diligent and wise, who always loved to associate with good and virtuous men." Following the custom of his predecessors, he obtained his consorts from the city of Madhurā. But, unlike the queens of the monarchs who immediately preceded him, they manifested great interest in the religion of the land of their adoption, and hearkening

[1] *M.V.*, xcvii, vv. 8–15.
[2] Translation of the *Vimāna-vatthu* (A.D. 1770), see below.

unto the Good Law, became Buddhists. With the zeal of new converts they gave themselves up to continuous devotion and to ceaseless acts of merit, and vied with one another in their piety and generosity, "like mines of virtue, showing much kindness and affection towards the inhabitants of Laṅkā, bestowing upon them as much love as mothers do upon their children."[1] They joined the king in persuading young persons to be robed as novitiates and causing them to be properly instructed in the doctrine, and they spent money on getting religious books written.[2] The king himself held many religious festivals, in one of which lamps were lit in all the shrines throughout the country. "Thus did the king make the face of the Island of Laṅkā look bright with shining lights, like the sky that is spangled with stars."[3] He caused preaching halls to be built in divers places, and, we are told, procured "with great trouble" many preachers of the law. In such manner did he attempt to bring about a revival of the faith and to provide even a scanty measure of religious knowledge for his people, whose minds had been starved. When he discovered that the Order of the Saṅgha was almost extinct in the land, he was immensely grieved, and, learning from the Dutch that Buddhism flourished in Pegu, Arakkan, and Siam, he sent an embassy to Ayodhyā in Siam to fetch a chapter of priests. The Dutch helped this mission by lending a ship for the voyage.[4] But the expedition proved disastrous, all except one person perishing in the sea. The survivor made his way to Pegu, whence he returned home to relate the sad news.[5] But the king was not disheartened; he sent a second embassy, and this time too with the help of the Dutch. The ambassadors were provided with suitable presents to the Siamese monks. At Batavia they left behind the presents and proceeded to Siam to inquire if monks were available to be

[1] *M.V.*, chap. xcviii, v. 18.
[2] Ibid., vv. 13–17.
[3] Ibid., xcviii, v. 64.
[4] Tennent, vol. ii, p. 61.
[5] Turnour's *Epitome*, pp. 53–5.

taken to Ceylon; the answer was in the affirmative, but on their return to Batavia they were told by their Dutch hosts that their good king was dead. They were advised not to convey the monks without first ascertaining the wishes of the ruling sovereign. They were compelled, therefore, to set sail for Ceylon reluctantly, their purpose unaccomplished. Unfortunately, however, on the voyage they were overtaken by a storm in which the majority of them perished, and only a handful of survivors were left to tell the doleful tale. Kīrti Srī Rāja-Siṃha, who was now on the throne, was a man of great wisdom and ability, imbued with great enthusiasm for the reform of all abuses. He studied the *Dhamma* with great care and assiduity, and caused it to be preached throughout his dominion. So anxious was he that the knowledge of the religion should be broadcast, that, we are told, he gathered many scribes together and had the whole of the *Dīgha-Nikāya* copied in one day.[1] Whenever copies of books were brought to him accurately and neatly made, he bought them and distributed them amongst the various monasteries. But the crowning glory of his work in the revival of Buddhism was the re-establishment of the *upasampadā* (ordination) in Ceylon.

At the time of his accession to the throne there was not even a single *upasampadā* monk in the whole of the island.[2] There were plenty of novices or *sāmaṇeras*, some of whom were good men and skilful, but owing to want of proper supervision the bulk of the priesthood were in a state of degeneracy. Ratanapāla *Thera*, who wrote a Sinhalese translation of the *Vimāna-vatthu* during the period (in the Śaka year 1692, i.e. A.D. 1770), has left us a short sketch of the condition of the monks before Rāja-Siṃha carried out his reforms.[3] "Ever since the time of Devānampiya-Tissa, the faith-

[1] *M.V.*, xcix, v. 31.

[2] Ibid., v. 175.

[3] This translation, with a few modifications, is taken from a paper on Kirti Sri's Embassy to Siam, read before the Royal Asiatic Society, Ceylon Branch, by Dr. Paul E. Pieris, and published in their *Journal*, vol. xviii, No. 54, pp. 17 foll.

ful-and wise kings who have reigned from time to time—aided by their great ministers and the efforts of pious priests, learned in the Law—had carefully swept away all schisms that had sprung up and preserved the doctrine inviolate. But in recent times the disappearance of such kings and ministers, followed by the oppression of the unbelieving Paraṅgīs and Damilas, had robbed the pious priests of the Four Necessaries ; and, as the religious young men of good families, who assumed the robe, had not the learning to study with care the three *Piṭakas*—which contain the *Vinaya*, *Sutta*, and *Abhidhamma*, —and to order their lives in consonance with the precepts contained therein, by degrees power fell into the hands of low-born priests of profane life, to the great injury of the Church. And, as for the priestly succession, beginning from Upāli *Thera* (whom the Buddha himself had named as the first in the knowledge of the *Vinaya*), and continued in the persons of Dāsaka, Sonaka, Siggava, Moggaliputta, Mahinda, etc., and recruited from all pious folk who assumed the robe without any distinction of family, in proper and perpetual succession of master and pupil, this they ignored. Confusing physical with spiritual kinship, they refused to allow pious young men of good family to assume the robe, and treated all the estates and wealth which generations of godly kings and ministers had dedicated to the service of the priesthood as if they had been dedicated to the use of their private families. Accordingly, for the sake of this wealth they had members of their own families ordained, so that, being robed, they might receive the due *rāja-kāriya*, pretending that this was the succession appointed by the church. But indeed that succession—which was maintained immaculate by disrobing all priests who had violated their oaths and by the ordination of religious and well-born youths—was reduced to a mockery ; and, save for a few holy priests, the majority were as men fouling themselves with hot ashes, while the gems lay before them. And, while the *Dhamma* and the *Vinaya*, subjects for unending study, lay in their path, they preferred the study of such profane matters as astrology, medicine, and devil-worship, all of which they practised in unbecoming fashion within and without the capital; and, thus winning the good-will of kings and powerful ministers, they obtained much wealth and high office. They led scandalous lives, and, ignoring the precepts of the Law, they betook themselves to cultivation and trade, accumulating jewellery and clothes, and making the support of their brothers and nephews an article of their faith. When, through the increase in the number of these shameless priests and the oppression of the unbelieving Paraṅgīs and Damilas, the Faith was on the brink of destruction, it came to pass that a valiant and powerful king of the name of Rāja-Siṃha succeeded to the throne of Laṅkā." Rāja-Siṃha was determined to put an end to this state of affairs. In the third year of his reign he sent an embassy to Siam to bring a body of monks from there, that he might reinstitute ordination in the island. The Dutch helped the mission by a loan of one of their sailing ships. The embassy was eminently successful. The King of Siam at the time was Dhammika, "a wise man who had devoted his whole life to the support of religion." He welcomed the Sinhalese ambassadors with all cordiality. Having heard their purpose, he held an assembly of monks, presided over by the Saṅgharāja (Hierarch) of Siam, and after due deliberation a chapter of more than ten monks was chosen for dispatch to Ceylon, at the head of them being Upāli *Mahā-Thera*. Along with them King Dhammika also sent copies of books on the *Dhamma* and the *Vinaya*, such as were not extant in Ceylon. Great were the rejoicings that attended the arrival of the Siamese monks in the Sinhalese capital. The king himself proceeded to greet them at the head of the whole army, with elephants and horses and other equipages. Thus in due time, 2,299 years [1] after the Parinibbāna (A.D.1756), in the month of Āsāḷha (July–August), the ceremony of *upasampadā* was held in Kandy amidst scenes of unparalleled pomp and ceremony. All the principal

[1] *M.V.*, chap. c, vv. 60 foll.

Sāmaṇeras received the higher ordination, and provision was made for their proper instruction by the monks who had come from Ayodhyā. Very soon afterwards the king had drawn up a *Katikā-vata* or Code of Conduct for the guidance of the monks, so that they might live in conformity with the rules of the *Vinaya*.

In all these measures of reform Kīrti Srī Rāja-Siṃha was assisted and inspired by the unflagging enthusiasm and most whole-hearted co-operation of a monk named Väliviṭa Saraṇaṅkara, who was destined to revive the glories of the faith for the benefit of future generations. Like a lonely star, he illumined this dark period of the history of the Ceylon Saṅgha, and the after-glow of his presence is felt even to-day. Born in the hamlet of Väliviṭa, near Kandy, in the Śaka year 1620 (A.D. 1698–9), he entered the Order as a *Sāmaṇera* at the age of 16, as a pupil of Sūriyagoda *Thera*. With commendable energy he addressed himself to the study of the Pāli language, so that he might learn and understand the sacred scriptures. But Pāli learning was then at such low ebb that no person could be found competent enough to teach him ; no complete copy of any Pāli grammar was available in spite of diligent search. Making the best of his opportunities and unbaffled by the difficulties that beset his path, the young *Sāmaṇera* travelled about from place to place, to allay his thirst for knowledge, collecting one drop of learning here and another there. Thus he studied the *Bālāvatāra* up to the chapter on nouns under a layman called Leuke Rāḷahāmi, and completed it under Palkumbure Atthadassi, himself a *Sāmaṇera* and known as Sāmaṇera-guru (novice teacher). Cherishing a strong desire to re-establish the priesthood in its full vigour, he wandered from place to place, preaching the *Dhamma* and exhorting his audience to rise up to their responsibilities. The fame of the young reformer spread like wildfire, and students flocked to him from all parts of the island. Always simple in his habits, he gave himself up to austerities, depending for sustenance only on what he received in his begging rounds. He thus came to be known as Piṇḍapātika Saraṇaṅkara. Already in the reign of Vimaladharma successor to Rāja-Siṃha II, he had received recognition at the hands of the king, who, we are told, caused to be made a gilt casket of one and a half cubits in height, and set it with seven hundred gems, and presented it to Saraṇaṅkara, together with many sacred books.[1] Later it was at his request that King Vijaya Rāja-Siṃha had sent two embassies to Siam to bring ordained monks from that country. And, when Kīrti Śrī Rāja-Siṃha came to the throne it was the inspiration and the encouragement of Saraṇaṅkara that guided him in his reform of the Saṅgha and enabled him to earn glory as a supreme benefactor of Buddhism in Ceylon. It was he that had written in Pāli the message that was to be taken to the King of Siam and the letter addressed to the Saṅgharāja of that country. The ministers who were to constitute the embassy were chosen on his advice, and the success of the mission was mainly due to his exertions. And after the re-establishment of the *upasampadā* in Ceylon, when the king was conferring honour on those who had helped to achieve it, Saraṇaṅkara's services received their due recognition. He stood pre-eminent among those who, according to the *Mahā-vaṃsa*,[2] had striven to " maintain the religion of the Conqueror, and had endeavoured long to restore to its former splendour the religion of the Sage, which had for a long time been often brought nigh unto the gate of destruction ". He was regarded as the " one who was diligent by day and night, and according to the measure of his wisdom and ability threw light on the doctrines and the precepts of the religion of the Sage ; one who shed light on religion by duly instructing many of his own pupils, and those of others also, in the doctrines and precepts of the religion ; one who was engaged in doing good to himself and to others, and who earnestly wished to maintain the religion of the Buddha for a

[1] *M.V.*, xcvii, vv. 54–7.
[2] Chap. c, vv. 102–8.

long time; one who was constant in devotion to a life of purity; one who in virtue and piety and austerity was like unto a mirror to all the sons of Buddha in Ceylon who sought to improve themselves". He was appointed Saṅgharāja of Laṅkā, the highest office that obtained amongst the priesthood. In that office, as the last representative of a long and glorious line of Hierarchs who had devoted their energies to the welfare of the national faith, he remained for many years leading a very active and useful life, till his death in 1778 at the ripe age of 81.[1] He was cremated on the grounds of the Ampitiya Vihāra, near Kandy, where a monument to his memory still exists.

The new lease of life thus given to the Saṅgha by the united efforts of Saraṇaṅkara and Kīrti Śrī Rāja-Siṃha resulted—as we might expect—in a renewal of literary activity as well. Saraṇaṅkara himself was the author of several important works. In order to facilitate the study of Pāli, which, as we saw above, had been greatly neglected, he wrote the *Rūpamālā*, a short treatise on the declension of Pāli nouns with numerous paradigms and examples; another of his original Pāli works is the *Abhisambodhi-alaṅkāra*, a poem in 100 stanzas, treating of the life of the Buddha Gotama from the time of his birth as the hermit Sumedha during the régime of Dīpaṅkara to his last birth as Siddhattha, when he attained to Enlightenment. The language and form of the poem show that it was not the work of a master hand; the style is weak, the similes and metaphors are borrowed from older works, and there is little originality. The following is the opening stanza:—

Buddhaṃ suddhaguṇākaraṃ dasabalaṃ devātidevaṃ Jinaṃ
Dhamman tena sudesitaṃ bhavanudaṃ dukkhāpahan nimmalaṃ
Saṅghañ cā'pi niraṅgaṇam munisutaṃ vandām'ahaṃ muddhanā
Buddho Dhammagatā Tathāgatavarā pālentu te maṃ sadā.

[1] The materials for the above sketch of Saraṇaṅkara are drawn chiefly from the *Saṅgha-rāja-vata* (a poem) and *Saṅgha-rājottama-sādhu-caritaya* (in prose), both written in Sinhalese by two of his pupils. For details of their works see Wickremasinghe's *Catalogue* under these titles.

There is an interverbal Sinhalese paraphrase, written by Saraṇaṅkara himself. His other works are in Sinhalese: the *Madhurārtha-prakāśanī*, a paraphrase, a commentary to the Pāli *Mahā-Bodhi-vaṃsa* in the Sanskritized Sinhalese of this period; the *Sārārtha-saṅgraha*, a treatise on various doctrinal teachings in Buddhism; a paraphrase of several Suttas used in the *Paritta*; the *Muni-guṇālaṅkāra*, a Sinhalese poem in praise of the Buddha; and an exhaustive Sinhalese *sanne* to the *Bhesajja-mañjūsā*. The last was perhaps inspired by the measures adopted by King Kīrti Śrī to ensure the physical well-being of the monks. "For in this world," says the *Mahā-vaṃsa*,[1] "there are two kinds of diseases to which novitiates and monks are liable, viz. those of the body and those of the mind. Of these, for the cure of diseases of the mind, the Buddha, the greater of men, has provided the *Vinaya* rules and the *Suttanta* discourses. But the monks, after they are instructed in the *Vinaya* and the *Suttanta*—remedies that are effectual in destroying lust and diseases of the mind—are liable to be afflicted with bodily diseases, by reason of which it is hard for them to practise the doctrines and precepts of religion." And we are told that, thus reflecting, King Kīrti Śrī devised ways and means to combat disease amongst the priesthood. The new interest displayed in medicine may have prompted Saraṇaṅkara to revive a study of the *Bhesajja-mañjūsā*, the only book on the subject, so far as we know, written by a Ceylon monk. Saraṇaṅkara gathered round him a galaxy of brilliant scholars, both laymen and monks, who studied under him and continued the revival of learning which he had so well begun. They established Pariveṇas (or places of instruction) in various parts of the country and imparted knowledge to whoever was imbued with love for it. Thus did they rescue from destruction whatever little of Sinhalese Buddhist culture had escaped the ravages of foreign invaders.

[1] Chap. xcix, vv. 179 foll.

Of Saraṇaṅkara's pupils, Attaragama Baṇḍāra Rājaguru, a layman, wrote three works on Pāli grammar. Of these the *Sudhīra-mukha-maṇḍana* is a short treatise dealing with *Samāsa* or compounds. It is meant to be used as a handbook in studying this section of Pāli grammar, and the rules are illustrated with copious examples. The *Kāraka-puppha-mañjarī* deals, as its name implies, with the *Kāraka* (or case relations), i.e. Pāli syntax. In the introductory stanza the author tells us :—

Kriyākārakasambandhaṃ ye na jānanti mānavā
pasubhis saha te tulyā khurasiṅgavivajjitā.

(" Those persons who do not know syntax are like beasts, without horns and hoofs ")—hence the purpose of this book, to give such knowledge.

The author quotes extensively from both Pāli and Sanskrit grammars. The text is accompanied by a Sinhalese interpretation which was written by Baṇḍāra himself.[1] His other work, the *Sadda-mālā*, is a comprehensive Pāli grammar, based on the *Kaccāyana*. The author follows closely the method adopted in the *Rūpa-siddhi*, and the work is divided into seven sections or *kāṇḍas* : *Saññā* and *Saṃhitā*, *Nāma*, *Samāsa*, *Taddhita*, *Ākhyāta*, *Kib-bidhāna* (affixes), and *Kāraka*. A section of *Uṇādi* (prefixes) is amalgamated, as in the *Rūpa-siddhi*, with the *Kib-bidhāna*, and, whereas both in the *Rūpa-siddhi* and the *Kaccāyana* the *Kāraka* section follows immediately after the chapter on *Nāma*, in the *Sadda-mālā* it is placed last of all, probably because the author felt it was the most difficult of them all ! The work contains, according to its colophon, 725 rules, and each of them is accompanied by a Sinhalese interpretation, written most probably by the author himself. The principal aphorisms are taken over from the *Kaccāyana*, while a number of secondary rules are also given to explain the aphorisms and sometimes to supply their deficiencies. These latter are mainly from the *Rūpa-siddhi*. Several references are made to the

[1] See Subhūti, *Nāma-mālā*, p. xciv.

grammatical works of Saṅgharakkhita—the *Sambandha-cintā* and the *Susadda-siddhi*. The Sinhalese colophon at the end of the work tells us that it was completed in the month of Āśleṣa in the year of Śaka, 1701 (July–August, A.D. 1779–80). To Attaragama Baṇḍāra is sometimes assigned also the authorship of a medical work in Sanskrit stanzas, the *Sāra-saṅkṣepa*.[1] Of Saraṇaṅkara's other pupils Tibbotuvāve Siddhattha compiled, at the king's request, the *Mahā-vaṃsa* from the reign of Parākrama-Bāhu IV of Kurunegala down to his own day.[2] Sitināmaluve Dhammajoti wrote the *Bālāvatāra-saṅgraha* and the *Bālāvatāra-liyana-sanne* (or the *Okoñdapola-sanne*), which have been referred to already in discussing the *Bālāvatāra*. Siddhattha Buddharakkhita compiled *Siyāmopasampadā-vata*, giving a description of the mission to Siam in search of the *upasampadā* (ordination), and the *Śrī Saddharmovāda-saṅgraha*, a popular work on Buddhism, exhorting men and women to lead the good life, that they may escape the round of rebirth. Ñāṇaratana *Thera*, incumbent of the Attanagalla Vihāra, composed a poem based on the *Attanagalla-vaṃsa*. At the king's special request Hīnaṭikumburē Sumaṅgala made a Sinhalese version of the *Milinda-pañha*, called *Śrī Dharmādāsaya* (*The Mirror of the Sacred Doctrine*). The author tells us in the colophon that he was the chief pupil of Attaragama Baṇḍāra, himself a pupil of Saraṇaṅkara, and that he wrote at the Uposatha Ārāma of the Mahā-vihāra at Sirivaddhana-pura (Kandy) in the year 2320 of the Buddhist era (A.D. 1777–8).[3] The Sinhalese translation follows the Pāli throughout, except that here and there it adds, by way of gloss, extracts from various Pāli works. It also puts into the mouth of the Buddha a prophecy not found in the Pāli original—that, as the Buddha lay on his deathbed, he saw by his power of clairvoyance that the discussion between Milinda and Nāgasena would take place about five hundred years after the Parinibbāna.

[1] Subhūti, *Nāma-mālā*, p. xciv.
[2] *M.V.*, xcix vv. 80–83, and Wickremasinghe, *Catalogue*, p. xxi.
[3] Colombo Edition, 1878.

Daramiṭipola Dhammarakkhita wrote a Sinhalese *Sanne* to the *Mahā-Sati-paṭṭhāna-sutta* of the *Dīgha-Nikāya*, and several other writers produced numerous works in Sinhalese, some of which are still held in high esteem.[1]

Probably to this period belongs the *Akkhara-mālā*, a short treatise on Pāli and Sinhalese alphabets. The author states that the alphabet which formed the basis of the Pāli was composed by a certain teacher of men at the beginning of the Kalpa, and this consisted of the present Pāli vowels and twenty-five consonants in five classes. The work is written in Pali stanzas, which are accompanied by a Sinhalese *Sanne*. Nāgasena is given in the colophon as the name of the author, but nothing else is known about him.

To the same period I would also assign the *Kāya-virati-gāthā* and the *Śṛṅgāra-rasa-ratna-mālā*. The former is a Pāli poem of 274 verses by an anonymous writer, divided into two sections, the first describing the formation of the body, its foulness, and the folly of bestowing any care on so worthless an object, the second dealing with the mind and the advantages of developing it regardless of the body, so that man may attain the emancipation of Nibbāna.[2] A Sinhalese translation made by the author himself usually accompanies the Pāli poem. Spence Hardy mentions the *Kāya-virati-gāthā-sanne* as one of the books which he consulted and translated in the preparation of his *Manual of Buddhism*, and tells us that it was read to condemned criminals "that they may not grieve at being obliged to leave a state that is connected with so many evils".[3] The *Śṛṅgāra-rasa-ratna-mālā* is a treatise on the eight forms of dancing. It is written in Pāli stanzas and is accompanied by a Sinhalese translation. It is the only work of its kind extant in Ceylon, written in Pāli. The eight forms of dancing are *śṛṅgāra* or lascivious, *hāsya* or comic, *karuṇā* or mournful, *rudra* or passionate, *vīra* or athletic, *bhayānaka*

1 See Wickremasinghe, *Catalogue*, p. xxii, introduction and text, *passim*.
2 Published in Colombo, 1881.
3 *Manual of Buddhism*, 2nd ed., p. 540.

or intimidating, *bībhatsa* or horrible, and *adbhuta* or extraordinary feats of skill. The author says that some have a ninth division called *Śyānta* or diverting, but he thinks that this last is included in the eight already mentioned. It is written in several metres, and is a most interesting work, if for nothing else, at least for its uniqueness.

CHAPTER XIV

THE MODERN PERIOD

KING KĪRTI ŚRĪ was followed by his brother, Rājādhirāja-Siṃha. He evinced the same interest as his predecessor had shown in the cause of religion and of learning, and, finding that the *Katikā-vata* drawn up by his brother needed revision, he summoned an assembly of monks and formulated a new *Katikā-vata*.[1] He was a scholar, well-versed in Pāli and Sanskrit and Sinhalese, and collected round him a band of brilliant literary men, whose *obiter dicta*,—apart from their original compositions—uttered most often in extempore verses, form very interesting reading.[2] The king himself was a poet of great merit, and his beautiful Sinhalese poem, the *Asadisa-Jātaka*,[3] is an elegant composition, full of melody and teeming with a wealth of poetic imagery.

It was during this reign that the British in 1782 first declared war against the Dutch in Ceylon, and in that very same year they captured Trincomali. British trade in India had grown during the preceding two centuries, and now the seizure of the Dutch possessions became essential to them, both for the protection of their own territory and also for the humiliation of the only formidable rival who then competed with Great Britain for the commerce of the Indian seas. Already in 1763 the English had sent an embassy to Kīrti Śrī in Kandy, to negotiate for an amicable treaty; the Sinhalese king received the overtures favourably, but nothing came of it.[4] In 1795 Holland found herself helplessly involved in the great war which was then agitating Europe, and the English in India eagerly seized the opportunity to capture the Dutch dominions in Ceylon. Rājādhirāja-Siṃha entered into an alliance with the English Governor at Madras, and, when,

[1] Wickremasinghe, p. xxii.

[2] These have been published in various anthologies of Sinhalese poetry (*Kavi-saṅgarā*).

[3] *M.V.*, Supplement to chapter c, vv. 13–14.

[4] Tennent, vol. ii, p. 46.

early in 1796, Colonel Stuart appeared before the Dutch garrison at Colombo and demanded their submission, they marched out without striking a blow. The capitulation of the Dutch was completed by a convention between the Dutch Governor and Colonel Stuart, and on the 16th of February, 1796, the British flag waved over the walls of Colombo.[1]

Two years later Rājādhirāja-Siṃha died, and the Adigār, or Prime Minister, nominated as his successor a nephew of the queen, an eighteen-year-old boy, who ascended the throne as Śrī Vikrama Rāja-Siṃha. The Adigār, whose name was Pilima Talauvé, was a traitor of the deepest dye, whose "vaulting ambition oft overleapt itself". He was fired by a treacherous desire to procure the death or the dethronement of the king and ascend the throne himself. With this end in view he spared no pains to spread disaffection among the king's subjects and ceaselessly plotted against his life. He entered into secret negotiations with Frederick North, who had come as the first British Governor of Ceylon, and the latter, instead of disclaiming any participation in the treacherous designs of Pilima Talauvé, disgracefully lent himself to "intrigues inconsistent with the dignity and the honour of his high office".[2] When the Adigār disclosed his plans for the ruin of the young king, North did not consider it unbecoming to discuss with him a matter so revolting and to enter into a bargain with the traitor. From this time onwards the life of Śrī Vikrama was in continual danger; he was dimly aware of the plots that were being hatched against him, but found himself helpless to arrest their progress. He was deprived of all peace of mind; on the advice of his evil associates he had recourse to intoxicating drink, that he might thus drown his sorrows.

There is extant a Pāli poem, written about this period, by a monk named Sumaṅgala of Kunkunāva, in the Kandyan district. The author calls himself a pupil of Rambukvellē

[1] Tennent, ii, p. 68.
[2] Ibid., pp. 76–8.

Thera, and mentions that he had studied under Saraṇaṅkara. The names of several of the eminent Elders of the time are given: Moratota Dhammānanda, Malvatte Sirinivāsa, Kaḍuvela *Thera*, Dhammapāla, Dhammānanda, Siddhattha, and Sunanda. The poem is called *Rāma-sandesa*, and is written in elegant Pāli stanzas. It purports to be a letter (*Sandesa*) addressed to the God Rāmā (Viṣṇu) at Rāma Dēvalā in Hañguranketa, praying to the god to shower his blessings on Śrī Vikrama Rāja-Siṃha. The poet praises the beauty of the capital, its palace and temples, and the river at Kandy. He then goes on to eulogize the king. From this account of the king's character, written before he began his downward career, which ended in sorrow both to himself and to his country, we gather that he was a man of artistic temperament—witness his efforts to beautify the capital with a lake, which yet remains its chief attraction—and that he was a great lover of learning.

But the feeling of insecurity and helplessness, which ceaselessly dogged his footsteps, hardened his heart against all finer emotions, and he gave himself up to savage excesses, unsurpassed by any recorded example of human depravity. North now openly began to assist Pilimatalauvé in exciting insurrections all over the country, and in forcing the king to commit an act of "sufficient aggression" which would serve as a pretext for the British to declare war upon the Kandyans.

North left Ceylon in 1805 and was succeeded by Robert Brownrigg. The traitorous Pilamatalauve was beheaded in 1812, detected in an attempt to assassinate the king. His nephew, Ehälepola, became Adigār, and, taking advantage of the universal horror with which the king's atrocities were regarded by his subjects, organized a general rebellion. The attempt proved abortive, and the king's vengeance knew no bounds. Ehälepola's wife and children were tortured and put to death with appalling cruelty. This awful occurrence was followed by promiscuous executions of all who were suspected of implication in the conspiracy; at length the limits of human endurance being passed, revolt became rife throughout the kingdom and Ehälepola again appealed to the British for help. In January, 1815, an army was on its march to the capital, and within a few weeks the king was taken captive. On the 2nd of March, 1815, at a solemn assembly of the Kandyan chiefs, the king was deposed, and his dominions were vested in the British Crown—contrary to what Ehälepola was given to expect, when the English lent him their support.

In their helplessness the chiefs acquiesced in the British Rāj, and a convention was drawn up whereby the Kandyan dominions were ceded to Great Britain. The Sinhalese nation, which had remained free for 2,358 years, now finally lost their independence and became subject to a foreign power. It is significant that in the treaty by which the island was handed over to the British one article laid down that the rites and ceremonies of the Buddhist religion should be declared sacred and inviolate, and that the Government should undertake to maintain and protect them. The safeguarding of the national religion was emphatically put forward as a condition of their voluntary submission. The unmitigated despotism of Śrī Vikrama had so dazed his subjects that they regarded the transfer of the kingdom to an alien power with almost perfect indifference. The chiefs had submitted to the inevitable force of circumstances with admirable grace, leaving to time the development of the result. It is not surprising, therefore, that before long attempts were made to regain their independence, as soon as they realized the true state of affairs. But all such attempts ended in failure, the country was too disorganized for a general insurrection and the sudden and premature rebellions which broke out proved abortive. Within a few years tranquillity was restored, and the people, too tired to fight, were contented under a mild and indulgent government. They returned to their ordinary avocations, and there was peace in the land.

Once the consummation of acquiring possession of the country had been achieved, the British Government applied with energy all its resources to develop the land. Roads were constructed, commerce encouraged in its utmost freedom, mountain forests felled to make way for the plantation of coffee, etc., civil organizations matured, revenue reformed, and measures adopted for the advancement of agriculture and industry.

Steps were also taken for the promotion of religion and education. The Portuguese had been freebooters and fanatics. Commerce was not their only object; they wished to convert the people to Christianity by every means in their power. For this power they had devised some sort of education, which—though proselytism was its chief aim—had served a useful purpose. The Dutch, though they occupied themselves less with conversion, manifested no disinterested concern at all for the elevation and happiness of their subjects, and, where care was bestowed upon the spread of education, their motives were such as to detract from the grace and the generosity of the act. The avowed object of their schools was to wean the young Sinhalese from their allegiance to the king and to impress upon them the might of Holland.[1] The great feature of their rule was the utter neglect of the country and its interests owing to the selfishness, egotism, folly, and want of energy of the general government.[2] Their religious policy was much more insidious than that of the Portuguese and much more useless. It was inspired more by a fury against the Church of Rome, which was in the island already, than by a desire for conversion. In 1658 a proclamation was issued, forbidding, on pain of death, the harbouring or concealing of a Roman Catholic priest.[3] The Presbyterian converts whom

[1] Tennent, ii, p. 57.

[2] M. Burnand, " The Dutch in Ceylon," *Asiatic Journal*, 1821, p. 444.

[3] Tennent, *Christianity in Ceylon*, pp. 41 foll.

they themselves made were not looked after at all in regard to either elementary teaching or spiritual instruction. In Jaffna alone there were 180,000 "Christians" under three clergymen! Yet all the time baptism was being carried on apace at every village schoolhouse, where attendance was compulsory. The amount of education given in these schools was infinitesimally small. It seldom went beyond teaching their pupils to read and write in the language of their district, and even this was discouraged by the authorities at Batavia. In a communication addressed to the missionaries of Ceylon they strongly expressed their opinion that "reading and writing are things not so absolutely necessary for the edification of these poor wretches as teaching them the fundamentals of the religion which are contained in a very few points: and to pretend to propagate Christianity by reading and writing would be both tedious and chargeable to the Netherlands East India Company".[1] And, in order to facilitate the work of conversion, proclamation was publicly made that no one could aspire to the rank of Modaliar (chief), or be even permitted to farm land or hold it under the Government, who had not first undergone baptism, become a member of the Protestant Church, and subscribed to the doctrines of the Helvetic confession of faith.[2] The number of nominal Christians was thus greatly increased. This system of political bribery, to encourage conversion, produced organized hypocrisy, whose results were pernicious and whose recoil and reaction, when it did come, was destructive of the object for the furtherance of which it had been resorted to unwisely. When the Dutch retired from Ceylon, they left behind them a superstructure of Christianity, prodigious in its outward dimensions, it is true, but so internally unsound and so unsubstantial, that within a few years it had disappeared almost from the memory of the people of Ceylon. A religion which

[1] Letter of the Governor-General of Batavia to Baldaeus, 18th Sept., 1662. See Baldaeus, *Descrip. of Ceylon, etc.*, p. 811.

[2] Tennent, loc. cit., p. 45.

required coercion and persecution to enforce its adoption was doomed to failure.

During the early years of the British régime but little was done to remedy this lamentable state of affairs, brought about by the artifice and corrupt inducement of the Portuguese priesthood and the alternate bribery and persecution of the clergy of the Church of Holland.[1] In 1806 Governor Maitland published a regulation abolishing the Roman Catholic disabilities imposed by the Dutch, and later an Act for the relief of the Roman Catholics was passed in 1829.[2] But even as late as 1850 nothing had been done to remove the difficulties under which the Buddhists were labouring. Even at that time no child could be legally registered without previous baptism by a Christian minister, and the clergy refused to solemnize the marriage of unbaptized individuals.[3] The people were made to understand that baptism conferred upon them some sort of civil distinction, and this resulted in the production of prodigious numbers of "Government Christians", who ostensibly professed Christianity, and we are told that "in point of character and conduct they were notoriously the most abandoned and reckless class of the community".[4] They were made to see in Christianity not only happiness in the world which is to come, but, what was more important to them, the promise of this life as well!

With the proclamation of liberty of worship to all sects of the Christian faith the island soon became a busy scene of the activity of various missionary bodies. The Baptists had already formed a colony in 1792: they were followed by the Wesleyan Methodists in 1814, the Americans in 1816, and the Church of England in 1818. They received every encouragement from the Government, both in the island and at Whitehall. When in 1808 Sir Thomas Maitland attempted to remove

[1] Tennent, ibid., p. 77.
[2] Ibid., pp. 75 and 91.
[3] Ibid., pp. 88–9.
[4] Ibid., p. 89.

the regulation which had rendered Christianity an essential qualification for office, he was promptly censured by the Secretary of State, and the necessity was urged upon him of "devoting every energy to the promotion of education, as essential to the extension, if not ultimately identified with the existence, of Christianity itself".[1]

The missionaries soon realized that the mere sprinkling of water on the face and the repetition of the formula of the baptismal rite were not sufficient to make the Sinhalese a Christian and sever him from his deep and tenacious attachment to his own national traditions. They therefore busied themselves with establishing schools in various parts of the island, manned and managed by missionary bodies. There the children were instructed in the principles of Christianity and the rudiments of elementary knowledge. Hitherto the temple had been the village school as well, and the monks had acted as the national instructors both in secular learning and spiritual wisdom. But in the chaotic conditions that prevailed during the preceding two centuries this system of education had become disorganized; and, although here and there the temple-schools yet maintained a precarious existence, the missionaries now launched forth a campaign for superseding the Buddhist priesthood in the department of education. These schools were supported by mission funds and subsidized by Government grants. In most of them no formal declaration of Christian belief was insisted upon as a preliminary to admission, but each student was required to be present at the morning and evening devotions of the school, and go through a course of instruction in the Christian faith. They had no opportunity of participating in their own religious observances.

The instruction imparted to them in these schools was arranged with a view to undermining the superstitions of their beliefs (as the missionaries were pleased to call all religions except their own), "to destroy the polypus vitality of their

[1] Tennent, *op. cit.*, p. 85.

faith," "to demonstrate the subtle errors of their idolatry, to expose the absurdities of their religion, and bring home to them the civilizing influences of Christian life."[1] It was to be a gradual process; the mind of the student was to be stirred, his inert faculties set in motion, his previous habits of thought disturbed; doubts made to assail his spirit, the deception of his original faith pointed out, followed by a displacement of unsoundness, the rejection of error and the dawnings of a desire for the substitution of truth. For this purpose men were imported with years of laborious experience amongst "heathens of every hue and in every quarter of the world".[2] The establishment of vernacular schools was soon followed by the organization of schools and seminaries for the study of English, and these followed the same lines of policy. The education of girls was not neglected, and the earliest efforts of the missionaries were directed to the establishment of girls' schools, especially of boarding schools, "where the girls could be domesticated in childhood, and kept pure and uncontaminated till married with the approbation of their Christian guardians."[3] Buddhism was held up to them as an object worthy of nothing else except ridicule and contumely, and every effort was made to defeat the influence of parents and relations in the matter of religion by condemning their idolatry and laughing to scorn their habits and pursuits of life.

As a result of all this, a cleavage and an estrangement, more deadly than had ever risen out of the institution of caste, began to creep in among the Sinhalese. The schools provided no access to their own literature: possibly it was recognized that national "superstitions" have ever found their surest allies in a national literature, with which their traditions and their tenets were almost imperceptibly blended. Instead their intellectual advancement was sought to be based

[1] Tennent, op. cit., pp. 142 and 276.
[2] Ibid., p. 143.
[3] Ibid., p. 159.

on books which were almost unavoidably adaptations from European literatures, abounding in ideas totally foreign to their customs and their habits of thought, and teeming with forms of expression neither familiar nor intelligible to them.

Other means were also adopted to ensure the grand consummation of the ultimate triumph of Christianity; the instrumentality of preaching and the printing press—education, exhortation, and the book. Padres went about preaching throughout the scattered villages, and the press looked after the universal distribution of the scriptures and scriptural tracts and publications designed to expose the delusions of the people's "idolatrous faith" and to exhibit the "supremacy and the divine origin of Christianity". The violence done to the Sinhalese language in these tracts and publications is extraordinary. The pliant dialect of the Sinhalese—so artistically inflected that by the variations of a single pronoun the speaker is enabled to supply it with delicate propriety, so as to convey no less than ten or twelve degrees of respect—is replaced in them by an artificial jargon lacking in nicety or tone or grace of style.

For the successful demonstration of their errors to the Buddhists, to assail their code of ethics and to point out to them the fallacies of the metaphysical subtleties of their faith, the missionaries now began to study Sinhalese and Pāli and to read the Buddhist scriptures. Their researches soon convinced them that the subjects of their study were full of literary treasures, whose value had not so far been sufficiently realized; this added a new zest to their work, and scholars like Charter, Lambrick, Clough, Spence Hardy, and Gogerly began to devote their attention more and more to the task of mastering the books which they found in Ceylon. They wrote grammars for the systematic study of these languages, and compiled dictionaries for the benefit of future students.[1]

[1] e.g. Charter's *Sinhalese Grammar* (1815); Clough's *Pāli Grammar* (1824) and *Sinhalese Dictionary* (1821); Lambrick's *Sinhalese Grammar* (1834).

They made translations of such books as would be useful to them in preaching against the Buddhists, and published them that they might be better known. Some of these books reached Europe and America, and there aroused in the hearts of various scholars a desire to learn more about the religion which the missionaries sought to condemn and the literature of which these books formed a part. The fervour which inspired the publication of such books was great. Spence Hardy in his *Manual of Buddhism*, which is a compilation from the sacred books of the Sinhalese, said : " This Manual will be received, I doubt not, as a boon ; and it will enable them (the messengers of the cross) more readily to understand the system they are endeavouring to supersede by the establishment of Truth. I see before me, looming in the distance, a glorious vision, in which the lands of the East are presented in majesty ; happy, holy, and free. I may not, I dare not, describe it ; but it is the joy of my existence to have been an instrument, in degree, however feeble, to bring about this grand consummation." (*Manual of Buddhism*, Preface, p. x.)

But the worm had already began to turn. The bewildering variety of religious beliefs which had been presented to the Sinhalese for acceptance by the various missionary bodies, under the régimes of the Portuguese, the Dutch, and now the English, had left them dazed, and later produced in them a listlessness and an indifference to all religion. The ostensible connexion which the churches had with the Governments of the day was associated in their minds with patronage and power, and being allured, as all ordinary men are, by the prospect of obtaining wealth and rank under the Government, they had changed from one faith to another as the expedience of circumstances had dictated to them. This had encouraged falsehood and brought about a certain debasement of character. They designated themselves the followers of the " Sopremād-āgama " (Government religion), and they formed a class " whose reputation and whose practice were alike an outrage on the religion in which they were born and an insult to that which they professed to have adopted ".[1]

Education had, as we saw earlier, been neglected for several generations, and this had produced an obtuseness and a torpor of intellectual faculties ; it had smothered all emotions of enterprise, emulation, and ambition, such as supply a stimulus to the intellect and organize the march of improvement. The Christianity which was imposed upon them was not made to appear as an institution of the land, to be cherished and supported as such ; its exotic nature was patent ; the missionary did not effectually accommodate his ministration to the habits of his flock, so as to gain upon their confidence, or to exert a sufficiently strong influence over their opinions and habits of thought. The " civilization " which it had brought in its trail and which meant chiefly the adoption of European ways and modes of life created artificial needs ; it is not surprising, therefore, that under its influence no art of any kind was developed, and no achievements of the mind, in the shape of literature, were produced.

But half a century of British rule worked remarkable changes ; it brought peace and tranquillity into the island, where strife and domestic discontent and despotism had reigned for nearly two centuries. British capital and enterprise helped in the development of the land and secured the enjoyment of certain personal comforts which had not been possible under the Portuguese or the Dutch ; new careers of occupation were opened up, and new energies called into exertion ; which resulted in the industrial and the material improvement of the people. The British followed a policy of general religious tolerance ; and though, for quite a long time yet, the Buddhists suffered from many disabilities, the more courageous of them were now able to profess their faith without fear of being openly persecuted. Governor North, in spite of his ignominious participation in the conspiracy to depose the last King of Ceylon, was a man of broad views, and in a statesman-

[1] Tennent, *Christianity in Ceylon*, p. 90.

like manner he adopted various measures to conciliate the people. Tennent tells us that his administration was characterized by signal success in the organization of civil government; the promotion of religion and education and commerce; the establishment of Courts of Justice; the reform of the revenue, and the advancement of native agriculture and industry.[1] In pursuance of this policy of the promotion of education he increased the number of parochial schools to 170 in various parts of the Island, and founded a "Seminary" at Colombo for the Sinhalese youths who wished to acquire a knowledge of English.[2] This "Seminary" was the first English school in Ceylon. Other schools soon followed, giving instructions, some in the vernacular and others in English, opened by various missionary bodies. Their avowed object was proselyzation; but, if the measure of their success be judged by the number of converts they have made, their efforts cannot be called productive of great results.

The grand consummation, which Hardy and his colleagues so devoutly prayed for, of Christianizing Ceylon seems yet as far off as ever. Apart from this, however, these schools served to diffuse over a wide area that general information which is the first essential of all knowledge. The English schools provided their students with facilities for the acquisition of English, and opened for them the door to a familiarization with the advances of modern science and modern education; these schools gave them the ability to investigate the problems that were put before them; the students learned, like the Jews of Beroea, to examine things for themselves and "search the Scriptures whether these things are so". In many instances the *alumni* of these institutions, instead of returning the care expended on them by the missionaries by seeking conversion to Christianity, became devout Buddhists, whose desire was the propagation of their own faith. Their education had given them

[1] Tennent, *Ceylon*, ii, p. 86.

[2] *Cey. Antiq.* and *Lit. Reg.*, ix, pt. ii, p. 145.

exercise of thought and exertion of intellectual power sufficient to realize the value of their own national faith, and now, by a strange Nemesis, they came forward as its strong adherents against the onslaught of the missionaries.

Meanwhile the missionaries themselves, more especially the Methodists,[1] had been studying the doctrines of Buddhism and the literature connected with it. The information they thus acquired was sedulously used by them in the preparation of tracts in Sinhalese, demonstrative of the errors of the Buddhist religion and illustrative of the evidences and institutes of Christianity. They acquired a command over the Sinhalese language, and their preachers went from village to village, distributing these tracts by the thousands, and questioning the truth of Buddha's teaching. The monks in their village temples, in the course of their sermons to the congregations that assembled at the Vihāra on the *Uposatha* days, attempted to refute the arguments adduced against Buddhism by the itinerant Christian preachers. Many of them, with characteristic broad-mindedness, invited the missionaries to their temples and gave them opportunities of addressing assemblies of monks, at the conclusion of which they would ask questions, relative to the proofs and principles of Christianity.[2] But the denunciation of Buddhism went on apace, till a young monk named Mohoṭṭivatte Guṇānanda, appeared on the scene and flung the gauntlet down in a challenge to the Christians to meet him in open debate. The Christian clergy at first treated him with indifference, even with contempt; but the young *sāmaṇera* (novice) assiduously studied the Christian scriptures and read with avidity such Rationalist Literature as he could obtain (printed in Europe) dealing with the fallacies of Christianity. He possessed

[1] The Methodists have at all times been the closest students of Buddhism and its sacred literature, and they produced men of great scholarship both in the classical and the modern languages of Ceylon, e.g. Clough, Gogerly, and Spence Hardy.

[2] Tennent, *Christianity in Ceylon*, pp. 307 and 312.

tremendous energy, and a masterful personality; his voice was compared to the roar of the ocean, deep and far-reaching; his flood of eloquence was unceasing. Well versed in the Buddha's teaching and armed with information against the Christians,[1] he went with meteoric rapidity from village to village, carrying the war into the enemy's camp, often at great personal risk. The fame of the young orator spread like wildfire, and his meetings, which were generally held in the open, were attended by thousands who flocked to hear him; he stormed several Christian strongholds, always throwing down his challenge to them to meet him in open debate, where the relative merits of the two religions could be discussed face to face. The challenge was at last accepted and debates took place at Udanviṭa (in the Four Korales) in 1866 and at Gampola in 1871. But the culmination of his efforts was the great Pānadura Controversy in August, 1873, which lasted for a week. Against him were ranged the foremost missionaries of the day; at the end the victory naturally lay for the people with Mohoṭṭivatte. The orderliness of the assembly was a great credit to all concerned, and, when the Christians retired from the conflict discomfited, the enthusiasm of the Buddhist camp was unprecedented. It was an epoch-making event; the enthusiasm it awakened amongst the Buddhists was immense; festivities were held in every temple in the Island to mark Guṇānanda's triumph, his effigy was carried in procession in every village, and he was the hero of the hour. From 1873 began the Buddhist Renaissance movement. Now that the truth of their religion had been vindicated, the Buddhists were determined to fight their Christian adversaries with their own weapons—" education, exhortation, and the Press."

The attention of Colonel Henry Steele Olcott, President-Founder of the Theosophical Society, was first drawn to

[1] He was also an accomplished scholar in Sinhalese. *Vide* his edition of the *Kāvya-śekhara* (Colombo, 1872).

Buddhism by a report of the Pānadura Controversy, which he happened to come across in a public library in the United States. He was a seeker after the truth in all religions, and, realizing the importance of the teachings of the Buddha in the development of man's spiritual nature, he came over to Ceylon to study Buddhism at first hand. His researches soon convinced him of the sublimity of the Buddhist faith, and, avowing himself a follower of the Teacher, he thenceforward became a staunch friend of the Sinhalese Buddhists, and to the best of his ability helped them in the tasks that awaited their attention.

Under his guidance in 1880 was started the Buddhist Theosophical Society at Colombo. The presence of Col. Olcott was an invaluable acquisition to the Buddhist forward movement; the Buddhist leaders rallied round him, and, acting under his counsel, they began establishing schools all over the Buddhist provinces. The enthusiasm thus awakened in the cause of Buddhist education still remains unabated; to-day the number of Buddhist schools in the Island, both English and vernacular, reaches nearly 500, and the instruction they impart compares favourably with that of schools maintained by missionary educational organizations in Ceylon.

Funds were wanted to carry on the campaign of educational propaganda. Volunteers were immediately forthcoming to act as itinerant preachers. They went from village to village, appealing for subscriptions to maintain the schools. The Buddhists, always generous in the support of religion, readily responded. Their devotion to the national faith, though submerged for a time under the flood of persecution, was inveterate, hereditary and insurmountable, and, as soon as their helplessness was removed, it found immediate expression. There are men and women still alive who have vivid memories of the tremendous enthusiasm that prevailed at these collection meetings.

The Christian Missions had been flooding the country with

many tracts [1] dealing with the fallacies they had discovered in Buddhism. To counteract their influence, and also to educate the Buddhists themselves in the knowledge of their own religion, the Buddhist leaders turned their attention to the publication of books. Printing was to them as yet quite a new art. It was unknown in Ceylon till about the year 1737, when the Dutch introduced printing in Sinhalese character for the purpose of translating and publishing Christian works in the language of the people. The Colombo Auxiliary Bible Society followed in the same lines about 1813 ; the Wesleyans established a press in 1815 ; the Church Missionary Society in 1822 ; the Baptist Mission in 1841 ; and the Roman Catholics in 1849. The Buddhists were too poor to afford a press of their own, and they appealed to the King of Siam, as the only Buddhist King of the time, for help in their enterprise. The king gladly responded, and the first printing press controlled by the Sinhalese Buddhists was established at Galle in 1862, under the name of the Laṅkōpakāra Press.[2]

Mohoṭṭivatte Guṇānanda, in his determination to fight the enemy in their own camp, had established his headquarters at Koṭahena, then, as now, a stronghold of the Roman Catholics ; there, with the help of his lay-supporters, he established in 1862 the Sarvajña-sāsanābhivṛddhi-dāyaka Press. The example thus set was soon followed by others : the Lakrivikiraṇa Press in 1863 and the Laṅkābhinava-viśruta Press in 1864. The most important work, and the most considerable in the point of size, among the first publications of these printing establishments was the *Milinda-praśnaya* (the Sinhalese translation of the *Milanda-pañha*). It was felt that the book would be most useful in refuting the

[1] It is a regrettable fact that the language used both in these tracts and in the rejoinders issued by the Buddhists was far from being refined or urbane. The vilest terms of abuse were sometimes employed in the discussion of the most sacred subjects of religious belief.

[2] I am indebted for this information to the Hon. Mr. W. A. de Silva, of Colombo.

arguments hurled at the Buddhists by their adversaries. The expenses of the publication were borne by five Buddhist gentlemen, whose names deserve to be mentioned here because their munificence paved the way for the right exercise of philanthropy later. They were Karolis Pīris, Abraham Livēra, Luis Mendis, Nandis Mendis Amara-Sekara, and Chārlis Arnolis Mendis Vijayaratna Amara-Sekara. The work was issued from the Buddhist Press at Koṭahena in 1877–8, under the editorship of Guṇānanda.[1]

The Buddhist Renaissance movement, thus inaugurated, found its pioneers in the foremost scholars of the day. The system of temple education which existed in ancient Ceylon had gradually fallen into decay and disorganization, and was now being slowly superseded by the schools, manned and managed wholly by laymen. The monasteries confined their attention mainly to the education of the monks. Secluded in their cloisters, and now happily free from persecution, and supported by an ever generous laity, they had been sedulously devoting their energies to the study of the old books, both sacred and secular, still preserved in places where the ravages of the persecutors had not penetrated. When men of learning were required to guide the destinies of the new Forward Movement, they came forth and offered their services.

Foremost among them was Hikkaduvē Siri Sumaṅgala. Born in 1827 in a small village near Galle, he entered the Order while yet quite young. With remarkable assiduity he mastered the books of the *Tipiṭaka* along with their commentaries under various teachers, and made himself very proficient in Sanskrit as well. In his boyhood he had witnessed the disabilities under which his co-religionists were labouring at the time, and while yet a *sāmaṇera* he did all that he could to encourage their adherence to the national faith and to foster their devotion to it in adversity. His fame as a preacher and an erudite scholar with a vast wealth of knowledge soon

[1] *Milinda-praśnaya*, Koṭahena, *B.E.* 2420 (1877–8 A.D.) pp. 628, 12, iv, 8°.

spread, and he was one of those that helped Guṇānanda at the Pānadura controversy, where, it is said, his speedy penmanship was especially of the greatest use in taking down the arguments addressed by the Christian spokesmen. Quite soon after that event some of the more prominent of the Buddhists in Colombo, impressed by his abilities and by his versatility, requested him to come over to the Metropolis and found a place of learning where both monks and laymen could acquire a thorough knowledge of Sinhalese, Pāli, and Sanskrit. The invitation was accepted, and in June, 1874, was started the Vidyodaya Pariveṇa, over whose destinies the Venerable *Mahā-Thera* presided till his death in May, 1911. The Vidyodaya Pariveṇa became a miniature of the old Mahā-Vihāra at Anurādhapura, one of the foremost places of learning in the East. Students flocked to it from all parts of the Island, and after having gone through a course of residence there they carried back with them the torch of knowledge which they had kindled at the feet of the Great Elder. It was a matter of common belief that no one who had had the good fortune of being taught by the Venerable *Mahā-Thera* would fail to achieve renown in the world, and amongst the last two generations of Ceylon Buddhists hardly a single person of eminence is to be found, either amongst the monks or amongst the laity, who, at some time or other in his life, had not received instruction at the hands of the President of the Vidyodaya Pariveṇa. Many of Siri Sumaṅgala's students established Pariveṇas in various parts of the country, and thus began once more the revival of learning which had remained in abeyance from Saraṇaṅkara's day. The fame of the Institution soon spread abroad, and thither came men in search of knowledge, not only from India, Burma, and Siam, but also from distant China and Japan and Europe and America. Siri Sumaṅgala himself was a hardworking student to the end of his days, and it is said that besides many languages of Asia he was able to read and understand several languages of Europe as well, and that at the time of his death, aged 80, he was studying Russian. On his death, in 1911, his chief pupil Mahagoda Siri Ñāṇissara [1] succeeded him as Principal of the Pariveṇa, and most ably continued the work which had been begun by his teacher. During his regime several improvements were effected in the courses of instruction, and English was made a regular subject of study. On Siri Ñāṇissara's death, in 1922, the reins of office were taken over by its present Principal, the Venerable Kahāve Siri Sumaṅgala Ratansarā, *Mahā-Nāyaka-Thera,* an Elder of wide scholarship, profound erudition and great ability.

This brief account of the literary revival in Ceylon during the last century would be incomplete without some reference, at least, to the exertions of the Europeans in the Island, missionaries, civil servants and others, whose researches it was that first brought home to the Ceylonese the glories of their own literature, when many of them had begun to treat it with neglect. Besides clergymen like Clough, Gogerly, Hardy and Copleston, who always evinced a deep interest in the languages and the literatures of Ceylon, there has been a succession of civil servants, who, having sympathy with the institutions and the learning of the people among whom their lot was cast, found in the garnering in of the harvest of knowledge which lay at their doors the greatest respite from the tedium of their official duties; men like Armour, Tolfrey, Turnour, Brodie, Tennent, Upham, Childers, D'Alwis and—greatest of them all—Rhys Davids, who realized the splendid opportunities they had of advancing their own inner and spiritual nature and at the same time being of immense service to the scholarship of the world. The results of their labours are too fresh in men's minds to need elaboration here. On the 7th February, 1845, was started the Ceylon Branch of the Royal Asiatic Society, "to institute and promote inquiries

[1] Besides preparing scholarly editions of several Pāli texts, Ñāṇissara made a Sinhalese translation of Vedeha's poem—*Samanta-kūṭa-vaṇṇanā.*

into the History, Religion, Literature, Arts, and Natural Philosophy of Ceylon, together with the social condition of its present and former inhabitants," and the first number of the Society's *Journal* was published the same year.

Along with the restoration of learning and the introduction of the printing press an impetus was given to fresh literary activity. The book-burnings and the persecutions of the preceding two centuries had brought about a scarcity in the number of books available for study. The first labours of scholars, therefore, were directed to the task of editing and publishing such books as were of immediate necessity to students in the prosecution of their studies. The Sinhalese had long been accustomed to have the benefit of the patronage of their kings in matters of this kind, but it was found that no such help could be expected from their present rulers. Printing was to them quite a novel thing; they had no experience in the art of collating manuscripts and editing them in a scientific manner; often the copies of the manuscripts that were accessible to them were defective and full of errors made by unlettered scribes. There was no proper organization, and the editors were not all men of learning. The result was that many of the books issued are replete with errors both of printing and of editing. The texts were often printed in parts of about eighty pages and published at irregular intervals, and several of them begun, perhaps, thirty years ago, yet remain to be completed!

In the *Journal of the Pāli Text Society* [1] Mr. W. A. de Silva has given a list of the books issued by the Sinhalese Press up to the year 1910. There we find, as he himself points out, that two classes of work have been published with a certain degree of abundance, namely Grammars for the Study of Pāli and a large number of translations into Sinhalese of isolated Suttas from the Five Nikāyas of the Pāli Canon. The reason for this preference is not far to seek. The study of Pāli had

[1] 1910–12, pp. 135 ff.

been long neglected, and when it was now revived, simple works on grammar were found necessary. The laity were more or less completely ignorant of Pāli, and hence the contents of their Sacred Literature were mostly unknown to them, except for what little they heard from the expositions of the monks in the village temples. It was to remedy this latter disadvantage that the translations were made and issued of some of the more well-known Suttas.[1] Both in Mr. de Silva's list and in the *Catalogue of the Temple Libraries of Ceylon*, prepared in 1885 at the request of the Ceylon Government by the late Louis De Zoysa,[2] there is another feature worthy of notice—the large number of books from Burma and Siam which seem to have been introduced into Ceylon during the nineteenth century; we do not hear of the existence of many of them in the Island earlier. We have seen that from the time of Vijaya-Bāhu in the twelfth century, there had been frequent intercourse between the countries above-mentioned and Ceylon, and scholars were in the habit of paying visits to each other across the seas. There is no reason to doubt that one of the results of these visits was the exchange of books. But during the political upheavals of the seventeenth and eighteenth centuries such intercourse had very largely ceased to exist, and the use of imported books does not seem to have at any time been prevalent to a large extent.

With the re-establishment of the *Upasampadā* by Saraṇaṅkara and Kitti Siri Rāja-Siṃha, however, the connexion with Siam was revived. When the Sinhalese embassy returned to Ceylon with the *Upasampadā* monks, we are told that they brought with them as a present from the King of Siam "books of diverse kinds, which were not extant in the Island".[3]

[1] It would be interesting to note, in view of what I have stated in an earlier chapter, that among the earliest of these translations was a compilation of the Suttas used in the chanting of Paritta.

[2] Govt. Printing Office, Colombo, 1885.

[3] *M.V.*, c, vv. 152–3.

The friendship thus renewed with Siam has ever since been maintained, and we saw how, when the Ceylon Buddhists desired to establish a press of their own, they appealed to the King of Siam for funds, and received a generous response.

Early in the nineteenth century certain events took place which drew Burma and Ceylon close together once more and freshened their bonds of affection. The Kandyan Kings were all strongly imbued with the prejudices of the Brāhmans and upheld the doctrines of polytheism and caste, and, when King Kitti Siri re-established the *Upasampadā* from Siam, he decreed that none but members of a particular caste, the Gahapati (Goigama) should be admitted to the higher order of monks. The monks of the maritime provinces, who belonged to the other castes, were justifiably indignant at this unrighteous exclusion and this maladministration of the religion. In 1798 therefore, as a protest, they organized an expedition to Burma to introduce the *Upasampadā* from that country. The embassy was led by Aṁbagahapitiye Ñāṇavimala-Tissa; he was accompanied by five *sāmaṇeras*. Their mission was eminently successful; the Saṅgharāja at Amara-pura received them with singular favour. The Emperor caused their ordination to be celebrated with all the pageantry of royalty, and five Burmese monks accompanied them on their return in 1802 to Ceylon, where they became the founders of the Amara-pura sect, which now forms a very influential body, with a large number of adherents. Seven years later, in 1809, a second expedition was led by Daḍalle Dhammarakkhita, who with four colleagues received the *Upasampadā* in Burma.

As a result of this close association between the two countries, several of the Ceylon monks went over to Burma and there specialized in the study of the Abhidhamma. On their return they brought with them a large number of works written in Pāli by Burmese authors. Many of these they edited and published in Sinhalese characters, and some of the more important were translated into Sinhalese.

Besides these translations, etc., to which reference has already been made, several original works have been written in Pāli during the last century.

In 1835 the Wesleyan Mission Press issued a Pāli translation of the New Testament. At the time of its publication there was a certain amount of misgiving in the minds of the Buddhists, because it was believed that one or two of the well-known Buddhist monks had a share in the work of translation, and that their action was ill-advised. These fears were soon laid to rest. It was found that the language of the translation was sufficient evidence against any such assumption. The book was not favourably received by the Christians, because they could not understand a word of what it contained, nor by the Buddhists, who would have nothing to do with it!

In 1876 Vaskaduve Siri Subhūti published the *Nāma-mālā*, a work on Pāli grammar, compiled at the suggestion of his erstwhile pupil, R. C. Childers (Professor at University College, London, after leaving Ceylon, in the last few years of his short life), author of the well-known *Pāli-English Dictionary*. The work was dedicated, by permission, to Edward VII, then Prince of Wales, who visited Ceylon. It is accompanied by prefaces in English and Sinhalese, the latter containing a most valuable historical account of works on Pāli grammar either written in Ceylon itself or used there. Subhūti had already published in 1865 an edition made by him of Moggallāna's *Abhidhāna-ppadīpikā*, with English and Sinhalese interpretations. Later, in 1893, he followed it up with a complete index of all the Pāli words, giving their meanings in Sinhalese.

In 1877, at the request of the Governor, Sir William Henry Gregory, Siri Sumaṅgala, assisted by Paṇḍita Devarakkhita Baṭuvantudāvē, brought out the edition of the *Mahā-vaṃsa*, completed from the time of Kitti Siri to the cession of the Island to the British in 1815. A few years later, in 1883, they made a Sinhalese translation of the whole work, and published it in two volumes.[1] Siri Sumaṅgala also brought out an edition of the *Bālāvatāra*, accompanied by a comprehensive original *ṭīkā* in Pāli.

In 1880 Ācariya Vimalasāra *Thera* published the *Sāsana-vaṃsa-dīpa*, a "history," as the author tells us, "of the Buddhist Church, written in Pāli verse and compiled from Buddhist Holy Scriptures, Commentaries, Histories, etc." He had published earlier another Pāli work, the *Sīmā-lakkhaṇa-dīpanī*, dealing with the oft-disputed question of the consecration of *Sīmā* or boundaries of ordination. The *Sāsana-vaṃsa-dīpa* is written in twelve chapters. It begins with the birth of the last Buddha as Sumedha, describes the twenty-four Vivaraṇas, and gives a history of his last life up to the time of the Parinibbāna. Chapters v–viii deal with the three convocations and the establishment of Buddhism in foreign lands; chapters ix and x deal with the establishment of Buddhism in Ceylon and the writing down of the Piṭakas and the Commentaries. Chapter xi is by far the most important, because it gives the names of authors who lived from the time of Buddhaghosa to the reign of Paṇḍita Parākrama-Bāhu, together with the works they produced. In spite of its faulty arrangement—because it follows no chronological order—this chapter is of great value. The last chapter deals with the measures adopted by various monarchs to re-establish the Sāsana, when it died down at various periods of its history for want of proper care and attention. It ends with the introduction of the Amara-pura Nikāya into Ceylon. In 1893 Siri Siddhattha Dhammānanda, Principal of the Parama Dhamma Cetiya Pariveṇa at Ratmalāna, published the *Lokōpakāra*, a didactic Pāli poem of 107 stanzas, written in *gāthā* verse, accompanied by a Sinhalese translation by the author himself. It is based on the *Saddhammōpāyana*, and deals with practically the same subjects.

In 1902 S. M. Burrows, Director of Public Instruction,

[1] Sihala Samaya Press, Colombo, 1883.

established the Committee on Oriental Studies to systematize the instruction given at the various Pariveṇas, make them conform to one common standard, if possible, and hold competitive examinations to encourage the students. The Government was to give an annual subsidy to such Pariveṇas as appeared to them to deserve it. The policy of the Committee was set forth as follows: "To make the Pariveṇas more attractive, progressive and useful, while zealously guarding their indigenous and independent character, without turning them into government-subsidized high schools."

The examinations have not been an unmixed blessing. The encouragement of competition has produced cram-work in place of erudition, and it is a lamentable fact that, even among the monks the winning of a medal or diploma has proved a greater incentive to work than disinterested love of knowledge. Knowledge for its own sake has given way to knowledge for recognition. There is also noticeable a tendency to pay far more attention to Sanskrit that to Pāli, which is bound to have an adverse influence on the growth of Pāli Literature. In 1909 there arose a bitter controversy among the Buddhists as to whether it was right for audiences to be seated on chairs or benches, while listening to the preaching of the Dhamma. The more educated among the Buddhists had found it more advantageous to adopt European costume, because it seemed to them to bring greater regard from their rulers. It was, however, discovered that European clothes did not conduce to comfort when the wearer sat on the floor—as had been the custom at the village temples for centuries—hence the controversy. Much rancour was shown on both sides and an appeal was made to the usage in Burma. One of the strongest opponents of the use of seats was Moraṭuve Medhānanda Thera. He had been to Burma to study the Abhidhamma, and in 1910 he publisheda book called the *Dhamma-gārava-dīpanī*,[1] written in Pāli *gāthā* verse, giving a history of the controversy and his own observations on the subject, together with the

[1] Moraṭuva, 1910.

opinions expressed to him by various eminent Theras of Burma whom he had consulted. The controversy gradually died down; a compromise seems to have been brought about whereby, if the preaching of the Dhamma was at the Vihāra itself, the audience should sit on the floor—while if the sermon be given at some place other than on the Vihāra precincts, the listeners may use seats at their option.

In 1911 Kodāgoda Upasena *Thera* wrote the *Sammoha-nāsanī*, on certain rules on the Vinaya connected with such subjects as the use of the begging-bowl, the modern umbrella, leather covering for the feet, etc. It is composed in Pāli verse, and divided into seven chapters. Two other works remain to be mentioned, to bring this history up to date. In 1917 Moraṭuve Medhānanda *Thera*, author of the *Dhamma-gārava-dīpanī* referred to above, published the *Jina-vaṃsa-dīpanī* (also called *Pabandha-siromaṇi*). It is an extensive Pāli poem of two thousand verses in thirty chapters. The author declares in his preface [1] that it is his ambition to write a Mahā-kāvya on the model of the Sanskrit *Raghu-vaṃsa* and *Kumāra-sambhava*, giving not only the life of the Buddha but also dealing with the cardinal points in his teaching. In this he has achieved remarkable success; the verses are written in several metres, some of them intricate and all of them composed with sedulous care. Medhānanda *Thera* has drunk deeply of the works of Sanskrit poets, and his composition abounds in metaphors and similes which bear close resemblance to their best productions. The language of the poem shows the strong impress of Sanskritic influence, and it is significant of the times that the dedicatory verses are written in classical Sanskrit. There is a Sinhalese paraphrase to the whole work by the author himself, and the book is prefaced by a very valuable historical introduction, dealing with some of the salient points of the history of the Saṅgha in Ceylon. He also gives a brief survey of Ceylon authors and their works. The *Jina-vaṃsa-dīpanī* has brought the learned

[1] p. ii (Colombo, 1917).

author recognition for his scholarship in his own lifetime, and it was no insincere compliment that his lay supporters paid to him when, on the day of its publication, they carried the book in procession round the town in which the great Elder had taken his residence. They were, in their own humble way, attempting to pay their respects and express their gratitude to the distinguished author who had laboured in the cause of religion and literature, two things which have always been closest to their hearts.

The other work is the *Mahā-Kassapa-carita*, published in 1924 by Vidurupola Piya-Tissa Nāyaka *Thera*,[1] a Pāli poem of 1,500 verses arranged in twenty cantos. The learned poet was born in 1880, and already at the age of thirty had distinguished himself as a brilliant scholar at the Final Examination of the Committee on Oriental Studies. This work from his pen has fulfilled the hopes of earlier years and holds out the promise of greater achievements in the future. The language of the *Kassapa-carita* is forceful and elegant, and the subject matter is well arranged. The materials for the biography of the great Elder, who was held in esteem only second to the Buddha himself, has been taken from the *Saṃyutta-atthakathā* and the *Aṅguttara-atthakathā*.

In 1913 Sir Robert (now Lord) Chalmers came as Governor of Ceylon. He had for some time past evinced great interest in Pāli literature, and had edited a portion of the *Majjhima-Nikāya* for the Pāli Text Society. His contributions to the *Journal of the Royal Asiatic Society* on subjects connected with Buddhism had been read with interest, and his translation of a part of the *Jātakas* for the Cambridge University Press had been studied with avidity. The people awaited his coming with eagerness, and, when he arrived, he was greeted with the utmost cordiality. Soon after he assumed office he declared in the course of a public speech his desire to bring out an edition of the Ceylonese Commentaries, which he proposed to call the Alu-vihāra Edition. "I have had the practical experience,"

[1] Colombo, 1924, Grantha-prakāśa Press, iii, 124, 8°.

he said, "of collating for my edition of the *Majjhima-Nikāya* not only Sinhalese MSS., but also the Mandalay MSS. from the Royal Library in Burma, and the King of Siam's printed edition, and, as a result of this experience, I have no hesitation in affirming—as I know the most distinguished of Pāli scholars in Europe will also affirm—that it is in the best Sinhalese MSS. that the soundest traditions of Pāli scholarship will be found. . . . It has always seemed to me that, with this unique tradition of scholarship on her part, Ceylon has failed in modern times to assert her historic claim to leadership in her own proper field. For instance, Siam, under the auspices of the late King, has taken the lead in issuing the *Tipiṭaka*, in the printed yellow-bound volumes which many of us know, and Siam has made at least a beginning with the printing of the *Atthakathā's* in Siamese character. . . . Ceylon must follow, but in following ought to improve upon Siam's example. Here, in Ceylon, we must have in Sinhalese characters, an edition both of the Canon and of the Commentaries, which will be worthy of the pre-eminent tradition of Pāli scholarship in Ceylon." [1]

It was with this noble ambition that the Alu-vihāra Edition was launched. But, alas! "the best laid schemes of mice and men gang aft agley", and Sir Robert's scheme was no exception. The Great War in Europe engaged all his attention, and later, in May, 1915, an unfortunate religious riot, which broke out between the Muslims and the Buddhists in Kandy, led to many a false move on the part of the officials, which plunged the country in gloom. Martial law was proclaimed, and under its régime many excesses were committed. All Sir Robert's constructive plans for the re-establishment of Ceylon's pre-eminence for Pāli scholarship had to be abandoned, and, when he left the Island, only one book, the *Papañca-sūdanī*, on the *Majjhima*, had been published. The work had been entrusted to the two foremost scholars of the

[1] Colombo, Public Hall, 27th February, 1915.

day, Ñāṇissara and Dhammārāma, and the result fulfilled all expectations.

But, fortunately, the work began under the inspiration of Sir Robert Chalmers was not destined to be left uncontinued, though by other hands and in other ways. On the 17th January, 1913, died Simon Alexander Hewā-vitārne, member of the well-known Hewā-vitārne family. He had been a pupil of the Ven. Siri Sumaṅgala, and was an earnest student of Abhidhamma. He had conceived the idea originally of printing the complete text of the *Tipiṭaka*, but, on the advice of Professor Lanman, of Harvard, later decided to bring out an edition of the Commentaries. Following this idea, he began, in 1911, to publish the Commentary on the *Saṃyutta-Nikāya*. The work was in progress when he died. In his will he left ample provisions for his plans to be carried out in their entirety. "I give, devise, and bequeath," it ran, "all such monies as may be found necessary for printing the Pāli text of the Commentaries which is being printed now, and all monies needful for bringing out a neat edition of the text of the *Tipiṭaka*." His executors have lost no time in carrying out his wishes. In 1917 appeared the first volume, Dhammapāla's *Commentary on the Peta-vatthu.*[1] Several others have appeared since then. The work of editing is in the hands of the most distinguished scholars of Ceylon, and the results of their labours have won unstinted approval from all quarters. It is a matter of great regret that no arrangements have so far been made to bring out carefully revised editions of the other Pāli works of Ceylon and the numerous valuable works written in Sinhalese, which form the national heritage of the people. The rulers of Ceylon in ages past have always extended their munificent patronage in the cause of literature, and it is to be hoped that the British Government will not fail to emulate the example of their predecessors in the sovereignty of the island. The incomes derived from the endowments made in former times for the

[1] Mahā-Bodhi Press, Colombo, 1917.

maintenance of the monasteries are being either wasted or misappropriated, for want of suitable legislation. If means are devised for the proper utilization of such funds as may be derived from them, the question of setting aside a sufficient yearly sum for the editing and publication of a literature of such great historical value as that of Ceylon, will be easily solved. A few hundreds a year for ten years would probably suffice—on the system followed by the Pāli Text Society—for the editing and publication of the whole. The conclusion of the war has ushered in a new era of prosperity, and it is fervently hoped that attention will be paid to this matter of urgency for the reputation of Ceylon in the scholarship of the world.

BIBLIOGRAPHY

ARUNĀCHALAM (Sir Ponnambalam): *Sketches of Ceylon History*, Colombo, 1906.

BARUA (B. M.): *A History of Pre-Buddhistic Philosophy*, Calcutta University, 1921.

BEAL (Samuel): *Buddhist Records of the Western World*, 2 vols., Trübner, London, 1884.

BODE (Mrs. Mabel H.): *The Pāli Literature of Burma*, R.A.S., London, 1909.

BURLINGAME (E. W.): *Buddhist Legends*, parts 1–3, Harvard Oriental Series, 1921; *Buddhist Parables*, Yale University, 1922.

CATALOGUES :—

Catalogue of Pāli MSS. in the Oriental Department, British Museum.

" " " " " " *India Office Library.*

" " " " " " *Bibliothèque Nationale*, Paris.

See also under D'Alwis, De Zoysa, and Wickremasinghe.

CHILDERS (Robert Cæsar): *A Dictionary of the Pāli Language*, Trübner, London, 1875.

COOMĀRA SWĀMY (Mutu): *Dāṭhā Vaṃsa*, Trübner, London, 1874.

D'ALWIS (James): *Sidat-Saṅgarā*, Colombo, 1852; *A Descriptive Catalogue of Sanskrit, Pāli, and Sinhalese Literary Works of Ceylon*, Colombo, 1870; *Attanagaluvaṃsa*, Colombo, 1870.

DE ZOYSA (Louis): *A Catalogue of the Temple Libraries of Ceylon*, Colombo, 1885.

DUTT (Sukumar): *Early Buddhist Monachism*, Trübner, 1924.

FLEET (J. F.): *Inscriptions of the Early Gupta Kings*, Calcutta, 1888.

FORCHHAMMER (Dr. Emil): *Report on the Pāli Literature of Burma*, Government of India Publication, 1879.

FRANKE (Dr. R. Otto): *Pāli und Sanskrit*, Strassburg, 1902.

GEIGER (Wilhelm): *The Dīpavaṃsa and Mahāvaṃsa* (English translation), Colombo, 1908; *Mahā-vaṃsa* (P.T.S.) and *Cūḷa-vaṃsa* (P.T.S.).

GILES (H. A.): *The Travels of Fa-Hsien*, Cambridge, 1923.

GRAY (James): *Buddhaghosuppatti*, Luzac, London, 1892; *Jinālankāra*, Luzac, London, 1894.

HARDY (R. Spence): *Eastern Monachism*, Williams and Norgate, 1860; *Legends and Theories of the Buddhists*, Williams and Norgate, 1866; *Manual of Buddhism*, Williams and Norgate, 1880.

HASTINGS (James): ed. *Encyclopaedia of Religion and Ethics*, T. and C. Clark (12 vols.), 1910–18.

Jātaka: ed. by V. FAUSBÖLL, 7 vols., Trübner, 1877–97.

Jātaka Tales: H. T. FRANCIS and E. J. THOMAS, Cambridge, 1916.

Jātaka Tales (translation): published by Cambridge Univ. Press, 7 vols., 1895–1913.

JOURNALS :—

Pāli Text Society.
Royal Asiatic Society, London.
„ „ „ Ceylon Branch, Colombo.
Bengal Asiatic Society, Calcutta.
Indian Antiquary, Bombay.
The Ceylon Antiquary and Literary Register, Colombo.
Calcutta Review, Calcutta.
Journal Asiatique, Paris.
Zeitschrift der Deutschen Morgenländischen Gesellschaft, Leipzig.

KERN (H.): *Manual of Indian Buddhism*, Strassburg, 1896.

LAW (Bimala Caran): *The Life and Work of Buddhaghosa*, Calcutta, 1923.

LEGGE (James): *A Record of Buddhistic Kingdoms*, Oxford, 1886.

MACDONELL (A. A.): *Sanskrit Literature*, Heinemann, London, 1899.

Mahā-vaṃsa: Pāli Text, ed. Sumaṅgala and Batuvantudāve, Colombo, 1905; *Ṭīkā*, ed. Sumaṅgala and Batuvantudāve, Colombo, 1895.

MITRA (Rājendra Lāla): *Buddha Gayā*, Calcutta, 1888.

NARIMAN (G. K.): *Literary History of Sanskrit Buddhism*, Bombay, 1920.

Nikāya-saṅgraha: Text, Government Printing Press, Colombo, 1907; translated by C. M. FERNANDO, and edited by W. F. GUṆAWARDHANA, Colombo, 1908.

OLDENBERG (Hermann): *The Vinaya Piṭakaṃ*, 5 vols., Williams and Norgate, London, 1879–83; *Dīpa-vaṃsa*, Williams and Norgate, 1879.

PĀLI TEXT SOCIETY: All publications, including the *Journal* and the *New Pāli Dictionary*.

PIERIS (Paul E.): *Ceylon and the Portuguese*, Ceylon, 1920.

PRIDHAM (Charles): *Ceylon and its Dependencies*, 2 vols., T. and W. Boone, London, 1849.

Rāja-ratnākara: ed. by SIMON DE SILVA, Colombo, 1907; see also Upham.

Rājāvaliya: Translated by B. GUṆASEKARA, Colombo, 1900; see also Upham.

RHYS DAVIDS (Mrs. C. A. F.): *Buddhism* (Home University Library), 2nd edition; *Buddhist Psychological Ethics*, 2nd edition, R.A.S., London, 1923; *Buddhist Psychology*, 2nd edition, Luzac, London, 1924.

RHYS DAVIDS (T. W.): *Buddhist Birth Stories*, vol. i, Trübner, 1880, and Routledge, 1924 (revised by Mrs. Rhys Davids); *Buddhist Suttas* (*Sacred Books of the East*, xi), Frowde, 1881; *Vinaya Texts* (*Sacred Books of the East*, xiii, xvii, xx), Frowde, 1881–5; *Dialogues of the Buddha*, 3 vols., Frowde, 1900–21; *Buddhism: Its History and Literature* (American Lectures), Putnam, 1896; *Buddhist India* (*Story of the Nations*), Fisher Unwin, 1903.

SENAVERATNA (John M.): *The Story of the Sinhalese*, 2 vols., Colombo, 1923.

SMITH (Vincent A.): *Early History of India*, Clarendon Press, 1st and 4th editions, 1904 and 1924; *Asoka* (Rulers of India Series), 1909; *Oxford History of India* (Oxford Univ. Press), 1st and 2nd ed., 1919 and 1923.

TENNENT (Sir James Emerson): *Christianity in Ceylon*, John Murray, London, 1850; *Ceylon*, 2 vols., Longmans, London, 1857.

TURNOUR (George): *Epitome of the History of Ceylon* (Ceylon Almanac), Colombo, 1823; translation of the *Māha Wanso*, vol. i, Cotta, Ceylon, 1837.

UPHAM (Edward): *Sacred and Historical Books of Ceylon*, 3 vols. (*Mahāvansī*, *Rāja-ratnācarī*, and *Rājā-valī*), Parbury, Allen and Co.

WICKREMASINGHE (D. M. de Z.): *Sinhalese MSS. in the British Museum*, London, 1900; *Catalogue of the Colombo Museum*, Government Oriental Library, Colombo, 1896; *Sinhalese Printed Books in the British Museum, London.*

WIJESINHA (L. C.): *Mahā Vaṇsa* (English translation), Colombo, 1909.

WINTERNITZ (Dr. M.): *Geschichte der Indischen Litteratur, Zweiter Band*, Leipzig, 1920.

SUPPLEMENT:
Corrections and Comments

Somapala Jayawardhana

p.1, lines 7ff. This second heading should also include the *ṭīkās*, or sub-commentaries, to the canonical texts.

p.1, lines 11ff. This third heading should also include the commentaries to the primary texts on history, grammar, and related subjects.

p. 18, lines 7ff. There seems to be no historical evidence to support the statement quoted from Gray's Introduction. His chronology regarding Ven. Buddharakkhita derives from an erroneous translation; see below, note to pp. 110-11. Further, Ven. Buddharakkhita of Rohaṇa was from southern Sri Lanka, not the maritime western division of the island.

p.22, lines 9-10. Malalasekera's statement that Asoka "*entered the Order*" is based on a mistaken rendering of the words in the Edict *saṅghe upayīte*, which literally mean "I drew near to the Order." Scholars are agreed that Asoka himself did not become a monk. Most probably the expression means that he came into close association with senior members of the Order and regarded them as his spiritual mentors.

p.22, lines 11-13. The words of the Edict, *ayāya sambodhim*, are now understood to mean that Asoka set out on a pilgrimage to the Bodhi-tree at Buddha-gayā, the site of the Buddha's Enlightenment.

p.23, line 10. Mahinda's descent was to Missaka Pabbata.

p.44, line 1. The Upāli who became the chief exponent of the Vinaya was not the eminent former Nigaṇṭha (a wealthy layman of Nālandā: see Majjhima Nikāya, Sutta No. 56), but the former barber of the Sakyans at Kapilavatthu.

p.51, line 10. The *Ariyavaṁsa* is a sutta in the Aṅguttara Nikāya (A.ii,27ff.) extolling the virtues of the monk's life. During this period of Ceylon's religious history it had become a popular theme for sermons. See Walpola Rahula, *History of Buddhism in Ceylon* (1956; rep. Dehiwala: Buddhist Cultural Centre, 1993), pp. 268-73.

p.66, lines 33-34. They disguised themselves as brahmins, not as members of the Buddhist Order.

p.99, line 13. There are traces of these old Sinhalese commentaries in quotations in Sinhalese works such as the *Dhampiyā-aṭuvā-gäṭapadaya* and the *Dharmapradīpikā*.

p.109, lines 12-14. Although a Ceylon tradition attributes the authorship of these two works to Ven. Buddhadatta, this ascription is only tenable in the case of the *Madhurattha-Vilāsinī*. On the authorship of the *Jinālaṅkāra* see p.110 and following note.

pp.110-11. The *Jinālaṅkāra* was composed by Ven. Buddharakkhita of Rohaṇa. The texts says that he was born in the seventeen hundredth year after the passing away of the Buddha (*not* the 117th year!); that is, in A.D. 1157. The author of the *ṭīkā* to the *Jinālaṅkāra* is not known.

p.113, lines 20-22. Ācariya Dhammapāla wrote the *ṭīkās* or subcommentaries to Ācariya Buddhaghosa's commentaries on the Dīgha Nikāya, Majjhima Nikāya, and Saṁyutta Nikāya.

p.114, lines 23-25. The *ṭīkās* to Buddhaghosa's commentaries on the *first three* Nikāyas are collectively called *Līnattha-ppakāsanā*.

p.117, line 10. Add the following: The author also tells us that he completed it in the 26th year of the reign of King Sirinivāsa Sirisaṅghabodhi, who has been identified as King Mahānāma (407-429). As the rulers who succeeded Mahānāma were usurpers, the author appears to have ignored them and stated the date reckoning from the coronation of the last lawful king.

p.134, lines 31-33. The *Dīpavaṁsa* cannot be regarded as forming "one continuous story."

p.135, line 3. To the statement that the *Dīpavaṁsa* attempts "*to create a composite whole*," Professor Jayawickrama has a marginal note: "It is itself composite."

p.157, line 8. For 'Dāṭṭhānāga' read 'Dāṭhānāga'.

p.160, lines 15-16; p.161, line 28. The *Anāgatavaṁsa-aṭṭhakathā*, also called the *Samantabhaddikā*, was composed by Ven. Upasena, not by a Ven. Upatissa.

p.160, lines 17-18. Ven. Kassapa of the Coḷa country wrote the *Moha-vicchedanī* and the*Vimati-vinodanī*. See p.179, and note to pp. 178-79 below. No work by the name '*Vimati-vicchedanī*' is known; this title appears to be a conflation of the names of the two works properly ascribed to Ven. Kassapa. The *Buddhavaṁsa* is a text in the Khuddaka Nikāya; no other work bearing this name is known.

p.160, lines 25-26. The authorship of the *Anāgatavaṁsa-ṭīkā* is not known.

p. 160, lines 29-32. This may be deleted.

p.178, line 30 - p.179, line 6. Ven. Mahākassapa of Dimbulāgala Vihāra is not identifiable with the Ven. Kassapa of the Coḷa country. The latter is the author of the *Moha-vicchedanī* (an Abhidhamma commentary) and the *Vimati-vinodanī* (a *ṭīkā* to Ācariya Buddhaghosa's commentary on the Vinaya). The authorship of the *Moha-vicchedanī-ṭīkā* is also ascribed to him.

p.185, lines 21-24. There seems to be a confusion between two Burmese monks named Chapaṭa and Chappaṭa, or Chappaḍa. The earlier, the pupil of the Elder Uttarajīva, accompanied his teacher to Ceylon in the twelfth century and received ordination from the Ceylon Sangha. He returned to Burma with four other bhikkhus, where he established a new ordination lineage. The second Chappaṭa was a Burmese monk who came to Ceylon during the reign of King Parākrama-bāhu VI (1412-1467), who had his capital at Jayawardhanapura. This latter Chappaṭa was also known by the name Saddhammajotipāla and is the author of the books discussed below (see pp.197, 201-203).

p.186, line 12. For *'Pañjikā-pradīpa'* read *'Pañcikā-pradīpa'*.

p.190, line 18. For *'pañjikā'* read *'pañcikā'*.

p.190, line 19. For *'Ratnamati-pañjikā-ṭīkā'* read *'Ratnamati-pañcikā-ṭīkā'*. For *'Pañjikālaṅkāra'* read *'Pañcikālaṅkāra'*.

p.192, lines 18-22. Ven. Sāriputta is properly credited with the *Sārattha-mañjūsā* (the *ṭīkā* on the Aṅguttara Nikāya), but the *Līnatthappakāsanā* (a collective name for the *ṭīkās* on the first three Nikāyas—the Dīgha, the Majjhima, and the Saṁyutta) is the work of Ācariya Dhammapāla.

p.192, line 30 - p.193, line 1. The earliest Pali *ṭīkās* were those composed by Ācariya Dhammapāla of Badaratittha, in South India, perhaps in the sixth century A.D. His *ṭīkās* include the *Paramattha-mañjūsā* (sub-commentary to the *Visuddhimagga*) and the *ṭīkās* to the first three Nikāyas (see the preceding note). As Ven. Dhammapāla was a South Indian and wrote long before the time of Parākramabāhu, Malalasekera's statement cannot be accepted. Two *ṭīkās* were composed after the Convocation of Polonnaruva: the *Sārattha-dīpanī* (a sub-commentary to the Vinaya) and the *Sārattha-mañjūsā* (a sub-commentary to the Aṅguttara Nikāya).

p.193, lines 19-20. The *Sārattha-mañjūsā* is not a sub-commentary to the four chief Nikāyas as a whole, but only to the Aṅguttara Nikāya.

p.196, lines 22-25. On the distinction between the two Chappaṭas, see the note to p.185 above.

p.200, line 3. For 'words' read 'works'.

pp.201-203. This is the second Chappaṭa, also known as Saddhammajotipāla; he wrote his works in the fifteenth century.

p.205, line 31. For 'A.D. 1197' read 'A.D. 1186'.

p.210, lines 23-28. The *Mūla-ṭīkā*, also known as the *Līnatthapada-vaṇṇanā*, explains the commentaries to the Abhidhamma Piṭaka.

p.215, lines 1-6. It appears that during the reign of this king an unknown author continued the *Mahāvaṁsa* from the date at which Mahānāma left off down to his own times. It was during this same period that there lived in Tambaraṭṭha an Elder who was also known as Dhammakitti.

p.217, line 19. For 'Vahiśvara' read 'Vāgiśvara'

p.221, line 27. For 'Dhammakitti's *Bālāvatāra*' read simply 'the *Bālāvatāra*'.

p.222, line 2. For '*Pañjikā-pradīpa*' read '*Pañcikā-pradīpa*'.

p.222, lines 19-26. Delete these two paragraphs, as they are confused and incorrect. There is no Pali text called *Sārattha-saṅgaha*. Perhaps what is intended is the *Sāra-saṅgaha* composed by Ven. Siddhattha, a pupil of Ven. Buddhapiya Dīpaṅkara. Buddhadāsa's work, the *Sārartha-saṁgraha*, is in Sanskrit.

p.226, lines 33-34. The *Sahassa-vatthu-ppąkaraṇa* has been published by Ven. A.P. Buddhadatta.

p.229, line 1. For '*Sārattha-saṅgaha*' read '*Sāra-saṅgaha*'

p.243, line 13. This Dhammakitti was the author of the *Bālāvatāra-sanne*, a paraphrase in Sinhala of the *Bālāvatāra*. The actual author of the *Bālāvatāra* is not known and some confusion in the editing of manuscripts has led to the unsupported assumption among several scholars that Dhammakitti was also the author of the *Bālāvatāra*.

p.243, line 24. See note to p.221, line 27, above.

p.244, lines 21-22. Delete 'who is usually identified with the author of the *Bālāvatāra* himself'.

p.244, line 29. For 'Siṭināmaluve' read 'Diyahunnate'

p.245, line 28. For 'India' read 'Thailand'.

p.251, line 20-21. For '*Moggallāna-pañjikā-pradīpa*' read '*Moggallāna-pañcikā-pradīpa*'. In line 22, for '*Pañjikā-pradīpa*' read '*Pañcikā-pradīpa*'; and in line 25, for '*Pañjikā*' read '*Pañcikā*'.

p.252, line 14. For '*Durgasiṁha-vṛtti-pañjikā*' read '*Durgasiṁha-vṛtti-pañcikā*'. And for '*Pañjikālaṅkāra*' read '*Pañcikālaṅkāra*'.

INDEX

Also from BPS

The Questions of King Milinda

An Abridgement of the Milindapanha

Edited by N.K.G. Mendis

Today the encounter between Buddhism and Western civilization has been hailed as a cultural event of far-reaching significance, promising to exercise a major impact on both partners to the meeting. However, the first encounter between Buddhism and the West took place long ago, in Northwest India during the age of Alexander the Great, and it issued in one of the most sublime works of Buddhist literature, *The Questions of King Milinda.* This work, preserved in the Pali language, is an imaginative record of a series of discussions between the Bactrian Greek King Milinda, who reigned in the Punjab, and the Buddhist sage Bhante Nāgasena. Their spirited dialogue—dramatic and witty, eloquent and inspired—explores the diverse problems of Buddhist thought and practice from the perspective of a probing Greek intellectual who is both perplexed and fascinated by the strangely rational religion he discovered on the Indian subcontinent. The present abridged edition has been adapted from existing scholarly translations, and includes in an easily readable style the most essential passages of the original classic.

Softback: 208 pages
U.S. $10; SL Rs. 280
140 mm x 214 mm
Order No. BP 217S

Also from BPS

King Aśoka and Buddhism

Historical and Literary Studies

Edited by Anuradha Seneviratna

King Aśoka, the third monarch of the Mauryan dynasty in the third century B.C., was the first ruler of a unified India and one of the greatest political figures of all time. After he embraced the teachings of the Buddha, he transformed his polity from one of military conquest to one of Dharmavijaya—victory by righteousness and truth. By providing royal patronage for the propagation of Buddhism both within and beyond his empire, he helped promote the metamorphosis of Buddhism into a world religion that spread peacefully across the face of Asia. The present collection of essays by leading Indological scholars draws upon both the inscriptions and the literary traditions to explore the relationship between King Aśoka and the religion he embraced. In highlighting the ways in which Aśoka tapped the ethical and spiritual potentials of rulership, these papers deliver a message highly relevant to our own time, when politics and spirituality often seem pitted against one another in irreconcilable opposition.

Contents: Richard Gombrich: *Aśoka—The Great Upāsaka*; Romila Thapar: *Aśoka and Buddhism as Reflected in the Aśokan Edicts*; Ananda W.P. Guruge: *Unresolved Discrepancies between Buddhist Tradition and Aśokan Inscriptions*; N.A. Jayawickrama: *Aśoka's Edicts and the Third Buddhist Council*; Anuradha Seneviratna: *Aśoka and the Emergence of a Sinhala Buddhist State in Sri Lanka*; John S. Strong: *Images of Aśoka*; Ananda W.P. Guruge: *Emperor Aśoka's Place in History.*

Softback: 180 pages, with maps — 140 mm x 214 mm
U.S. $12.00; Rs.300 — Order No. BP 410S